EZEKIEL
A Christian Interpretation

James E. Smith, Ph.D.

Originally published as part of the
Bible Study Textbook Series
by College Press, 1979.
Revised Edition 2008

Scripture Translation of chs 1-39
is that of the Author;
For chs 40-48 the
American Standard Version of 1901
has been utilized.

DEDICATED TO

Jerry and Kay Williams

With Delightful Memories
Of Wednesday Evening Bible Study
In the Williams' Home

ISBN 978-1-4357-1725-1

PREFACE

The Book of Ezekiel stands fourth among the Major Prophets in the English Bible. It ranks second in actual word count among the prophetic books (39,407 words as compared to Jeremiah's 42,659). It stands third in size in the entire Bible (behind Psalms and Jeremiah). In spite of its size this book may well be the most neglected of the prophets. Previous surveys have convinced the average Bible student that he cannot possibly understand this material. Ezekiel is regarded as one portion of Scripture with little spiritual value and even less contemporary relevance. Those who do attempt a more serious study of the book often fail to make it past the intricate visionary details of the first ch. This is most unfortunate. Ezekiel has a vital message for God's people, a message not duplicated elsewhere in the sacred canon.

While the Book of Ezekiel has been neglected by the church as a whole, it has come to be the happy hunting ground of cultists, critics and curiosity mongers. The modern negative critics regard Ezekiel as pivotal in their topsy-turvy reconstruction of Old Testament history that views the tripartite priesthood as a scribal concoction from Babylon rather than a divine revelation from Sinai. Ezekiel is cited by self-styled "students of prophecy" as proof that God's plan for the future includes the modern Zionist movement (Jews returning to Palestine in unbelief), an imminent Russian invasion of Israel, and the reinstitution of the Mosaic animal sacrificial system in a temple shortly to be constructed in Jerusalem. Science fiction buffs have scoured the Book of Ezekiel in search of spaceships and extra-terrestrial beings who pretended to be God. Mormons regard Ezekiel 37:15-23 as the prophetic allusion to the Book of Mormon (stick of Ephraim) being added to the Bible (stick of Judah). If for no other reason the Book of Ezekiel merits careful study so that the man of God may be able to silence these modern day "empty talkers and deceivers" who are upsetting so many families (Titus 1:10-11). The best defense against a thousand and one errors is the truth.

There is something more positive to be said in favor of diligent study of Ezekiel. The book is full of profound theology, not the least of which is the doctrine of individual responsibility. God's sovereign grace, his absolute holiness and justice, and his universality are presented here as clearly as in any other portion of Scripture. In spite of difficult details the theme of ultimate victory for God's people is forcefully developed in this prophecy These mother lode truths, plus priceless nuggets of revelation too numerous to mention, will make the serious student of this book spiritually wealthy. Let not those who will prospect for this treasure become discouraged by the exegetical bogs that here and there challenge the resolve as well as the intellect.

Ezekiel invites investigation not only because of what he said, but also because of how he said it. The book is fascinating. It is replete with visions, allegories, and action parables. Not without reason has Ezekiel been dubbed the "audio-visual aids prophet." If a picture is worth a thousand words then Ezekiel must be regarded as artfully verbose. His prophecy is a gallery of word pictures interspersed with mini-stages upon which the prophet performed divinely inspired monodrama. Ezekiel's delightful antics should draw students to his book in these days even as they attracted observers to his door in his day.

The commentary follows the ch divisions of the book. The translation of the text is that of the author, at least up to ch 40. For the tedious "blueprint" chs 40-48 the American Standard Version of 1901 has been followed with only minor adaptation. Verse-by-verse comments follow the translation of the individual units of the text.

James E. Smith
Florida Christian College
January 2008

ABBREVIATONS

PERIODICALS

BAR *Biblical Archaeology Review.*
BIES *Bulletin of the Israel Exploration Society.*
BS *Bibliotheca Sacra.*
BT *Bible Translator.*
BTB *Biblical Theology Bulletin.*
CBQ *Catholic Biblical Quarterly.*
CTJ *Calvin Theological Journal.*
CTM *Concordia Theological Monthly.*
ET *Expository Times.*
HAR *Hebrew Annual Review.*
HUCA *Hebrew Union College Annual.*
IEJ *Israel Exploration Journal.*
Inter *Interpretation.*
JAOS *Journal of the American Oriental Society.*
JBL *Journal of Biblical Literature.*
JETS *Journal of the Evangelical Theological Society.*
JSOT *Journal for the Study of the Old Testament.*
JTS *Journal of Theological Studies.*
NTS *New Testament Studies.*
PRS *Perspectives in Religious Studies.*
RB *Revue Biblique.*
TB *Tyndale Bulletin*
TBT *The Bible Today.*
VT *Vetus Testamentum.*
ZAW *Zeitschrift für die alttestamentliche Wissenschaft.*

ENGLISH VERSIONS

ASV *American Standard Version* (1901).
BV *Berkeley Version* (1958).
KJV *King James Version* (1611).
NAB *New American Bible.*(1970).
NASB *New American Standard Bible* (1963).
NIV *New International Version* (1978).
RSV *Revised Standard Version* (1952).

OTHER WORKS

ANET James B. Pritchard (ed.) *Ancient Near Eastern Texts Relating to the Old Testament*. Third edition; Princeton, New Jersey: University Press, 1969.

IDB G.A. Buttrick, ed. *The Interpreter's Dictionary of the Bible*. New York: Abingdon, 1962.

NBD J.D. Douglas, ed. *The New Bible Dictionary*. Grand Rapids: Eerdmans, 1962.

CONTENTS

INTRODUCTION

TRANSLATION AND COMMENTARY

INTRODUCTION

The study of a prophetic book is rewarding but not easy. The serious student must be willing to take time to immerse himself in the historical context that gave birth to the book. He must attempt to walk awhile in the sandals of the prophet who wrote the book—to understand his motives and manners, his actions and attitudes. He must come to grips not only with what the book says to and about men, but also with what men have said about the book. All of this takes years of study. But, as the wise one has said, the journey of a thousand miles begins with a single step. This first ch contains an historical, biographical, and literary introduction to the Book of Ezekiel.

STEPPING INTO EZEKIEL'S WORLD

Do men make the times, or do the times make the men? That is the age-old question. History is replete with examples of ordinary men catapulted into prominence by circumstances over which they had no control. So it was with Ezekiel. For him the crucial moment came on March 16, 597 BC. On that day King Jehoiachin opened the gates of Jerusalem to the mighty Nebuchadnezzar. The king and some ten thousand of his subjects—including Ezekiel—were carried away to Babylon. But for that event and the subsequent prophetic call that came to this priest-in-exile, history probably would not have accorded to Ezekiel so much as a footnote. Therefore to evaluate the historical context of this man of God one must look backward and then forward from the crucial date March 16, 597 BC.

Judah Prior to Ezekiel's Deportation

Ezekiel was born in the eighteenth year of Josiah, 621 BC. Those were bright and promising days for tiny Judah. The shock of seeing their sister kingdom to the north carried away into the far corners of the Assyrian Empire a century earlier had now largely disappeared. Young King Josiah successfully had thrown off the oppressive yoke of those same Assyrians. A vigorous religious reformation led by the prophets Zephaniah and Jeremiah, the priest Hilkiah, and the king himself seemed to be correcting the basic moral and religious flaws of the nation. Visible signs of idolatry had been purged from the land, but, as it turned out, not from the hearts of the people.

The heroic efforts of that mighty coalition of crown, priest and prophets proved to be in vain. The reformation came to an abrupt halt in 609 BC. That was the year when Josiah met his untimely death as a result of the wounds received in the unfortunate and ill-advised battle of Megiddo. For some unexplained reason Josiah had challenged unsuccessfully the army of Pharaoh Neco. The good king's second son Shallum was elevated to the throne by the people of the land. Shallum assumed the throne name of Jehoahaz.

At the end of three months Jehoahaz was deposed by Pharaoh Neco. The Egyptian was still encamped at Riblah about two hundred miles from Jerusalem. Neco placed Eliakim, an older son of Josiah, on the throne of Judah as his vassal. Eliakim ruled under the throne name Jehoiakim. When Neco was defeated by Nebuchadnezzar at Carchemish on the Euphrates (Jer 46:1), Jehoiakim shifted his allegiance to the Babylonian sovereign. Daniel and several other prominent hostages were sent to Babylon at this time (Dan 1:1).

Jehoiakim served Nebuchadnezzar for three years (2 Kgs 24:1), probably the years 604-601 BC. When the Babylonian king received a setback on the borders of Egypt, Jehoiakim withheld tribute and declared Judah to be independent. Nebuchadnezzar marched against Jerusalem in order to punish the infidelity of his Judean vassal.

Jehoiakim died a natural death or was assassinated before the arrival of the Chaldean troops. His son, the eighteen-year-old Jehoiachin, had to face the wrath of Nebuchadnezzar's army. After three months or so of siege Jehoiachin surrendered himself and his capital. The king and ten thousand of his chief people—Ezekiel among them—were carried away to far-off Babylon.

Nebuchadnezzar installed Mattaniah, another son of Josiah and uncle of the most recently deposed king, on the throne of Judah. His name was changed to Zedekiah (2 Kgs 24:10-17).

Judah after Ezekiel's Deportation

The blow that fell against Jerusalem in 597 BC did not cure the country of its vice and immorality. The inhabitants of Judah continued to be a rebellious and impudent people (Ezek 2:4; 3:7). They refused to walk in the statutes of God (Ezek 5:6-7). They defiled the sanctuary of Yahweh with idolatrous paraphernalia (5:11) and practices (ch 8). Pagan high places, altars and images were conspicuous "upon every high hill and under every green tree" (Ezek 6:13). In ch 22 of Ezekiel Yahweh recites against Judah a catalogue of abominations that would make a pagan people blush—idolatry, lewdness, oppression, sacrilege and murder. Such sin permeated all classes of society. Perhaps Ezek 9:9 best summarizes the complete corruption of Jerusalem in its last decade: *The iniquity of the house of Israel and Judah is exceeding great, and the land is filled with blood. The city is full of perversion, for they say, Yahweh has forsaken the land! Yahweh does not see!*

That Ezekiel in no way exaggerated the corruption in his native land is attested by Jeremiah who lived through those dark days. In a vision the subjects of King Zedekiah were represented to the mind of this prophet as a basket of rotten figs (Jer 24:8). By intellectual madness and spiritual sophistry the inhabitants of Judah had convinced themselves that they were heaven's favorites to whom the land of Palestine had been given for a possession (Jer 11:15). They believed their city was impregnable (Jer 11:3). These delusions were stoked by false prophets. In Zedekiah's fourth year, exactly one year before Ezekiel began his ministry, one of these false prophets dramatically announced in the temple that God was about to shatter the yoke of Babylon within two years (Jer 28:1-4). In vain Jeremiah warned of the imminent overthrow of Jerusalem and the final deportation of its population (Jer 21:7; 24:8-10; 32:3-5; 34:2-3).

Encouraged by the optimistic predictions of his favorite prophets King Zedekiah got involved in a treasonous coalition against Nebuchadnezzar. An embassy from the kings of Edom, Moab, Ammon, Tyre and Sidon assembled in Jerusalem (Jer 27:3). Unfortunately for Zedekiah the plot was reported to the great king in Babylon. Zedekiah was required to make a trip to Babylon to set things straight with his overlord (Jer 51:59).

Five years later Zedekiah reneged on his vassal pledge. He openly broke with Babylon (2 Kgs 24:20). Tyre and Ammon joined Zedekiah in this revolt. He probably was supported by promises of aid from Pharaoh Hophra (Jer 27:15). Nebuchadnezzar was swift to move his army into Palestine to punish Zedekiah and the other rebellious vassals. The siege of Jerusalem was a gruesome ordeal that, with one brief interruption, lasted for eighteen months.

On July 3, 586 BC the supposed impregnable Jerusalem fortress fell. Zedekiah was captured as he attempted to flee the city. He was taken in chains to Riblah where he watched his sons executed. Zedekiah was then cruelly blinded, bound in chains, and carried off to Babylon (cf. Jer 32:4; Ezek 12:13).

A pitiless massacre of Jerusalem's inhabitants followed the successful capture of the city. A month later the great king had the city walls and palaces razed and burned. Those who escaped the slaughter were herded off to join the captives on the River Kebar in Babylon. Only a handful of the poorest were left on their native soil (2 Kgs 25; 2 C 36; Jer 39, 40, 52).

Situation on the Kebar

Reactions among the Jews taken captive in 597 BC were mixed. Some of the more pious may have realized that their removal from the homeland was a divine stroke against an apostate nation. They sat down by the rivers of Babylon and wept as they remembered the sacred precincts of Jerusalem (Ps 137:1). Others continued in the old idolatrous ways of their fathers (Ezek 20:30). While they pretended to be interested in the revelation of God's prophet, they were setting up idols in their hearts (Ezek 14:4). They enjoyed Ezekiel's preaching (33:32) and pondered his parables (20:49); but they never intended to do as he directed them.

On one point virtually all members of the exilic community agreed. The stay in Babylon was to be short. God would not abandon his chosen city and people to the Babylonians. This delusion was promoted by a bevy of false prophets who predicted peace for Jerusalem (Ezek 13:16). Thus they caused the exiles to trust in lies (Ezek 13:19).

From distant Jerusalem Jeremiah did what he could to combat these pretenders. A letter from his pen was carried by royal ambassadors to Babylon. The prophet wisely counseled the exiles to settle down quietly in their new home. They should try to make the most of their situation. Jeremiah categorically denied that there would be any speedy deliverance. Only after seventy years had expired will God intervene on behalf of his people (Jer 29:5-14).

The delusions of speedy deliverance and the inviolability of Jerusalem were not easily dislodged. One prophet by the name of Shemaiah fired back a letter to the high priest in Jerusalem suggesting that Jeremiah was mad; he should be taken into custody (Jer 29:24-29). Jeremiah's letter may have been one external stimulus that caused a young priest named Ezekiel to step forth as a prophet of Yahweh. In any case, Ezekiel waged valiant battle against the delusion of speedy deliverance during that decade before the Babylonian destruction of Jerusalem.

GETTING ACQUAINTED WITH EZEKIEL

The only source of information concerning the life of Ezekiel is the book that bears his name. Outside of his own book he is mentioned only by Josephus[1] and Ben Sira,[2] neither of whom add any significant detail to the prophet's biography.

Name

The fourth book of the Major Prophets takes its name from its principal prophetic figure and author. The Hebrew form of his name (*y^{e}chezqēl*) means *God strengthens*, or perhaps *God is strong*. In the Greek Old Testament the name appears as *Iezikiei*, and in the Latin Vulgate *Ezechiel* from which the English spelling is derived.

Ezekiel's name is used only twice in the book that he wrote. Another Ezekiel—a priestly dignitary of David's day—is mentioned in 1 Chr 24:16. It is possible, though not likely, that the prophet Ezekiel was named for the earlier namesake.

It cannot be determined whether the name Ezekiel was the prophet's birth-name conferred on him by his parents, or an official title assumed when he commenced his prophetic vocation. In either case the name is appropriate to the character and calling of this man of God. Ezekiel was to preach to a people who were *stiff-hearted* (*chizqê-lēbh*) and of a *hard forehead* (*chizqê-mētsach*). Yahweh, however, gave assurance that he had made the prophet's face *hard*

---

[1]*Antiquities* 10.5.1; 6.3; 7.2; 8.2.

[2]Ecclesiasticus 49:8.

(*ch"zaqîm*) against their faces and his forehead hard against their foreheads (2:5; 3:7-8).

Family and Station

Like Jeremiah, Ezekiel was a priest before he was a prophet. Nothing is known of his father Buzi.[3] Circumstantial evidence in the book suggests that Ezekiel was of the Zadokite line of the priesthood.[4] This line of priests was descended from Zadok, the great priest of Solomon's day (1 Kgs 2:35), and ultimately from Eleazer the son of Aaron. The Zadokites came into prominence during the reformation of Josiah (621 BC). They were considered part of the Jerusalem aristocracy. This accounts for the fact that Ezekiel was carried off to Babylon in 597 BC.

Did Ezekiel have a ministry in Jerusalem prior to being carried away to Babylon? No certain answer to this question can be given. It has been suggested that Ezekiel became a temple priest, or at least a priestly trainee, during the reign of King Jehoiakim (609-598 BC). No positive evidence exists, however, that Ezekiel performed priestly functions before his deportation. The rabbinic tradition[5] that Ezekiel already had commenced his prophetic activity in Palestine likewise finds no support in the biblical materials.

Unlike Jeremiah who was under divine directive not to marry, Ezekiel had a wife whom he tenderly cherished as "the desire of my eyes." It is not clear whether he was married at the time of his deportation. The likelihood is that he married in Babylon. He may have chosen a wife in response to Jeremiah's letter to the exiles instructing them to settle down and marry.

In the ninth year of his captivity, four years after he had begun his prophetic ministry, Ezekiel's wife died (ch 24). There is no indication that any children were born to this union.

---

[3]One Jewish tradition understands the name Buzi (*despised one*) to refer to Jeremiah. However, Jeremiah never married.
[4]Ezekiel 40:66; 43:19; 44:15-16.
[5]*Mekilta Bo* 1b; Targum Ezekiel 1:3.

Influences on Ezekiel

We cannot know all the factors that made Ezekiel the man he was. It is clear from his writings, however, that this prophet was deeply influenced by four circumstances in his early life.

First, Ezekiel must have been deeply stirred by the heroic reform efforts of good King Josiah. This reformation began in the eighth year of the young king's reign, intensified in his twelfth year, and climaxed in his eighteenth year (621 BC). This was the year Hilkiah the high priest found a lost law book in the temple. That law book became the basis for the most thoroughgoing reform movement ever launched in Judah. Ezekiel's childhood (up to about age thirteen) coincided with this vigorous governmental effort to bring tiny Judah back to the paths of spiritual fidelity.

Second, Ezekiel was also deeply impressed by the elaborate temple services in Jerusalem. Like the young Samuel, he may have spent many of his boyhood hours assisting the priests in their temple duties. In any case, large blocks of his book betray his interest in priestly ritual.

Third, during his youth Ezekiel surely was exposed to the energetic ministry of the prophet Jeremiah. The priestly prophet from Anathoth may have been the teacher of Ezekiel. The two men lived in close proximity to one another for a quarter of a century. The stamp of Jeremiah can be seen in the words, phrases, sentences and even complete paragraphs of the Book of Ezekiel.

Finally, Ezekiel's deportation to Babylon in 597 BC must have been a major influence on his life. Like the other captives he was treated humanely. Ezekiel was among those captives who settled in the city of Tel Aviv (3:15) in the midst of a fertile district near the river Kebar (1:3).

Unlike his fellow exiles Ezekiel did not view the exile as a temporary and inconsequential setback for Judah. He had been indoctrinated by Jeremiah too thoroughly to accept that superficial view of the situation. Ezekiel knew the servitude to Babylon was to last seventy years (Jer 25:11). He knew that the deportation of 597 BC was the first stage of a process that was to climax in the overthrow of the Judean state.

For five years Ezekiel kept silent in Babylon. He heard others who claimed to be prophets—Ahab, Zedekiah, Shemaiah—proclaim speedy deliverance. He surely must have read the letter written by

Jeremiah to Babylon rebuking these deceivers and pronouncing God's judgment upon them for presuming to speak in the name of Yahweh when they had received no message from God (Jer 29). His confidence in the truthfulness of Jeremiah's message must have been strengthened when two of that trio of false prophets were seized by Nebuchadnezzar and roasted in a fire. The point is that Ezekiel had five years in Babylon to pray and meditate, to sift and sort, and to ponder and evaluate. He had time to seek to comprehend the full theological significance of what had happened in 597 BC, and what was about to happen in 586 BC.

Ministry of Ezekiel

Ezekiel was thirty when he received his call to the prophetic ministry (1:1). He carried out his assigned mission until at least his fifty-second year. How long after that he lived cannot be determined. Did he live to see King Jehoiachin released from prison in 562 BC? (2 Kgs 25:27ff; Jer 52:31). There is no way to tell. A Jewish legend—and it is nothing more than that—has Ezekiel executed by a Jewish prince on account of his prophecies. According to this legend Ezekiel was buried in the tomb of Shem and Arphaxad.

Ezekiel was a contemporary of Jeremiah; but he never mentions the name of his co-laborer. He does, however, mention Daniel 3x (14:14, 20; 28:3). The early sixth century before Christ saw a flowering of the prophetic institution the likes of which had not been seen since the mid-eighth century when Hosea, Amos, Isaiah and Micah were all flourishing. The mid-eighth century has been called the golden age of Hebrew prophecy; the early sixth century could just as well be dubbed the silver age of the prophetic movement.

A. Tone

Ezekiel's mission was primarily, if not exclusively, to the Judean exiles in Babylon. His preaching was meant for their ears. He worked among them as their prophet. The fall of Jerusalem in 586 BC was the pivotal event in the prophet's career. That disaster served to divide Ezekiel's ministry into two distinct phases.

In phase one of his ministry (593-586 BC) Ezekiel was a prophet of doom. In various ways, both by deed and word, he announced that Jerusalem must fall. His threat seemed unconditional. Again and again Ezekiel dashed to pieces the desperate hope of the exiles that they would return swiftly to their homeland. Ezekiel's basic thesis during these years was that sin had severed the union of Yahweh and Jerusalem. For the exiles to have faith meant to free themselves from their dependence on the temple city, to understand the judgment upon it, and to accept that judgment as being the will and purpose of God.

Following the destruction of Jerusalem the tone of Ezekiel's ministry changed. His audience was crushed, despondent and spiritually shaken. The primary tenet of their man-made theology had been demonstrated to be false. Their faith was shattered. Ezekiel sought to comfort those who had lost hope by raising their vision to see the glorious future that God had in store for his people. He sought to guide those who wished to return to Yahweh. Like Jeremiah, Ezekiel followed the path from a demand for repentance to a promise of deliverance.

B. Preaching

As with most prophets preaching played the primary role in the ministry of Ezekiel. "Prophets were not writers in the study, but rather impassioned speakers in the market-places."[6] Twice Ezekiel was told to write something—the name of the day (24:2), and names on two sticks (37:15-16)—but in so doing he was only underscoring or illustrating the spoken word. Once he was told to draw (21:18-23), but the sketch that he made in the sand only served as a visual aid to his preaching. Dozens of times in the book, however, Ezekiel is instructed by God to verbalize the divine message; *prophesy...say* (6:2-3; 13:2; 34:2; 36:1); *speak...say* (14:4; 20:3; 33:2); *propound a riddle, speak an allegory...say* (17:2-3); *take up a lamentation...say* (19:1-2). Like Jeremiah, Ezekiel probably had a scribe to date and record the various oracles that he delivered.

An oracle is a type of prophetic speech in which the prophet becomes the mouthpiece for God. In an oracle Yahweh speaks in the first person. By way of contrast, in a sermon the prophet speaks about God in the third person. An oracle is normally introduced by the formula *thus says Yahweh.* In Ezekiel the oracles usually conclude with one of three formulas: 1) *oracle of Yahweh*, the standard oracular conclusion; 2) the affirmation formula, *I, Yahweh have spoken*; or 3) the recognition formula, *and you/they will know that I am Yahweh.*

---

[6]John Weavers, *Ezekiel, The Century Bible, New Series* (Camden, New Jersey: Nelson, 1969), 11.

The book of Ezekiel is rich in the variety of the prophetic oracles that it contains.

C. Symbolic Actions

More than any other prophet Ezekiel communicated his message through symbolic actions. The purpose of such actions was twofold. First, they were designed to illustrate or render the oral word more concrete. Second, they were sufficiently bizarre to arouse interest on the part of the audience. As a rule the prophet appended to his symbolic action an interpretative oracle that expanded upon the meaning of what he had done.

The symbolic act was considered to be *the word of Yahweh* as much as any oral discourse that the prophet delivered. Each of the mini-dramas is introduced by the expression *the word of Yahweh came to me.* These actions are not to be attributed to the creative genius of Ezekiel. The prophet himself bears testimony to the fact that God directed him in the execution of these acts.

D. Visions

Visionary experiences were also a prominent part of the ministry of Ezekiel. Each vision in the book is introduced by the technical phrase *the hand of Yahweh was upon me*. There is no hint that Ezekiel experienced any traumatic physiological reaction to these visions as did Isaiah (ch 21), Habakkuk (Hab 3:16), and Daniel (Dan 10:7-8). Each vision account contains relevant interpretative oracles that are intended to convey a divine message to the prophet and/or his audience. Dialogue between God and the prophet in the visionary experience is common.

Presumably Ezekiel related to the captives all of the visions that he received from God. The prophetic vision was similar to, but not identical with, a dream experience. Categories of time and space became meaningless. Ezekiel could be physically in Babylon, but then suddenly be in Jerusalem (8:33) or on a high mountain (40:2), or in the midst of a valley (37:1). Scenes change rapidly and illogically. Time is compressed. The measuring of the new temple will have taken considerable time; but in vision this is compressed into but a moment.

Unlike a dream the vision did not occur while sleeping (8:1). The prophet was conscious of entrance into and departure from the visionary state (cf. 8:1 with 11:24b). Ezekiel's visions occur in four sections of the book. The book opens (1:1-3:15) with the vision of the magnificent throne-chariot of God. This was Ezekiel's inaugural vision, the basis for his prophetic ministry. Chs 8-11 contain the prophet's visions of the terrible abominations being practiced back in the Jerusalem temple. The most famous vision in the book is undoubtedly that of the valley of dry bones (ch 37). This vision sets forth in bold symbolism the resurrection of the nation Israel following the Babylonian exile. The Book of Ezekiel closes with a lengthy vision of a future temple in a new era (chs 40-48). Ezekiel devotes more space to recording his visionary experiences than any other prophet in the Old Testament.

Character of Ezekiel

Ezekiel was endowed with great intellectual capacity, clear perception, lively imagination, and eloquent speech. He certainly was acquainted with the sacred books, institutions and customs of his own people. He also was acquainted with the learning and culture of the world in which he lived. So accurate is his knowledge of Egypt and Tyre that one wonders if perhaps he had traveled to these places in his youth.

Ezekiel possessed boundless energy, firm resolution, and amazing self-control (3:15, 24, 26; 24:18). He evidently was a man of deep personal humility as is indicated by the title applied to him some 93x in the book, *son of man*. This title as used in Ezekiel sets forth man's finite dependence and lowliness in the presence of God's infinite power and glory.

Ezekiel was a man of intense moral earnestness (chs 22, 23). He was a powerful orator (33:32) and a poet of the first rank (15:1-5; 19:14-21; 21:14-21). Though perhaps not as intense as Jeremiah, Ezekiel nonetheless was a warm and sympathetic soul (9:8; 19:1, 14). A deep undertone of pity for the fallen nation of Judah is discernible throughout the third main division in the book. While earlier prophets focused on the nation as a whole, Ezekiel was concerned for individual souls.

Wellhausen referred to Ezekiel as a "priest in a prophet's mantle." So he was. From the moment he was told to eat the scroll containing God's word this man was endowed with the spirit and message of Yahweh. From that point on he became the very embodiment of the word that Yahweh desired the exiles to hear. His overt actions were fully as significant as the words he spoke.

Ezekiel immersed himself in his prophetic duties for some twenty-two years. Like his two illustrious contemporaries Jeremiah and Daniel, Ezekiel possessed an invincible fortitude that kept him faithful through long years of rejection and dejection.

Ezekiel's propensity for visions, dramatized signs and trance-states has been interpreted as a symptom of a more or less profound mental disturbance. Albright, for example, states that Ezekiel became one of the greatest spiritual figures of all time "in spite of his tendency to psychic abnormality."[7] Others see evidence of schizophrenia or catalepsy[8] in his personality.

It is ridiculous in the extreme to attempt amateur psychoanalysis on a person of another culture and age who has been dead for twenty-five hundred years. One is on safer ground to speak of Ezekiel as "a highly developed mystic who was able to utilize channels of communication not normally available to others."[9] The fallacy of suggesting that Ezekiel was in some sense deranged can be easily demonstrated from a study of his words. His thought processes are normal, his ideas are completely comprehensible, his sentences are coherent and the sequence of ideas yields meaningful continuity.

Fohrer[10] has observed three paradoxes in Ezekiel: 1) burning passion on the one hand, pedantic casuistry on the other; 2) bold hopes for the future, but also a sober sense of reality; and 3) on occasion he speaks coldly and bluntly, while on other occasions he feels full sympathy for both the devout and the wicked.

Message of Ezekiel

The fall of Jerusalem and captivity were necessary measures for God to employ in order to correct his disobedient people. Ezekiel's

---

[7]W.F. Albright, *From the Stone Age to Christianity* (2nd ed.; Garden City, NY: Doubleday, 1957), 325.

[8]Catalepsy is a pathological condition akin to autohypnosis. The afflicted person manifests a tonic rigidity of the limbs to the point where they can be placed and maintained in various positions for long periods of time.

[9]R.K Harrison, *Introduction to the Old Testament* (Grand Rapids: Eerdmans, 1969), 851.

[10]George Fohrer, *Introduction to the Old Testament* (Trans. David Green; Nashville: Abingdon, 1968), 415.

prophetic duty was to explain that Judah—the theocracy in its outward form—must come to an end because of sin. Exile, however, was not the end of the story. God will one day re-gather a penitent remnant of his chastened people. He will bring them back to their homeland where they will share in a glorious latter-day theocracy. Thus the basic message of Ezekiel is that God is faithful to his eternal purpose. The sinful nation must be destroyed, yet God will not forsake his own people. At first his messages were not well received (14:1, 3; 18:19, 25). In time, however, Ezekiel's prophecies produced fundamental change in the idolatrous tendencies of the nation.

Ezekiel was a priest as well as a prophet. In many passages the interest of a man of priestly origin is apparent. His concern with the cult, priesthood and sanctuary doubtlessly influenced the attitude of the postexilic Jews toward the temple. Ezekiel, however, was not a priestly ritualist whose only concern was with the minutiae of liturgy and worship. He makes important contributions to biblical theology.

A. Doctrine of God

In Isaiah the focus is on the *salvation* of Yahweh; in Jeremiah, the *judgment* of Yahweh; in Daniel, the *kingdom* of Yahweh; and in Ezekiel the focus is on the *glory* of Yahweh.[11] To Ezekiel God was the supreme, self-existent, almighty (1:24) and omniscient (1:18) One.[12] The God of Israel was no mere local or national deity. He was infinitely exalted above the earth, clothed with honor and majesty. Yahweh was the ruler of the celestial hierarchies as well as all that dwell on earth. Men and nations yield to his sovereign decisions. Egypt, Babylon and all heathen peoples were bound to obey him. The mighty Nebuchadnezzar was but a tool in his hand.

To Ezekiel God was the Holy One (39:7) whose name was holy (36:21-22; 39:25). He was a God who could make no compromise with sin, who could not overlook the guilty, whether individual or national. Because of the sin of his people Yahweh withdrew his glory from Jerusalem and the temple (10:18; 11:23). This holy God placed in the mouth of his prophet terrible denunciations against the wickedness of Israel and Judah. In fact, Ezekiel's denunciation of the spiritual waywardness of Judah is more severe than that of his contemporary Jeremiah.

---

[11]Charles L. Feinberg, *The Prophecy of Ezekiel* (Chicago: Moody, 1969), 12.

[12]Thomas Whitelaw, *Ezekiel* in "Pulpit Commentary" (New York: Funk and Wagnals, 1909), xxix. The theological summary that follows is adapted from Whitelaw.

On the other hand, the God of Ezekiel was a God of boundless grace who had no pleasure in the death of the wicked (18:23, 32; 33:11). Amidst the threats of judgment Yahweh woos his people to repentance (14:22; 16:63; 20:11). Although they were undeserving of his mercy (36:32), yet Yahweh promised the penitent a glorious future.

B. Doctrine of Messiah

The Messiah is not as prominent in Jeremiah and Ezekiel as in Isaiah. Nonetheless, some striking teaching about the Promised One does appear in this book. The Messiah is represented as a *tender twig* taken from the highest branch of the cedar of Judah's royalty. He was to be planted upon a high mountain (17:22-24). He is the one to whom the diadem of Israel's sovereignty rightfully belonged, and to whom it will be given after it had been removed from the head of the wicked Zedekiah (21:27). The messianic David will be a faithful prince among God's restored people. He will perform all the functions of a true and faithful Shepherd (34:23-24), ruling over them as king (37:24). This Prince will eat and drink before Yahweh in his capacity of special representative of God's people (44:3).

C. Doctrine of Man

Ezekiel viewed man as God's creature and property (18:4). He shows awareness of the biblical teaching of the original innocence of man (28:15, 17). Man, however, had fallen; man is sinful (18:21-30). His heart needs to be softened and renewed (18:31). For his wickedness he is held individually accountable (18:4, 13, 18). He is a free moral agent. He is responsible for his own reformation of life and purification of heart[13] (33:11; 43:9). God will give a new heart (11:19; 36:26; 37:23) to those willing to receive it. Among the Old Testament prophets Ezekiel has earned the title "the champion of individualism."

D. Doctrine of God's Kingdom

Ezekiel never uses the terminology "kingdom of God;" but the book certainly points to the concept of God's reign over the hearts of redeemed men. Ezekiel stressed one point that was considered rank heresy by his countrymen, viz. that the kingdom of God was not inseparably connected with the political existence of Judah. He saw an inner spiritual kernel of the nation existing in the lands of the disper-

[13]Ezekiel is expanding on a theme proclaimed by Jeremiah (Jer 31:34).

sion (12:17). This nucleus was constantly growing as penitent men were added to it (34:11-19). Eventually Ezekiel saw a new Israel with Messiah as its prince (34:23-24; 37:24). That new Israel will walk in the law of Yahweh (11:20; 16:61; 20:43; 36:27) and dwell in the land of Canaan (36:33; 37:25). God will enter into a new covenant with that people[14] (37:26-28). He will walk in close fellowship with them (39:29; 46:9). Upon them he will pour out his Holy Spirit (36:27; 39:27).

Mission of the Prophet

Ezekiel's special task was to act as a watchman to the house of Israel (3:17; 33:7). He was to warn the wicked of the danger of persisting in wickedness. He was to warn the righteous of the peril of turning from the path of fidelity.

A. Dimensions of his Mission

To be more specific, Ezekiel's task can be seen as having a fourfold thrust. First, he had the task of demolishing delusions. Ezekiel was to refute the shallow theology that argued that Jerusalem could not be destroyed. He was to defuse the potentially dangerous deception that the exile will soon end with the overthrow of Babylon. Ezekiel had a clear and accurate assessment of the moral and religious situation both in Judah and in Babylon.

Second, Ezekiel was to expose apostasy. Thereby he was to present God's rationale for the past and future judgments on the Judeans. He was "to interpret for Israel in exile the stern logic of her past history."[15]

Third, Ezekiel was to awaken repentance. Thereby he could raise up from the ruins of old Israel a new people who might inherit the promises that had been given to Abraham, Isaac and Jacob.

Finally, Ezekiel was to stimulate hope for a better tomorrow with the promise of restoration after the seventy years of Babylonian supremacy had ended.

---

[14]The classic Old Testament promise of a new covenant is Jer 31:31ff.

[15]Whitelaw, *Pulpit Commentary*, x.

B. Comparison with Other Prophets

Ezekiel's mission stands in stark contrast to that of Daniel, his illustrious contemporary and fellow captive. Daniel was God's messenger to the mighty monarchs of Babylon and Persia. He rubbed elbows with royalty and never, so far as is known, preached to his fellow exiles. Ezekiel, on the other hand, conducted most of his ministry from his home. He apparently never undertook journeys to distant colonies of exiles, but restricted his prophetic utterances to those who sought him out at his dwelling (8:1; 14:1; 20:1; 24:19). Some of his sermons, however, may have been delivered before larger audiences.[16] Most of his utterances were first spoken before being written. His foreign nation oracles (chs 25-32) and his elaborate description of the messianic temple (chs 40-48) were probably never spoken orally.

Like most of the prophets, Ezekiel was commissioned by God to deliver a series of oracles against foreign nations. The messages were intended to sound a note of warning to the nations that were harassing Israel and exulting in her overthrow. Ezekiel argued that the destruction of Israel was nothing over which the nations should gloat because Israel's destruction was a pledge of their own doom. These foreign nation oracles also served the purpose of beginning the consolation that Ezekiel had for his own people. Israel should derive comfort from the thought that God was preparing for their recovery by pouring out his wrath upon their foes.

BOOK OF EZEKIEL

Before undertaking an exegesis of the prophecies of Ezekiel, some introductory and critical matters pertaining to the book must first be treated.

Authorship of the Book

A. Claims of the Book

The view that Ezekiel the son of Buzi, the sixth century exile, authored the entire book that bears his name is supported by good evidence. First, the book claims to be by this Ezekiel (1:1;

[16]Sermons on Judah's sins (chs 6, 7, 13, 16); sermons on repentance (chs 33, 36); and sermons on the justice of God (chs 18, 33).

8:1; 33:1; 40:1-4). A unity of theme is observable throughout the forty-eight chs—God's vengeance in Israel's destruction and God's vindication in Israel's restoration. Thirteen prophecies are dated and localized in such a way as to point to the life and times of Ezekiel. Similarity of thought, style, phrasing and arrangement make it clear that the entire book is the work of one mind. The evidence for the authenticity and unity of Ezekiel is so convincing that some scholars who otherwise take a critical view toward the Old Testament have written in support of the essential Ezekielian authorship (e.g., Cornill, and Driver). The work as a whole bears the decided imprint of a single personality.

B. Clouds over the Book

The traditional view of Ezekielian authorship is clouded by two curious statements in Jewish literature. The first is in the Talmud (fifth century AD) where it is said that "the men of the Great Synagogue wrote Ezekiel and the Twelve."[17] A second curious statement is found in Josephus (first century AD): "But not only did he [Jeremiah] predict to the people [the destruction of Jerusalem], but also the prophet Ezekiel who first wrote two books about these things and left them [for posterity.][18]

The Talmud statement probably means nothing more than that the men of the Great Synagogue in the days of Ezra edited and copied the original writing of Ezekiel, The *two books* referred to by Josephus probably are a reference to the two major divisions of the present Book of Ezekiel. Young[19] suggests that chs 1-32 may have constituted the first book, and chs 33-48 the second.

Canonicity of the Book

The Book of Ezekiel was one of five antilegomena—books spoken against—in the Hebrew canon. Certain rabbis were convinced that the teaching of this book was not in harmony with Mosaic Law. The Torah (Law), for example, prescribed two bullocks and seven lambs and one ram be offered at new moon celebrations (Nm 28:11).

---

[17]*Baba Bathra* 15a.

[18]Josephus, *Antiquities* 10:5.1.

[19]Edward J. Young, *An Introduction to the Old Testament* (Grand Rapids: Eerdmans, 1960), 256.

Ezekiel, however, speaks of only one unblemished bullock, six lambs and one ram (Ezek 46:6).

Rabbi Hananiah vigorously defended the book before those who argued that it should be removed from the canon. Legend has it that he burned the midnight oil—300 jars of it—in harmonizing Ezekiel with the Pentateuch.[20] Hananiah's effort at harmonization must not have satisfied all Jewish scholars. The Talmud (*Menach.* 45a) states that when Elijah comes (cf. Mal 4:5) the discrepancies between Ezekiel and the Pentateuch will be explained.

Modern scholars are not concerned about the differences between the worship system described in Ezekiel and that set forth by Moses. Ezekiel was describing the worship of a new age and a new covenant.

The Book of Ezekiel certainly belongs in the Christian Bible. It apparently was found in Nehemiah's collection of "the acts of the kings, and the prophets, and of David, and the epistles of the kings concerning holy gifts" (2 Macc 2:13). Ezekiel was included in the Septuagint translation that was initiated about 280 BC. Josephus, the famous Jewish historian, numbered this book among the books held sacred by the Jews in his day.[21] The majority of the rabbis defended the book against the disparagement of those who were concerned about the discrepancies with the Pentateuch. The Book of Ezekiel was listed in the Talmud (*Baba Bathra* 14b) as belonging to the canon. In Christian circles the canonicity of Ezekiel never has been questioned seriously. Among early Christian scholars the book was acknowledged as canonical by Melito (AD 172) and Origen (AD 250).

Modern Criticism

Modern criticism of the Book of Ezekiel goes back to the Dutch Jewish philosopher Spinoza in the seventeenth century. From that time to the present the attacks on the book have taken four forms.

A. Attack on Authenticity

In the nineteenth century some critics began to argue that the entire Book of Ezekiel was a literary fraud. One group of critics dated the book to the Persian period (Zunz, Geiger), and another group to as late as the Maccabean age (Seinecke). C.C. Torrey, with his charac-

---

[20]*Shabbath* 14b; *Hagiga* 13a; *Menachoth* 45a.
[21]*Against Apion* 1:8.

teristic propensity for out radicalizing the radicals, proposed in his book *Pseudo-Ezekiel* (1930) that the whole book was a pseudepigraphic work composed centuries after the time of Ezekiel.[22] Another critic, James Smith [no relation to the present writer], argued that the book was actually written in the time of King Manasseh early in the seventh century, a century earlier than Ezekiel.

Bentzen contends that "the book as it now stands is no authentic work of the prophet Ezekiel."[23] One basis for such an assertion is the dogmatic contention that a prophet cannot hold forth both doom and promise. Critics imagine that the historic Ezekiel must have been a preacher of doom who offered the nation no ray of hope. Nearly all Old Testament prophets who speak of doom, however, also hold out some hope of restoration for God's people. The mixture of gloom and discouragement on the one hand, and hope and optimism on the other can be observed in the discourses of any great preacher of the word.

In response to these conjectures the opinion of another respected critic needs to be heard. Fohrer thinks Ezekiel was active in the period defined by the dates given in his utterances. "There is no evidence in favor of a date different from that suggested in the book of Ezekiel."[24]

B. Attack on Unity

In the eighteenth century questioning the unity of ancient documents came in vogue. The unity of nearly every Old Testament prophetic book became suspect at this time. G.L. Oeder suggested that chs 40-48 were added to the Book of Ezekiel long after the prophet was dead.

C. Attack upon Integrity

Modern critics will not allow that Ezekiel was responsible for the arrangement and assembling of the utterances and reports that make up his book. Others must have done this work. These critics disagree among themselves as to whether this rather extensive editorializing was a long process (Freedman), a single editor (May) or a particular circle of disciples (Zimmerli). In any case, the critics believe that the evolution of the book continued even after the editors put it together.

---

[22] Torrey dated the book about 230 BC. Browne dated the book to the time of Alexander the Great, and van den Born to the days of Ezra-Nehemiah.
[23] Aage Bentzen, *Introduction to the Old Testament* (5th ed.; Copenhagen: Gad, 1959), 2:125.
[24] Fohrer, *Introduction*, 406.

They postulate later "literary accretions" by scribes who copied the work.[25]

Most critics will allow that the sixth century Ezekiel wrote some part of the present book; but they attribute to him only a bare minimum of the total vv in the book. This trend began with Jahn (1905) who proposed that scribal notes from the margin of ancient manuscripts were later inserted into the text of the Book of Ezekiel. Hoelscher (1942) wielded the knife of literary criticism mercilessly. He argued that only 170 vv of the 1273 in the book actually belonged to Ezekiel.[26] William A. Irwin (1943) did a little better for the prophet. He gave him 251 vv of the book. H.G. May in the *Interpreter's Bible* generously assigns about half the book to Ezekiel.

On what basis do these critics deny these large chunks of material to Ezekiel? Hoelscher and Irwin take the distinction between poetry and prose as the criterion of genuineness. They deny Ezekiel's authorship of everything that cannot be fitted into a pre-determined poetic style. Fohrer takes to task other critics for denying large sections of the book to Ezekiel. He then asserts: "Nevertheless, the material preserved under the name of Ezekiel contains a series of later passages deriving from various authors and various periods."[27] Fohrer himself denies about 111 vv to Ezekiel.

Each critic seems to have his own criteria for deciding what is genuine and what is not. The subjectivity of this approach is manifest. Harrison raises an appropriate question: "How is it possible to establish canons of genuineness, and what in fact constitutes an oracle thus defined?"[28]

Setting of the Book

A. Babylon or Jerusalem?

In 1932 Herntrich introduced the suggestion that Ezekiel actually lived and ministered in Palestine rather than in Babylon as the book plainly states. Later editors were responsible for the literary framework of the book that makes it appear that Ezekiel lived in Babylon. Other critics have suggested that the locale shifted during Ezekiel's

---

[25]Ibid.

[26]Harrison (*Introduction,* 824) refers to Hoelscher's work as "one of the most radical treatments to which the book of Ezekiel has ever been subjected."

[27]Fohrer, *Introduction*, 410.

[28]Harrison, *Introduction*, 840.

ministry. Ezekiel is said to have returned to Palestine from Babylon (May) in 591 BC, or to have commenced his ministry in Palestine and subsequently to have gone to Babylon (Bertholet). Some complicate the matter further by postulating a double shift in Ezekiel's ministry. Pfeiffer will have Ezekiel first in Babylon, then back in Jerusalem, and finally back among the exiles in Babylon.[29]

B. Evidence Evaluated

Five arguments have been advanced in support of the view that Ezekiel spent part of his time ministering in Palestine. First, many of the oracles in chs 1-24 are relevant to Jerusalem and Judah rather than to the exiles.

Actually very little is known about the religious attitudes of the exiles apart from the Book of Ezekiel. How then can one be so sure that what Ezekiel says was not appropriate to the situation in Babylonia? The exiles apparently considered themselves still a part of Jerusalem society. They optimistically expected to return to the homeland shortly. Therefore invectives against Jerusalem society are far from meaningless to the exilic audience. Furthermore, some of Ezekiel's utterances may actually have been carried back to Jerusalem by travelers.

Second, in ch 16 Ezekiel was told to "make known to Jerusalem her abominations." A message to a society, however, does not demand the physical presence of the prophet. Numerous examples can be cited of prophets who resided in Jerusalem who addressed oracles to foreign nations they had never seen or visited. Therefore the fact that one or two prophecies are directed to Jerusalem and Judah is no evidence that Ezekiel must have been in Palestine at that particular moment.

Third, prophecies are directed to "the house of Israel," the "rebellious house" that might refer to the inhabitants of Palestine. The exiles, however, considered themselves a part of the house of Israel. The concept of national solidarity made the exiles corporately part of the rebellious house.

Fourth, Ezekiel betrays an intimate acquaintance with what is going on in the temple in chs 8-11. In response it must be recognized that Ezekiel's priestly background provided him with vivid recollection of the temple structure and worship. Furthermore, Jer 29 proves

---

[29]Bentzen (*Introduction*, 2:128) suggests that Ezekiel was a Babylonian secret agent who was allowed to return to Palestine a few years before the fall of Jerusalem.

that contacts between Jerusalem and Babylon were greater than one might think. News of recent developments in Jerusalem could have reached the prophet's ears by means of those who traveled between the two places. Finally, Ezekiel may have received his knowledge of the temple idolatries through divine revelation.

Fifth, ch 11 demands clairvoyant powers on the part of Ezekiel if he were living in Babylonia. How could he have known that Pelatiah had died immediately in response to the oracle that he had just given?

Answer: It may be that the statement in 11:13 that Pelatiah died immediately in response to the oracle is itself a part of the vision. If so, no problem exists. On the other hand, through divine revelation Ezekiel may have known immediately that Pelatiah died in accordance with the prophetic word.

The theory of a Palestinian ministry for Ezekiel creates more problems than it solves. Far-reaching textual alterations are necessary in order to support the theory. Whole sections of the book must be pronounced spurious. Fohrer, himself a radical critic, has stated: "Nothing suggests Jerusalem as one or the only location of Ezekiel's ministry; on the contrary, everything points to Babylonia."[30] Of the utterances of Jeremiah he is familiar essentially with those from the period before 597 BC. Not one shred of evidence can be produced to suggest that Ezekiel spent the crucial years under Zedekiah in Jerusalem, or experienced the bitter siege of that city. Besides, no one has ever successfully explained what an editor possibly could have gained by transferring the ministry of a Palestinian prophet to Babylon.

The critical studies of the Book of Ezekiel over the past eight decades or so have largely cancelled out each other. The situation now is much the same as it was prior to 1924 (the work of Hoelscher) when the unity and integrity of the book were generally accepted by the critics.[31] H.H. Rowley (1953) defended the essential unity of the book and took issue with those who transferred the prophet from Babylon to Palestine or from the sixth century to some other time-frame.

---

[30]Fohrer, *Introduction*, 407. Even among critical scholars the trend is to support an exclusively Babylonian ministry for Ezekiel as can be seen in the works of Howie (1950), Cooke (1960) and in West (1971).

[31]H.L Ellison, "Ezekiel, Book of," *The New Bible Dictionary* (ed. J.D. Douglas; Grand Rapids: Eerdmans, 1962), 407.

Literary Characteristics

A. General Comments

Most modern critics give Ezekiel low marks on literary style. Driver referred to him as the most uniformly prosaic of the earlier prophets. It is wrong, however, to analyze the book on the naive assumption that the author was essentially a poet as some critics have done (e.g., Hoelscher and Irwin). It is true that the book is characterized by what moderns might consider excess verbiage. The sentences are often long and involved. Ezekiel's style, however, is enriched by uncommon comparisons. The straight forward and unembellished narration is at times punctuated by passages sublime in both thought and expression. If at times Ezekiel smothers his readers with comparatively dry and uninteresting details (e.g., 40:6-49), at other times he overwhelms them with a barrage of scintillating images (e.g., ch 27). At times he halts and staggers (ch 17); at other times he emotionally plunges forward.

B. Specific Details

To be specific, the Book of Ezekiel is marked by at least seven stylistic characteristics. First, the book is *permeated with the supernatural.* It is impossible to reduce Ezekiel to an ordinary or even an extraordinary man of genius. The book is not the result of the subjective meditations of Ezekiel about the condition of his people. Ezekiel insists that every vision, every symbol, every oracle be understood as divine communication of which he was merely the intermediary.

Second, the book is marked by *highly idealistic coloring.* Challenging visions, allegories, parables and the like are found throughout. God no doubt chose to communicate his word in forms suitable to the poetic temperament of this prophet. This type of imaginative discourse is eminently suited for capturing the attention of reluctant listeners. It impresses vividly upon their minds the truths of God. Scholars differ among themselves as to the source of Ezekiel's imagery. Was he influenced by the art of Babylonia? Many sculptured shapes found in that area have points of analogy to Ezekiel's cherubim. Keil has argued, however, that all the symbolism in the book is derived from the Israelite sanctuary. It is the logical outcome of Old Testament ideas and views.

Third, Ezekiel makes *extensive use of earlier Scriptures.* He displays an intimate knowledge of the works of the eighth century prophets—Hosea, Amos and Isaiah—as well as those of his own century—Jeremiah and Zephaniah.[32] Most certainly Ezekiel was acquainted with the Pentateuch.[33]

Fourth, the book reflects a *cosmopolitan outlook*. Ezekiel exhibits a remarkable acquaintance with several foreign lands. Some scholars have even suggested that he may have visited these lands in his youth.

Fifth, Ezekiel employed *cultured diction*. He was an aristocrat; and there is something aristocratic about his style.[34]

Sixth, the book is marked by *originality*. Ezekiel freely reproduced the sentiments of the earlier writers "with the stamp of his own individuality" upon them."[35] Among the expressions and thoughts original in the book are the following: *son of man; rebellious house; hand of Yahweh was on me; the word of Yahweh came unto me; set your face against; they will know that I am Yahweh; they will know that a prophet is in their midst; thus says Lord Yahweh*. A long list of Hebrew verbs and nouns peculiar to Ezekiel could also be produced.

Seventh, the book is full of *repetition and deliberate redundancy*. If his visions are obscure and mystical Ezekiel's sermons are simple. He believed in the technique of emphasis by repetition. He wanted to make it impossible for his hearers to misunderstand his prose discourses.

Interpretation of Ezekiel

The interpreter faces his greatest challenge in the first ten and in the last nine chs of the book. Ezekiel was the great mystic among the prophets. It is probably because of the difficulty of interpreting his visionary and symbolic prophecies that Ezekiel is the most neglected of all the prophets.[36] Hall has put his finger on the reason for the difficulties in Ezekiel. He regards the book as "a transition from regular prophetic literature with its annunciations and denunciations to the

---

[32]See Whitelaw, *Pulpit Commentary*, xxv for a list of passages reflecting the writings of Jeremiah.
[33]An extensive list of passages indicating widespread acquaintance with the Pentateuch can be found in Whitelaw, *Pulpit Commentary*, pp. xxv-xxvi.
[34]Ibid.
[35]Ibid.
[36]Feinberg, *Ezekiel*, 13.

highly figurative apocalyptic literature of works such as Daniel and Revelation."[37]

Ezekiel is a mixture of prosaic and poetic, historical and prophetical, literal and symbolic, realistic and idealistic discourse. Each type of literature must be interpreted according to its own hermeneutical principles. Ordinarily it is not too difficult to identify clearly these various types of literature. Obviously the visions and symbols are the most difficult. Ezekiel's visions seem to have been based on actual scenic representations that were present to his mind's eye during moments of ecstasy. In regard to his symbolic acts the question arises: were they actual occurrences, or were they merely carried out mentally by the prophet and reported to the captives? Were they external (Plumptre) or merely internal occurrences (Keil; Hengstenberg)?

There is no reason to doubt that Ezekiel did physically perform some of his symbolic acts, e.g., carrying stuff from his house (11:7); sighing bitterly before the eyes of the people (21:6). In other instances the question is not so easily answered. This much is clear: If Ezekiel did not actually perform the actions before his auditors in his own house, it at least seemed to him while in the ecstatic state that he did.[38]

Text of Ezekiel

Harrison describes the Hebrew text of Ezekiel as "poorly preserved."[39] He attributes the difficulties in the Hebrew text to the obscurities, technical expressions and *hapax legomena* that led subsequent copyists into frequent error. It is interesting, however, that the fragments that could be detached from the Ezekiel scroll found in Cave 11 at Qumran show that the Hebrew text was fixed in a form similar to the standard Masoretic Text by the middle of the first century BC at the latest.

The Septuagint (Greek) text of Ezekiel was translated by a fairly literal translator, although he occasionally paraphrases when the text is difficult. At times he gave such a literal rendering of the Hebrew that his translation makes for impossible Greek. He often omitted re-

---

[37]Bert Hall, "The Book of Ezekiel," in vol. III of *The Wesleyan Bible Commentary*. (ed. Charles W. Carter. Grand Rapids: Eerdmans, 1967), 369.
[38]Whitelaw, *Pulpit Commentary*, xxix.
[39]Harrison, *Introduction*, 854.

repetitious words and phrases so as to make for a simpler form of the text. Sometimes he appears intentionally to change the text in accordance with a different point of view.

Structure and Arrangement

The Book of Ezekiel has been carefully constructed. It is to Ezekiel himself that the credit for this arrangement belongs. The fall of Jerusalem was the mid-point in the ministry of the prophet and also in the book. Chs 1-24 come from the period prior to the fall of Jerusalem; the last twenty-four chs in the main are post-fall.[40] In terms of subject matter the book breaks down into three divisions—oracles against Israel (1-24), oracles against foreign nations (25-32); and a second section pertaining to Israel (33-48).[41]

Chart 1 STRUCTURE OF EZEKIEL		
Oracles Concerning Israel	**Oracles Concerning Nations**	**Oracles Concerning Israel**
Chs 1-24	**Chs 25-32**	**Chs 33-48**
Prior to Fall of Jerusalem	**During Siege of Jerusalem**	**After Fall of Jerusalem**
Condemnation & Catastrophe		**Consolation & Comfort**

Whatever interruption of strict chronological sequence that the book displays is best accounted for as the work of Ezekiel himself, not some perplexed editor. The prophet at times desired to group his prophecies by the subjects to which they related rather than by the dates on which they were spoken.

The Book of Ezekiel displays a chronological system[42] unparalleled in any prophetic book save Haggai. Sixteen dates are given in

[40]Because of the importance of the destruction of the temple, some divide the book at 33:21.

[41]The structure of Ezekiel is similar to that of Isaiah in the Hebrew Bible and Jeremiah in the Greek Bible where the oracles against foreign nations are grouped in the middle of the book.

[42]K.S. Freedy and D.B. Redford, "The Dates in Ezekiel in Relation to Biblical, Babylonian and Egyptian sources," *JAOS* 90 (1970): 462-485.

fourteen passages. In two cases (1:1-2; 40:1) a double dating is employed utilizing two different counting systems. In the following chart the chronological references are tabulated and converted into the modern calendrical system.

The dating in the Book of Ezekiel is based on the years of the deportation of King Jehoiachin. This young king went captive in 597 BC. Apparently he was still considered by many of that time the legal ruler of Judah *vis-à-vis* Zedekiah who was looked upon as a mere regent of Nebuchadnezzar.[43]

Chart 2
EZEKIEL'S CHRONOLOGICAL SYSTEM

REFERENCE	YR/MO/DAY	CONVERSION
1:2	5/4/5	Aug 1, 593
8:1	6/6/5	Sep 19, 592
20:1	7/5/10	Aug 14, 591
24:1	9/10/10**	Dec 29, 588
29:1	10/10/12	Dec 31, 588
30:20	11/1/7	Apr 30, 587
31:1	11/3/1	Jun 21, 587
26:1	11/ ? /1	Sep 18, 587*
33:21	12/10/5	Jan 4, 585
32:1	12/12/1	Mar 4, 585
32:17	12/ ? /15	Mar 18, 585*
40:1	25/1/10	Apr 29, 573
29:17	27/1/1	Apr 26, 571

* Since the month is not given in the Hebrew text the date is conjecture. See discussion at the relevant passage. The conversion column is based on the assumption that Ezekiel used the Spring calendar that was common in Babylon rather than the Autumn calendar that at various times was employed in Palestine.
**Ezekiel here is using the dates of Zedekiah for this event as in 2 Kgs 25:1.

Harrison[44] follows Brownlee in suggesting that the Book of Ezekiel is "a literary bifid," i.e., the book reveals a two part arrangement.

---

[43]Even after his deportation to Babylon, Jehoiachin appears to have possessed land in Palestine. A seal of his steward, dating after 597 BC, has been found in Palestine, See W.F. Albright, "The Seal of Eliakim and the Latest Pre-Exilic History of Judah, with Some Observations on Ezekiel," *JBL*, 51 (1932): 77-106.
[44]Harrison, *Introduction*, 848-49.

Harrison puts a great deal of emphasis on the statement of Josephus (*Ant.* 10:5.1) that Ezekiel left behind *two* books. These books, originally separate productions of the prophet, have been combined in the present book. Harrison thinks that chs 1-23 constitute Book One and chs 24-48 Book Two. The following chart indicates parallels between the two "books" of Ezekiel.

Chart 3
HARRISON'S TWO BOOK THEORY

BOOK ONE Chs 1-23	**BOOK TWO Chs 24-48**
Vengeance of Yahweh against his People	Vindication of Yahweh through his People
Name Ezekiel appears once (1:3)	Name Ezekiel appears once (24:24)[45]
Commissioning of the prophet (3:25-27)	Commissioning of the prophet (33:1-9)
Commission followed by dumbness (3:25-27	Commission followed by release from dumbness (33:21f)
Divine glory forsakes temple (chs 8-11)	Divine glory returns to sanctify land (43:1-5)

[45] Such renewed claim to authorship is made by Thucydides in his *History* (5:26), the probable beginning of the second roll of his work.

TRANSLATION AND COMMENTARY

EZEKIEL 1
INAUGURAL VISION[46]

Before a prophet could speak to others God had to speak to him. A special call vision catapulted the young priest Ezekiel into the prophetic ministry. The vision of the divine chariot—the *Merkabah* as it is known in Jewish literature—is a fitting introduction to his career. Jewish mystics have always been fascinated with this material. More recently science fiction writers have subjected the *Merkabah* to the most detailed scrutiny in search of evidence that spaceships from other worlds have landed on this planet.

Much has been written on this ch. Often the discussion has centered on the mechanics of the *Merkabah* rather than the message that God is trying to communicate through this vision. In ch 1 Ezekiel discusses the setting (vv 1-3) and the substance (vv 4-28) of his inaugural vision.

SETTING OF THE VISION
1:1-3

The first three vv are a preface to the Book of Ezekiel. Two distinct statements can be identified here. Verse 1 is in the first person and vv 2-3 are in the third person.[47] Some critics think two distinct superscriptions are used, superscriptions that at one time headed separate collections of Ezekiel's writings. It is better, however, to regard vv 2-3 as a parenthetical insertion by Ezekiel himself designed to explain the puzzling, indefinite expressions in v 1.

That vv 2-3 are an integral part of this book can be seen in the fact that they provide, in addition to the date for the book, the customary information about the author. The following chart sets forth the differences between the autobiographical superscription and the parenthetical explanation that follows.

[46]Leslie Allen, "The Structure and Intention of Ezekiel I," *VT* 43 (1993): 145-61.
[47]Verse 3 is the only v in the book in which Ezekiel's personal experiences are described in the third person.

Chart 4 SUPERSCRIPTION TO THE BOOK		
	Verse 1	**Verses 2-3**
Form	First Person	Third Person
Date	Thirtieth Year Fourth Month Fifth Day	Fifth Year of Jehoiachin's Captivity Fifth Day
Place	In the midst of the captives by the River Kebar	In the land of the Chaldeans by the River Kebar
Experience	Heavens were opened, I saw visions of God	Word of Yahweh came assuredly unto Ezekiel. Hand of Yahweh was upon him.
Recipient		Ezekiel son of Buzi the priest

The double preface to the Book of Ezekiel (vv 1-3) presents the setting for the inaugural vision of the prophet. These vv set forth information regarding the recipient; the time; the place; and the nature of the vision.

Preface
1:1

Now it came to pass in the thirtieth year, the fourth month, the fifth day of the month that I was in the midst of the captives beside the River Kebar. The heavens were opened and I saw visions of God.

A. Personal Dating (1:1a)

Ezekiel's inaugural vision receives double dating.[48] In v 1 the vision is dated in terms of Ezekiel's own life; in v 2, according to the captivity of King Jehoiachin.

Ezekiel was thirty years old when he received the divine call to be a prophet.[49] From v 2 it can be computed that the call vision fell in the

[48]N.H. Tur-Sinai, "The Double Dating of Ezechiel 1-3," *BIES* 23 (1959): 5-7.

[49]This interpretation of the *thirtieth year* in 1:1 seems to have been proposed first by the church father Origen (d. AD 253). The objection has been raised that it is rather unusual for a prophet to call attention to his age. It must be remembered, however,

year 593 BC. This means that Ezekiel was born about 622 BC, during the reign of good King Josiah. He was born four years after Jeremiah began his ministry, and one year before the discovery of the lost book of the law in the temple. The dated prophecies in this book cover a span of twenty-two years. Thus Ezekiel engaged in his prophetic ministry between the ages of thirty and fifty-two.

It is strange that nothing is said in the Old Testament or in Jewish tradition about the age at which a priest began to serve. Under the Law of Moses, however, Levites entered into their service at the age of thirty (Nm 4:23, 30). The probability is rather strong that this was the normal age for entering priestly service as well.[50] If this is so, then Ezekiel never functioned as a priest prior to his deportation in 597 BC, for as v 2 clearly shows, his thirtieth year fell in 593 BC.

While he never officiated in the temple Ezekiel must have studied for years the intricate details of priestly ritual. His thirtieth birthday must have been particularly sad for the son of Buzi because he knew he would never succeed his father in the sacred vocation for which he had prepared throughout his youth. This was a crucial time in the life of Ezekiel. Since it would not be possible for this godly man to serve Yahweh as a priest God called him to another and even more vital sphere of service.

Some scholars regard the thirty years as reckoned from some fixed point in Babylonian or Jewish history. Thus in one scheme the thirty years are counted from the accession of Nabopolassar in 626 BC. This yields a date of 596 BC, one year after the deportation of Ezekiel and ten thousand of his countrymen. This computation will not square with the fifth year of the captivity of Jehoiachin mentioned in v 2. Even less justification exists for counting the thirty years from 621 BC when the lost law book was discovered in the Jerusalem tem-

---

that Ezekiel was an unusual prophet. Verse 1 presents certain unique characteristics on any interpretation. See Harrison, *Introduction*, 838; James Miller, "The Thirtieth Year of Ezekiel 1:1," *RB* 99 (1992): 499-503; S.G. Taylor, "A Consideration of the 'Thirtieth Year' in Ez 1:1," *TB* 17 (1966): 119-20; C.F. Whitley, "The 'Thirtieth' Year in Ezekiel 1:1," *VT* 9 (1959): 326-30.

[50]It was at this age that Jesus commenced his priestly ministry. John the Baptist was also in his thirtieth year when he began to preach on the banks of the Jordan.

ple.[51] As important as this event was in the history of the monarchy, no example of reckoning time from this year can be adduced.[52]

So important was the inaugural vision in the life of Ezekiel that he dates it as to month and day as well as year. The call came in the fourth month. Ezekiel here follows the normal pre-exilic custom of numbering rather than naming the month. In postexilic times the fourth month was known as Tammuz. Converted into modern day equivalents Ezekiel's call vision occurred on August 1, 593 BC.

B. **Place of Vision** (1:1b)

Ezekiel was in *the midst of the captives* when he received his majestic vision. What a mixed group they were! Some had given up on God because of the misfortunes that had befallen them. They had compromised with the materialistic culture of Babylon. Others clung desperately at the outset to the illusion that God would never let Jerusalem be destroyed—that God would shortly bring them back to their homeland.

Ezekiel was *by the River Kebar* at the time God called him to the prophetic ministry. The Jewish captives were not in confinement, but were restricted to a certain area of the land. It is now known that the River Kebar was not actually a river, but an enormous irrigation canal known as Naru Kabari, the Grand Canal. The remains of this canal are known as *Shalt en Nil*. The canal started at the Euphrates above Babylon. It flowed southeasterly sixty miles through Nippur. It reentered the Euphrates near Uruk. Evidence of one large Jewish settlement near Nippur has come to light.

C. **Manner of Vision** (1:1c)

In the preface of his book Ezekiel states in a general way what he will amplify in the rest of chs 1-3. The vision began when *the heavens were opened*[53] revealing the unseen spiritual world. Whether to the prophet's mental "eye" or to his physical eye, the heavens unfolded like curtains of a stage to reveal to him the divine glory.

---

[51]An interpretation advocated in the Targum and in S. Fisch, *Ezekiel*, "Soncino Books of the Bible," (London: Soncino, 1950), 1.

[52]For a host of other interpretations of the thirtieth year, see Andrew W. Blackwood, Jr. *Ezekiel, Prophecy of Hope*. Grand Rapids: Baker, 1965), 35-36. Blackwood overstates the difficulty of the expression when he calls the interpretation here "an insoluble puzzle."

[53]This is the only place in the Old Testament where the heavens were opened in a vision. The concept appears twice in the NT (Acts 7:55-56; Rev 4:1-8.

The phrase *visions of God* could legitimately be understood in more than one way. Often the Hebrews add the name of God to a noun to express greatness or majesty. For example, Psalms 36:6 in the Hebrew refers to *the mountains of God* by which is meant great mountains.[54] Thus, *visions of God* could be regarded as great or majestic visions.[55] Currey, however, is correct when he observes that "the visions were not only supremely majestic, but visions of the majesty of God."[56] The Hebrew, then, may also be translated "divine visions," i.e., visions concerning God, or devised by God.

Amplified Preface
1:2-3

In the fifth day of the month (it was the fifth year of the captivity of King Jehoiachin) 3 the word of Yahweh came most assuredly to Ezekiel son of Buzi, the priest in the land of the Chaldeans beside the river Kebar; and the hand of Yahweh came upon him there.

A. National Dating (1:2)

The vision is further dated to the fifth year of King Jehoiachin's captivity. Jehoiachin was taken captive by Nebuchadnezzar when he surrendered to the Chaldean conqueror on March 16, 597 BC. The fifth year of the captivity coincided with 593 BC. Most of the dates in Ezekiel are given in terms of the captivity of Jehoiachin. It has been suggested that Ezekiel regarded Jehoiachin as the legitimate ruler of the Jews even though he had reigned only for three months after the death of his father Jehoiakim (2 Kgs 24:8).[57] This, however, may be reading too much into Ezekiel's dating system. The captivity of Jehoiachin involved Ezekiel as well. It may simply have been the most convenient way of measuring time for the captives.

---

[54]See also Ps 80:10; 65:9.

[55]Visions of God could also be translated in the singular: *a divine vision.* Millard Lind, *Ezekiel, Believers Church Bible Commentary* (Scottdale, Pa: Herald, 1996), 27. Cf. NEB. This expression is used also of the two other extended visions in the book (8:3; 40:2).

[56]G. Currey, "Ezekiel," in vol. VI of *The Holy Bible with Explanatory and Critical Commentary* (ed. F.C. Cook; New York: Scribner, 1892), 18.

[57]Keith Carley, *The Book of the Prophet Ezekiel* (Cambridge: University Press, 1974), 10.

B. Manner of Vision (1:3a)

The visions of God are further identified as being *the word of Yahweh*. The expression appears some 50x in Ezekiel. This is the most frequently used expression in the Old Testament to affirm that a prophet had received direct communication from God.[58] The phrase is not to be restricted to the oral directions that came to Ezekiel in ch 2. Rather *the word of Yahweh* embraces all the revelatory experiences of the prophet. The messages Ezekiel preached were not of his own choosing—not necessarily of his own liking. What he spoke came from above.

The problem of authority was crucial for Ezekiel. The somewhat shocking nature of his message required that his credentials be impeccable. For this reason Ezekiel makes the strongest possible claim that he was commissioned by God. The word of Yahweh *came most assuredly*[59] to him. No doubt existed in his own mind that he had in fact received a heaven-sent vision. The claim to have heard the divine word is found often in Old Testament prophecy (cf. Amos 7; Hos 1).

C. Recipient of Vision (1:3c)

The author of the book identifies himself as Ezekiel the son of Buzi. The name *Ezekiel* means *God strengthens*. Nothing further is known of Buzi beyond what is said here. The title *the priest* properly belongs to the name Buzi as is indicated by the Hebrew accent marks. Ezekiel was also a priest, however, because the Mosaic priesthood was hereditary.

The first three chs of Ezekiel describe that moment when the young priest was called to be a prophet. A prophet is one who speaks for another (Ex 7:1; 4:16). This involved speaking for God to man through sermon and oracle. It also involved speaking for man to God in intercessory prayer. While the priesthood was hereditary, one could only become a prophet when he was divinely chosen.

Prophets interpreted history in the light of the law, urged compliance to the spirit of the law, and announced God's plans for the near and distant future. While both priest and prophet fulfilled vital functions, the ministry of prophet was somewhat broader and less affected by time. Priests were concerned with old covenant law and ritual—the types and shadows that according to God's grand plan were to pass away. Prophets were concerned with timeless principles and with

---

[58]See 1 Sam 15:10; 1 Kgs 12:22; Isa 38:4; Jer 1:2; Hosea 1:1; Joel 1:1.
[59]Hebrew infinitive absolute.

the ultimate developments of God's program for this earth. The names of even the greatest priests are scarcely known today; but the prophets through their writings continue to instruct, challenge, guide and rebuke the sons of men.

D. Location of Vision (1:3d)

The inaugural vision took place *in the land of the Chaldeans*. Originally the Chaldeans and Babylonians were ethnically distinct groups; but at this stage of history the two terms were used interchangeably. The land of the Chaldeans is the southern Mesopotamian basin. It is not certain when the Chaldeans began to filter into this region from the Syro-Arabian desert. The Assyrian kings found the Chaldeans a formidable force under the leadership of Merodach-Baladan in the late eighth century. Under Nabopolassar (626-605 BC) the Chaldeans were able to extricate southern Mesopotamia from the grip of the Assyrians. They founded what was destined to become the most powerful and wealthy empire that had heretofore existed on the face of the earth.

E. Empowerment of Messenger (1:3e)

God not only gave the captive priest a message, he also endowed him with the power to deliver that message. Such is the import of *the hand of Yahweh came on him there.* The *hand of Yahweh* designates something felt rather than seen. Proclaiming the unpopular word of God is never easy. Furthermore, relatively young men like Ezekiel were to be seen, not heard. All wisdom resided in the elders of the nation! Thus Ezekiel needed the unseen hand of Yahweh to guide, strengthen and protect him.

Reference to *the hand* of Yahweh (or God) is frequent in the Old Testament. This anthropomorphism refers to the authority, power or protection of Yahweh. In reference to individuals the expression is used somewhat sparingly. The hand of Yahweh is said to have come upon Elijah (1 Kgs 18:46) and Elisha (2 Kgs 3:15). In the former case, the hand of Yahweh bestowed upon the prophet unusual physical power and endurance; in the latter case, oracular power was imparted.

Elsewhere in Ezekiel the expression *the hand of Yahweh* is used 4x to introduce a visionary experience (3:22; 8:1; 37:1; 40:1). In two passages *the hand of Yahweh* refers to the divine constraining or sustaining power as it manifested itself in the physical stamina of the prophet (3:14; 33:22).[60]

The evidence points to the following definition for this expression: *the hand of Yahweh* refers to the supernatural manifestation of divine power in the life of a prophet that enhanced his physical abilities and enabled him to see what the unaided human mind can never ascertain.

SUBSTANCE OF THE VISION 1:4-28

Ezekiel's call vision is replete with strange and even grotesque figures. Ancient rabbis warned teachers not to expound the mystery of creation in the presence of more than one person, and the mystery of Ezekiel's chariot-throne not even to the one, unless he was unusually wise and discreet.[61]

The point of the vision is that God is arriving to be with his people. This visionary account creates a sense of awe, mystery, and irresistible power. If only this much can be learned from the account the prophet will have accomplished his purpose. If the reader misses this in the reading of ch 1, detailed analysis of the vision will be of little value.

The interpretation of the details of the throne-chariot description is notoriously difficult. The Jewish rabbis declared that if anyone could master the secrets of the *Merkabah* (chariot) he will know all the secrets of creation. The difficulties involved here are not in the English translation. The problem lies in the poverty of human language when it comes to describing the celestial and supernatural; and the lack of spiritual imagination on the part of the interpreters of this book. In any case, it is the message of the throne-chariot, not the mechanics that is important.

The account of the call is written in cumbersome and grammatically inappropriate Hebrew. This seems to be deliberate rather than scribal. Perhaps it is due to the emotional jolt that the vision gave to the prophet.[62] Ezekiel's pen stuttered as surely as did Moses' lips (Ex

---

[60]Cf. Rev 1:17; Dan 8:18; 10:10.

[61]M. *Hagiga* 2:1. Cited by Blackwood, *Ezekiel*, 39.

[62]D.I. Block, "Text and Emotion: A Study in the 'Corruptions' in Ezekiel's Inaugural Vision (Ezekiel 1:4-28)," *CBQ* 50 (1988).

4:10). The corrective for Ezekiel came when he consumed the sacred scroll (ch 3).[63]

Ezekiel's inaugural vision is discussed under its five chief aspects: the storm cloud (v 4); the creatures (vv 5-14); the wheels (vv 15-21); the platform (vv 22-25); and the throne (vv 26-28).

Storm Cloud
1:4

I looked, and behold a stormy wind was coming from the north, a great cloud with fire flashing forth, and a radiant splendor round about. From its midst there was something that appeared like polished bronze from the midst of the fire.

The words *I looked and behold* are the common introductory formula to visions that occurs 9x in the book.[64] The first sight to meet the eyes of Ezekiel was a *stormy wind*.[65] Association of deity with storm phenomena and fire is quite common in Hebrew thought.[66] The mighty thunderstorm is but the attendant of the throne of God. This storm must be a symbol of God's omnipotent power. Within six more years Jerusalem will be destroyed by this stormy wind. Chs 4-24 recount in detail Ezekiel's description and prediction of that forthcoming judgment.

The stormy wind comes from the north. The direction of the storm is unusual for either Palestine or Mesopotamia.[67] Jeremiah spoke of an enemy coming from the north against Judah (1:14; 4:6). God will employ a ruthless foe from the north—the Chaldeans—to bring about the final destruction of Jerusalem.[68]

---

[63]Daniel Fredericks, "Diglossia, Revelation, and Ezekiel's Inaugural Rite, *JETS* 41/2 (June 1998): 189-99.

[64]1:4, 15; 2:9; 8:2, 7; 10:1, 9; 37:8; 44:42. Cf. 40:4-5.

[65]John Taylor suggests that it was while Ezekiel was meditating on a black northern storm cloud that this vision developed. "The physical and visible led into the spiritual and visionary." *Ezekiel*, "Tyndale Old Testament Commentaries" (London: Tyndale, 1969), 54. See also Blackwood, *Ezekiel*, 40-41.

[66]E.g., Ex 3:2; 19:16-19; Ps 18:7-15; 29:3.8.

[67]Storm clouds normally come from the southwest in Mesopotamia, and from the west in Palestine. In neither place do storms normally arise in the fourth month. W.H. Brownlee, "Ezekiel 1-19" in vol. 28 *Word Biblical Commentary*. (Waco, Tx: Word, 1986), 11.

[68]H.L. Ellison thinks the reference is to the Babylonian myth that the gods lived in the north. The storm cloud from the north means that Yahweh had vanquished the pagan deities before coming to Ezekiel. This interpretation seems a bit forced. *Eze-*

Accompanying the stormy wind was *a great cloud.* The cloud may be a portent of impending calamity,[69] or perhaps better, a symbol of approaching deity. God will be present in the judgment that comes on Jerusalem. Three aspects of the cloud are described.

First, Ezekiel does not dwell on the blackness of the cloud. He emphasizes rather its radiance. From that cloud *fire* was *flashing forth.* The Hebrew phrase is literally "a fire taking hold of itself," i.e., a succession of outbursts of flame.[70] The fire is probably lightning streaking across the blackness of the heavens. Those who see in this fire an indication that the Jerusalem temple was to be burned[71] are probably reading too much into this descriptive detail.

Second, surrounding the cloud was a *radiant splendor (nōgah).* This dazzling sight is not to be explained with Taylor[72] as the brightness of the desert sun lighting up the edges of the cloud. Still less was the radiant splendor produced by the fire that was flashing forth from the cloud.[73] It is rather the splendor of the glory of God that is being observed by Ezekiel in connection with the great cloud and stormy wind. It is almost impossible to talk about God for any length of time without mentioning light.

Third, in the midst of the great cloud was something that appeared like (lit., "as the eye of") polished bronze (*chašmal*). The Hebrew word occurs only 3x in Ezekiel (cf. 1:27; 8:2). Some uncertainty exists as to its precise meaning. The Septuagint and Vulgate have "electrum," a substance composed of silver and gold. Cooke, however, traces *chašmal* back to an Akkadian word meaning "polished bronze."

---

kiel: The Man and His Message (Grand Rapids: Eerdmans, 1956), 22. Even more forced is the contention of Currey (*Bible Commentary,* 18) that the north was felt by the Jews to be the peculiar seat of the power of Yahweh, an interpretation based on an erroneous understanding of Ps 48:2.

[69]Fisch, *Ezekiel*, 3.

[70]Currey (*Bible Commentary*, 19) understands this to mean that the fire formed a circle of light about the cloud.

[71]Fisch, *Ezekiel*, 3.

[72]Taylor, *Ezekiel*, 54.

[73]Fisch, *Ezekiel*, 3.

Creatures
1:5-14

A. Appearance (1:5-8a)

From its midst [I saw] the likeness of four living creatures. This was their appearance: they possessed the likeness of a man. 6 Each of them had four faces and four wings. 7 Their feet were straight feet, and the soles of their feet were like the sole of a calf's foot, and they glistened like the appearance of polished bronze. 8 Under their wings upon their four sides were hands of a man.

Ezekiel observed four *living creatures* emerging from the midst of the flashing cloud. These creatures supported the platform (1:22f) on which stood the throne of Yahweh. The living creatures were basically human in appearance.[74] The Greek version uses the word *zoon* (animal, living creature), the same word employed of the four living creatures of Rev 4:6.

The number *four* has special significance throughout the Bible. It suggests primarily the idea of completeness and totality. As a secondary import this number stands for the created world. Thus the Old Testament speaks of "the four corners of the earth" (Isa 11:12), "the four winds" (Ezek 37:9) and so forth. Ezekiel's predilection for the number four can be seen in the four wings, four faces, four hands, four sides and four wheels of the inaugural vision. In ch 8 he presents four scenes of false worship and in ch14 he refers to four plagues.

As to the specific features of the creatures Ezekiel speaks first of *their feet.* Probably in the first use of *foot* (*regel*) the term is used in the wider sense of *legs*. These legs are said to be *straight*, i.e., unjointed.[75] Such at least is the old Jewish understanding of the word. The creatures then did not bow, crouch or lie down. Throughout the vision they remained perfectly erect.

The *feet* of the creatures resembled the hoof of a calf. This probably means nothing more than that their feet were rounded.[76] This en-

---

[74]Brownlee (*Word*, 11) proposes a different vocalization of the word translated *man* (*'ādām*) and reads "carnelian" (*'ōdem*), i.e., they had a reddish appearance. The many references to colors in this text make this the only Technicolor vision in the Bible.

[75]W.B. Barrick, "The Straight-Legged Cherubim of Ezekiel's Inaugural Vision (Ezekiel 1:7a)," *CBQ* 44 (1982): 543-50.

[76]Groping for significance in the *feet like a calf*, Taylor (*Ezekiel*, 55) suggests that the calf symbolizes nimbleness.

abled the creatures to move freely in every direction. The feet are said to *glisten (nōttsîm)* like polished bronze.

Second, in addition to the four wings each creature had *hands*. Some question exists as to whether each creature had four hands or two hands. Probably the latter is correct. These hands will be put to good use a bit later (cf. 10:7).

B. Wings and Faces (1:8b-10)

Now as for the faces and wings of the four of them, 9 their wings were joined together, they did not turn when they moved; each went straight ahead. 10 The likeness of their faces was as the face of a man, and the four of them had the face of a lion on the right, and a face of a bull on the left, and the four of them had the face of an eagle.

1. Wings of the creatures (1:8b-9): When in flight the outstretched wings of the creatures appeared to be joined together. This means that the wing tips touched one another. Since each creature had a face on four sides they did not turn around when their course was altered. The face toward the intended course moved forward in that direction. Wherever they went they always moved forward, since each creature had a face in the appropriate direction. This detail may point to the resoluteness of purpose that these creatures manifested.

2. Focus on the faces (1:10): Each of the living creatures had four faces (cf. v 6). Something of great importance is thus signified. Those creatures associated most intimately with God could see in all directions. The shape of the face differed on the four sides: the face of a man in front, of a lion on the right side, of an ox on the left side, and of an eagle behind.[77] At the very least these faces symbolized the highest forms of life that are found in the various realms of creation. The Jewish rabbis commented:

> Man is exalted among creatures; the eagle is exalted among the birds; the ox is exalted among domestic animals; the lion is exalted among wild beasts; and all of them have received dominion, and greatness has been given them yet they are stationed below the chariot of the Holy One.[78]

---

[77]According to Targum Jonathan, there were four faces in each direction, so that each creature had sixteen faces.

[78]Midrash Rabbah *Shemoth*, 23.

There may be more to the quadruple faces. Representations of lion, ox and eagle were common in Babylonian art. They were particularly suggestive to the mind of the exiles there. Four-faced statuettes of gods have also been found in Babylon. I.G. Matthews suggested that these were common symbols for the chief deities of Babylonia in Ezekiel's day.[79] The vision may then be proclaiming that Yahweh, not the gods of Babylon, controlled history.

The living creatures formed a square. The human face of each creature faced outward. From whatever angle one looked at the four creatures a different face was seen from each. All four faces were visible at the same time from any angle.[80]

C. **Movements** (1:11-14)

Their faces and their wings were separated above. Each had two that joined another, and two covering their bodies. 12 Each went straight ahead. Wherever the spirit was to go, they went; they did not turn as they went. 13 As for the likeness of the living creatures, their appearance was like burning coals of fire, like the appearance of torches. Fire[81] was going to and fro between the living creatures. The fire had a radiant splendor, and from the fire lightning was going forth. 14 The living creatures were running back and forth like lightning bolts.

The creatures had four wings (cf. v 6).[82] [83] For the sake of modesty two of these wings were used to cover the naked bodies of these creatures. The other two wings were in the act of flying. They were so stretched out that the tip of each touched the wing tip of a fellow living creature on the right and on the left (cf. v 9). This symbolized their unity of purpose. When the throne-chariot came to a stop the second pair of wings was let down (cf. 1:24). The creatures appeared at times to be connected to one another at the wing tips; but their

---

[79]The ox-face was associated with Marduk, the eagle-face with Ninib (god of war), the human face with Nabu (god of revelation) and the lion-face with Nergal (god of the underworld). Cited by Brownlee, *Word*, 11.

[80]Taylor, *Ezekiel*, 55.

[81]The Hebrew actually uses a feminine pronoun, but the reference is obviously to the fire.

[82]By way of contrast, the angelic seraphim of Isa 6 had six wings, two of which were used to cover the face, two to cover the feet (possibly a euphemism for pudenda), and two to hover in mid-air.

[83]Reliefs and statuettes of four-winged creatures have been found in Mesopotamia.

faces and their wings were separated above, i.e., they were not physically connected.

The creatures did not need to turn their heads as they moved in various directions (cf. v 9). Apparently the living creatures were not capable of independent movement. The entire throne-chariot of which they were a part moved as a single unit under the impulse of *the spirit,* i.e., the Holy Spirit.

Ezekiel compares the appearance of the living creatures to *coals of fire* and *torches* (*lappidîm*). They must have had a pulsating or glowing quality about them. In the midst of the hollow square formed by the four creatures Ezekiel observed a bright *fire* that seemed to move back and forth among the living creatures. Periodically *lightning* flashed forth from the interior of the "chariot."[84] This fire no doubt symbolized the judgment that at that moment of history was in the center of God's concern.[85]

Initially the movements of the living creatures seemed to Ezekiel to be erratic. The creatures were seen *running back and forth like lightning bolts*, i.e., the throne-chariot moved to and fro with the speed of lightning.

D. Creatures: Interpretation

The living creatures had their[86] groundwork in the Old Testament cherubim. Little is known about the angelic order of cherubim, although they are frequently mentioned in the Bible. The cherubim of the Mosaic ark and the Solomonic temple probably did not resemble those that are here in view. This explains why Ezekiel when he first saw these creatures on the bank of the Kebar did not recognize them as cherubim.

The cherubim as they appear throughout the Bible are symbols, not likenesses. This is why the appearance of these creatures differs from passage to passage. In place of the four-faced figures seen by Ezekiel, John saw each living creature having only one face.

---

[84]Verse 13 is extremely difficult. The Greek version makes the whole v a description of what was in the midst of the living creatures. According to the Hebrew text, followed here, the first part of the v contains two similes descriptive of the creatures. The latter part of the v describes a flashing fire that was *among* or *between* the creatures.

[85]Ellison (*Ezekiel*, 24) thinks it is the spirit of God that is symbolized by the pulsating light coming from within the square formed by the creatures.

[86]Lind (*Ezekiel*, 30) points out that the pronouns referring to the creatures alternate in gender. The significance of this is not clear.

These living creatures are symbols; but of what are they symbolical? The oldest and probably the correct explanation is that the living creatures are symbolic representations of heavenly beings.[87] This is not to say that the living creatures represented any four particular angels. The main point is this: heavenly beings serve the King; how much more should the sons of men.

The general import of the living creatures is not difficult to ascertain. Their facial features suggest that they have the specific function of representing the earthly creation before Yahweh. Yahweh, the God of creation and redemption, rules over all the earth. It is most appropriate that the throne-chariot of the heavenly Sovereign should be borne by those who represent the whole earth over which Yahweh holds sway.

Wheels
1:15-21

A. Location (1:15)

Now as I saw the living creatures, behold [I saw] a wheel on the earth beside each of the living creatures on its four sides.

Beside each of the living creatures was *a wheel*. The wheels of the throne-chariot were not functional. The only reason the wheels are mentioned is so that the chariot imagery can be maintained. That the wheels were not essential to the movements of the throne-chariot is seen in the fact that the vehicle traveled in the air and not on the ground. Ellison[88] suggests that the wheels symbolize inanimate nature just as the four creatures represent the living creation. In ancient Jewish teaching the wheels were thought to symbolize some order of heavenly beings.[89]

---

[87]The Jewish commentator Kimchi thought the four living creatures represented the four great empires symbolized by the various beasts of Dan 7. Irenaeus saw in these creatures figures of the four Gospel evangelists. J. Kenneth Grider thinks they represent the forces of Nebuchadnezzar. "The Book of the Prophet Ezekiel," in vol. 4 of *Beacon Bible Commentary* (ed. A.F. Harper, *et al.*; Kansas City: Beacon Hill Press, 1966), 538.

[88]Ellison, *Ezekiel*, 25.

[89]See the pseudepigraphic Book of Enoch 61:10; 70:7.

B. Appearance (1:16-18)

The appearance of the wheels and their works was like the color of topaz. The four of them had one likeness. Their appearance and their works were as a wheel in the middle of a wheel. 17 When they went, they went toward their four sides. They did not turn about in their going. 18 As for their rims, they were high and awesome. Their rims were filled with eyes round about the four of them.

As to the appearance of the wheels Ezekiel makes two points. First, the wheels resembled *topaz* (Heb., *taršîš*).[90] Second, they were so constructed as to facilitate movement in any direction. They were omnidirectional wheels. Each wheel actually consisted of two wheels, i.e., *a wheel in the middle of a wheel*. The two wheels were probably solid discs that bisected each other at right angles. This is Ezekiel's way of describing what today would be called caster wheels.

The caster-like wheels allowed movement of the chariot in any direction without the wheels being turned. Apparently there was no steering mechanism connected to the wheels.

The *rims* (*gabbōt*) of the wheels were *high*, i.e., the wheels were huge in comparison to the entire chariot.[91] Because they were full of *eyes* the rims were *awesome*, i.e., terrifying.[92] The eyes may have been no more than dazzling spots that added to the brilliancy of the wheels. It seems more likely, however, that they had a symbolical meaning.[93] The eye in the ancient world was a symbol of intelligence. God sees and knows what is happening throughout his world, including the camps of Jewish captives in Mesopotamia.

C. Movement (1:19-21)

When the living creatures went, the wheels went beside them. When the living creatures were lifted up from upon the earth, the wheels were lifted up. 20 Wherever the Spirit was to go, they went;

---

[90]Opinions differ on the identity of this stone. Jasper and beryl have been suggested. The ancient versions have "chrysolite," whatever that may have been.

[91]Some have seen in the word *high* the power of raising the throne chariot. Something like hydraulic wheels may be intended.

[92]The RSV emends the text of v 18 so that it reads: "the four wheels had rims and they had spokes." The Hebrew text in v 18 is difficult, but this in no way justifies the arbitrary change of the RSV.

[93]Some have suggested that the "eyes" on the rims were bosses or studs designed to improve traction on rough and uneven roads. Bruce Vawter and Leslie Hoppe, *Ezekiel: A New Heart* in "International Theological Commentary" (Grand Rapids: Eerdmans, 1991), 28. Others see in the eyes and the unattached character of the wheels an indication that the wheels were in some sense living creatures. Brownlee, *Word*, 13.

there was the spirit to go, and the wheels lifted up opposite them, for the spirit of the living creatures was in the wheels. 21 In their going, they went, and in their standing still, they stood still. When they were lifted up from upon the earth, the wheels were lifted up opposite them, for the spirit of the living creatures was in the wheels.

Ezekiel takes up from v 17 the wheel movement. He adds three points to what he previously said. First, the wheels themselves had no capacity for independent movement. They always moved in conjunction with the living creatures.

Second, the creatures in turn were under the control of the *Spirit* of God. The Spirit of God was in the creatures; and *the spirit of the living creatures,*[94] as it were, was in the wheels. God from his throne exercised an influence upon the spirits of the living creatures. He coordinated their movements. Amid all the uncertainties and tragedies of life the Spirit of God is at work providentially directing all discordant aspects of life.

Third, there is no indication that the wheels were attached to the living creatures. In v 21 Ezekiel repeats and amplifies the thought that when the creatures moved in any direction the wheels moved with them. The effortless mobility of God's throne-chariot is a way of depicting the grand theological theme of God's omnipresence.

Platform
1:22-25

A. General Appearance (1:22)

Over the heads of the living creatures was something like a platform, gleaming terribly like ice, stretched forth over their heads above.

Over the heads of the creatures was what appeared to be a platform (*rāqî'a*). It is not certain how this platform was supported, whether by the wings of the cherubim or by some other means.[95] The platform was gleaming like *ice* (*qerach*). The ice was terrible in the sense of being awesome because of its glittering brightness.

In this dazzling platform the glories of heaven are symbolized. In Rev 4:6 this platform becomes a "sea of glass." Some commentators

---

[94]A singular is used in v 20 in a collective sense as in 10:20.
[95]Ellison (*Ezekiel*, 24) argues that it is better to regard the wings of the cherubim as forming a protective square around the throne. Cf. Rev 4:6.

think that this expanse was dome-shaped. There is, however, no indication of this in the word itself or in the context.

B. Sound under Platform (1:23-24)

Under the platform their wings were straight, one to another. Each one had two wings covering his body on either side.[96] 24 Then I heard the sound of their wings like the sound of great waters, as the sound of the Almighty as they went, the sound of noise like the sound of an encampment. When they stood still they let down their wings.

The entire persons of the living creatures including their outstretched wings were under the platform. Each creature had one pair of wings stretched straight out. Another pair modestly covered their bodies.

The audio portion of the vision is referred to in vv 24-25. The four pairs of outstretched wings vibrated powerfully as the throne-chariot moved. Three similes are employed to try to depict the awesome sound produced by the theophonic chariot. The noise was like that produced 1) by great (or many) waters; 2) by the voice of the Almighty, i.e., rolling thunder,[97] and 3) by an army on the move. When the movement of the chariot ceased, the living creatures lowered their wings. Consequently the dreadful noise ceased.

C. Voice above Platform (1:25)

From above the platform that was over their heads came a voice when they stood and let their wings down.

The movement of the throne-chariot was directed by a voice that came from above the platform. This voice must be that of God.[98] No words are attributed to him at this point; but the author prepares the way for the later words of that One who was enthroned above the living creatures.

---

[96]Literally, "each one had two covering on this side, and each one had two covering on that side, their bodies."

[97]Cf. Job 37:4-5; Ps 29:3, 5; Rev 10:3.

[98]Currey (*Bible Commentary*, 22) thinks the reference is to the voices that were praising God above the tumult in 3:12.

Throne
1:26-28

A. Location (1:26a)

Above the platform that was over their heads was what appeared to be a sapphire stone, the likeness of a throne.

With obvious hesitation the prophet describes what he saw *above* the platform. God can be visualized only in terms of "likeness." For this reason the vision abounds in terms like *as* (*k^{e}*), *resembling*, *looked like* (*d^{e}mût*), *like* (*k^{e}mareh*), and *appearance* (*mareh*).

Ezekiel saw what resembled a throne of *sapphire*.[99] What Ezekiel saw may be compared to the vision of Moses who saw under God's feet "a pavement of sapphire stone, like the very heaven for clearness" (Ex 24:10). The throne is an obvious symbol of universal sovereignty.

B. Occupant (1:26b-27)

Upon the likeness of the throne was a likeness of the appearance of a man upon it above. 27 I saw as the color of polished bronze, as the appearance of fire, as an enclosure to it round about, from the appearance of his loins and upward. From the appearance of his loins and downward I saw the appearance of fire. There was a radiant splendor round about him.

He who sat upon the throne had *the likeness of the appearance of a man*. Ezekiel is careful to place as much distance as possible between the deity and a mere man. The upper portion of this human-like figure flashed like polished bronze. These bright flashes resembled fire (lightning?). Similarly the lower half of the figure flashed like fire. A *radiant splendor* characterized the whole being.

Anthropomorphism—describing God in human terms—is quite common in the Old Testament. The use of this literary device has occasioned the charge that the concept of God in the Old Testament is primitive. Anthropomorphism, however, serves a useful function. It aids in describing the indescribable; but it does more than that. Anthropomorphism underscores the basic theological proposition of the Old Testament, viz. God is *living*. Furthermore, anthropomorphic description causes men to appreciate even more the truth that man bears

---

[99]Some think the *lapis lazuli* stone is intended. In either case, the throne was made of a most precious stone.

in his person the divine image. In theophanies like that in Ezek 1 only the human form was appropriate to represent Yahweh.

C. Divine Glory (1:28)

As the appearance of a bow that is in a cloud on the day of rain, so was the appearance of the radiant splendor round about. This was the appearance of the likeness of the glory of Yahweh. When I saw it I fell upon my face. And I heard a voice speaking.

The brightness was multi-colored, much like the beautiful colors of a rainbow. This rainbow is more than simply a sign of glory and splendor. It is a token of mercy and promise as well. Ezekiel was to preach about the coming storm of judgment; but he was to look beyond that dark hour to the dawning of a new day and the resurrection and restoration of the people of God.

The final v of ch 1 interprets what Ezekiel has described in the previous vv. He has been describing *the appearance of the likeness of the glory of Yahweh.* God revealed his magnificent person to Ezekiel to prepare him for ministry. The Lord continued to appear to Ezekiel in this same fashion throughout the book to encourage him that he was a servant of almighty God.[100]

The term *glory* was a technical term used to denote the presence of Yahweh among his people. To look on the face of God meant death (Ex 33:20). God's presence, however, could be described in terms of blinding light or dazzling fire within a protective cloud (Ex 19:16-18; 40:34-38). At the dedication of Solomon's temple the glory of Yahweh filled the sanctuary. It took up permanent residence in the Holy of Holies (1 Kgs 8:10). As time went on God became linked more and more to Judah and the temple. It was left to the prophets of God to champion the ancient doctrine that Yahweh was Lord of all the earth.

Ezekiel's vision of the glory of God is truly remarkable in that he sees this manifestation at a spot far removed from the Jerusalem temple. Those who were captive in Babylon felt cut off from Yahweh because geographically they were unable to participate in temple wor-

---

[100]Cf. 3:12, 23-24; 8:2-4; 9:3; 10:1-20; 11:22-23; 43:2-4.

ship. This vision gives evidence that God's presence could be experienced in a foreign land.

Ezekiel's vision centers on God, not the creatures or the wheels as interesting as they may be. However symbolic this vision may have been it was a genuine vision of God. Ezekiel saw as much as God permits to be seen by man. The true spiritual significance of Ezek 1 is ascertained when the various details of the vision are interpreted as revealing *theological* truths. The search for spaceships and visitors from other planets in this ch is ludicrous if not downright blasphemous!

In contemplating God under the form of a man Ezekiel helps pave the way for that grand revelation of God in Christ Jesus. Paul describes Jesus as the image of the invisible God (Col 1:15) and the brightness of God's glory and the express image of his person (Heb 1:3). John declares that the word was made flesh and dwelled among us; and we beheld his glory, the glory of the only begotten of the Father, full of grace and truth (Jn 1:14). Currey is correct when he argues

> We are therefore justified in maintaining that the revelation of the divine glory here made to Ezekiel has its consummation or fulfillment in the person of Christ, the only begotten of God....[101]

The whole vision of the throne-chariot and the divine presence had a marked effect upon Ezekiel. He fell to his face. He was thus prepared to hear the word of Yahweh. The experience of Ezekiel was akin to that of Isaiah (Isa 6) and Daniel (Dan 7:9ff).

EZEKIEL 2-3
CALL OF THE PROPHET

Heavenly visions were not granted to biblical saints merely to excite their (and our) curiosity. The visions were intended to incite them to proclaim the divine word. Chs 2-3 contain the commission that came to Ezekiel in connection with his inaugural vision.[102] As in

---

[101]Currey, *Bible Commentary*, 25.

[102]A prophetic call experience generally consisted of 1) a divine confrontation, usually in the form of a vision; 2) the commission that described the task at hand; 3) objections from the candidate; and 4) reassurances from Yahweh. See N. Habel ("The

the case of Jeremiah the commissioning came in stages separated presumably by some time intervals. For the most part these intervals cannot be determined. At each stage of the process Ezekiel was given time to assimilate the message before the commissioning continued.

The material in chs 2-3 can be discussed under the following four heads: call to service (2:1-7); preparation for service (2:8-3:15); responsibilities of service (3:16-21); and restrictions on service (3:22-27).

CALL TO SERVICE
2:1-7

Following his mind-boggling visionary experience Ezekiel heard the call of God to prophetic service. He was told in no uncertain terms where and how he was to serve. In this paragraph Ezekiel was 1) strengthened (2:1-2); 2) warned (2:3-5); and 3) charged (2:6-7).

Ezekiel Strengthened
2:1-2

And he said unto me, Son of man, stand upon your feet and I will speak to you. 2 And the Spirit came into me as he spoke unto me. He caused me to stand upon my feet. Then I heard one speaking unto me.

Yahweh took the lead in the commissioning of the prophet. It was his voice (1:28), rather than that of one of the creatures, that Ezekiel heard giving him the first command.

The title *son of man* occurs over 90x in the Book of Ezekiel. In most cases it precedes a command of God. The term "son" often is used in Hebrew to denote membership in a class. Thus a *son of man* is a member of the class of man, i.e., a mortal. The designation emphasizes human frailty as over against the awesome might and majesty of God who had just revealed himself to Ezekiel. By this title Ezekiel was reminded continually that he was dependent on the Spirit's

---

Form and Significance of the Call Narrative," *ZAW* 77 [1965]: 297-323). All four elements are found in Ezekiel's commission.

power. The Spirit enabled him to receive the message of God and to deliver it in the power and authority of Yahweh.

Ezekiel had been privileged to see the majestic heavenly vision of God's throne-chariot; but he was nevertheless nothing more than a human being. Within a few years Daniel will use the title *son of man* in a technical sense of that divine-human one who will receive a kingdom from the Ancient of Days (Dan 7:13). Jesus' application of the title *son of man* to himself seems to be based more on Daniel's usage than on Ezekiel's.

The first command given to Ezekiel in the book is the command to *stand upon your feet.* The standing position is apparently the correct posture from which to hear the divine commission.[103] It is service, not servility, that God desires most. Davidson comments: "It is man erect, man in his manhood, with whom God will have fellowship and with whom he will speak."[104]

Even as Yahweh issued this command to Ezekiel *spirit* came into him. The term *wind/spirit* (*rüach*) occurs about 53x in this book. In the light of 3:24 it is best to understand this spirit as the Spirit of God. The Spirit came into the prophet compelling him and enabling him to comply with the command just issued. That Spirit supplemented and revived Ezekiel's physical powers like a fresh breath of life.[105] What a blessed truth is intimated here. Frail and feeble man can be empowered and indwelt by the Holy Spirit. God supplies the power to perform his special service.

Ezekiel Warned
2:3-5

God sets forth the difficulties that Ezekiel will confront in his ministry and the duty that will be his as God's spokesman. He likewise seeks to encourage Ezekiel in the discharge of his ministry.

---

[103]Another view is that Ezekiel is told to stand so that he can more readily obey the following command to go preach.

[104]A.B. Davidson, *The Book of Ezekiel* in "The Cambridge Bible for Schools and Colleges" (Cambridge: University Press, 1896), 15.

[105]Feinberg (*Ezekiel,* 23) sees the entrance of the Spirit as forming the basis of Ezekiel's prophetic inspiration.

A. Record of Rebellion (2.3)

And he said unto me, Son of man, I am sending you unto the children of Israel, unto rebellious nations that have rebelled against me. They and their fathers have transgressed against me until this very day.

Ezekiel was to be God's representative to the children of Israel. In earlier prophets the term *Israel* is used of the northern kingdom that was carried away captive in 722 BC. The kingdom of Israel, as distinct from the kingdom of Judah, had long since ceased to exist by the time of Ezekiel. Thus *Israel* here is not the northern kingdom.

The term *Israel* is used two ways in the Book of Ezekiel. Sometimes Ezekiel employs the name *Israel* for all of the people who had joined in the covenant with God at Sinai. In other words, *Israel* is the entire community of faith. On other occasions Ezekiel refers to the inhabitants of Judah and Jerusalem as *Israel.* After the destruction and deportation of the northern kingdom, the inhabitants of the Judah claimed this honored title for themselves.

Ezekiel's mission was ultimately to the whole contemporary generation of Israelites, both those who were in Judah and those who were in exile. To be sure his ministry had impact back in Judah, at least in the period between 593 and 586 BC. His immediate audience, however, was near at hand—his fellow exiles. Ezekiel does not clearly distinguish between Israelites in Judah and those in Babylon. Often he seems to ignore the miles that separate the two groups.

The present generation had *rebelled* against Yahweh. They had refused to adhere to strict monotheism. In their apostasy the present generation was but following the example of their fathers. They too had *transgressed* against Yahweh. The rebellion of Israel was intergenerational.

The audience is described as *rebellious nations that have rebelled against me*. The plural *nations* may be a reference to Israel and Judah.[106] The term *nations* (*gōyim*), however, usually is restricted to the heathen peoples as over against God's people. Perhaps the word is here used contemptuously. By virtue of their rebellion against God Israel and Judah had become no better than heathen nations. The plural also points to the fact that the children of Israel at this time are not *one nation*. They are scattered and disunited.

---

[106]Fisch (*Ezekiel*, 9) thinks the two *nations* intended were the two tribes Judah and Benjamin that formed the southern kingdom after 931 BC. In Gn 35:11 Israel's tribes are called nations.

B. Their Intransigence (2:4)

The sons are hard of face and stout of heart. I am sending you unto them, and you will say unto them, Thus says Lord Yahweh!

The sons, i.e., the present generation, are further described as being *hard of face and stout of heart*. The first phrase describes the brazenness of the hardened sinner who displays no shame. The second phrase describes that stubborn, unyielding disposition that continues in the path of error in spite of repeated warnings and harsh chastisements.

Ezekiel's mission field did not look promising! God wanted him to have no illusions about this work. There was little prospect for success. The important thing, however, was that Ezekiel was to preach only the word of God. His message was to be punctuated with the phrase *thus says Lord Yahweh*. This so-called messenger formula is common in the prophets. It also appears in a secular context (Gn 32:3-4; 2 Kgs 19:9-10).

C. Opportunity for Enlightenment (2:5)

But as for them, whether they will hear or refuse (for they are a house of rebels), then they will know that a prophet is in their midst.

In the word *rebels* there may be an allusion to the insane and suicidal rebellions that foolhardy patriots were continually plotting. Nebuchadnezzar was the God-ordained ruler of the world. To rebel against him was to be in rebellion against the will of God. Over 12x Ezekiel refers to his auditors as a *house of rebels*, lit., "house of rebellion."

Ezekiel was not required to be successful, only faithful. The recognition formula *they* [or *you*] *will know* appears in the book about 60x. It underscores how Israel and the nations will come to recognize Yahweh as Lord of history. Here the people come to realize that a prophet had been in their midst.[107] They will be forced to recognize Ezekiel as a true prophet when the calamities predicted by him came upon them.

---

[107]The past tense probably indicates that they will not recognize him as a prophet until after his death.

Ezekiel Charged
2:6-7

But as for you, son of man, do not fear them or be afraid of their words; for thorns[108] and thistles are with you. You are sitting upon scorpions! Do not fear their words. Do not be dismayed at their looks, for they are a rebellious house. 7 But speak my words unto them, whether they hear or refuse, for they are rebellious.

Unlike Moses and Jeremiah, Ezekiel had no opportunity to protest his inability and timidity. God moved to forestall such excuses with earnest exhortation. Ezekiel will face terrible opposition. God tells his prophet 4x not to be afraid. Such words of reassurance are part of the calls of other prophets (Josh 8:1; Jer 1:8). They usually occur, however, only after the candidate has expressed reluctance. Ezekiel has given no indication of hesitation about his mission; but Yahweh may be addressing his unspoken fears.

Such an exhortation is in order because his hearers are *thorns and thistles*.[109] This preacher must have a tough hide to endure the digs, scratches, abrasions and stinging sarcasm that a hostile audience heaps on him.

Dwelling among those thorns and thistles are *scorpions* with deadly stings. There will be threats to his life. He will be pierced through on many occasions by this ungrateful and irresponsive crowd. At such times he must remember that this kind of conduct is entirely in character as far as these exiles are concerned for *they are a rebellious house*. For this reason Ezekiel must not *fear their words* or *be dismayed* (lit., "shattered") at their looks.

This section of explanation and exhortation closes with renewed appeal to be faithful to his preaching ministry regardless of the audience reaction.

---

[108]The Hebrew word is not elsewhere found in the Bible and is of uncertain meaning. Context favors the traditional rendering *briers* or *thorns*.

[109]Margaret Odell, "The Particle and the Prophet: Observations on Ezekiel 2:6," *VT* 48 (1998): 425-32.

PREPARATION FOR SERVICE 2:8-3:15

Following the call to service God begins a process of education to prepare this man for the assigned task. Three steps can be distinguished in this educational process. The prophet needed to assimilate the message of God (2:8-3:3), have assurance of divine power (3:4-9) and have a correct assessment of his future congregation (3:10-15).

Assimilate the Message 2:8-3:3

A. Appearance of a Scroll (2:8-10)

As for you, son of man, hear what I am about to speak unto you. Do not be rebellious like the rebellious house. Open your mouth and eat what I am about to give you. 9 I saw, and behold a hand was extended unto me, and behold in it the roll of a book. 10 He spread it before me, and it was written on front and back. There was written on it lamentations, mourning and woe.[110]

God addressed Ezekiel with four imperatives: *hear, be not rebellious, open, eat*. Ezekiel must not be rebellious like the house of Israel. He must *eat* what God gives him. Once again God forestalls any reluctance on Ezekiel's part by these words of warning. Disobedience will mark Ezekiel as no better than the rebellious people to whom he was to preach.

Ezekiel makes four observations about the scroll. First, it was extended. The stage was set for this initial test of obedience. To his surprise (*behold!*) Ezekiel saw a *hand* (cf. Jer 1:9) come forth to him from the throne-chariot. The hand was either that of one of the creatures or that of the One on the throne itself. The hand contained a *roll of a book*, i.e., a scroll (v 9).[111] This scroll was probably made of papyrus rather than animal skins. Papyrus is edible. It can easily be cut in pieces column by column.[112] By sewing many pieces of this mate-

---

[110]Ehrlich suggests that *lamentation, mourning and woe* was the heading of the scroll. Cited in Fisch, *Ezekiel*, 12.

[111]The prophecies of Jeremiah and Isaiah were written down after oral delivery (Isa 8:16; Jer 36). Many of Ezekiel's prophecies may first have been written down (Lind, *Ezekiel*, 35).

[112]Vawter and Hoppe, *Ezekiel*, 32.

rial together a scroll of twenty feet or more in length can be constructed.[113]

Second, the scroll was unrolled. Unlike the sealed scroll in Rev 4, this scroll was open. It was no mystery what God was about to do to Jerusalem.

Third, the scroll was full. The scroll contained *writing*. The ancients regarded the written word as far more definite and unalterable than the spoken word. The writing on the scroll was God's authoritative word for the children of Israel. The writing was on the scroll before Ezekiel received it. The message he will preach originated with God. It was a written word—a fixed and unchangeable divine declaration.

The scroll was somewhat unusual in that it contained writing on both sides. Normally scrolls were inscribed on only one side. Is there symbolic significance in this fact? Perhaps it simply means that God had a lot to say to his people through Ezekiel. On the other hand, maybe the scroll was completely inscribed so as to eliminate the possibility of Ezekiel adding anything to the divinely received message.[114] Then again perhaps the writing on front and back symbolized the abundance of the calamities that were to befall Jerusalem.[115]

Fourth, the scroll was sad. Until the fall of Jerusalem in 586 BC, Ezekiel preached a message of doom such as might be characterized as lamentation, mourning and woe. The scroll thus set forth prophetically what will shortly befall Jerusalem and Judah.

B. Eating of the Scroll (3:1-3)

He said unto me, Son of man, eat what you discover; eat this roll and go speak unto the house of Israel. 2 I opened my mouth, and he fed me this roll. 3 He said unto me, Son of man, your belly will eat and your inward parts will be full with this roll that I am giving unto you. So I ate it, and it became in my mouth like honey for sweetness.

---

[113]Some think Ezekiel's scroll vision was inspired by a remembrance of the events in Jer 36 where King Jehoiakim destroyed the scroll of Jeremiah. Ezekiel may have witnessed this event. Like Jeremiah's scroll, this scroll 1) was inscribed on both sides; and 2) contained "lamentation, mourning and woe." Ezekiel 2 served as a model for Rev 10:8-11, and possibly for Zech 5:1-4.

[114]Ellison, *Ezekiel*, 28.

[115]Unlikely is Fineberg's suggestion (*Ezekiel*, 26) that the front side of the scroll symbolizes truths of a more obvious nature, the backside those of a more concealed nature.

Again God addresses four imperatives to Ezekiel. He is to *eat, eat, go*, and *speak*. He is to *eat this roll*. The word of God must be internalized, digested and assimilated by one who will serve as God's messenger.[116] Ezekiel himself must become the message. Coming on the heels of the command to eat the scroll is the command to *go speak unto the house of Israel*. Immediately following the reception of the word there must be the proclamation of it.

Ezekiel attempted to comply with Yahweh's command. He opened his mouth. At this point the gracious God intervened and aided in the consumption of the document. Further encouragement came from Yahweh to the effect that Ezekiel should swallow and digest the scroll that he had been given. Ezekiel complied. Ezekiel himself becomes the embodiment of the divine word.

Much to his surprise, Ezekiel found that the scroll tasted sweet like honey (cf. Jer 15:16; Ps 119:103). This sweetness in no way indicates that Ezekiel took some morbid delight in his message of doom. Rather the sweetness of the scroll lay in the privilege of knowing and proclaiming the word of God.[117]

Ezekiel did not eat a literal scroll. This action was done in a vision. A person does strange things in dreams; and so it was also in this heaven-sent vision. The point is that Ezekiel must familiarize himself with the word of God by reading the scroll as eagerly and attentively as one eats food to satisfy hunger. The fact that God caused him *to eat the scroll* may point to supernatural aid that the prophet received in comprehending and mentally preserving the minutest detail of this unpleasant message.

Assurance of Divine Power
3:4-9

A. Need for Divine Power (3:4-7)

He said unto me, Son of man, go unto the house of Israel and speak with my words unto them. 5 For you have not been sent unto a people of obscure language and heavy tongue, but unto the house

---

[116]Thus while the passage clearly teaches verbal inspiration, it does not set forth mechanical dictation. The message had to be assimilated before annunciated in the prophet's own unique way. Cf. Margaret Odell, "You Are What You Eat: Ezekiel and the Scroll," *JBL* 117 (1998): 229-48.

[117]Cf. Ps 19:10; 119:103: Jer 15:16.

of Israel. 6 Not unto many people of obscure language and heavy tongue whose words you cannot comprehend. Surely if I had sent you unto them they would hearken unto you. 7 But as for the house of Israel, they are not willing to hearken unto you because they are not willing to hearken unto me; for all the house of Israel are strong of forehead and hard of heart.

The ingested scroll symbolizes empowerment to preach. The command to go to the captives with the word is repeated in v 4: *Go ... speak*. He is to preach *with my words*. He is to convey God's message to them in the very tongue in which he had received it. The exiles were beginning to use the Aramaic tongue of the Chaldeans; but they were still familiar with the Hebrew.

Unlike Jonah, Ezekiel is not being sent to a people whose language was utterly incomprehensible. The expression *obscure language* means literally "deep of lip." The same expression is found in Isa 33:19 where it refers to a foreign language that cannot be comprehended. *Heavy tongue* is a tongue that is sluggish and dull (cf. Ex 4:10), or one that is tiresome to understand. Many foreigners were in Babylon. Communication with them will not be easy.

Lack of communication between Ezekiel and his audience will not be due to any language barrier. It was to the *house of Israel*—his own compatriots—to whom he is sent. But this in no way will aid the communication process. Sometimes the home missionary has a more difficult task than he who ventures into foreign lands to preach the gospel in exotic tongues. Strange languages are more easily mastered than the technique of communicating with unbelieving hearts. Ezekiel's chances of "getting through" to his audience would have been greater if he were speaking to people with a hard language rather than a hard heart.

Nothing personal will be involved in Israel's rejection of the message of Ezekiel (cf. 1 Sam 8:7-8). The basic problem with the house of Israel was that they had no interest in hearing what God had to say. The people will show an aversion to Ezekiel simply because he was the bearer of the divine word. Therefore the opposition that Ezekiel was warned to expect was not to be regarded as unusual, or directed against him personally. The exiles were deaf to the voice of God that had spoken through various natural disasters as well as through his human spokesmen. It was therefore unlikely that they will give any heed to Ezekiel.

B. Provision of Divine Power (3:8-9)

Behold I have made your face strong against their face, and your forehead strong against their forehead. 9 Like a diamond[118] harder than flint I have made your forehead. Do not fear them. Do not be dismayed before them for they are a rebellious house.

The first hurdle for Ezekiel's ministry was the natural fear that will arise over the prospects of preaching an unpopular message to an unsympathetic multitude. For this task God will endow Ezekiel with courage. Yahweh will make Ezekiel's face *strong against their face* and his forehead *strong against their forehead.* The latter figure is taken from horned animals that vie for supremacy by butting heads. Ezekiel will be able to match their obstinacy with sanctified stubbornness of his own. He will be as zealous for truth as they were for falsehood. They were as hard as *flint*; he will be as hard as a *diamond* (*šāmîr*). Ezekiel's firmness will cut like a diamond into the flint-like hearts of the men of Israel.

Ezekiel need have no fear or be dismayed before that rebellious people. Given the circumstances that he faced, how appropriate was this prophet's name, Ezekiel—"God strengthens" or "God hardens."

Congregation Assessed 3:10-15

A. Obligation of the Prophet (3:10-11)

And he said unto me, Son of man, all my words that I will speak unto you receive into your heart. With your ears hear. 11 Then go unto the captives, unto the children of your people. Speak unto them and say unto them, Thus says Lord Yahweh; whether they will hear or whether they desist.

The first priority of any preacher is to be in harmony with the word of God. God called upon Ezekiel to hear all the words that he will speak to him. He must not only hear them with the ears, he must also *receive* them into his heart. He must *understand* and *believe* the message he is to preach. *All my words that I will speak* suggests that there will be future revelations that the prophet will also have to assimilate and subsequently announce. It is interesting to note that God

---

[118]The Hebrew word *šāmîr* is rendered "diamond" in Jer 17:1, "adamant" in Zech 7 12.

will communicate to Ezekiel in *words*, not just in abstract thought and ambiguous visions. Here is *verbal* revelation.

Once Ezekiel understood the divine word and personally yielded to it he will be prepared to undertake his mission to the Babylonian captives. He must *go* to them and *speak* what God had spoken to him. He was not to be influenced by their reactions to his words. His job was faithfully to proclaim the word. He was to speak authoritatively. A *thus says Yahweh* was to characterize all of his preaching. He was to preach on regardless of whether or not they gave heed. There may be a touch of irony in the expression *your* people rather than *my* (God's) people.

B. Change of Scene (3:12-15)

Then the Spirit lifted me up. I heard behind me the sound of great shaking— Blessed be the glory of Yahweh from his place—13 even the sound of the wings of the living creatures touching each other, and the sound of the wheels beside them, even the sound of great shaking. 14 And the Spirit lifted me up and took me so that I came with bitterness in the heat of my spirit; and the hand of Yahweh was strong upon me. 15 And I came unto the captives at Tel Aviv who were dwelling beside the river Kebar, and to where they dwelled.[119] And I sat there seven days astonished in their midst.

At this point the Holy Spirit *lifted* Ezekiel up to whisk him from this mountain-top visionary experience to the valley of prophetic service (cf. 2:2). This is the first of several places where the prophet describes his supernatural transports. In his vision Ezekiel experienced a subjective feeling of being airborne. This was much like the feeling one has in a dream of soaring through the air. The prophet had been in the presence of the theophany—the visionary throne-chariot—during all that has been narrated to this point (1:4-3:12). When he was *lifted up* and *carried away* it seemed to Ezekiel that he was leaving the theophany behind.

Simultaneous with the Holy Spirit entering Ezekiel the magnificent throne-chariot departed the scene. As it did so *the sound of a great shaking was heard.*

A voice pronouncing a blessing on the glory of Yahweh accompanied the shaking noise. This voice is unidentified. It may be the voice that was heard from above the firmament in 1:24-25; or it could

---

[119]Another reading, that involves a change in the Hebrew text, is: "and I sat where they were sitting."

be the voice of the creatures praising Yahweh.[120] The phrase *from his place* is problematic. It probably refers to the place where the glory of God revealed itself in the vision.[121] To state the matter differently, the glory of Yahweh yet remained in the place from which it was departing because his place is universal.[122]

The sound of great shaking of v 12 is identified as the whirring of the wings of the living creatures and the rumble of the wheels. When the throne-chariot was stationary the living creatures did not touch each other. When they were in flight, however, the creatures raised their wings so as to touch each other. See on 1:11.

After the departure of the throne-chariot Ezekiel describes what happened to him in these words: *the Spirit lifted me up and took me away*. This seems to indicate that Ezekiel was miraculously transported from one spot to another in Mesopotamia. At the very least it means that Ezekiel, guided and impelled by the Holy Spirit, went forth among his countrymen. This suggests that the site of the vision was some distance from the exile settlement for it is to the latter place that Ezekiel now returned.

Ezekiel describes his feelings as he departed the scene of his visionary experience. He went *in bitterness,*[123] *in the heat of my spirit*. Anger was the dominant emotion in his heart at this moment. Why did he feel this way? Was he resentful at having been thrust into such a terrifying task? Possibly. It is more likely, however, that the word of Yahweh that had been eaten and digested had created within him a righteous anger against the sin of Israel.[124]

Ezekiel filled with God's indignation. He also was conscious of being strengthened and guided by the hand of Yahweh.[125] Even though the vision was over, he still felt that the unseen hand was upon him.

---

[120]Blackwood imagines that the throbbing pulsations of the creatures seemed to chant this doxology.

[121]Currey, *Bible Commentary*, 28.

[122]Another view is that *his place* refers to Jerusalem.

[123]The Hebrew *mar* (*bitter*) can express fierce temper, discontentment or wretchedness.

[124]Fisch (*Ezekiel*, 15) thinks the meaning is that Ezekiel was deeply distressed over having to deliver such a calamitous message. The *heat of my spirit* he explains as descriptive of the state of exaltation that he felt as the result of his vision. This interpretation is forced.

[125]The purpose of the hand of God was not, as Fisch (*Ezekiel*, 15) contends, to counteract the reluctance of the prophet.

Following the visionary experience, Ezekiel rejoined his fellow captives in Tel Aviv, the chief center of the exiles in Babylon. The name *Tel Aviv* means "heap of grain ears." The place probably got its name from the fertility of the area.[126]

For *seven days* Ezekiel sat *astonished* among the exiles. Keil understands the term to mean motionless and dumb. This was a time for reflection, meditation and readjustment. Various explanations of the seven days have been given. This was the period of prescribed mourning in certain periods of Old Testament history (Job 2:13). The period for the consecration of a priest was also seven days (Lv 8:33). Thus Ezekiel may have regarded this period as his time of personal consecration to the prophetic office. The simplest explanation, however, is that Ezekiel was waiting for further instruction. In this case there is no particular significance in the number seven.

RESPONSIBILITY OF SERVICE 3:16-21

The focus now shifts from the national to the individual aspects of Ezekiel's mission. In the midst of the general visitation that will fall upon the nation as a whole each individual was to stand before Yahweh to have his faith and works rewarded or punished. This passage underscores the basic moral principle that each person is individually responsible for his own conduct. Another principle enunciated here is that God's messengers must face up to the responsibility to warn all men of the consequences of their ways.

Ezekiel as Watchman 3:16-17

And it came to pass at the end of seven days that the word of Yahweh came unto me, saying, 17 Son of man, I have appointed you a watchman for the house of Israel. Hear the word from my mouth, and give them warning from me.

At the end of the seven days of silence *the word of Yahweh* came to Ezekiel, i.e., he had another revelation from God. This is the first

[126]Others interpret the name to mean "mount of the flood." The name has been resurrected in the name of the largest city in the modern state of Israel.

of some sixty occurrences of the revelation formula in the book.[127] The expression implies the experience of a *possessing word* or influence.[128] In this *word* Ezekiel receives both instruction and further commission to carry out his ministry.

Ezekiel learned in this revelation that God had appointed him to be a *watchman for the house of Israel.*[129] Watchman was not a new name for the prophet of God; but it was not common. Yet it is used at the beginning of Ezekiel's commissioning. It is repeated and amplified at his re-commissioning in 33:1-9. Evidently the term brings out a prominent feature of Ezekiel's ministry.

Ellison puts his finger on the significance of the title *watchman* when he notes that Ezekiel was not merely to be God's messenger to the people in general; he was to be God's messenger to the individual in particular.[130] He was to be a personal evangelist as well as a public orator. Only the facts of his public ministry have been preserved; but this in no wise nullifies the conclusion here reached. Ezekiel was to engage in a pastoral ministry such as priests in Old Testament times were supposed to perform.[131] The chief contribution of Ezekiel to Old Testament theology is his emphasis on individual responsibility.

In his capacity as *watchman* Ezekiel was to wait and watch for the word from the mouth of God. He then was to warn the people of impending calamity. The life and safety of a community were in the hand of a city watchman. So also the life and safety of the people of God were in the hands of Ezekiel. Four different cases are discussed so that Ezekiel might clearly assess his responsibility as Israel's watchman.

---

[127]This formula is used in reference to Samuel (1 Sam 15:10), Nathan (2 Sam 7:4), Gad (2 Sam 24:11), a Bethel prophet (1 Kgs 13:20), Jehu (1 Kgs 16:1), Elijah (5x), and Isaiah (2 Kgs 20:4). With variations, the formula appears in Jeremiah some 30x.

[128]Vawter and Hoppe, *Ezekiel*, 36.

[129]Earlier usage of the watchman concept: Isa 21:6; 52:8; 62:6; Hab 2:1; Jer 6:17. A fuller description of the watchman phase of Ezekiel's ministry is found in ch 33.

[130]Ellison, *Ezekiel*, 28.

[131]See Lv 10:11; Dt 24:8; Mal 2:7; 2 Chr 17:7ff.

Watchman Scenarios
3:18-21

A. Unwarned Wicked (3:18)

When I say to the wicked, You will surely die, and you do not warn him or speak to preserve his life, he is the wicked one who will die in his iniquity; but his blood I will seek from your hand

In his role as Watchman Ezekiel will encounter two types of individuals. First, he will encounter the wicked—those destined to die for the sin they had committed. Ezekiel's job was to warn him of his wicked way, i.e., of the consequences of continuing his wicked course of conduct. The wicked are those who do not serve God. On the contrary, they live in open defiance of him.

God told Ezekiel that the penalty for the wicked is death. *He will die in his iniquity*. Some see nothing more involved here than the end of physical life. It should be noted, however, that it is not Ezekiel who speaks; it is Yahweh. The question is not the level of understanding of the doctrine of retribution or the doctrine of the afterlife in the sixth century BC. Still less is the full meaning of the utterance to be determined by ascertaining how Ezekiel or his contemporaries may have interpreted the word *die*. The teaching of the Bible is that those who die unforgiven "die" for all eternity in a conscious existence elsewhere known as the lake of fire (Rev 20:15). That a premature death may also be involved cannot be denied; but to contend that premature death exhausts the meaning of the statement is to disregard the total biblical teaching that eternal retribution follows the physical death of the wicked.

If the prophet fails faithfully and forthrightly to sound the alarm he will be held accountable for the death of that sinner—*his blood I will seek from your hand*. The focus changes from *them* to *him*—the individual. The teaching harks back to the principle expressed in Gn 9:5f. The blood of a murdered man demanded retribution by the nearest kinsman. So a man dying unwarned will be regarded virtually as the victim of murder committed by the unfaithful Watchman. Ezekiel himself would have to die for his negligence. Though this utterance is metaphorical it nonetheless emphasizes the enormous responsibility that was Ezekiel's. The Christian responsibility to warn the lost is no less (1 Jn 5:16).

B. Non-repentant Wicked (3:19)

But as for you, when you warn a wicked one, and he does not turn from his wickedness and from his wicked way, he in his iniquity will die; but as for you, your life you have delivered.

Nothing but good can result from the discharge of responsibility to warn the wicked. If he heeds the warning and alters his course of conduct he will *live*, i.e., save his soul. If he refuses he will suffer the consequences of death; but the messenger thereby has done his duty. Thus he has delivered his own life of blood-guiltiness. An important principle of Old Testament jurisprudence is illustrated in this passage: the failure to save life corresponds to murder.

C. Straying Righteous (3:20)

And when a righteous man turns from his righteousness and does evil, and I place a stumbling block before him, he will die; because you did not warn him in his sin, he will die; his righteousness that he has done will not be remembered; but his blood I will seek from your hand.

On occasion Ezekiel will encounter a man whose basic orientation was righteous, but who momentarily had strayed from the path of fidelity. Sometimes God permits a stumbling block to be placed before such a one—some trial, some difficulty, some occasion for sin. For an example of such a stumbling block see 7:19 and 44:12. It is true that God tempts no man in order to bring about his destruction. Through his providence and permissive will, however, he allows men to be tried that their faith may be found true. Stumbling was not inevitable. A moral choice was always involved. Furthermore, God provided the Watchman to warn where the stumbling blocks were located.

Should one who was outwardly pious depart from the path of righteousness, the past righteous acts[132] of that man will not be remembered. To neglect to warn such a person will result in his death and the Watchman's guilt.

D. Righteous Penitent (3:21)

But as for you, if you warn a righteous man that a righteous man does not sin, and he does not sin, he will surely live because he has been warned. As for you, you have delivered your life.

---

[132]The verb is plural. In the marginal notes of the Hebrew Bible, the Masoretic scribes suggest that the noun should also be read as a plural.

If a righteous man who had stumbled into sin repented he will thereby save his soul. In any case, the Watchman is free from any responsibility so long as he sounded the alarm.

RESTRICTIONS ON SERVICE 3:22-27

New Meeting with God 3:22-23

And the hand of Yahweh came upon me there. He said unto me, Rise, go out into the plain. There I will speak with you. 23 And I arose and went out unto the plain. Behold there the glory of Yahweh was standing like the glory that I saw beside the River Kebar. I fell upon my face.

The protracted period of commissioning comes to an end with a second glimpse of God's glory.[133] Following the lesson at Tel Aviv *the hand of Yahweh*, i.e., the power and guiding influence of God,[134] came upon Ezekiel. He was told to go out *into the plain*. There God will teach Ezekiel yet another lesson about his ministry. The word *plain* means literally "valley," the area between two mountains. Perhaps Ezekiel frequented this place in his periods of solitude.[135] It may well have been in this same "valley" that Ezekiel later received his vision of dry bones (37:1).

Ezekiel complied with the divine command. When he reached the designated spot he saw a second vision of *the glory of Yahweh*. The vision was very much like what he had seen by the Kebar. Ezekiel sums up the whole of that vision by his reference to the One who rode the chariot—*the glory of Yahweh*. As on the earlier occasion Ezekiel reacted to this majestic manifestation by falling on his face.

---

[133]Some commentators postulate a time gap between 3:21 and 3:22 during which Ezekiel conducted a ministry as a watchman. The chronology of the book, however, does not allow for a significant interval at this point.

[134]Cf. Blackwood (*Ezekiel*, 54) thinks *the hand of Yahweh* refers to an inward, spiritual experience. Blackwood follows Davidson in contending that Ezekiel's trip to the plain did not involve any *physical* motion.

[135]Taylor, *Ezekiel*, 72.

New Instructions
3:24-27

A. Movement Restricted (3:24-25)

And the Spirit came on me. He made me stand upon my feet. He spoke to me and said: Go shut yourself up in the midst of your house. 25 And as for you, son of man, behold fetters will be placed upon you. You will not go out in their midst.

Again the Holy Spirit entered into Ezekiel, giving him the strength and confidence to stand on his feet. Ezekiel now received a new command. He was told to shut himself within his house.

In his house Ezekiel will be bound with *fetters*. No evidence exists that Ezekiel was ever literally bound by his auditors. The fetters must be symbolic or metaphorical of self-imposed (or God-imposed) restraint. Perhaps the restraints were placed on the prophet by his fellow captives. It seems that Ezekiel's movements outside his house were severely restricted, if not actually curtailed.

B. Speech Restricted (3:26)

And your tongue will cleave unto the roof of your mouth so that you will be dumb. You will not become to them a man of reproof; for they are a rebellious house. 27 But when I speak with you, I will open your mouth. You will say unto them, Thus says Lord Yahweh. The one who hears let him hear, and the one who desists let him desist; for they are a rebellious house.

Divine restrictions were placed upon the speech of Ezekiel as well as on his movements. His tongue will cleave unto the roof of his mouth. Because of the rebelliousness of the house of Israel the prophet should (or will) be silent.

During that period of self-imposed (or God-imposed) dumbness Ezekiel will not serve as a man of reproof to the exiles.[136] This ministry of silence seems to have been intended to demonstrate to the exiles that they were indeed a rebellious house.[137]

Ezekiel will only communicate with his fellow exiles at such times as he had a divine communication to share with them. From

---

[136]Cf. R.R. Wilson, "An Interpretation of Ezekiel's Dumbness," *VT* 22 (1972): 91-104.

[137]C.F. Keil suggests that the silence also was designed to help prepare Ezekiel for the successful performance of his ministry. *The Prophecies of Ezekiel.* "Biblical Commentary on the Old Testament" (Grand Rapids: Eerdmans, 1950 reprint), 1:65.

time to time God will commit to his Watchman a revelation that was to be passed on to the captives. Ezekiel was to preface every spoken word with *thus says Yahweh.*

The silence of Ezekiel was to last for a limited time. When Jerusalem fell six years later the restraints were removed from the prophet (33:22).[138] This was, to use the language of Taylor, ritual dumbness. Ezekiel did not suffer from catalepsy or some nervous disorder. Rather the idea is that he was to speak only when under a divine compulsion to do so. The reaction to these God-given pronouncements will confirm men in their attitude toward God. Men will either obey it or they will despise it. In the former case they will find grace; in the latter, condemnation. By his preaching and non-preaching Ezekiel continuously confronted his auditors with the life and death alternatives.

SPECIAL NOTE
Ezekiel 3:25-27

The interpretation of this paragraph is extremely difficult. The problem is not so much in what is said—though that is difficult enough—but in the timing of it. How can the previous commands to preach the word be squared with the thought that Ezekiel was to be dumb? How can his being bound with cords be harmonized with subsequent chs that show him moving about freely? Those who have wrestled with these questions may be divided into two broad categories. First, some think in terms of a literal period of silence. Even among those who hold to a literal period of silence at least four different positions have been taken:

1. Some think the episode is chronologically out of place. They think this command was issued after ch 24. The passage has been placed in its present position because of topical considerations. It does, after all, partake of the nature of a commission.

2. Others suggest that there was a period of dumbness prior to the launching of the ministry of proclamation. This is the obvious solution to the problem were it not for the difficulty of finding time for such a period of dumbness in the known chronology of Ezekiel's life.

[138]There are two references along the way to the prophet's silence—24:27 and 29:21.

3. David Kimchi offered the intriguing suggestion that the silence was divinely imposed so as to prevent Ezekiel from speaking until he had received the entire revelation that God reveals in chs 1-11. He was not to speak prematurely.

4. Finally, some suggest that the silence was the first of a series of prophecies that Ezekiel acted out.

Another approach to this passage regards the fetters on Ezekiel as symbolic or metaphorical. These scholars see the restraint upon the prophet as a symbol of the bitter opposition of his fellow exiles to his prophesying. Ezekiel preaches; but the exiles do not listen. Since no real communication takes place it will be as though Ezekiel were dumb. Still others interpret the entire passage as saying simply that Ezekiel will refuse to speak to his neighbors about ordinary matters. He will speak only when he had a divine revelation.[139]

EZEKIEL 4
DRAMATIC PARABLES

The use of symbolic actions by Old Testament prophets was a proven way of gaining an audience and underscoring a point.[140] The great prophets Isaiah and Jeremiah found the symbolic act a useful tool when they could no longer obtain a hearing for their message.[141] Ezekiel performs four dramatic parables in this section depicting the siege of Jerusalem (4:1-3); national sin (4:4-6); the siege famine (4:9-17); and the nation's fate (5:1-4).

These dramatic parables were performed in the fifth year of Jehoiachin's captivity. At that time any thought of Jerusalem's overthrow was, according to any human prognostication, highly improbable. Zedekiah ruled in Jerusalem as Nebuchadrezzar's vassal. Zedekiah's lands were diminished and his military strength exhausted. No one could imagine that he would be so stupid as to provoke his over-

[139]The prophets normally moved among their people, speaking God's message as they observed the contemporary situation. Ezekiel, however, was to remain in his home, except to dramatize God's messages (cf. 4:1-5:17). He was to remain mute (v 26), *except* when God opened the prophet's mouth to deliver a divine message (v 27). Instead of Ezekiel's going to the people, the people had to come to him.

[140]Early examples of the use of symbolic prophecy are 1 Sam 15:27f; 1 Kgs 11:29ff; 22:11; 2 Kgs 13:14-19.

[141]E.g., Isa 20:2; Jer 13:1-7; 19:1, 2; 27:2-3.

lord. Yet Ezekiel joined Jeremiah in affirming that destruction was the ultimate fate of Jerusalem.

PARABLE OF JERUSALEM'S SIEGE 4:1-3

Preparation 4:1-3a

But as for you, son of man, take to yourself a tile and place it before you. Inscribe upon it a city, Jerusalem. 2 Lay siege against it; build an assault tower and construct a mound about it. Set against it encampments, and place battering rams round about. 3 As for you, take to yourself an iron pan. Place it as a wall of iron between you and the city.

In his first symbolic action Ezekiel was to sketch a diagram of Jerusalem on a tile or brick (RSV). In Mesopotamia the clay tablet was the common writing material. While the clay was moist and soft the inscription was engraved upon it with a stylus; then the tablet was exposed to the sun for hardening. Large numbers of such tablets have been recovered. Some of these have diagrams of buildings upon them similar to what an architect might devise.[142] It would be natural under the circumstances for a Hebrew exile to make use of the Babylonian writing material.

Ezekiel was instructed to *lay siege* against the city he had drawn. By a common figure the prophet is here represented as doing what he portrays. Perhaps he drew on the tile the plan of a siege. On the other hand, it may mean that he was to model the various siege weapons around the brick. A third possibility is that the armament of the besieging troops was represented on other tiles. Four common siege techniques are named:

An *assault tower* (*dāyēq*) provided the elevated platform from which archers could attack the defenders on the walls. Sometimes these towers were of enormous height, as much as twenty stories.[143]

---

[142]A brick map of Nippur, a city close to Tel Aviv, is presently displayed in the museum of the University of Pennsylvania (*IDB*, 3:553).
[143]Currey, *Bible Commentary*, 32.

Such towers are frequently depicted in Mesopotamian art. According to 2 Kgs 25:1 assault towers were used in the final siege of Jerusalem.

Mound (*sōlᵉlāh*) was a bank of soil heaped up to the level of the walls of the besieged city. Such mounds could serve as observation posts. If close enough to the walls they could also serve as ramps for the battering rams.

Encampments (machᵃnōt) were military detachments that surrounded the city.

Battering rams (kārîm)) were iron-shod beams transported by a wheeled tower.[144] Often the battering ram was found in the lower part of the siege towers mentioned above.

The prophet was to place an *iron pan* between him and the inscribed tile. This was a kind of flat plan—virtually no more than a sheet of metal—such as was used for baking a thin cake of bread (cf. Lv 2:5). This pan represented a *wall of iron*. Normally walls provided protection or containment. The pan probably represents the siege wall around Jerusalem erected by the Babylonians.[145]

Action
4:3b

Set your face against it. It will enter a state of siege, and you will besiege it. It is a sign to the house of Israel.

With his symbolic objects in place Ezekiel was to perform a symbolic action. He was to set his face against the city;[146] and to lay siege to it. The prophet was to assume the part of the attacking army. Since Ezekiel was God's representative his actions underscored the point that God was fighting against Jerusalem. Perhaps *laying siege* (RSV, "press the siege") indicates the gradual movement of the clay models of siege instruments nearer and nearer the doomed city.[147] The tile

---

[144]Blackwood, *Ezekiel*, 58.

[145]Others take the pan to be a symbol of 1) Jerusalem's wall in which the Jews put so much trust; 2) the iron-like severity of the siege against the city, i.e., no escape; 3) the impenetrable barrier that had arisen between God (as represented by Ezekiel) and Jerusalem; 4) another siege implement—the shield that attackers erected as protection for archers; and 5) a symbol of Ezekiel's protection (cf. 2:6) as he carries out his prophetic assignment.

[146]The command *set your face against* occurs with variations 11x in the book. This is a symbolic act in which the face is turned toward or against the object of judgment. The act regularly was accompanied by a judgment oracle.

[147]Ellison, *Ezekiel*, 33.

diagram and the objects pertaining to it were designed to be *a sign to the house of Israel.*

Ellison pictures Ezekiel silently acting out these parables much to the chagrin of the growing numbers who assembled each day to watch his antics. When the crowd was ready to listen Ezekiel gave the verbal explanation of his actions (5:5-7:27).[148] The term *house of Israel* here embraces both those Jews who were in exile and those who remained in Judah.

ISRAEL'S SIN 4:4-8

In 4:1-3 Ezekiel impersonated Jerusalem's enemies. His role is now reversed. Here Ezekiel symbolizes the apostate people of God. He is to lie first on his left side, then on his right side, *to bear the iniquity* of the house of Israel and the house of Judah. The Oriental habit was to face eastward when indicating points of the compass.[149] Facing east one has north on his left side and south on his right. Hence the left side represented the house of Israel, the northern kingdom that had been taken captive in 722 BC. The right side symbolized the house of Judah, the southern kingdom that was in its dying days at the moment Ezekiel received this revelation. The number of days that the prophet spent on each side symbolized the number of years that each kingdom stood under the condemnation of God.[150]

General Observations

A few observations about this action parable need to be made before the difficult question of the numbers found here is taken up:

---

[148]Ibid. Others think that Ezekiel never actually performed these parables, but only described to the captives vividly what he had seen in vision.

[149]Feinberg, *Ezekiel*, 33.

[150]Ralph Alexander takes the 390 + 40 = 430 years as a prediction of future punishment for Israel. Counting from Ezekiel's chronological reference point (597 BC), the 430 years denote the punishment inflicted by conquering foreign powers on the children of Israel and Judah from the deportation of Jehoiachin, their recognized king, to the inception of the Maccabean rebellion in 167 BC. During the Maccabean period the Jews once again exercised dominion over Judah. "Ezekiel" in vol. 6 *The Expositor's Bible Commentary* (ed. Frank E. Gaebelein. Grand Rapids: Zondervan, 1986) 770.

1. The action of the prophet in lying first on the one side, then on the other, was commanded by God. Therefore there is no reason to suspect that Ezekiel suffered from epileptic seizures or catalepsy.

2. Verse 4 seems to suggest that the time periods do not represent the time of Israel's sinning, but the period during which the people of God had been, or will be, punished for their sins.

3. The longer period of punishment for Israel, the northern kingdom, indicates the greater guilt of that nation.

4. Part of the time Israel and Judah bore the penalty of their sin simultaneously. The periods of punishment overlapped.

5. The end of the period of punishment was the same for both kingdoms—539 BC.

6. In dealing with prophetic numbers one must allow for approximations or rounding off.

7. Such great diversity of opinion exists as to the *terminus a quo* of the figures in vv 5-6 that dogmatic assertions are out of place.

8. Inherent in these figures is a hint of hope. The period of punishment, though long and terrible, will not be interminable.

9. It is not necessary to assume that Ezekiel was in the prone position day and night. Other activities are said to have been performed during this period. Hence the symbolic prone position must have lasted only part of each day.

Ezekiel on the Left Side
4:4-5

As for you, lie upon your left side. Set the iniquity of the house of Israel upon it. The number of days in which you lay upon it you will bear their iniquity. 5 For I have appointed to you the years of their iniquity, according to the number of days, 390 days. So will you bear the iniquity of the house of Israel.

In his prone position Ezekiel was to *bear the iniquity* of the two kingdoms. The term *iniquity* in the Old Testament can refer to the sin itself or the punishment that comes upon that offense. In the present passage the term seems to have the latter connotation. Ezekiel is to symbolize through his personal suffering of physical restraint the punishment of God's people in being cut off from the holy land and the temple.

Ezekiel was to lie on his left side 390 days. If the Hebrew text be retained there seems to be only one possible *terminus a quo* for this period,[151] viz. the division of the Israelite kingdom in 931 BC. Allowing for round figures—something very common in prophecy—the 390 years terminate with the fall of Babylon in 539 BC. Through that entire period the citizens of the northern kingdom were under the wrath of God because of their apostate activities.[152]

Ezekiel on the Right Side
4:6

When you have finished these days then lie a second time upon your right side, and bear the iniquity of the house of Judah 40 days; one day for each year I have appointed you.

From what point are the forty years of Judah's punishment to be counted? The figure forty is reminiscent of the period of Israel wandering in the wilderness (Nm 14:34). In Ezekiel's day the nation came into "the wilderness of the peoples" (20:35). From the final deportation of Jews to Babylon in 582 BC (Jer 52:30) until the fall of Babylon and the end of the Babylonian exile in 539 BC is a period of forty-two years. The prophet is probably referring to this period with the symbolic number forty, the period during which God's people, because of their sin, were denied access to the Promised Land.

Some scholars find difficulty in fitting the 430 days of this action parable into the chronology of the early ministry of Ezekiel. Ellison argues that this action parable must be fitted into the year and two months that elapsed between 1:2 and 8:1. According to the Jewish system of reckoning time this is equivalent to 413 days.[153] Ellison

---

[151]W. Eichrodt points out that 390 + 40 = 430, the number of years the Israelites were in Egypt (Ex 12:40). He suggests that the period of Egyptian servitude is used as a pattern for the exile. The larger figure for Israel may symbolize the longer exile of the northern kingdom. *Ezekiel, a Commentary* in "The Old Testament Library" (Philadelphia: Westminster, 1970), 85. Van den Born suggested that the technique of *gematria* has been applied to the words *days of siege (ymy mtsr)* in 4:8. The numerical value of the letters of these two words is 390. Cited in Vawter and Hoppe, *Ezekiel*, 42.

[152]Many prefer to follow the Greek text that gives 190 as the figure here. From the fall of Samaria in 722 BC until the time of Ezekiel's vision was about 150 years. Add to this the forty years mentioned in 4:6 and the figure 190 is reached. However, it is more likely that the Greek translators deliberately altered the text. There is no logical explanation of how any accidental change in the text could have occurred here.

[153]The Jewish year was a lunar year of 354 days. Periodically an extra month was intercalated so as to bring the lunar calendar into harmony with the seasons. If the

therefore argues that the forty days on the right side must have been concurrent with the last forty days of the 390 days on the left side.[154] In the fulfillment of this prophecy the forty years of Judah's punishment were in fact concurrent with the last forty years of Israel's punishment. In the symbolic action, however, the days seem to be consecutive—390 on the left side followed by forty on the right side. Therefore one must conclude either 1) that during the period between 1:2 and 8:1 a month had been intercalated; or 2) that the symbolic prostration extended beyond the time stipulated in 8:1. Of course if the prophet's prostration occurred only in a vision, as some scholars contend, it is not necessary to fit the 430 days into the chronology of Ezekiel's life.

Other Details
4:7-8

So unto the siege of Jerusalem you will set your face. Your shoulder will be uncovered. You will prophesy against it. 8 Behold I have placed bands upon you, and you will not turn yourself from one side to the other until you have completed the days of your siege.

During the entire time that he was lying on his side Ezekiel was to fix his gaze upon the tile that depicted the besieged city of Jerusalem. The fixing of the gaze indicates steadfastness of purpose. He was to have his arm uncovered like a warrior prepared for battle (cf. Isa 52:10). By these actions he was prophesying against Jerusalem.

Verse 8 underscores the discomfort that Ezekiel must have experienced while carrying out this symbolic act. He was not to turn from one side to another. There may be a hint of special divine aid in the statement *I lay bands upon you.*[155]

---

year that elapsed between 1:2 and 8:1 was such a leap year, the maximum number of days would be 442.

[154]Ellison, *Ezekiel*, 34.

[155]Taylor (*Ezekiel*, 81) takes the expression literally, and pictures Ezekiel's body trussed with cords during his daily period upon his side.

JERUSALEM'S FAMINE
4:9-17

How could Ezekiel be commanded to make bread while lying bound upon his side? Several commentators think that this inconsistency is proof that all of these symbolic actions transpired in vision where such a thing is possible.[156] If the prophet's immobilization, however, occupied only a part of each day there is no inconsistency. Once Ezekiel had performed his daily demonstration—lying facing the model of the besieged city—he apparently arose and performed the other symbolic acts that related to the siege.

Original Directive
4:9-13

A. Food Quality (4:9a)

Now as for you, take for yourself wheat and barley, beans and lentils, millet and fitches. Put them in a vessel, and prepare them as food for yourself…

The nature of Ezekiel's food was restricted. His bread was to be made of an odd mixture of grains and seeds. Instead of the normal wheat flour, various kinds of cereals were to be mixed so as to obtain sufficient quantity to make a cake of bread. Those besieged in Jerusalem will have to eat what they could get. Six different kinds of cereal grains are specified: 1) *wheat* and 2) *barley* are frequently mentioned as foods in the Old Testament; 3) *beans* (*pol*) are mentioned elsewhere only in 2 Sam 17:28; 4) *lentils*, 5) *millet*, and 6) *fitches* (*spelt*, RSV), a species of wheat.[157]

The various grains were to be placed in one vessel. In the Law of Moses it was forbidden to "sow the ground with mingled seeds" (Lv 19:19; Dt 22:9). Though not specifically condemned, the mixing of these grains and seeds in flour seems to be banned under the same

[156]E.g., Blackwood, *Ezekiel*, 60; Fisch, *Ezekiel*, 21.

[157]M. Greenberg cites the Babylonian Talmud (*Erubin* 81a) to the effect that an experiment had shown that a dog will not eat bread made in this fashion. *Ezekiel 1-20* in "Anchor Bible" (Garden City: Doubleday, 1983), 106.

principle.[158] In a city under siege and in foreign exile the Jews will not be able to be so scrupulous about their diet.

B. Duration of the Diet (4:9b)

according to the number of days in which you are lying upon your side, 390 days and you will eat it.

The dietary restrictions were to be in force during the 390 days of bearing the iniquity of the people of God. Here again the question of the duration of Ezekiel's symbolic siege of Jerusalem is raised. Verse 9 seems to suggest that the prophet lies upon his side only 390 days. What happened to the forty days he was to lie upon his right side? Some assume that the 390 days are inclusive of the forty days. This interpretation, however, runs counter to the explicit statement in v 6 that Ezekiel was to lie on his right side *after* he had finished the 390 days on his left side. One must conclude either 1) that the dietary regulations of this paragraph were to be observed only during the time when Ezekiel was on his left side; or 2) that the dietary restrictions were observed during the forty days on the right side as well, even though the text does not explicitly so state. Any other interpretations will put v 9 at variance with v 6. God's people were to be exiled from the sacred temple precincts for 390 years, the northern kingdom from 931 to 539 BC, and the southern kingdom for the last forty years of that period.

Ezekiel's symbolic diet during the days of his "siege" was designed to set forth two basic thoughts: 1) the scarcity of food that will exist in Jerusalem during the final siege; and 2) the impure food that those exiled from Judah will be forced to eat. This point he established during the 390 days on his left side. Continuing this phase of the demonstration during the period he lay on his right side would have been superfluous.

C. Food Quantity (4:10-11)

Your food that you eat will be twenty shekels in weight for a day. Once each day you will eat it. 11 As for water, you will drink the sixth of a hin by measure. Once each day you will drink it.

The *quantity* of his food was limited.[159] Ezekiel's diet during the 390 days was to consist of twenty shekels of food and the sixth of a

---

[158]Taylor, (*Ezekiel*, 82), does not think that any ritual defilement was involved in mixing these grains.

hin of water. This amounts to about eight ounces of food and two cups of water daily. This is insufficient for maintenance of physical well-being. Only with supernatural assistance would Ezekiel have been able to follow this regime during the symbolic days of siege. In a hot climate this limitation on water is very oppressive. Rationed water is called the water of affliction (1 Kgs 22:27; Isa 30:20). The fact that food was weighed rather than measured indicates the most extreme scarcity (cf. Lv 26:26; Rev 6:6).

The prophet was to partake of his unpalatable meals literally "from time to time." The rabbis interpreted this phrase to mean once in a twenty-four hour period. Currey concurs. The instruction is to partake of the food at the appointed interval of a day and at no other time.[160]

D. Food Consumption (4:12-13)

As a barley cake you will eat it, and with human dung you will bake it in their presence. 13 Yahweh said, In this way the children of Israel will eat their unclean food among the nations where I will drive them.

The meager food was to be eaten *as barley cake*, i.e., he is to eat his meal with all the relish that one customarily gives to barley cakes. Both the eating and the preparation of the food were to be *in their presence*, i.e., so the exiles could observe. Thus will they come to understand it as a sign of what had befallen them already, and of what will yet befall their brethren in Jerusalem.

One of the usual calamities of a siege is lack of fuel. To further dramatize siege conditions Ezekiel was to prepare his food with unclean fuel. The prophet was told to use human dung as cooking fuel, that which was revolting as well as ceremonially impure and defiling (cf. Dt 23:12ff). Barley bread was prepared on hot stones (1 Kgs 19:6) that were to be heated by human excrement. For the moment the ceremonial law was to be overridden so as to make a moral point.

The significance of the disgusting instruction regarding the use of human dung for fuel is given in v 13. Those Israelites who yet remained in Jerusalem will be forced to eat unclean food among the nations where God will drive them (cf. Hos 9:3). Foreign lands were

---

[159]What Ezekiel prophesied here, his contemporary Jeremiah experienced. See Jer 37:21.

[160]Currey, *Bible Commentary*, 35. 1 Chr 9:25 makes it clear that *time to time* refers to a recurring action that takes place at the same time each day.

regarded by the Israelites as unclean.[161] Even those who attempted to maintain the dietary code will be eating unclean bread because the ritual first fruits of the harvest will not be able to be offered in the temple of Yahweh.[162] In addition to the specific prediction being set forth in this action parable, Ezekiel is making a significant point: Israel's position as a separate, sanctified people will be destroyed during the Babylonian exile.[163]

Mitigation
4:14-15

A. Ezekiel's Protest (4:14)

Then I said, Ah, O Lord Yahweh! Behold my soul has not been polluted, and a corpse or that which was torn in pieces I have never eaten from my youth until now. Abominable meat has never come into my mouth.

The command to prepare his food with human dung as fuel shocked the conscientious young priest. He obliquely requested relief from this phase of the object lesson. The first words that Ezekiel speaks in this book are an emotional outburst: *Ah Lord Yahweh!* (cf. Jer 1:6). The godly prophet was not so much concerned with what displeased his taste as what offended his conscience.

From exasperation Ezekiel moved to narrative prayer that is introduced with *behold. My soul* (i.e., *I*) *has not been polluted.* He meticulously had sought to abide by the dietary laws *from my youth until now.* Even in the deprivations of captivity and the spiritual confusion of that episode he conscientiously had attempted to follow the law of God.

Ezekiel cites three examples of how he faithfully had observed the Old Testament law. 1) He had not eaten of a corpse, i.e., an animal that had not been properly slaughtered. Such meat was forbidden (Lv 17:15; Dt 14:21). 2) He had not eaten what was torn in pieces, i.e., an animal that had been killed by a wild beast. Such was forbidden to the Israelite because the blood had not been properly drained. 3) Abominable meat (*piggûl*) had never come into his mouth. In its more restricted sense the Hebrew term refers to sacrificial flesh ren-

---

[161]Fisch, *Ezekiel*, 23.
[162]Cf. Amos 7:17; Dan 1:8.
[163]Feinberg, *Ezekiel*, 34-35.

dered unfit by disregard for the laws of sacrifice.[164] In a broader sense the term is used of any forbidden food.[165]

B. Yahweh's Compassion (4:15)

Then he said unto me, See, I have appointed for you cattle dung instead of human dung. You will prepare your food with it.

The gracious Lord acquiesced in the request of his prophet. He permitted Ezekiel to substitute animal dung for the prescribed human dung. Dried cow dung was not as physically disgusting as human dung.[166] So in the case of Ezekiel there was a mitigation of the defilement; but still defilement remained. The point is that in the exile the people of God were subjected to defilement.

Explanation
4:16-17

He said unto me, Son of man, behold I am about to shatter the staff of bread in Jerusalem. They will eat food by weight and with concern. Water by measure and in dismay they will drink 17 because bread and water will be scarce. They will be dismayed one with another. They will waste away under their punishment.

Shortly God will *shatter the staff of bread* in Jerusalem. Bread is the staff of life because man is so dependent upon it (cf. Lv 26:26; Ps 105:16). The inhabitants of that doomed city will be forced to *eat food by weight* and drink water *by measure.* The food and water will be so scarce as to give rise to grave concern and even dismay. Faced with this lack of food the populace will gradually *waste away under the punishment*[167] of Yahweh.

---

[164]More precisely, meat of an offering, if kept to the third day, was abominable and could not be eaten by the priests (Lv 19:7).

[165]Cf. Lv 7:18; Isa 65:4.

[166]Brownlee (*Word*, 78) reports that in rural Near Eastern communities today, little girls are often assigned the task of collecting animal droppings in a basket. They and pat them while still moist into patties. In dry weather these patties are dried on the roof for fuel.

[167]Could also be translated, "in their iniquity."

EZEKIEL 5
REBELLION AND RETRIBUTION

The first four vv of ch 5 probably belong as the concluding vv of ch 4. The three discourses in chs 5-7 are related in that they elaborate on the symbolism of 5:1-4. Each of these discourses, however, has its distinctive thrust. The first is characterized by the dual themes of rebellion and retribution (5:5-17). The focus is on disobedience and desolation in the second discourse (6:1-14). In his third sermon Ezekiel speaks of chaos and calamity (7:1-27).

Whether these sermons were delivered during the later part of the time of the symbolic siege of Jerusalem or sometime afterwards cannot be determined. In either case the symbolic actions gained for Ezekiel an attentive audience. It appears that during the period of these public discourses he was generally treated with respect (cf. 8:1; 14:1; 20:1).

PARABLE OF THE NATION'S FATE
5:1-4

Shaving of the Hair
5:1a

And as for you, son of man, take to yourself a sharp sword for a barber's razor. Take it, and cause it to pass over your head and your beard.

During the days of his symbolic siege of Jerusalem Ezekiel performed another act. He shaved his head and beard with a sharp sword that he used like a barber's razor.[168] The sword symbolizes the invading Chaldean army. Ezekiel symbolizes the land of Judah.

The coming invader will scrape the land barc (cf. Isa 7:20). He will bring upon it disgrace and mourning. Again Ezekiel was com-

[168]Grammatically it is difficult to determine whether Ezekiel took a sword or a razor-sharp knife symbolizing a sword. In either case the message is the same.

manded to violate the ceremonial law so as to make a prophetic application. The hair of the priest was a mark of his consecration to God's service (Lv 19:27). Shaving the head was a sign of mourning (Isa 3:24; 22:12). If an Israelite priest shaved his head he was defiled (Lv 21:5). Ezekiel defiled and humiliated himself as a symbol of the humiliation of the people of Judah who were defiled and no longer holy to Yahweh. Nothing was left to do but to mourn their death as a nation.

The hair removed from face and head was to be divided by weight into three parts. The *balances* that Ezekiel was to use may symbolize justice just as is still the case today. God's judgment is measured, accurate and fair (cf. Jer 15:2).[169]

Distribution of the Hair 5:1b-2

Take to yourself balances, and divide them. A third part you will burn in the fire in the midst of the city when the days of the siege are fulfilled. 2 Take a third part, smite with the sword around about her. And a third part you will scatter to the wind. And I will unsheathe a sword after them.

Ezekiel's shorn hair symbolizes the population of Jerusalem. The manner of the disposal of the hair indicated the various fates that awaited those rebellious Jews. A third of the hair was to be burned *in the midst of the city*, i.e., on the tile that depicted the city of Jerusalem.[170] These hairs symbolized those who will die in the horrors of warfare—fire, sword, famine and pestilence—when the city was besieged.[171]

Another third of the hair was to be smitten with the sword *round about her*, viz. the city. This symbolized the fate of those who tried to escape Jerusalem either during or after the fall. A prime example is King Zedekiah and his associates (cf. 2 Kgs 25:4 ff).

The last third of the hair was to be scattered to the wind. These hairs symbolize those who will be dispersed to foreign lands. Though they had escaped the holocaust at Jerusalem they will not find peace

---

[169]Weighing and numbering are ominous signs of impending judgment (cf. Dan 5:24-28).

[170]Another view is that the actual city of Jerusalem is meant. If all these action parables are *visionary,* this could be a possible interpretation.

[171]For a similar prophecy of a much later time, see Zech 13:8-9.

for *I will unsheathe a sword after them.* Jeremiah predicted the same fate for the exiles (Jer 9:15), as did Moses before him (Lv 26:33).[172]

Gathering of the Hair
5:3-4

Take a few in number, and bind them in the hem of your garment. 4 From them take again and cast them into the midst of the fire and burn them. From it a fire will go out into all the house of Israel.

In this bleak passage there is a hint of hope. A few of the hairs—presumably those that had been scattered to the wind—were to be retrieved and bound in the hem of Ezekiel's garment. A remnant of those carried off to exile will survive.

Though some will survive their situation will be desperate. From the hairs retrieved Ezekiel was to take some and cast them into the fire. The fire here may represent persecution through which some of the Jewish remnant will die. On the other hand, *the fire* may represent the fire that will destroy *Babylon*. Those who refused to heed the prophetic admonition to flee Babylon will face this fate.[173]

Thus the general drift of this parable is clear. Ezekiel foresaw the total destruction of Jerusalem and dispersion of the populace. True faith, however, will survive in a faithful remnant.

The expression *from it fire will go out into all the house of Israel* is difficult. Perhaps the thought is that even the faithful remnant in Babylon will suffer new hardships because of the suicidal rebellion launched by the leadership in Jerusalem.

EXPLANATORY DISCOURSE
5:5-17

In this unit the four symbols found in 4:1-5:4 are directly and forcefully explained. Ezekiel may have preached this homily as he lay upon his side illustrating the siege of Jerusalem. After briefly reciting the sin of Jerusalem (5:5-6) the prophet enunciates two dreadful

---

[172]Cf. Jer 40-44 and the trials that befell the Jewish remnant in Egypt.

[173]The remnant theme can be traced through the following references: 2 Kgs 25:22; Isa 6:13; 10:22; Jer 23:3; Ezek 6:8-10; 9:8; 11:13; Zech 13:8-9.

threats against the city (5:7-12). He then describes the results of the judgment (5:13-15). He closes this discourse with yet another direct threat (5:16-17). This first discourse describes the privilege, perversity and punishment of Jerusalem.

Sin of Jerusalem
5:5-6

A. **Jerusalem's Central Position** (5:5)

Thus says Lord Yahweh: This is Jerusalem! In the midst of the nations I have placed her, and lands are round about her.

Through the siege signs of 4:1-5:4 Ezekiel has made it clear that disaster was going to overtake the inhabitants of a besieged city. It remained only for Ezekiel to make known the identity of the city. The sense of drama is sustained as the prophet tersely announces, *This is Jerusalem*. His auditors can no longer speculate that the map portrayed some other city.

Jerusalem's sin was grievous because of the position that she occupied. God had placed Jerusalem *in the midst of the nations*. This is no manifestation of Jewish pride. It is rather an indication of the basic premise of Old Testament religion, viz. the election of Israel. Geographically Canaan was in the midst of the great civilizations of the ancient Near East.[174]

The habitation assigned to the chosen people was carefully chosen by Yahweh. The people of God were to be the great witness to monotheism in the ancient world. Jerusalem, however, was unfaithful to her mission. The ancient Jews thought of God as inexorably connected with physical Jerusalem. The continued physical existence of the walls and buildings known as Jerusalem was not what concerned God. He was concerned about the mission and message of that city. This concept the contemporaries of Ezekiel found hard to accept.

B. **Jerusalem's Blatant Rebellion** (5:6)

She has rebelled against my judgments for evil more than the nations, and against my statutes more than the lands that are round about her; for they have refused my judgments, and in my statutes they have not walked.

---

[174]The same idea is elevated to a higher level in 38:12. The future Israel dwells *in the middle* (lit., "navel") *of the earth*.

Jerusalem's sin was grievous in view of the fact that she had received special divine revelation in the form of judgments and statutes. The rabbis taught that *judgments* (*mišpāṭîm*) pertained to a man's duty to his fellowman; *statutes* (*chuqqōt*) spelled out his duty to God.[175] Certainly greater light involves greater responsibility before God. An Egyptian and an Israelite may commit the same overt act; but the deed was a far greater crime for the Israelite because Israel had divine law and light.

The grievousness of Jerusalem's sin is indicated by the verbs of v 6. She had *rebelled* (r. *mrh*) against, and her population had *rejected* (r. *m's*), the judgments of God. She refused to walk in the statutes of God.

First Threat
5:7-10

A. Basis of the Threat (5:7)

Therefore thus says Lord Yahweh: Because you are more tumultuous than the nations that are round about you—in my statutes you have not walked, and my judgments you have not done, nor have you done according to the judgments of the nations that are round about you.

The word *therefore* introduces further indictment. This is common in oracles of judgment. It is almost as though Yahweh is hesitant to pronounce the sentence. At the very least he wants to establish a firm legal basis for that sentence before it is uttered.

The word translated *tumultuous* (r. *hmn*) is of uncertain meaning. It seems to be connected with the noun *hāmōn* that refers to a tumultuous crowd. They raged in their opposition against God. Such a description is appropriate to these lawless ones who rejected the judgments and statutes of Yahweh. Judah had not even measured up to the standards of heathen nations. Judah had sunk even deeper into wickedness than pagan nations. The thought here may be that of Jer 2:10f, viz. that the heathen were more loyal to their non-gods than was Israel to the God of creation.

---

[175]Carley (*Ezekiel*, 38) sees the distinction being that judgments were conditional laws (casuistic law) and *statutes* were unconditional commands or prohibitions (apodictic law).

B. Specifics of the Threat (5:8-10)

Therefore thus says Lord Yahweh: Behold I, even I, am against you, and I will execute judgments in your midst in the sight of the nations. 9 And I will do in you what I have not done, and the likes of which I will not do again because of all your abominations. 10 Therefore fathers will eat sons in your midst, and sons will eat their fathers. I will execute judgments in you. I will scatter all your remnant to every wind.

The second *therefore* in the unit introduces Yahweh's word of judgment. Five specific details concerning the forthcoming judgment of God are set forth in 5:8-10.

First, the future judgment is the work of the sovereign ruler of Judah. Yahweh is *Lord*, i.e., sovereign. It is he who has become the adversary of Judah. The formula *I am against you* seems to be derived from the background of hand-to-hand combat. The dreadful thought that God has entered into mortal combat against Jerusalem is underscored by the emphasis on the first person pronoun—*I, even I, am against you.* The great sovereign God declares his hostility toward Jerusalem. He also announces his intention to execute judgments in the midst of that city. The last expression is repeated in v 10.

Second, the judgment will be public. Repeatedly Ezekiel emphasizes this thought.[176] Judah publicly had profaned the honor of God. Thus the Holy One of Israel publicly must be vindicated. The death of Judah will be a hideous example to other nations.

Third, the judgment will be unprecedented. The *abominations*[177] of Judah were without precedent; so also will be the manifestation of God's judgment. Modern students find it easy to criticize the spiritual blindness and obduracy of Israel in refusing to believe the prophetic threats against Jerusalem. This v should serve to explain in part the bewilderment and incredulity that this message of destruction produced. There was no precedent to prepare for the disaster. Currey observes that

> The punishments of God are cumulative. The calamities of the Babylonian were surpassed by the Roman siege (Mt 24:21), and these

---

[176]See Ezek 20:9, 14, 22, 41; 22:16; 28:25; 38:23: 39:27.

[177]The term *abominations* (*tō'ēbhāh*) is used 42x in Ezekiel. It refers to idolatry. Cf. Dt 7:25-26; 13:12-14; 17:2-4.

again were but a foreshadowing of still more terrible destruction at the last day.[178]

Fourth, the judgment is unthinkable. It will result in horrible barbarisms. In the extremities of the forthcoming siege cannibalism will be practiced in Jerusalem. That children will be devoured during that brutal period had been prophesied already.[179] The gruesome fulfillment is recorded in Lam 4:10. Ezekiel, however, here goes beyond previous threats in that he predicts that sons will eat their fathers. "Human plight can know no greater depths."[180]

Finally, the judgment will be *devastating.* The judgment involves the scattering of God's people. Ezekiel alludes to those Jews who will flee from the Babylonian invasion as well as those who will be carried off to Babylon or sold into slavery in distant lands.

Second Threat
5:11-12

A. General Picture (5:11)

Therefore as I live (oracle of Lord Yahweh) surely because my sanctuary you have defiled with all your detestable things and with all your abominations; therefore I will cut you short. My eye will spare not, nor will I have pity.

Again the first *therefore* introduces the basis for the second threat. The second *therefore* sets forth the threat itself. This dire threat is in order because the inhabitants of Jerusalem had defiled God's temple with their *detestable things* and their *abominations*, i.e., their idolatrous paraphernalia. History records how King Manasseh erected an idol in the temple precincts (2 Kgs 21:7). Ahaz replaced the divinely ordained altar with an Assyrian model (2 Kgs 16:11).

Because of such brazen presumption God will *cut short* Jerusalem without mercy. There is no evidence that the Israelites were overtly wickeder than neighboring peoples. They, however, had violated the first and most basic commandment in that they rendered allegiance to what was less than God.

178Currey, *Bible Commentary*, 37.
179Lv 26:29; Dt 28:53; Jer 29:9.
180Feinberg, *Ezekiel*, 38.

B. Specifics of the Threat (5:12)

A third part of you with pestilence will die. With famine they will be consumed in your midst. A third part will fall by the sword round about you. A third part I will scatter to every wind. A sword I will unsheathe after them.

Ezekiel alludes to the symbolic act that he had performed with his shaven hair (5:1-4). A third of the populace will be consumed by pestilence and famine in the midst of the city. A third will fall by the sword in trying to defend the city or escape from it. A third will be scattered in every direction. This latter group includes both those who might manage to escape to surrounding nations and those who will be carried into foreign exile.

Divine retribution will continue to pursue these folks even on foreign soil. The *sword* that God will unsheathe after these refugees symbolizes the persecution that they will continue to experience. The horrors of the Babylonian siege were but the beginning of sorrows of the nation. The prophecy may reach beyond the limits of the Babylonian era. Ezekiel may here be foretelling the continuous misery that the once favored people of God will experience.

Results of the Judgment 5:13-15

Then my anger will end. My wrath I will cause to rest in respect to them, and will be comforted. They will know that I Yahweh have spoken in my zeal when I have finished my wrath on them. 14 And I will make you a desolation and a reproach among the nations that are round about you, before everyone who passes by. 15 And it will be a reproach, and a taunt, a lesson and an astonishment to the nations that are round about you when I execute against you judgments in anger, wrath and furious rebukes. I Yahweh have spoken it.

Three results of Jerusalem's judgment are mentioned in these vv. First, only when Jerusalem was in ruins and her few survivors scattered abroad is God's anger (*'aph*) and wrath (*chēmāh*) assuaged. The strongly anthropomorphic expression *my wrath I will cause to rest in respect to them* is used in three other places in the book.[181] Evil actions have tragic results. In this first discourse the only note of hope is

---

[181]Ezek 16:42; 21:22; 24:13.

that once Jerusalem is destroyed the righteous anger of God will be satisfied.

Second, through the fulfillment of the predicted punishment they will recognize that the calamity was initiated by God and was not due to mere chance. Ezekiel uses the terms *zeal/jealousy* (*qin'āh*) and *wrath* (*chēmāh*) synonymously.[182] God's zeal or jealousy is provoked by idolatry (8:3, 5; cf. Ex 20:3-5).

Third, the retribution against Jerusalem earns for the people of Judah the contempt of all neighboring nations, and passers-by as well. The ruins of the once proud capital of Judah will serve as a *reproach*, *taunt*, a warning *lesson* and a source of *astonishment* to the neighboring nations. At this point Ezekiel mentions only this one good that will result from the fall of Judah. From the tragedy of Israel the nations will learn that Yahweh is in control of history. They will learn that he is a righteous God.

Third Threat
5:16-17

When I send against them the evil arrows of famine that are for destruction that I will send against you to destroy you, then I will increase famine upon you. I will shatter your staff of bread. 17 I will send against you famine and wild beasts, and they will bereave you. Pestilence and blood will pass through you. I will bring a sword upon you. I Yahweh have spoken it.

In the third threat of this discourse Ezekiel enumerates six calamities that will befall Judah. First, God was about to send against his people *the evil arrows of famine*, i.e., blasting, mildew, locusts and other plagues that will lead to a scarcity of food. Second, God will *increase the famine*. He will withhold the rain. Thus will he *shatter the staff of bread* (cf. 4:16).

Third, *wild beasts* will become a problem. They will especially attack children. Thus will the wicked mothers and fathers be bereaved. Fourth, *pestilence*, i.e., plagues, will take their toll against man and beast. Fifth, others will die by violence as *blood* passed through their midst. Finally, they will face the *sword* of divine retribution, the Chaldean enemy.

---

[182]See 16:38, 42; 23:25; 36:6.

Three times in this first discourse Ezekiel stressed the fact that *I Yahweh have spoken* (vv 13, 15, 17). It is really Yahweh, the God of revelation and redemption, who has made these threats. He is a God who reveals himself in acts as well as in words. His acts accredit and validate his words. The dire threats of this ch were certain to befall Judah.

In summarizing the first discourse, three stages of backsliding can be observed. First, the Jews had rebelled against the ordinances of God in their hearts (v 6). Second, they ceased to walk in God's statutes in the outer life (v 6). Finally, they were so brazen that they defiled God's sanctuary (v 11).

With regard to Jerusalem's punishments again a threefold progression is observable. First, God was against his people (v 8). Second, God will execute judgments on his people (v 8). Finally, those judgments will be executed in anger and wrath (v 15).

CHAPTER 6
DISOBEDIENCE AND DESOLATION

In his second discourse Ezekiel zeroes in on the places of idolatrous worship that were located in the mountains and valleys of Judah. These pagan sanctuaries, once known for their shady trees, will become desolate. There is throughout this ch a frequent change from *their* to *your*, and from *your* to *their*, when the same persons are spoken of. This is consistent with the manner of Ezekiel. The sermon contains three points of emphasis: a dire prediction (6:1-7); a confident expectation (6:8-10); and a distressing lamentation (6:11-14).

A DIRE PREDICTION
6:1-7

Address
6:1-3a

And the word of Yahweh came unto me, saying: 2 Son of man, set your face toward the mountains of Israel, and prophesy against them. 3 Say, O mountains of Israel, hear the word of Lord Yahweh. Thus says Lord Yahweh concerning the mountains and hills, concerning the ravines and valleys…

The *word of Yahweh* directed Ezekiel to *set his face* toward, and *prophesy* against, *the mountains of Israel.* Apparently the prophet actually assumed a posture that demonstrated determination and anger, i.e., he faced westward as he spoke these words.[183] Just as the anonymous prophet of 1 Kgs 13 addressed an oracle to the illegitimate Bethel altar, so Ezekiel spoke directly to *the mountains of Israel.* It is as though the people of Judah were so hopelessly meshed in idolatry that Ezekiel might as well speak to the mountains of the land.[184]

The mountains are not to be understood as geographical symbols of the land of Judah, but rather as theological symbols. The mountains were the places where Israel practiced idolatry. This oracle goes beyond the previous discourse in that it asserts that the judgment will include the pagan shrines scattered throughout the land as well as in Jerusalem. The distraught exiles on the monotonous plains of Babylon might pine for the beloved Judean hills. Those mountains, however, were contaminated and doomed.

While the mountains were directly addressed the message pertains to *the hills, ravines and valleys* as well. All of these areas had been contaminated by the presence of pagan high places. Remains of such high places have been discovered at Taanach, Gezer, and Petra. The standard features of a Canaanite high place were an altar, stand-

---

[183]Cf. 13:17; 20:46; 21:2. The idiom of setting the face is a well-attested travel formula in the Bible and in the literature of the ancient Near East. Ugaritic texts attest its use in the imperative addressed to messengers of gods and kings in the sending out of a messenger. Brownlee, *Word Biblical Commentary*, 96.

[184]Another view: like *house* of Israel, the *mountains* means the inhabitants of the mountains (Vawter and Hoppe, *Ezekiel*, 50).

ing stones, a wooden pole symbolic of Asherah, and a laver. Hezekiah in the eighth century and Josiah in the seventh century made determined efforts to remove these theological cancers from the nation. Unfortunately later kings tolerated and/or encouraged pagan practices (2 Kgs 18:4; 23:5). Both Jeremiah and Ezekiel testify to the resurgence of this corrupt worship following Josiah's valiant reform effort.

Slaughter
6:3b-5

Behold I, even I, am about to bring against you a sword, and I will destroy your high places. 4 Your altars will be made desolate. Your incense stands will be broken. I will cast down your slain before your idols. 5 And I will put the carcasses of the children of Israel before their idols. I will scatter your bones around your altars.

Yahweh will bring the sword of destruction against the pagan high places. The term *sword* (*cherebh*) can denote any kind of destructive instrument. Here the term is symbolic of the invading forces of Nebuchadnezzar that will bring death, destruction and desolation to the land. The sexual license and child sacrifice that marked the pagan worship were an abomination to God. They had to be judged. When the judgment of God falls the pagan high places will be desecrated. The sacrificial *altars* and smaller *incense stands*[185] will be destroyed.

The corpses of the slain Israelites will not even be accorded the dignity of burial. They will be left to rot before their helpless *idols.*[186] Yahweh will fulfill the covenant threat of Lv 26:30.

The bones of the idolaters will be scattered around the altars. Death defiled (cf. Nm 9:6-10; 2 Kgs 23:14, 16). Hence the altars will be made desolate, rendered permanently unclean and unsuitable for worship. A similar threat was made by Jeremiah (Jer 8:1f). They had defiled the land with their idols; they will yet further defile it by their dead bodies. The fragrance of incense offered to pagan deities will be replaced by the stench of rotting bodies.

---

[185]Small limestone altars with "horns" too small for offering any sacrifice other than incense have been found in Palestine. *IDB*, 2:699-700.

[186]The term for *idols* (*gillūlîm*) is one of contempt used 39x in the book. Ezekiel may have coined this term that means something like "dung ball." The term is closely related to the word used for human excrement in 4:12, 15.

Ruins
6:6-7

In all of your dwelling places the cities will become waste. The high places will become desolate that they may be laid waste. Your altars will bear their guilt. Your idols will be broken and cease to be. Your incense altars will be cut down. Your works will be wiped out.
7 The slain will fall in your midst. You will know that I am Yahweh.

In characteristic emphasis by repetition Ezekiel underscores the threat against the idolatrous shrines in vv 6-7. Here the people are directly addressed rather than the mountains. In all of their dwelling places the cities will become waste and their high places desolate. *Altars, idols* and *incense altars* will be destroyed. The work of their hands, i.e., their idols, will be wiped out.[187] The slain of Judah will fall throughout the land. No idol will be able to prevent the massacre. In that terrible day when man-made gods proved impotent the sovereignty of Yahweh will be admitted by all.

The expression *you will know that I am Yahweh* occurs 4x in ch 6 (vv 7, 10, 13, 14) Ezekiel indicates that God's supreme motivation in all his acts of judgment or mercy is that people might *know*, i.e., experience him anew. This major thrust of the book (mentioned over 65x) called for an intimate relationship with Yahweh rather than a destructive allegiance to impotent idols.

---

[187]The same order had been given regarding the Canaanites who occupied the land before Israel, Since Israel had adopted the ways of Canaan, they and their worship will now come under the same divine edict.

CONFIDENT EXPECTATION 6:8-10

Preservation 6:8

But I will leave a remnant in that you will have those who escaped the sword among the nations when you are scattered among the lands.

Not all will die in the bloodshed that will befall Judah. A remnant will survive on foreign soil. In the midst of the thundering severity of God's wrath the prophet underscores the tenderness of God's mercy. The nation is rejected; but faithful individuals will be spared. These godly souls will become the prototype and the nucleus of the New Testament Israel of God.[188] The nation will die in 586 BC, but faith will live on.

Conversion 6:9-10

And those of you who escape will remember me among the nations where they have been taken captive, that I was shattered by their adulterous heart that turned aside from me, and by their eyes that committed adultery after their idols; and they will loath themselves in their sight for the evils that they committed, for all their abominations. 10 And they will know that I am Yahweh; not in vain have I said that I will do this evil to them.

Four facts about the remnant are brought out in these vv. First, there will be a new focus on Yahweh. The remnant will *remember*[189] Yahweh among the nations where they had been taken captive. The word *remember* implies more than the recollection of past events. The exiles will seek to restore their relationship to God by repentance.

Second, there will be a new understanding of Yahweh. When they remember Yahweh the remnant for the first time will come to realize

---

[188]Key passages for the study of the remnant theme in the Old Testament are: Isa 1:9; 10:20; Jer 43:5; Zeph 2:7; 3:13, Zech 10:9; Rom 9:6-13; 11:5.

[189]Simon DeVries, "Remembrance in Ezekiel: A Study of an Old Testament Theme," *Inter* 16 (1962): 58-64.

the anguish[190] that their loving Father had experienced because of their flirtations with idolatry. Those wanton hearts will be changed. Through the fires of punishment the surviving remnant was purged of impurity.

Third, there will be a *new* attitude toward sin. The remnant will come to *loath themselves* for the evils that they had committed. They will then regard all their idols as abominations. *Abomination* is a favorite term of Ezekiel for a practice that led to religious impurity. He uses this term mainly of idolatry, but sometimes of adultery.

Finally, there will be a new appreciation for God. The remnant will know in that day that Yahweh is sovereign God. His word had not been spoken in vain. The ultimate aim of the national chastisement was to produce a faithful remnant. God's purpose will thus be accomplished.

DISTRESSING LAMENTATION 6:11-14

Dramatized 6:11

Thus says Lord Yahweh: Clap your hands and stamp your feet and say, Alas, because of all the evil abominations of the house of Israel! With sword, famine and pestilence they will fall.

With a dramatic action Ezekiel was to underscore what he had just said.[191] He was to *clap* his *hands and stamp* his *feet*. These were gestures expressive of intense emotion and excitement generated either by intense joy or sorrow.[192] There is no reason to assume that Ezekiel is exulting over the impending fall of Judah. This prophet hated the evil practiced by his people; but he did not long for their destruction. Like Jeremiah, he commiserated with the people of Judah

---

[190]Literally, "I have been broken" or "shattered." The RSV has followed some of the ancient versions by rendering, "when I have broken their whorish heart."

[191]One must always reckon with the possibility that this oracle was not delivered on the same occasion as the preceding vv.

[192]Others have interpreted Ezekiel's actions as indicating malicious satisfaction, joy, triumph as well as horror, indignation and sorrow. Still others think Ezekiel exhibited God's delight over the comprehensive eradication of pagan shrines and practices from Israel.

in their misfortune (cf. 11:13). It was with a broken heart that Ezekiel spoke to and about his people.

The prophet's gesture of distress was accompanied by the customary wail *Alas!*[193] Because of all the evil abominations (idolatry) of Israel the nation will fall with *sword, famine and pestilence.*

Justified 6:12-14

He who is far off will die with the pestilence; and he who is near will fall by the sword; and he that remains and is besieged will die in the famine. Then I will bring to an end my wrath against them. 13 And you will know that I am Yahweh when their slain ones will be in the midst of their idols round about their altars upon every high hill, in the tops of the mountains, and under every green tree and under every leafy oak, the place where they presented a sweet savor to all their idols. 14 And I will stretch out my hand against them. I will make the land a desolation and waste more than the wilderness of Diblah in all their dwelling places. They will know that I am Yahweh.

The one *far off* from the scene of battle will die by pestilence; the one near the battle, by the sword. Those in the besieged capital will die of famine. Distance will make no difference. Wherever they were the inexorable and relentless wrath of God will overtake them (cf. Zech 1:6). There will be no escape. With these terrible calamities the wrath of Yahweh will come to an end.

For the third time in this ch the prophet underscores the dramatic impact that these judgment works will have on the hearts and minds of the surviving remnant. They will see their slain comrades lying about their once sacred altars within sight of their lifeless idols. Then they will finally come to confess the sole sovereignty of God.

---

[193]Ellison (*Ezekiel*, 37) proposes the rendering *Ha*. "Ezekiel is called upon to rejoice that the accumulated evil of centuries is to be swept away."

In order to emphasize the extent of the godless worship Ezekiel enumerates the different locations where Canaanite rites were practiced. Their hilltop-sanctuaries and mountain retreats—the shady bowers where once the fertility orgies of Baal and Asherah were practiced—will be desecrated. Ezekiel uses ribald humor in his allusion to the *sweet savor* of incense being offered before dung ball idols (*gillūlîm*). Here is the irony: "They perfumed their stinky idols."[194]

The hand of Yahweh will be stretched out against the land. It will become a desolate waste. The reference to *Diblah* is difficult. Some translate, "from the wilderness to Riblah" (RSV). They see here a reference to the extent of the disaster. From the edge of the southern wilderness to Riblah on the Orontes River is a distance of 150 miles. This understanding necessitates two changes in the Hebrew text.[195] The second approach is to see in this phrase a comparison. The land of Judah will become a greater desolation than Diblah. The location of Diblah is uncertain.[196] The discourse closes with a fourth assertion that this divine judgment will serve to turn people to Yahweh.

EZEKIEL 7
CHAOS AND CALAMITY

Ch 7 is a sermon in the form of a lamentation. It is characterized by frequent repetitions designed to underscore the certainty and severity of the coming calamity. The ch is written in what has been called poetic prose. The sentences are choppy, broken, and oozing with emotion. Division of the material into discussion units is admittedly arbitrary. It seems, however, that the prophet first announces the coming calamity (vv 1-9) and then describes it (vv 10-27).

---

[194]Lind, *Ezekiel,* 64.

[195]The change of *d* to *r* as the first letter of the place name, and the addition of the article to the word *wilderness*. The interchange of *d* and *r* is attested in Nm 1:14 and 2:14.

[196]A Diblathaim on the eastern border of Moab is attested in Nm 33:46-47 and Jer 48:22 (ASV).

CALAMITY ANNOUNCED 7:1-9

First Announcement of the End 7:1-4

A. Announcement of Yahweh (7:1-2)

The word of Yahweh came to me, saying: 2 As for you, son of man, thus says Lord Yahweh concerning the land of Israel: An end! The end has come upon the four ends of the land.

Ezekiel announced that *an end* had come to *the land of Israel*. Yahweh was not merely calling a halt to Israel's wrong doing. He is bringing down the curtain on Judah's national existence (cf. Amos 8:1-3). There is no hope in this message for any future for Israel. In this period of history *the land of Israel* was equivalent to the kingdom of Judah. The end or destruction will come upon *the four ends of the land*, i.e., the devastation will be geographically total. No city or village will escape.

B. Anger of Yahweh (7:3-4)

Now is the end upon you. I will unleash my anger against you. I will judge you according to your ways. I will bring upon you all of your abominations. 4 My eye will not have pity upon you, nor will I have compassion; but your ways I will bring upon you while your abominations are in your midst; and you will know that I am Yahweh.

Ezekiel contends that *now is the end upon you*. The anticipated destruction is close at hand. The prophet refers to the destruction of Jerusalem in 586 BC. This destruction will not be a mere accident of history. It will be a manifestation of the anger of God. God will unleash his anger. The destruction will be a just act of retribution. The people will be judged according to their ways, i.e., their conduct. God will bring upon them all their abominations, i.e., he will hold them accountable for their association with abominable idols (vv 3, 4, 8).

In this destructive judgment God will not manifest mercy or compassion toward the nation of Judah. The meaning is that God will carry out his pre-announced intention to destroy Jerusalem. He will not relent. There is, of course, mercy for the remnant of the nation as other passages clearly show. In a sense the exercise of justice was itself an act of mercy. Its aim was purification from sin and restoration of harmony between God and man.[197]

The judgment will fall on Jerusalem while their abominations (idols) were still in the midst of the city. They will cling to their idols to the bitter end. No further evidence need be presented to prove that the actions of God were justified. Through the horrible destruction, the surviving Jews will come to realize that it was truly Yahweh, God of covenant and redemption, who had made these dire threats.

Second Announcement of the End 7:5-7

Thus says Lord Yahweh: A disaster, a unique disaster, behold it comes. 6 An end has come, the end has come! It has awakened against you; behold it comes. 7 The turn has come upon you, O inhabitant of the land; the time has come, the day of tumult is near, and not joyous shouting upon the mountains.

The disaster facing Judah was unprecedented (lit., "one disaster"). The *unique* catastrophe that overshadowed all the rest was the destruction of the temple. This disaster will not only be *an* end, it will be *the* end.

The judgment is described as the *turn* (*tsᵉphîrāh*). The meaning of the term is uncertain. Modern translations prefer to render it "doom."[198] The basic idea, however, may be something round,[199] hence a cycle or turn. The turn of events had come to Judah. To use a modern idiom, the tables were about to be turned. Judgment inevitably follows sin as day follows night.

The predicted end will awaken. The long dark night of prophetic threat was about over; the day of Yahweh was about to dawn. A play on words in the Hebrew cannot be reproduced in English. The end (*qēts*) has *awakened* (r. *qîts* in Hiphil).

The coming day will be a day of *tumult,* i.e., clamor and confusion. This tumult will not be the joyous shouting upon the mountains

[197]Fisch, *Ezekiel*, 34.

[198]RSV, NASB. This translation is based on a cognate Arabic noun.

[199]Cf. Isa 28:5 where *tsᵉphîrāh* is rendered "crown."

that one might hear in connection with a harvest festival (Isa 16:10; Jer 25:30) or idolatrous worship. This tumult will be the din and confusion of military invasion. In the popular mind the day of Yahweh was a day of triumph over national enemies. Beginning with Amos the prophets blasted this concept. The day of Yahweh refers to God's triumph over all unrighteousness whether in Israel or among the Gentiles.

Anger of Yahweh
7:8-9

Now I will shortly pour out my wrath upon you. I will finish my anger against you when I have judged you according to your ways. I will bring upon you all your abominations. 9 My eye will not pity, nor will 1 have compassion; I will bring upon you according to your ways while your abominations are in your midst. You will know that I Yahweh Makkeh.

These vv are virtually a repetition of vv 3-4, with some variation, to give added emphasis to the warning. God's anger against Judah will be complete once he had recompensed them for their ways.

No compassion will be shown toward the *nation* in that day. Through the experience of judgment the Judeans will come to know, i.e., personally experience, Yahweh by a new name: *Yahweh Makkeh*, i.e., "Yahweh who strikes the blow." The notion of an indulgent deity will have to be abandoned in that day.

CALAMITY DESCRIBED
7:10-27

In describing Judah's coming day of visitation, Ezekiel stresses four points: the social disruption (vv 10-13); the military dismay (vv 14-18); the economic distress (vv 19-22); and the political disorder (vv 23-27).

Social Disruption
7:10-13

A. Nearness of Judgment (7:10-11)

Behold the day! Behold it comes; the turn has come forth; the rod has blossomed, arrogance has budded. 11 Violence has risen up for a rod of wickedness; none of them (will remain) and none of their multitude, and none of their wealth or any wailing among them.

The third oracle in ch 7 focuses on the imminence, comprehensiveness, and readiness of judgment.[200] The judgment rod of God—Babylon—had blossomed into an arrogant superpower.[201] *The violence* practiced by the Jews had *risen up for a rod of wickedness*; i.e., the evil practices of the Jews had created the rod that will smite them.[202] In that day the whole population will be affected. None will escape. They will either perish or be carried away into exile. Nothing will remain of the *multitude* of the people or their *wealth*. So great will be the loss that survivors will not wail over the dead.

B. Result of Judgment (7:12-13)

The time has come, the day has arrived. As for the buyer, let him not rejoice; and as for the seller, let him not mourn; for wrath is upon all its multitude. 13 For the seller will not return unto what is sold, although they be yet alive; for the vision concerns the whole multitude that will not return; neither will they strengthen themselves, a man whose life is in his iniquity.

The coming day will result in a complete socio-economic upheaval. Selling an inherited piece of property was normally an occasion of deep grief in the Old Testament world. The seller of real estate, however, will no longer be concerned with such sentimentality. On the other hand, the one who purchased that property will have no reason to rejoice. In the day of God's wrath land holdings will be immaterial. Both the wealthy land buyer and the poverty-stricken seller will be faced with deprivation and death.

---

[200]Alexander, *Expositor's Bible Commentary*, 777.

[201]Others think the rod in v 10 is the royal house of Judah that had blossomed with arrogance.

[202]Cf. Isa 10:5 where Assyria is called the rod of God's anger; and Jer 50:31 that underscores the arrogance of Babylon.

Never will the land seller be able to repossess his inheritance even though he might live through the judgment (lit., “though their life be yet among the living”). Jubilee observance, where all property reverted to original owners, will not be possible in the land of exile. According to the vision that Ezekiel had received, the Jews will be driven from their homes never to return during their lifetime.

At first sight this prophecy seems to contradict Jeremiah (32:15, 37, 43) who predicted that properties again will be bought and sold in Judah following the exile. Ezekiel, however, is speaking of his contemporaries. They will not live to reclaim their family inheritances. The men who lived a life of iniquity will not be able to strengthen themselves so as to withstand punishment. Those driven out will not return, and those who remained in the land will die in their sins.

Military Dismay
7:14-18

They have blown the trumpet. All is made ready, but none is going to the battle; for my wrath is against all its multitude. 15 The sword is without, the pestilence and the famine within; the one who is in the field will die by the sword, and as for the one who is in the city, famine and pestilence will consume him. 16 Should fugitives escape they will be upon the mountains like doves of the valleys, all of them moaning, each in his iniquity. 17 All hands will droop. All knees will run with water. 18 They will gird themselves with sackcloth. Terror will cover them. Shame will be upon every face, and baldness upon all their heads.

Organized resistance to the coming invasion will fail. Sin had destroyed the moral courage of the nation. Preparation for war had been made, but the troops had neither strength nor courage to withstand the enemy. The alarm trumpet sounded, but the terrified troops refused to enter into battle. God’s wrath saps their powers of resistance. Courage flees before the forces of God. Their fear is justified, however, because the wrath of God had gone forth *against all its multitude*, i.e., army.

Death will stalk the whole land. The sword of the Chaldean army will cut off all escape beyond the walls of Jerusalem. Within the city itself famine and pestilence (disease) will take their toll.

The “no escape” of v 15 is immediately qualified. The few refugees who will escape the city will take to the mountains. Like *doves of the valleys* they will occupy the lofty heights and deep ravines. There they will bemoan their fate as they realized that the disaster was the result of their iniquity.

Despair will render the fugitives helpless. All hands will droop in dismay. The knees will *run with water*, i.e., because of their fear those refugees will not be able to control their bodily functions.[203] The refugees will openly manifest their dismay. Sackcloth will be worn upon the body; but they will act as though they were covered with *terror* (*pallātsūt*). Heads will be shaved. Shame (*būšāh*) will be etched on every face—shame because of what had happened; greater shame because of why it had happened.

Economic Distress
7:19-22

They will cast their silver into the streets. Their gold will become an unclean thing. Their silver and their gold will not be able to deliver them in the day of the wrath of Yahweh; they will neither satisfy, nor will they fill their inward parts; because their iniquity has become a stumbling block. 20 As for their beautiful adornments, they appointed them for their pride. They made the images of their abominations, their detestable things with it. Therefore I have given it to them for an unclean thing. 21 I will place it in the hand of strangers for spoil, and to the wicked of the earth for booty; and they will profane it. 22 I will turn my face from them. They will profane my secret place. Robbers will come into it, and they will defile it.

Worldly wealth will be worthless in that day. *Silver* and *gold* will come to be regarded as an unclean thing, (lit., "something defiled by menstrual impurity," Lv 20:21). The precious metal only proves cumbersome to those who are fleeing for their lives. In that day of Yahweh's wrath men will be able to purchase neither deliverance nor food for their bellies.

Their wealth had been the cause of their sin (cf. Hos 2:10). These precious metals and *their beautiful adornments* (i.e., jewelry) they had fashioned into objects of pride and images of their detestable gods. They had committed the same sin as the Sinai generation in

[203]Others interpret the phrase metaphorically as expressive of complete paralysis of strength. Still others think the reference is to sweat caused by fear.

fashioning a graven image of their jewelry. Because they had so abused God's gifts Yahweh will bring them into circumstances in which these precious substances will be regarded as filthy and unclean.

The wealth of Judah will become the possession of *strangers*, i.e., the invading army. In the hands of the *wicked of the earth* these riches, once devoted to sacred albeit illegitimate services will be profaned.

The Jews will be deprived of their material support. They will also be denied spiritual support. God will turn his face from them. The turning of God's face from the people is the reverse of the priestly blessing that invoked God to *make his face shine upon* them (Nm 6:25f). The temple will provide no protection. The invader will *profane* God's *secret place*, i.e., the holiest part of the temple. The sacred precincts will be plundered by the greedy thieves. God had no desire for mere outward forms of worship when that worship had been perverted by the devices of wicked men.

The despoliation of Judah and the temple were a necessary part of God's plan for reclaiming a remnant of Israel. With material possession gone and the temple in ruins the people of God were forced to cast themselves completely on Yahweh. As it turned out "the death of material security turned out to be the resurrection of faith."[204]

Political Disorder
7:23-27

Make the chain; for the land is full of bloodshed and the city is full of violence. 24 Therefore I have brought the worst of nations. They will possess their houses. I will make to cease the pride of the strong. Their sanctuaries will be profaned. 25 Horror is coming! They will seek peace when there is none. 26 Calamity upon calamity will come. Rumor will be upon rumor. They will seek a vision from the prophet. Instruction will perish from the priest, and counsel from the elders. 27 The king will mourn. The prince will be clothed with astonishment. The hands of the people of the land will become feeble. According to their way I will deal with them. According to their judgments I will judge them. They will know that I am Yahweh.

[204]Blackwood, *Ezekiel*, 70.

Apparently Ezekiel performed yet another symbolic act. He made *a chain* that symbolized the coming exile.[205] This punishment is necessary because Judah was full of bloodshed and violence.[206]

God will employ *the worst of nations* against Judah. This is one of the rare instances when Ezekiel speaks derogatorily of the Babylonians. In 28:7 and 30:11 he refers to the Babylonians as *the terrible of the nations*. But his language here is not so much intended to abuse the invaders as to show how low Israel had fallen. The people of God must indeed be wretched for God to send against them men who make no pretense of maintaining just behavior. The ruthless invaders will possess their houses. By means of this invader God will make to cease *the pride of the strong*, i.e., he will humble the proud rulers of Judah, especially the monarchy and priesthood. The sanctuaries of Judah—both the pagan and the proper—will be profaned by these invaders.

Efforts to placate the foe and arrange some peaceful accommodation will fail. There will be no escape from this horrible fate. Israel had gambled on a precarious political balancing act by pitting one power against another. She gambled, and she lost.

The false prophets had assured the Judeans that peace was possible. They will now discover that those optimistic predictions were unfounded. The future judgment will become progressively worse. *Calamity upon calamity* and *rumor upon rumor*. News of one blow will immediately be followed by news of another.

In their desperation people will turn at last to their spiritual leaders for guidance. They will find none (cf. Lam 2:9). The false *prophets*, who had for so long misled the people with their made-to-order "visions," will have nothing to say in that hour when their optimistic prognostications proved to be false. The *priests* will have no *instruction*, the *elders* no useful political *counsel* in that day. The crisis will leave them without direction from their religious and national leaders (cf. Jer 18:18). If the reference in v 26 is to faithful spiritual leaders then the idea is this: they had for so long rejected the words of God's spokesman. Now in the hour of judgment God will no longer communicate with them through these godly men.

The political as well as the spiritual leaders will be unable to cope with that day. The *king* will only be able to *mourn* as he saw his peo-

[205]Cf. Jer 27:2; Nah 3:10.

[206]The Hebrew reads literally, "judgments of bloods," which may refer to capital crimes.

ple suffering and his crown slipping from his grasp. Other members of the ruling class—*the prince*—will be *clothed with astonishment*, i.e., they will be dumbfounded in the face of what will transpire.

Without guidance from spiritual leaders and leadership from the royal family, the *people of the land*[207] will be incapacitated by fear. They will be helpless to defend themselves for their hands will become feeble. This judgment will be a just recompense. God will deal with his people as they had dealt with others. He will judge them as unmercifully as they had judged one another. When all these predictions come to pass all the survivors will know that Yahweh had really spoken these ominous words.

EZEKIEL 8 DEGRADATION OF JERUSALEM

In chs 8-11 Ezekiel recounts a new series of visions. The purpose of these visions is to show that the divine judgments against Judah were justified. A year and two months have elapsed since the call vision (cf. 1:3 and 8:1). At the time this series of visions was received Ezekiel was in the 420th day of his symbolic siege of Jerusalem.[208] He was at this time lying on his right side depicting the judgment for Judah's iniquity (cf. 4:6). These visions of Jerusalem's judgment were most appropriate at this time.

This section of the book can be divided into three major units: the degradation of Jerusalem (8:1-18); the destruction by Yahweh (9:1-10:22); and the declarations by the prophet (11:1-25).

In ch 8, after describing his visionary transmigration to Jerusalem (vv 1-4), Ezekiel relates the terrible abominations that were being practiced in the holy city (vv 5-16). He concludes this ch with a brief announcement of judgment (vv 17-18).

---

[207]The phrase *people of the land* has various meanings in the Old Testament. Here the phrase probably refers to the general populace.

[208]The assumption here is that the year that elapsed was an ordinary year of twelve months and not a leap year of thirteen months. If a leap year was involved, then Ezekiel had this visionary experience twelve days after he ended his symbolic siege of Jerusalem.

ASCENT OF THE PROPHET 8:1-4

Vision of God 8:1-2

A. Circumstances of the Vision (8:1)

It came to pass in the sixth year, in the sixth month, in the fifth day of the month when I was sitting in my house, and the elders of Judah were sitting before me, that the hand of Lord Yahweh fell upon me there.

At the time Ezekiel received these visions a company of *elders of Judah* was sitting before him. Apparently these leaders had retained their rank and prestige in the exilic community.[209] They were sitting *before* Ezekiel as his students. Perhaps they had come specifically to inquire about the state of affairs in the homeland. The initial rejection that Ezekiel met seems now to have given way to respect, at least among these elders. His antics of the previous year were fascinating. Auditors were drawn as by a magnet to Ezekiel's house. Perhaps these men had been coming for months. During the course of the prophetic lesson *the hand of Yahweh fell* upon Ezekiel. The verb *fell*, used only here, marks the suddenness and power of the experience on this occasion.

B. Focus of the Vision (8:2)

I saw and behold the likeness of the appearance of a fire;[210] from the appearance of his loins and downward—fire; and from his loins and upward like the appearance of brightness, like the luster of glowing metal.

In his trance-like state Ezekiel saw again the divine person who had appeared to him initially atop the heavenly throne-chariot. In the present passage Ezekiel has taken a step back from anthropomorphism of 1:26-27 by focusing only on the dazzling appearance of *fire* and *brightness* (*zōhar)* that characterized the lower and upper parts of

---

[209]Plumptre (*Pulpit Commentary*, 143) suggests that these elders were actually visitors from Judah.

[210]Some ancient versions read "man" here.

the visionary body. The glory of Yahweh is seen now in the glow of fire without the milder, more hopeful brightness of the rainbow mentioned in 1:28. The cherubim are absent in the present vision. What Ezekiel sees is but a *likeness* of the ineffable glory, an image of the Unseen.

Transmigration
8:3-4

A. Description (8:3a)

He stretched forth the form of a hand and took hold of me by a lock of my head; and the Spirit lifted me between earth and heaven…

Carefully avoiding anthropomorphism the prophet describes how the divine figure put forth *the form of a hand* out of that blazing glory. Ezekiel felt as though he were being lifted up by a lock of his hair. At the same time he felt the Spirit gently lifting him from the earth to mid-air. Both the *hand* and the *Spirit* are metaphors for him who can neither be imagined nor described.[211] The actions of *the hand* serve to underscore the reality of Ezekiel's feeling of physical removal from his home.[212]

No *physical* transmigration of Ezekiel to Jerusalem takes place in this passage.[213] God, of course, could have transported Ezekiel to Jerusalem in the body.[214] The words *in divine visions* (lit., "visions of God"),[215] however, prove that all that follows took place mentally.

Further indication that these experiences were in the realm of the visional is found in the nature of what Ezekiel saw in Jerusalem—much of which cannot be taken literally—and by actions that hardly seem to be physically possible (e.g., 8:8). Thus Ezekiel was transported in spirit, not in body to Jerusalem.

---

[211]Blackwood, *Ezekiel*, 72.

[212]A conscious imitation of the present passage can be found in the apocryphal story of Bel and the Dragon, v 36.

[213]Brownlee (*Word Biblical Commentary*, 129) argues for interpreting Ezekiel's journey to Jerusalem as literal.

[214]Cf. 1 Kgs 18:12; 2 Kgs 2:16; Acts, 8:39.

[215]The word is not the same as that commonly used by Daniel (*chazōn*) and often by Ezekiel (7:13: 12:22-23 etc.). The word here is *mareh,* which implies a more direct act of intuition. See Plumptre. *Pulpit Commentary*, 144. The word is again used in 11:24 and 43:3.

B. Destination of Transmigration (8:3b)

And brought me to Jerusalem in divine visions unto the entrance of the gate of the inner court that faces north where the seat of the image of jealousy that causes jealousy was located.

To understand the visions of ch 8 one must be familiar with the geography of the temple area. Solomon's temple stood on Mount Moriah along with the royal palace complex.[216] The temple had its own courtyard (called the inner court) as did the palace. But the entire complex of buildings on Mount Moriah was surrounded by a walled courtyard known as the great court or outer court.

After his visionary transmigration Ezekiel found himself in the familiar precincts of the Jerusalem temple. To be more precise, he was set down in the outer court in front of the northern gate[217] that led to the inner court. This was one of the most conspicuous spots in the temple complex. Prior to the reforms of King Josiah this had been the *seat of the image of jealousy*. This image may have been the graven image of Asherah[218] that King Manasseh had erected (2 Kgs 21:7). This image provoked God to jealousy because he alone is God (Ex 20:1-3) and his name is Jealous.[219]

C. Discovery (8:4)

Behold the glory of the God of Israel was there, like the vision that I saw in the plain.

On the very spot where once the image of jealousy had stood Ezekiel saw *the glory of God*. This is the same vision of God's presence that he had seen previously in the plain (3:23) and at the River Kebar (1:1ff). The idea is that Yahweh already had deserted the holy of holies; but because of the reforms instituted by Josiah the glory of God had not yet completely abandoned the temple.

---

[216]See C.D. Gross, "Ezekiel and Solomon's Temple," *BT* 50 (1999): 207-14. Gross uses archaeological data to reconstruct the prophet's movements during his visionary journey.

[217]*The door of the gate of the inner court* is called *the altar gate* in v 5. It may be *the upper gate* of 9:2, "the higher gate" of Jer 20:2, "the upper gate" of 2 Kgs 15:35, and "the new gate" of Jer 36:10.

[218]Probably the *image of jealousy* is also to be identified with the Queen of Heaven in Jer 44. For an opposing view, see H.C. Lutzky, "On 'the Image of Jealousy'" *VT* 46 (1996): 121-25.

[219]Ex 34:14. See also Ex 20:5; Dt 4:24; 5:9; 6:15; Josh 24:19.

ABOMINATIONS
8:5-16

There are two views as to what Ezekiel is seeing in ch 8. Some think he is seeing what is going on in Jerusalem at that very moment. This means that various forms of public idolatry were being tolerated in Jerusalem during the reign of Zedekiah. The problem with this view is that no public apostasy during the reign of Zedekiah is attested in the books of Kings, Chronicles or Jeremiah. In fact, Jer 44:18 seems incompatible with the notion that pagan practices had been officially introduced following Josiah's reformation. The decline after Josiah (Jer 7:1-15), however, and the political pressures of those desperate days quite conceivably could have led to the adoption of such foreign religious practices.[220]

Another view is that ch 8 is a symbolic picture of the false beliefs that held sway in Jerusalem "though they may have had only a restricted public expression."[221] The four abominations here mentioned represent what is known to have been the false religious tendencies during the last century or so before the exile. According to this view each of the abominations mentioned represents the religious deviations of a different section of the Jerusalem community.[222]

Whichever view regarding the abominations of ch 8 is correct this much is certain: the holy city had been desecrated by the most reprehensible pagan abominations. The fact that Jeremiah did not inveigh so heavily against pagan influences in the temple should not cause scholars to question the evidence here.[223] Ezekiel's account has the ring of sober reality.

Yahweh provided Ezekiel with a guided tour of the temple. He pointed out to the prophet four abominations: the image of jealousy (vv 5-6); the secret animal cult (vv 7-13); the Tammuz cult (vv 14-15); and the worship of the sun (v 16).

---

[220]Carley, *Ezekiel*, 51.

[221]Ellison, *Ezekiel*, 41.

[222]The image of jealousy related to the king and people; the animal worship related to the elders; the weeping for Tammuz involved the women, and the sun worship had attracted the priests and Levites. See Taylor, *Ezekiel*, 96-97.

[223]Contra Y. Kaufmann, *The Religion of Israel* (Chicago: University Press, 1960), 426-36.

Image of Jealousy
8:5-6

He said unto me, Son of man, set, I ask you, your eyes to the way of the north. Behold north of the altar gate was this image of jealousy in the entrance. 6 He said unto me, Son of man, do you see what they are doing? [Do you see] the great abominations that the house of Israel are doing here that I should go far away from my sanctuary? But you will yet see greater abominations.

Ezekiel was told to look to a place outside the temple courtyard into the greater court. There he saw another *image of jealousy*. Such an image was an outrage. Israel's God was provoked by all images (Ex 20:3-5). The presence of the image in the vicinity of the temple provoked Yahweh to *jealousy*, i.e., the desire to vindicate his own exclusive rights.

The image was associated with popular religion, for it was located *outside* the northern gate of the temple in the great public court. The old Canaanite paganism was flourishing in Jerusalem, though perhaps without official support. The image was probably the Canaanite goddess Asherah. It may be that they were thinking of this goddess as the wife of Yahweh.[224] If so, the image of jealousy represents Canaanization of Israelite worship. This debased concept must have dominated the popular mind in Jerusalem although the image had not been officially reinstated in the temple.

Divine interrogation called the prophet's attention to men worshiping before the image. Such practices justified, yea compelled, God's withdrawal from the temple. The image of jealousy was only the tip of the iceberg. Ezekiel would soon see worse things.

Animal Cult
8:7-13

A. Instructions (8:7-9)

He brought me unto the entrance of the court. I looked and behold a hole in the wall. 8 He said unto me, Son of man, dig now in

---

[224]Cf. 1 Kgs 15:13; 2 Kgs 21:7. In the fifth century Jewish cult at Elephantine Egypt, Yahweh was represented as having a wife. In most pagan cults the chief deity had a consort.

the wall. When I dug in the wall behold a door. 9 He said unto me, Go in and see the evil abominations that they are doing here.

Ezekiel was now led onward as through successive stages of an inferno of idolatry.[225] He was first escorted through the door of the gate that opened from the inner to the outer court. This court was surrounded by chambers or cells (Jer 35:4). There he discovered a hole in the outer wall of the temple. This hole he was told to enlarge until he could crawl through it. Digging is still a metaphor for searching out the truth.

Inside the side chambers of the temple Ezekiel saw a door that was used by those who were involved in illicit worship. The divine voice commanded Ezekiel to pass through the door so that he might observe firsthand the abominations secretly being practiced by the leaders of the nation.

B. Observations (8:10-11)

So I went in and I saw. Behold every form of creeping thing and detestable beasts and all the idols of the house of Israel were portrayed upon the wall round about. 11 Standing before them were seventy men of the elders of the house of Israel, and Jaazaniah the son of Shaphan was standing in their midst, each man with his censer in his hand; and a thick cloud of incense was going up.

How shocked Ezekiel must have been when he walked through that door! The religious perversion was worse than he had ever imagined. Upon the walls of that chamber the prophet saw the representation of all manner of creeping things (small animals)[226] and beasts (larger domestic animals). The figures on the walls are said to be *detestable* either because they were animals declared to be unclean in Mosaic Law, or because of the use to which they were being put as objects of veneration. It appears that some of the leaders of Judah had adopted the Egyptian custom of animal worship.[227]

---

[225]Plumptre, *Pulpit Commentary*, 144.

[226]*Creeping things* (Heb. *remes*) designates all animals in Gn 9:3, water animals in Ps 104:25. However, usually the word indicates all creatures that appear to move close to the ground.

[227]G.A. Cooke points out that certain aspects of Babylonian religion fit this description equally well. *A Critical and Exegetical Commentary on the Book of Ezekiel* in "International Critical Commentary" (Edinburgh: T. and T. Clark, 1936), 94. Ellison (*Ezekiel*, 42) thinks Ezekiel is referring to all the foreign cults—especially from Assyria and Babylonia—that had poured into the country in the time of Ahaz and Manasseh, but which had influenced mainly the ruling classes.

Various Egyptian cults made idols of the cat, the crocodile, the hawk, the scarab beetle and other animals. This abomination may have come into Judah during the brief period when King Jehoiakim had been a vassal of Pharaoh Neco (608-605 BC). At the very time when Ezekiel is said to have had this vision, in Jerusalem King Zedekiah was making political overtures to Egypt. Perhaps this vision is setting forth the idea that some of Judah's leaders were looking to Egypt for spiritual and political support.

Standing before the engraved images were *seventy elders* of the nation. The figure *seventy* is probably to be understood in contrast to the twenty-five of v 16. Perhaps both figures are to be taken symbolically. Virtually all the elders were involved in this idolatry, whereas a smaller percentage of the priests had taken the final plunge into apostasy in v 16. The *seventy* are probably not to be understood as any official governing body.[228] Acting as their own priests these leaders were offering to those pictorial gods the incense that none but the sons of Aaron were to offer, and that none but Yahweh was to receive.

Jaazaniah is singled out for special mention because of the prominence of his family. He was *the son of Shaphan*, the scribe who played such an influential role in the reform efforts of Josiah (2 Kgs 22:10f). Jaazaniah[229] must have been the proverbial black sheep of this otherwise godly family.[230]

In the actions of the seventy elders there is a combination of "secrecy and despair."[231] These men were ashamed openly to go back on the covenant made under Josiah; but they had opened their hearts to the idolatries and memories of the past. They were not successful in hiding their abominations. Five hundred miles away Ezekiel knew what they were doing.

---

[228]From the earliest times, Israel had a ruling body of seventy men. See Ex 24:1; Nm 11:16. In the intertestamental period this body came to be known as the Sanhedrin.

[229]Another Jaazaniah, the son of a certain Jeremiah, appears in Jer 35:3; yet another, the son of Azur is mentioned in Ezek 11:1.

[230]Two other sons of Shaphan, Gemariah and Ahikam, apparently were pious Israelites (Jer 36:10; 39:14).

[231]Ellison, *Ezekiel*, 43.

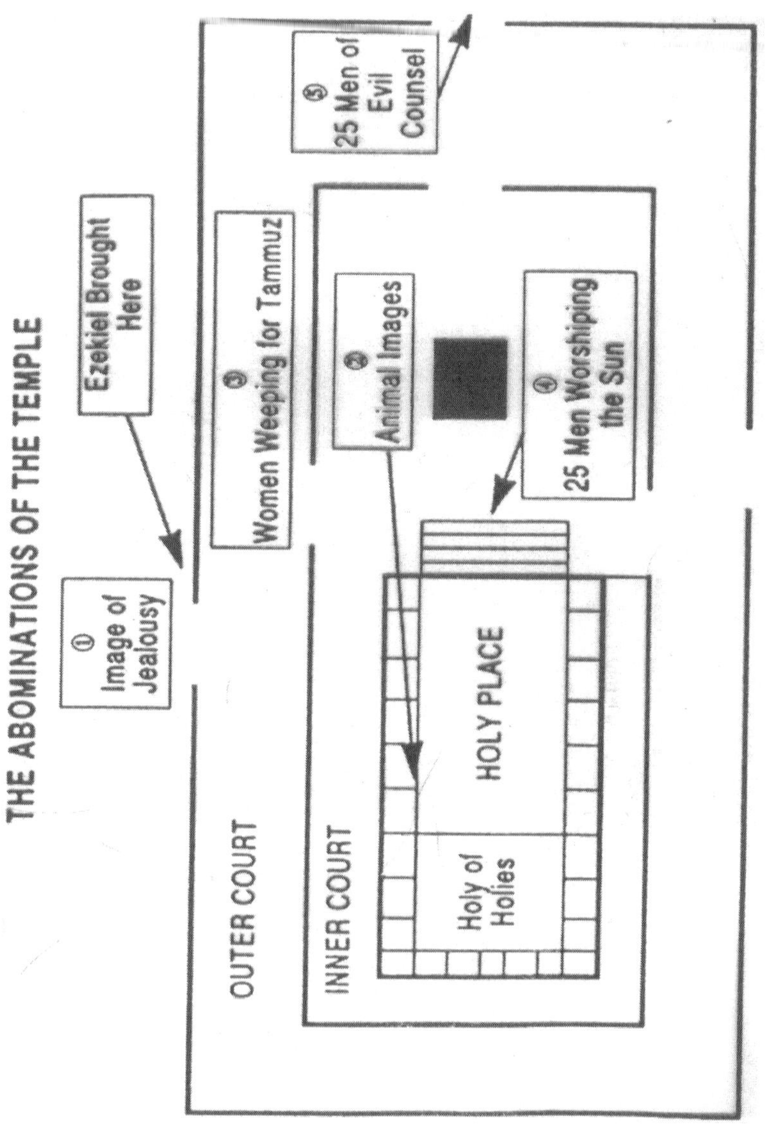

C. **Explanation** (8:12-13)

He said unto me, Son of man, have you seen what the elders of the house of Israel are doing in the darkness, each in his chamber of imagery? For they are saying, Yahweh does not see us; Yahweh

has forsaken the land. 13 He said unto me, Again you will see yet greater abominations that they are doing.

To underscore the tragedy of this scene Yahweh asked the prophet if he had observed what was taking place in those private chambers. Two additional details are added in v 12. The elders were practicing the pagan rites *in the darkness.* Furthermore, the pagan rites were being performed individually, as well as collectively, by the elders, *each in his chamber of imagery.* Apparently each worshiper had his own private cubicle where the Egyptian rites were performed [232]

Yahweh, who knows the hearts of all men, revealed to Ezekiel the inner attitudes of those apostate elders. They affirmed (in their heart, if not openly) that Yahweh did not see their actions. By this they meant either God was not omniscient, or, what is more likely, God was totally disinterested in the affairs of his people. The very name of their leader Jaazaniah—*Yahweh is listening*—should have warned them that God heard their blasphemous boasts.

The apostate elders also held to the belief that Yahweh had forsaken the land of Judah.[233] To them Yahweh was no more than a local deity who had abdicated. They were free to do as they pleased without fear. They saw in the tragedies that recently had befallen the land abundant proof that God had abandoned his people. Why continue to worship a God who will not care for his people? Such is the logic of the carnal mind. Sorrows should not cause a man to question whether God has forsaken him, but rather whether he has forsaken God.

The first phase of Ezekiel's tour of the Jerusalem temple ended with the assurance that other abominations were yet to be observed.

Tammuz Cult
8:14-15

He brought me unto the door of the gate of the house of Yahweh that was upon the north. Behold there the women were sitting weeping over Tammuz. 15 He said unto me, Son of man, do you see this? You will again see yet greater abominations than these.

---

[232]Others interpret *each in his chamber of imagery* to refer to the imaginations of those concerned; still others think the reference is to the homes of the worshipers.

[233]Here is the first of a series of popular half-proverbs—thirteen in all—that are cited in Ezekiel. See 11:3; 12:22; 18:2, 19; 33:10; 37:11.

The prophet was next conducted into the inner court in front of the northern gate of the temple. Ezekiel observed a group of women weeping for Tammuz. This is the only reference to this ancient Babylonian cult in Palestine. Tammuz (or Dumuzi) was the son and/or lover of Ishtar. He was a vegetation god. A myth taught that he died and went to the nether world each fall only to make his return to the land of the living in the spring.[234] As the vegetation withered and rivers dried up the annual death of Tammuz was lamented with public dirges. Women joined Ishtar in mourning her dead lover in the intense drought of summer. The fourth month of the Hebrew calendar bears the name Tammuz. Ezekiel's vision, it will be recalled, dates to midsummer when Palestine is parched by the summer sun.

Tammuz worship survived into the Middle Ages and vestiges of it can still be observed among the Yezidis of Kurdistan.[235]

Women seem to have led out in religious exercises in this period of biblical history.[236] Women were the most conservative element in Oriental religious life. The women of the nation had fallen into the cesspool of filthy idolatry and false theology. Could there be any hope for the nation?

It was terrible to find the women of Judah participating openly in such perverse practice; but the prophet was still to observe greater abominations.

Sun Worship
8:16

He brought me unto the inner court of the house of Yahweh. Behold at the door of the temple of Yahweh, between the porch and the altar, [there] were about twenty-five men with their backs toward the temple of Yahweh and their faces toward the east. They were worshiping the sun toward the east.

In the final phase of his temple tour Ezekiel was brought again into the inner court. This time, however, he was brought from the northern gate to the eastern side of the temple between the porch and

---

[234]Some scholars question the validity of the resurrection theme in Tammuz worship. Cf. Edwin Yamauchi, "Tammuz and the Bible," *JBL* 84 (1965): 283-90).

[235]Fisch, *Ezekiel*, 44.

[236]According to 2 Kgs 23:7, women wove hangings for the Canaanite female deity Asherah. Jeremiah conducted a lively debate with some apostate female worshipers in the land of Egypt (Jer 44:9, 15-19).

the sacrificial altar. This was a sacred area to which only the priests had access.

Ezekiel discovered twenty-five men facing the rising sun and worshiping before it. Facing eastward their backs were toward the temple of Yahweh.[237] This was not merely the debasing of Yahweh worship by linking it with pagan ritual. This was the outright rejection of Yahweh and the enthronement of the Babylonian god Shamash, the sun god.[238] By their actions these men were proclaiming that the gods of Babylon had defeated Yahweh. The heavenly body that should have reflected the glory of God was actually detracting from his glory.

That those participating in this sun worship were priests and/or Levites is reasonable to assume. In 9:6 they are called elders so they must have held senior standing. Ezekiel estimated that about twenty-five were participating in the sunrise service. If there is any significance in this number it may be as follows: twenty-four of the men may represent the twenty-four priestly courses (1 Chr 24:4-19) with the high priest at their head. [239] The thrust of the passage is that apostasy prevailed in the ranks of the priesthood as well as among the tribal leaders and women.

JUDGMENT
8:17-18

He said unto me, Have you seen, son of man? Is it a light thing to the house of Judah that they are committing abominations that they have done here? For they have filled the land with violence, and they have provoked me still more. Behold they are putting the branch to their nose. 18 Therefore also I will deal with them in fury; my eye will not have compassion nor will I take pity. When they cry in my ears with a loud voice I will not hear them.

Judah was ripe for judgment. The abominations practiced throughout the land were viewed by most as *a light thing*. But to Yahweh they were a provocation. *Do you see this, son of man?* sug-

[237]Normally priests prayed facing the temple.

[238]Moses had warned against this worship (Dt 4:19). Josiah had attempted to eliminate it from the land (2 Kgs 23:4-5).

[239]Feinberg, *Ezekiel*, 52.

gests that Ezekiel was a little uncertain in his own mind as to the necessity of the judgment that he had been preaching (cf. Jer 5:1-3).

The breakdown in devotion to God led to social chaos. The people had *filled the land with violence*. Proper theology must undergird proper morality. Such social injustice only provoked Yahweh that much more. "If the root of faith is severed, there can be no fruit of righteousness."[240]

Commentators vie with one another in the ingenuity with which they attempt to explain the charge that *they are putting the branch to their nose*. Certainly some grossly offensive act is intended. Brownlee[241] suggests that the branch was cedar, a symbol of immortality associated with Tammuz and Ishtar. Holding the cedar under the nose would be an effort to inhale the life-giving powers of the deity. Rabbinic tradition lists this phrase among the few deliberate emendations of the ancient scribes. The original reading was: "they put the branch to *my* nose." If this reading is correct then thrusting the branch of cedar under Yahweh's nose identifies him openly and explicitly as the dying and reviving fertility god.

Saggs offers another proposal. A bundle of Tamarisk branches was held up to the nose at daybreak as hymns were sung to the rising sun.[242]

On the basis of the evidence presented in ch 8 God had no alternative but to deal with these people in fury. Compassion for the nation was out of the question. Prayer was useless. No matter how loudly they cried he will not hear them. The day of grace was over; the day of wrath had come.

EZEKIEL 9
SLAUGHTER IN JERUSALEM

The visions that are recorded in chs 9-10 follow logically the terrible indictment of the previous ch. A four-fold development is evident in the visions at this point: Ezekiel first sees Jerusalem destroyed by slaughter (9:1-11), and then by fire (10:1-8). His attention is then

---

[240]Blackwood, *Ezekiel*, 76.

[241]Brownlee, *Word Biblical Commentary*, 137f.

[242]H.W.F. Saggs, "Notes and Studies: The Branch to the Nose," *JTS* (October 1960): 318-29). Such a custom is reported by Strabo (15:3, 14) as being observed by the magi when engaged in prayer.

drawn again to the divine throne-chariot (10:9-17), and finally to the departure of the divine presence from the Jerusalem temple (10:18-22).

Whereas the vision in ch 8 was symbolically descriptive, the one in ch 9 is symbolically predictive. Here Ezekiel saw in dreadful symbolic detail what was to befall Jerusalem six years later in the catastrophe of 586 BC.

AGENTS ASSEMBLED 9:1-2

A great voice called in my ears, saying, Bring nigh the overseers of the city each one with his weapon of destruction in his hand. 2 Behold six men were coming from the way of the upper gate that faced northward, each with his weapon of destruction in his hand. One man was among them clothed in linen with a scribe's writing case at his side. They came and stood beside the bronze altar.

The prophet's attention was first attracted to a loud voice summoning the divinely appointed executioners to discharge their duty. The voice came from the human form (seen as a theophany) in the midst of the divine glory. Each of these agents of judgment was to come prepared for the dreadful deed with *a weapon of destruction in his hand*.

Six *men* answered the summons. Jewish tradition is probably correct in identifying these men as angels.[243] These angels symbolized the armies of Babylon that will crush Jerusalem. Therefore they came *from the north*, the usual attack route against Jerusalem. Each angelic agent carried *a weapon of destruction in his hand*. The Hebrew word implies an instrument used for crushing into fragments. Probably a battle-ax or mace is intended.[244]

A seventh angelic agent was in the midst of the first six. He was *clothed in linen*, the material used for priestly garments and for the clothing of others in authority. Daniel once encountered an angel wearing linen (Dan 10:5f). Hence white linen is the apparel of the hosts of heaven as well as priests on earth. The material is probably

[243]Cf. the "men" (angels) who visited Sodom (Gn 19). Blackwood (*Ezekiel*, 77) supposes that the six represent Babylonian generals.

[244] The same Hebrew word is used in Jer 9:2. A cognate word in Jer 51:20 is translated "battle-ax." The Septuagint gives that meaning here.

intended to symbolize purity. This angel of mercy had a *scribe's writing case* at his side. A scribe carried his pens and receptacle for mixing ink in a case. Sometimes these cases were made of silver. They were elaborately and beautifully engraved. Most writing at this time was done with a reed pen on papyrus or parchment.[245]

All seven angelic agents of God entered the temple courtyard and stood beside the bronze altar. Both judgment and salvation proceed from the altar of God. The angels are seven in number because that is the number of perfection or completeness throughout the Bible.

AGENTS DISPATCHED 9:3-7

Agent of Mercy 9:3-4

The glory of the God of Israel was going up from upon the cherub on which it had been unto the threshold of the house. He called unto the man clothed in linen who had the scribe's writing case at his side. 4 Yahweh said unto him, Pass over in the midst of the city, in the midst of Jerusalem, and set a mark upon the brows of the men who sigh and cry over all the abominations that are done in the midst of her.

Ezekiel next saw the glory of God move from over the cherubim in the holy of holies. In the Old Testament God is said to be enthroned above the cherubim that were molded over the ark. The glory of God moved over *the threshold of the house* as if to direct the action of the seven angels. Yahweh first dispatched the man clothed in linen who carried the scribe's writing case.

The heavenly scribe was told to place a mark upon the brows of all the men of Jerusalem who *sigh and cry* over all the idolatrous practices done in the city. How many concerned citizens there may have been cannot be determined. Six angelic agents, however, were needed to execute the act of judgment. Only one was needed to administer the mark of salvation. Conditions were so terrible in Jerusa-

---

[245]There is probably a connection between this angelic scribe and the oft-recurring thought of the heavenly book of life and death. See Ex 32:32; Ps 69:28; 139:16; Isa 4:3; Dan 12:1; Phil 4:3.

lem at this time that those who were faithful to the worship of Yahweh could only show their faithfulness by lamentation over the national apostasy.

The *mark* to be placed on the brow of the faithful was a *tav*, the last letter of the Hebrew alphabet. In ancient Hebrew script the letter *tav* was shaped like an X.[246] As early as the church father Origen[247] the significance of this was noted. Those who were saved bore the sign of the cross. Is this a mere coincidence? Or was Ezekiel seeing something far more profound than he could ever have imagined?[248] This passage is the background for the scene in Rev 14:1 where the redeemed wear the name of Christ on their foreheads.

Agents of Judgment
9:5-7

To these others he said in my hearing, Pass over in the city after him and smite; do not let your eyes look with compassion, and do not have pity. 6 Slay utterly old, young man, maiden, child and women; but do not approach any man who has the mark upon him; And begin at my sanctuary. Then they began with the elders who were before the house. 7 He said unto them, Defile the house, and fill the courts with slain; go forth. And they went forth and smote in the city.

The six executioners were to follow the angel of mercy through the city. They were to deal a deadly blow to all who did not bear the mark (*tav*) upon their foreheads. They were to exercise absolutely no compassion. All segments of the population were to experience the judgment—old and young, male and female. Only those with the seal of salvation were to be spared.

The judgment was to begin *at my sanctuary*. The *elders* who had turned their backs upon the temple to perform the rites of Shamash the sun god (8:11) were to be the first to experience the wrath of God. It is fitting that the punishment should commence in the spot where the guilt had culminated. The temple was intended to be a place of refuge from violence. Now, however, the God of that temple ordered

---

[246]Cf. J. Finegan, "Crosses in the Dead Sea Scrolls: A Waystation on the Road to the Christian Cross," *BAR* 5 (Nov.-Dec. 1979): 40-49.

[247]This interpretation was also advanced by Tertullian (*Adv. Marcion* 3:22).

[248]Jewish interpreters suggest that since *tav* is the last letter of the Hebrew alphabet, it here denotes completeness. *Tav* is also the first letter of the word *tōrāh* (law).

the courts to be defiled with the bleeding corpses of those who had polluted that place with idolatrous rites.

The final order was given: *Go forth*. The six executioners obediently began their dreadful mission.

INTERCESSION
9:8-10

Prayer Presented
9:8

It came to pass when they were smiting and I was left that I fell upon my face and cried out and said, Ah Lord Yahweh! Will you destroy all the remnant of Israel when you pour out your wrath upon Jerusalem?

Ezekiel was not a passive witness in this visionary experience. He saw the slain falling all about him in the temple courtyard. At last only the angels of judgment and the prophet were left in that spot. As the executioners turned about to carry the slaughter into the rest of the city Ezekiel fell on his face in mighty intercessory prayer.[249] *Ah, Lord God!* he cried in desperation. Anxiously he asked Yahweh if he would completely destroy *the remnant of Israel* in this outpouring of divine wrath.

Northern Israel had fallen in 722 BC. Her citizens had been dispersed throughout the length and breadth of the Assyrian Empire. Several thousand of the inhabitants of Judah already had been carried away by Nebuchadnezzar in the deportations of 605 and 597 BC. Now Ezekiel asks if the remaining people of God will also be wiped out. The question is in reality an oblique request that God spare what was left of the once proud nation of Israel.[250]

---

[249]Only twice in the book does Ezekiel engage in prophetic intercession, both times in this vision (9:8; 11:13).

[250]Cf. the intercessory prayers of Amos in response to the visions of the destruction of Israel (Amos 7:1-6).

Prayer Answered
9:9-10

He said unto me, The iniquity of the house of Israel and Judah is exceedingly great, and the land is filled with blood. The city is full of perversion, for they say, Yahweh has forsaken the land! Yahweh does not see! 10 As for me also, my eye will not have compassion nor will I show pity. Their way I will bring upon their head.

The sovereign God is not compelled to justify his actions to man. It is a pure act of grace when he chooses to do so. Here Yahweh cites four reasons why the destruction of the state of Judah was an absolute necessity. First, God declared that *the iniquity of the house of Israel and Judah is exceedingly great.* The evil had gone too far.[251] The coupling of the names *Israel* and *Judah* is significant. What justified the yet future destruction of Judah also justified the past judgment against Israel.

Second, Yahweh points to widespread bloodshed. The land of Judah was *filled with blood*, i.e., the violence that leads to bloodshed. No doubt the reference is to the mistreatment of the poor and helpless. Third, Jerusalem was *full of perversion* (*mutteh*), i.e., the wresting of judgment. The miscarriage of justice probably led to the bloodshed mentioned above. To Ezekiel social evils were merely the by-product of a wrong relationship with God.

Finally, the Judeans had lost confidence in Yahweh. They had begun to utter blasphemous charges against him. *Yahweh has forsaken the land! Yahweh does not see!* A similar proverb is cited in 8:12. The faith of the people had been shaken by recent calamities because their faith was built upon a faulty theological foundation. They believed that prosperity was the reward for faithful religious ritual. Misfortune could only be interpreted in the light of the proposition that God was either powerless or pitiless. He either could not prevent what was happening, or else he simply did not care. Such is the logic of doubt.

Because of all their sin God will be forced to deal with his people in wrath. He could show no compassion or pity in dealing with these sinners lest his absolute holiness be called into question. He had no

---

[251]This note is sounded many times in the exilic period. E.g., Ezek 11:13; 14:14; Jer 17:16; 11:14; 14:11; 15:1.

choice but to bring down *their way upon their head*, i.e., recompense them for their conduct.

OMINOUS REPORT 9:11

Behold the man clothed in linen who had the writer's case at his side reported, saying, I have done as you commanded me.

The vision concludes with the report of the agent of mercy. The blessed scribe had done his work. Those who truly had remained faithful to God in the midst of national corruption had been sealed with the sign of promise. In his despair the prophet had forgotten about those who were to receive the mark upon their foreheads. They were the true remnant. In effect God answered the intercessory prayer of Ezekiel by allowing him to overhear the report of the angel of mercy. The true Israel of God will in fact survive the calamity that was about to befall Jerusalem.

EZEKIEL 10 JERUSALEM DESTROYED

FIERY DESTRUCTION 10:1-8

Divine Directive 10:1-2

A. **Source** (10:1)

Then I looked and behold upon the platform that was above the head of the cherubim there appeared something like a sapphire stone, as the appearance of the likeness of a throne.

The man clothed in linen had completed his God-assigned task of marking the faithful for salvation (9:11). It was time for the six executioners to expand their work from the court of the temple to the rest of Jerusalem. Yet in all of ch 10 these agents of God are not mentioned. They disappeared from the scene. Only the man clothed in linen remained. To this beneficent character, however, a new role was as signed. He now became the agent of fiery judgment. Jerusalem was to be destroyed by sword and by fire. These two aspects of the judgment are successively portrayed to the prophet in chs 9-10.

Again the throne-chariot of Yahweh appears before the prophet's mind. He saw the platform over the heads of the cherubim upon which stood the sapphire-like throne of the Almighty (cf. 1:26). The throne was initially empty, waiting for Yahweh once again to occupy it (cf. 10:18). The relationship between the glorious presence of God and the throne in these chs is a bit difficult to follow.

For the first time it becomes clear in 10:1 that the *living creatures* in Ezekiel's throne vision (1:5ff) were *cherubim*. It is useless to speculate as to why Ezekiel waited until this point to make this identification. The delay is surely not due to the fact that Ezekiel did not know what cherubim actually looked like until he saw the interior of the temple.[252] Surely as a member of a priestly family he had received such information.

Chart 5 LOCATION OF THE GLORY OF GOD				
In the Holy of Holies	Temple Threshold	In the Holy of Holies	At the Eastern Gate	Mt. East of Jerusalem
On the Throne	Separate from the Throne	On the Throne	On the Throne	On the Throne
8:4	9:3; 10:4	10:18	10:19	11:23

The cherubim are assigned a variety of roles in the Old Testament. They first appear in connection with the Garden of Eden where they guarded the entrance to the tree of life (Gn 3:24). In Solomon's temple they served as symbolic guardians of the holy of holies (1 Kgs 6:23). They were depicted on the lid of the ark of the covenant with their heads bowed and their faces looking downward toward the mercy seat as if in silent adoration (Ex 25:18-20). Ezekiel sees the cherubim in their traditional role as guardians. They protect access to the holy fire.

In a number of passages Yahweh is described as being enthroned on (or above) the cherubim.[253] In at lcast one passage God is said to

[252]As suggested by Taylor, *Ezekiel*, 104.

[253]E.g., 1 Sam 4:4; 2 Sam 6:2; 2 Kgs 19:15; Ps 80:1.

ride on a cherub (Ps 18:10). This is very much like the function performed by cherubim in Ezekiel's vision where these heavenly beings bear up the throne of God and provide locomotion for the entire throne-chariot.

The connecting link between the previous and the present ch—the man with the linen garment—appears in v 2. Ezekiel heard the voice of the Almighty speaking again to this anonymous angel.[254] In 9:3 the divine Presence had departed from the throne-chariot and had stood at the threshold of the sanctuary. Now, however, the divine Presence is connected with the throne-chariot again.

B. Recipient (10:2)

He spoke unto the man clothed in linen and said, Go in between the wheels[255] under the cherubim and fill your hands with coals of fire found between the cherubim. Scatter them over the city. And he went in my sight.

The man in linen garb was instructed to go into the midst of the wheels of the throne-chariot and pick up with both hands the hot coals that he found there (cf. 1:13). Hot coals apparently symbolize judgment and purgation (Isa 6:6f). That both hands are to be employed in the task points to the severity of the anticipated judgment. The agent was to scatter the coals over the wicked city of Jerusalem. As the vision continued Ezekiel actually saw the linen-clad man begin to carry out those instructions.

The symbolic import of this part of the vision is obvious. The judgmental fire that was to fall on Jerusalem will come from the Holy One of Israel. The tragic theology of the day denied that God could ever turn against the city where he was enthroned between the cherubim.

The Babylonian exiles could not (or would not) listen to Ezekiel. Desperately the prophet proclaimed the incredible truth that Yahweh will purge Jerusalem. Six years later when Jerusalem received that awful baptism of fire only a few recognized it as being the fire of God. Those few had been prepared by the preaching of men like Ezekiel.

---

[254]Later writers attempted to identify the man in the linen as Gabriel or Raphael.

[255]A singular noun used in the collective sense. The same is true for the noun *cherubim* that follows.

Circumstances
10:3-5

Now the cherubim were standing on the right of the house as the man entered. Smoke filled the inner court. 4 The glory of Yahweh had arisen from over the cherubim and was over the threshold of the house. The house was filled with the cloud. The courtyard was filled with the brightness of the glory of Yahweh. 5 The sound of the wings of the cherubim was heard to the outer court, like the voice of almighty God when he spoke.

Verses 3-5 parenthetically describe in vivid detail the situation in the temple at the moment the linen-clad man proceeded to execute the command of Yahweh. The *cherubim were standing on the right* (i.e., south) side of the temple, far removed from the ritualistic abominations being practiced on the north side of that house (cf. 8:14). The *cloud*[256] that accompanied the divine glory filled the inner court.

That deep and dark cloud filled the inner court and house because *the glory of Yahweh had arisen* and was now over the threshold of the house. This is the first stage of the God's departure from that place (cf. 9:3). The cherubim had been left behind to perform a significant task, viz. to give the divine messenger of destruction the means of destroying the city. *The house* (i.e., the holy place) was also filled with the divine glory. This explains the presence of the glory in the inner court in the previous v.

Because of the presence of the glory of Yahweh the outer court was filled with ineffable radiance (*nōgah*). From within the temple the sound of the wings of the cherubim could be heard even to the outer court. The sound resembled *the voice of almighty God* (*El Shaddai*).[257] Psalm 29 equates the voice of Yahweh with the roar of thunder. Probably Ezekiel intends the same comparison here. Normally the wings of the cherubim were motionless and made no sound. In this vision, however, they made a loud noise when God spoke (cf. 1:24). Nevertheless, the voice of God was not thereby drowned out. It was heard both by Ezekiel and the linen-vested minister. The thundering pulse of those angelic wings signaled the imminent departure of those heavenly creatures.

---

[256]This cloud is mentioned also in 1 Kgs 8:10-11 and Isa 6:1-2. The Jews called this cloud the *Shekinah*.

[257]The name *El Shaddai* expresses the fact that God rules over all nature. The name was more common in the early stages or Old Testament history. See Ex 6:3.

Compliance
10:6-8

It came to pass when he had commanded the man clothed in linen, saying, Take fire from between the wheels, from between the cherubim. And he went and stood beside the wheels. 7 The cherub put forth his hand from between the cherubim unto the man who was between the cherubim and he lifted up and gave unto the hands of the man clothed with linen. He took it and went out. 8 The cherubim appeared to have the form of a man's hand under their wings.

Verse 6 continues the narrative from v 2 following the parenthetical interjection of vv 3-5. The divine voice had bidden the linen-clad angel to enter among the cherubim and take hot coals from between the wheelwork or chariot (*galgal*).[258] Without any hesitation the man made his way to one of the magnificent wheels that moved in conjunction with the cherubim.

Before the man dressed in linen could fill his hands with hot coals, one of the cherubim—presumably the one closest to Ezekiel—put forth his hand into the fire. He drew forth hot coals and placed them in the hands of the "man." This was possible, v 8 parenthetically explains, because there appeared under the wings of each of the cherubim the form of a man's hand. Perhaps the lesson here is that even an angelic messenger like the man clothed in linen had to keep his distance from the awful throne of God.

It was appropriate that one of the guardians of the fire should actually give the fire to the destroying angel. Having received those coals of judgment fire the man with the linen garment *went out* from the temple to execute the command to set fire to the city (cf. v 2). This visionary and symbolic representation of the burning of Jerusalem found fulfillment in 586 BC.

---

[258]The word is singular and collective. It means literally, "the whirling thing." It is used elsewhere of the wheel of a war chariot (cf. Isa 5:58). Perhaps in this context the word could be translated "chariot."

THRONE-CHARIOT OF GOD
10:9-17

Focus on the Wheels
10:9-13

I looked and behold four wheels beside the cherubim, a wheel beside one cherub, and another wheel beside another cherub. The appearance of the wheels was as the color of a tarshish stone. 10 Now as for their appearance, the four had the same likeness as when a wheel is in the midst of a wheel. 11 When they moved they moved unto their four sides. They did not turn as they moved, but to the place that the head turned they followed. They did not turn as they moved. 12 All their body, their backs, their hands and their wings, as well as the wheels were full of eyes round about, i.e., the wheels that the four had. 13 As for the wheels, they were given the name "the chariot."

One might expect to find in the remaining vv of ch 10 a graphic description of the conflagration that was to befall Jerusalem. Such, however, is not the case. Instead the prophet again describes the throne-chariot that had occupied his attention in ch 1. The variations in the two descriptions serve to underscore the visionary and symbolic import of the entire narrative. Five points of new information are brought out here.

First, a tarshish-colored[259] wheel appeared alongside each of the four cherubim. Second, the four wheels were identical, each appearing to consist of a wheel within a wheel (cf. 1:16). Third, the wheels were such that they could move in any direction without benefit of a turning mechanism (cf. 1:17). Whichever direction *the head*, i.e., the cherub,[260] looked the wheel followed. The cherubim were the principal driving force of the chariot. The spirit of the living creatures (cherubim) was in the wheels. That gave unity to the whole operation.

Fourth, whereas in ch 1 the *rims* of the wheels were full of eyes (1:18); here the eyes are everywhere. The entire bodies of the cherubim—their backs, hands and wings—as well as the wheels are cov-

---

[259]Literally, "like a tarshish stone." This was obviously a precious stone, perhaps yellow jasper.

[260]Others take *the head* to refer to the front wheel.

ered with eyes.[261] Multiplied eyes are here, as always in Scripture, symbolic of omniscience.[262] Finally, the elaborate wheels were identified in the hearing of Ezekiel as being *the chariot* (*haggalgal*). He recognized that as the correct name for the mysterious and complex visionary object.

Focus on the Cherubim
10:14-17

Each one had four faces. The first face was the face of the cherub, the second the face of a man, the third the face of a lion, and the fourth the face of an eagle. 15 The cherubim were lifted up. These were the living creatures that I saw at the River Kebar. 16 When the cherubim went, the wheels went beside them. When the cherubim lifted up their wings to rise above the earth, these same wheels did not turn from beside them. 17 When these stood they stood; and when they were lifted up, they lifted themselves up, for the spirit of the living creatures was in them.

Attention shifts from the wheels to the cherubim themselves. As in ch 1 each cherub had four faces. Three of the faces are the same as those seen in ch 1— the man, the lion, and the eagle. The face of the ox (1:10), however, is now described as *the face of the cherub*. In ch 1 this face was third in order; here it is first. The ox-like face that looked straight forward is thus assumed to be the primary or real face of each cherub. The definite article—the face of *the* cherub—possibly indicates that this was the particular cherub that had given the coals of fire in v 7.

Ezekiel then observed the cherubim—the living creatures of ch 1—mount up. The method by which the throne-chariot became airborne is described in vv 16-17. The main point here is that the wheels moved in conjunction with the flight of the cherubim (cf. 1:19, 21).

---

[261]Others limit v 12 to the wheels. This interpretation maintains the harmony between ch 1 and the present vision. The term *backs* is taken to mean *rims* or felloes (as in 1:18). The *hands* are understood as axles. What part of a wheel, however, could be designated as a *wing*?

[262]Zechariah saw seven eyes on the messianic stone set symbolically before the high priest Joshua (Zech 3:9). The living creatures of Rev 4:6 were covered with eyes.

DEPARTURE OF THE GLORY 10:18-22

At the Eastern Gate 10:18-19

The glory of Yahweh went out from over the threshold of the house and stood over the cherubim. 19 The cherubim lifted their wings. They went up from the earth in my presence. When they went out, the wheels were beside them. It stood at the entrance of the eastern gate of the house of Yahweh. The glory of the God of Israel was over them above.

The throne-chariot was ready for the heavenly rider. The glory-cloud took its place again upon that throne. The departure route was by way of the eastern gate of the temple where for a time the throne-chariot stood. The eastern gate was the most important gate since it faced the front of the temple. The temporary stand at the eastern exit has no further significance other than to dramatize the divine departure.[263] The departure clears the way for the destruction of the city. Through this same gate Ezekiel will later see the glory of Yahweh return to his temple (43:4).

Details about the Cherubim 10:20-22

These were the living creatures that I saw under the God of Israel by the River Kebar. I knew that they were cherubim. 21 Each had four faces. Each had four wings. The likeness of the hands of a man was under their wings. 22 As for the likeness of their faces, they were the faces that I saw beside the River Kebar, their appearances and themselves. Each went straight ahead.

Ezekiel underscores the fact that the throne-chariot that he saw in the temple was the same that he had seen in his first vision by the River Kebar. The living creatures[264] were cherubim each of which had

---

[263]Moses had declared that this departure would occur if the people forsook God (Dt 31:17; cf. Hosea 9:12). Once again, in Ezekiel's day God wrote *Ichabod* (*without glory*) over Jerusalem and Judah. Cf. 1 Sam 4:26.

[264]Singular in Hebrew used collectively.

four faces, four wings and the likeness of man's hand under their wings. The faces of the creatures in both visions were the same. So also was the fact that the heavenly vehicle could move straight forward in any of the four directions that the four faces faced.

EZEKIEL 11
DECLARATIONS BY THE PROPHET
11:1-25

Ch 11 sets forth two declarations by the prophet in his vision. The first (11:1-13) denounced the leaders in Jerusalem. The second brought comfort to the exiles in Babylon (11:14-21). To these declarations is attached a note about the conclusion of this vision (11:22-25).

JERUSALEM LEADERS DENOUNCED
11:1-13

The leading citizens of Jerusalem were convinced of the impregnability of the holy city. In 11:1-13 Ezekiel was commissioned to smash this vain delusion. Blackwood succinctly summarizes Ezekiel's declarations within his vision: Jerusalem will die; but faith will live.[265]

Men of Evil Counsel
11:1-3

A. Observation (11:1)

A spirit lifted me up and brought me unto the eastern gate of the house of Yahweh, the one that faces east, and behold in the entrance of the gate twenty-five men. I saw in their midst Jaazaniah ben-Azur and Pelatiah ben-Benaiah, princes of the people.

---

[265]Blackwood, *Ezekiel*, 84.

Ezekiel feels himself swept off his feet and carried by a spirit/wind to another part of the temple. See on 11:24. From the inner court where he was last said to be standing (8:16) the prophet was transported to the eastern gate of the outer court. This was the spot where the throne-chariot momentarily had set down (10:19). This area just outside the sacred temple precincts was traditionally a place of public assembly (cf. Jer 26:10).

At the eastern temple gate Ezekiel saw twenty-five men. Are these the same men Ezekiel observed worshiping the sun in 8:16? Probably not.[266] The former company was a priestly group; these twenty-five appear to have been lay leaders. Furthermore, the two groups are seen in different localities.

What significance there may be in the number twenty-five cannot be ascertained.[267] The men seem to have been members of a political pressure group. Two of the twenty-five men easily were identified by Ezekiel. Jaazaniah[268] and Pelatiah were prominent statesmen, *princes of the people.*[269] This term refers to the ruling class of Judah, not necessarily the royal family.[270]

B. Explanation (11:2-3)

He said unto me, Son of man, these are the men who devise iniquity, and give wicked counsel in this city; 3 who say, It is not near, let us build houses.*[271] *It is the pot, and we are the meat.

The twenty-five men are said to be those who *devise iniquity and give wicked counsel in this city*, i.e., Jerusalem. Exactly what this iniquity and counsel[272] may have been is not certain. Since this narra-

---

[266]Many capable commentators do make the identification between the two groups.

[267]Various conjectures: 1) two from each tribe of Israel with the king at their head; 2) two from each of the twelve divisions of the army with their commander; 3) two representatives from each of the twelve regions of the city with their president.

[268]Not to be confused with the Jaazaniah of 8:11 who was the son of Shaphan. This Jaazaniah was the son of Azur. An Azur was the father of Hananiah the false prophet (Jer 28:1). Could this Jaazaniah have been the brother of Hananiah?

[269]Brownlee (*Word Biblical Commentary*, 157) argues for a more precise translation of *sārē hā'ām* = "commanders of the army." The same expression is so translated in 1 Chr 21:2 in RSV, JB, NAB.

[270]See Jer 26:10, 12, 16, 21; 36:14, et al.

[271]Lit., "not in the near (future) the building of houses."

[272]Brownlee (*Word Biblical Commentary*, 157) thinks the counsel is military. Jerusalem's defenses had been so strengthened that the commanders felt that the place was battle-ready for the impending attack of the Chaldean army. More housing, however, would be necessary for those flocking in from the countryside for protection.

tive dates from the latter half of Zedekiah's reign. Jeremiah's experiences with the princes may give some indication. In open contradiction to Jeremiah's constant proclamation of certain doom for Jerusalem, the princes optimistically proclaimed the city's invulnerability. This anti-Babylon faction constantly agitated for revolt against the authority of Nebuchadnezzar. Such policies were tantamount to rebellion against the will of God (Jer 27:12ff). These policies were, therefore, politically and spiritually disastrous.

The defiant boast of these evil counselors is cited in v 3. *It* (the judgment of which the true prophets spoke) *is not near*;[273] *let us build houses*. Jeremiah had bidden the exiles in Babylon to build houses and settle down for a long stay (Jer 29:5). The evil princes urged that houses be built[274] in Jerusalem, that business proceed as usual. Jeremiah had threatened the inhabitants of Jerusalem with the image of the seething pot (Jer 1:13); but the rebel party regarded Jerusalem as the caldron that will protect the meat—the inhabitants of the city—from the fire of destruction. The schemers thus assured themselves that the walls of Jerusalem afforded them adequate protection in the event of an attack by the army of Babylon.

Message for the Rebels
11:4-8

A. Accusation (11:4-6)

Therefore prophesy against them, prophesy, O son of man. 5 The Spirit of Yahweh fell upon me and said unto me, Speak! Thus says Yahweh: You have said thus, O house of Israel, and the things of your spirit I surely know. 6 You have multiplied your slain in this city, and you have filled its streets with slain.

In his vision Ezekiel heard himself bidden to do the true work of a prophet in rebuking the defiant rebels. God had an urgent message concerning these Jerusalem leaders. The repetition of the command to prophesy underscores this urgency.

---

[273]The Greek version turns this into a question, "Is not the time at hand to build houses?"

[274]Many modern commentators prefer the translation "the time is not near to build houses." The idea is then that all attention should be devoted to war against Babylon, not house-building. While this translation is possible, the explanation is farfetched.

As in 2:2 Ezekiel felt the Spirit of God fall upon him. He knew that he spoke the word of Yahweh inerrantly. For this reason he prefaced his visionary oracle with the phrase *thus says Yahweh.*

Ezekiel's message was addressed to *the house of Israel*, a term that in Ezekiel's day was restricted to the people of Judah—the remnant of Israel. God knew what the leaders of Israel had been saying. He knew their thoughts as well.

Ezekiel makes a serious accusation against the Jerusalem leadership: *You have multiplied your slain in this city.* This has been taken by some to be prophetic invective against the violence of the Jerusalem leadership.[275] The term *slain* is often used in classical Hebrew prophecy to refer to the helpless victims of social and political iniquities.[276] Plenty of examples from the biographical narratives of Jeremiah can be adduced to substantiate the charge of ruthlessness against the national leaders in Jerusalem.

Context seems to point in the direction of another interpretation of the accusation. It might be called a predictive accusation. The defiant attitude of the anti-Babylonian party will result in the streets of Jerusalem being filled with those slain by Babylonian swords. The princes or governmental leaders were ultimately responsible for this needless slaughter.

B. Rebuttal (11:7-8)

Therefore thus says Yahweh: Your slain that you have put in your midst, they are the meat, and it is the pot; but you will be brought forth[277] from its midst. 8 A sword you have feared, and a sword I will bring against you (oracle of Lord Yahweh).

The prophet was led of Yahweh to respond to the derisive and defiant caldron simile. The evil practices of Jerusalem's rulers had resulted in a situation in which the city walls will only serve to entrap, not protect. The gullible inhabitants of Jerusalem were bound together within the city for slaughter. The Jerusalem caldron was a pot of death. The leaders were responsible for the *slain*—the corpses—that will fall in the streets of that city. At least those slain will remain in

---

[275]Wevers, *Ezekiel*, 94. Brownlee (*Word Biblical Commentary*, 158) suggests that there had been a military coup of the pro-Egyptian party over against the pro-Babylonian party in Jerusalem. This coup may account for Zedekiah's reversal of allegiance to Babylon.

[276]E.g., Isa 1:21-23; Amos 2:6-8; Hos 4:1-3; Mic 3:1-3.

[277]Another reading is, "I will bring you forth."

Jerusalem, interred in their native land. For the war-mongers a worse fate was in store. They will fall into the hand of the ruthless Nebuchadnezzar. They will be brought forth by him out of the midst of Jerusalem.

Stripped of metaphor v 7 states simply that Jerusalem will afford no protection to the inhabitants. Many will be slain; others will be carried away into captivity on foreign soil. With all their talk about security, the leaders really feared an attack by the sword, i.e., Babylon. These fears, Ezekiel announced, will finally materialize.

Warning Amplified
11:9-12

I will bring you out from its midst. I will place you in the hand of strangers. I will execute judgments among you. 10 With the sword you will fall, upon the border of Israel I will judge you. You will know that I am Yahweh. 11 It will not be your pot, nor will you be in its midst as meat; but I will judge you upon the border of Israel. 12 You will know that I am Yahweh in whose statutes you did not walk, and whose judgments you did not execute, but have done according to the judgments of the nations that are round about you.

Ezekiel becomes more specific about the expulsion of the leaders from Jerusalem. In so doing he eliminates any ambiguity in his previous statement. Their expulsion from Jerusalem will not result in escape to safe refuge. God will deliver them into the hands of strangers, i.e., the Babylonians. Through the instrumentality of these foreigners God will execute his judgments upon the rebels.

Ultimately the leaders will fall by the sword. They will taste the judgment of Yahweh *upon the border of Israel*. This prediction was fulfilled when the princes of Judah were massacred at Riblah (Jer 52:9-10) on the frontier of the old northern kingdom (cf. 1 Kgs 8:65; 2 Kgs 14:25). When this prediction came to pass they would know that *I am Yahweh*—that Yahweh is not indifferent to the conduct of man.

Ezekiel reiterates the predictions of the previous vv for emphasis. Jerusalem will not serve as a caldron to protect the meat, i.e., these leaders, from the fire of the Babylonian army. Rather, they will experience divine judgment *upon the border of Israel*. The fulfillment of these predictions will establish that the One who spoke through the prophetic mouthpiece was really Yahweh, the God who will not leave the wicked unpunished. These leaders had disregarded the statutes and ordinances of Yahweh. They had followed heathen customs and practices. They were therefore deserving of divine wrath.

Death and a Prayer 11:13

Now as I was prophesying Pelatiah ben-Benaiah died. Then I fell face down and cried out in a loud voice, Ah, Lord Yahweh! Will you completely destroy the remnant of Israel?

As Ezekiel prophesied in his vision a dramatic event took place. One of the leaders, Pelatiah ben-Benaiah, dropped dead.[278] Was the death of Pelatiah an actual event that is incorporated into the vision?[279] or was it is purely a symbolic and visionary occurrence.[280] In either case Ezekiel was startled by this occurrence. He began to fear once again (cf. 9:8) that God would destroy all the remnant of Israel.

Following his natural impulse as prophetic intercessor Ezekiel fell on this face in earnest supplication before Yahweh. In a loud voice he cried out his exasperation, *Ah Lord God!* A question conveys an oblique petition on behalf of his people.[281] *Will you make a full end of the remnant of Israel?* The remnant of Israel consisted of those who were left in Jerusalem after the Babylonian siege in 597 BC. The prophet interpreted the death of Pelatiah, one of the chief counselors of the city, to mean that the entire population of Jerusalem was about to share a similar fate.

---

[278]Cf. the death of the false prophet Hananiah (Jer 28:17).

[279]Taylor (*Ezekiel*, 110) thinks Pelatiah actually died in Jerusalem at the very moment that Ezekiel had his vision. Subsequent reports of the incident reaching the exiles confirmed the authenticity of the vision and Ezekiel's supernatural power.

[280]For an analysis of eight different views of the death of Pelatiah, see Brownlee, *Word Biblical Commentary*, 160.

[281]Compare the prayer in 9:8.

JEWISH EXILES ENCOURAGED 11:14-21

Removed 11:14-16

A. Attitude of Jerusalemites (11:14-15)

The word of Yahweh came unto me, saying, 15 Son of man, your brethren, your kinsmen, and all the house of Israel—all of these are they of whom the inhabitants of Jerusalem have said, Go far away from Yahweh; the land has been given to us for a possession.

In response to the desperate prayer-question of Ezekiel concerning the future of Israel, God granted to the prophet a special revelation of comfort. Ezekiel was first reminded that the remnant of Israel about which he was concerned embraced others besides those who still inhabited Jerusalem. The exiled Israelites were also his brethren and kinsmen. Indeed *all the house of Israel* included the exiles of the northern kingdom as well as those of Judah.

All the exiles were despised by those who remained in Jerusalem. The fact that they were left in possession of the land and temple was interpreted as being an evidence of God's blessing on them. Conversely, they regarded those who had been carried away to foreign lands as being cursed of God because they were far from the land, i.e., Yahweh's domain and presence.

B. Promise of God (11:16)

Therefore say, Thus says Lord Yahweh: Although I have removed them far among the nations, and although I have scattered them among lands, yet I will be a sanctuary for a little while for them in the lands where they have come.

Yahweh rebuked the haughty attitude of the Jerusalemites. The proof that the exiles were God's people is seen in what he had done already for them, and what he promised yet to do for them. It was true that the exiles had been scattered among the nations by Yahweh. Yet this in no way implied that he had cast off these people.

The exiles were separated by miles from Mount Zion and God's house. Now God himself will serve as their sanctuary during the *little while*[282] they were in captivity. Those exiles were really nearer to the presence of God than those who worshiped in the Jerusalem temple from which Yahweh had now departed. He was their protection and source of strength. The phrase *little while* suggests that the captivity was temporary. For Ezekiel, as for Jeremiah, the people in exile were the "good figs" (cf. Jer 24:1) and those in Jerusalem the rotten figs. The exiles were the remnant for which there was a hope of better things.

This passage suggests that it is the presence of Yahweh that makes the sanctuary, not the sanctuary that secures the presence of God. The physical temple was not absolutely essential to the relationship between God and his people. Although the exiles had lost the temple they had not lost the presence of God.

Transformed
11:17-21

A. Gathering (11:17-18)

Therefore say, Thus says Lord Yahweh: I will gather you from the peoples, yes I will assemble you from the lands where you have been scattered, and I will give to you the land of Israel. 18 And they will come there, and they will remove all her horrible things and all her abominations from her.

For those despised exiles God had something wonderful in store. He will gather the exiles from among the nations where they had been driven. Furthermore, he will give the land of Israel to them. This is the first mention of a future restoration in Ezekiel. If this prophet emphasized Mosaic threats of judgment he also embraced the Mosaic predictions of restoration (Lv 26:40-45; Dt 30:1-10).

The prophecy of restoration began to be fulfilled in the work of Zerubbabel, Ezra and Nehemiah. The gathering of God's people, however, goes on today wherever and whenever the gospel is preached. Men and women baptized into Christ become part of the Israel of God (Gal 6:16) and inherit the Jerusalem that is from above (Gal 4:26).

Those exiles brought home by God will be spiritual persons. Immediately upon returning they will remove all horrible things and

---

[282]The charming translation "little sanctuary" (KJV) is not accurate. Even today Jews call their synagogues "a little sanctuary" in allusion to this v.

abominations, i.e., idols, and the paraphernalia of idolatry. Repentance must precede God's work in the heart of men. God can do nothing for the person who does not recognize his sins and turn from them.

B. Consecration (11:19-20)

And I will give to them one heart, and a new spirit I will put within them. I will take away the heart of stone from their flesh. I will give them a heart of flesh 20 in order that they will walk in my statutes, and keep my ordinances, and do them. They will be my people, and I will be their God.

In the new Israel God will give his people *one heart*. Here Ezekiel is introducing the great prophetic theme of unity among the people of God, a theme that he will later amplify by a symbolic action (37:15-22). The long-standing cleavage between north and south, Israel and Judah, will disappear. Oneness of purpose and of action will characterize the new Israel of God. The unity in Christ of Jew and Gentile, male and female, bond and free is a grand theological fact that in practice, unfortunately, God's people do not display before the world.

The means of achieving this grand unity of God's people is the divine gift of a *new spirit*.[283] The prophet speaks here of the spirit of loyalty, obedience and unselfishness.[284] God sets up his covenant; he also provides all the qualifications for living under the covenant. The new spirit is God's Spirit. The new Israel of God will be infused with divine energy. Such a prediction can only be fully understood in the light of the gift of the Holy Spirit to God's people on Pentecost.

A *new heart* also will be given to the individual members of the new Israel. The stony heart is that which is hardened (3:7; cf. Zech 7:12) against inducements to repentance.[285] The *heart* to the Hebrews was the center of the will and the mind, the intellectual basis for emotion and action.

The new spirit and new heart will manifest themselves in a new life—a life of righteousness. In sincere obedience the members of new Israel will live by the statutes and ordinances of God. In acts of

---

[283]The new covenant promised in Jer 31:31-34 provided for 1) a change of heart and 2) a new spirit.

[284]In this prophecy of the new spirit Ezekiel echoes the thoughts and even the words of Jer 31:31-33; 32:37-39 and Dt 30:11-16.

[285]Zech 7:12 speaks of those who made their hearts "harder than an adamant stone."

formal worship and in their daily dealings they will act in accordance with God's revealed will.

The new spirit, new heart and new life make possible a new—or perhaps more accurately, a renewed—relationship with God. Restored Israel will be his people; he will be their God. Ultimately this theme reaches its fulfillment in the blessed state of eternity (Rev 21:3-5).

C. Warning (11:21)

But as for those whose hearts go after horrible things and abominations, I will recompense their way upon their head (oracle of Lord Yahweh).

The glorious promises of this oracle come to an end with a stern warning to those Israelites who may be hardened in unbelief. Certainly the inhabitants of Jerusalem are in view; but the warning is not limited to them. Those who continued to walk after idolatry will face the judgment of God. He will bring their way upon their own heads, i.e., he will give them their just deserts. In the economy of God every set of promises has a corresponding set of punishments that fall upon those who do not through faith and obedience appropriate those promises (cf. Dt 11:26; Mt 7:13f).

CONCLUSION OF THE VISION 11:22-25

Chariot Movement 11:22-23

Then the cherubim lifted up their wings and the wheels beside them. The glory of the God of Israel was above them. 23 And the glory of Yahweh went up from over the midst of the city. It stood upon the mountain that was east of the city.

The throne-chariot of God had paused at the eastern gate of the temple court (10:19). Now Ezekiel saw those cherubic wings begin to whir. The entire throne-chariot with the glory of God over it became air-borne.

The heavenly chariot came down on the Mount of Olives east of Jerusalem. From that same spot centuries later the Son of Man "beheld the city and wept over it" (Lk 19:41). From that same hill he, the very embodiment of heavenly glory, ascended into heaven. It is not altogether clear why the *Shekinah* glory paused on the Mount of Olives in the course of departure.[286] There is no need to trace further the journeys of the throne-chariot. Ezekiel already had seen it in Tel-Aviv.

Ezekiel Movement 11:24-25

Afterwards a spirit lifted me up and caused me to go like a vision by the Spirit of God unto the captivity. So the vision that I had seen went up from me. 25 And I spoke unto the captivity all the things of Yahweh that he had showed me.

The long vision—actually a series of related visions—that commenced in 8:1 comes to an end in 11:24-25. In his vision Ezekiel felt himself transported by a spirit/wind—perhaps an angel—to Chaldea, the land of captivity.[287] Immediately the state of prophetic ecstasy came to an end.

When Ezekiel awoke from his vision he began to reveal to his fellow-exiles all that he had seen and experienced. Therefore the prophetic purpose of the visional experience was to serve, not as a message to the inhabitants of Jerusalem, but rather to those in Babylonian captivity.

EZEKIEL 12 SYMBOLS AND SERMONS

The introductory phrase *the word of Yahweh came to me* indicates the beginning of a new series of messages. In all likelihood the symbolic actions and oracles recorded here date from the same time as those in the preceding section, viz. in the summer of 592 BC. In chs 12-19 Ezekiel's purpose is to defend and reinforce the announcement of Jerusalem's coming judgment.

---

[286]Jewish tradition sees in this pause evidence that God was still looking for repentance within the city. Others suggest that the purpose of the delay was to enable the glory-cloud to direct the judgment on the city.

[287]In 11:24 the transporting spirit/wind is clearly distinguished from the Holy Spirit.

In ch 12 Ezekiel was commanded to demonstrate to the captives in Babylon, through the medium of symbolic actions, the certainty of Judah's destruction. In the parable of the fugitive he assumes the role of a refugee who tries to flee a beleaguered city (12:1-16). The second parable sets forth the hardships that will be experienced when Jerusalem comes under siege (12:17-20). Prophecies of speedy deliverance were current in both Jerusalem and Babylon. The teaching of this section is especially aimed at countering this false optimism.

FUGITIVE PARABLE 12:1-16

Preliminary Observation 12:1-2

The word of Yahweh came unto me, saying, 2 Son of man, you are sitting in the midst of a rebellious house. They have eyes to see, and do not see, ears to hear, but do not hear, for they are a rebellious house.

Ezekiel's congregation in Babylon was enough to discourage the most ardent preacher. They were indeed a *rebellious house*; they refused to see or hear the truth.[288] Ezekiel had been warned of this in his commission (2:3-8); but now he experiences the reality of that truth. The exiles had refused to listen to the inspired explanation of their plight that Ezekiel had conveyed to them in sign and word during the previous twelve months. They clung desperately—irrationally—to the conviction that God ultimately would deliver Jerusalem. Still the prophet must try to get through to them. The preacher's knowledge that his words will be ignored is never to be used as an excuse for not uttering those words. The truth must forthrightly be preached if only to justify the hearer's condemnation.

[288]Similar statements regarding spiritually blind eyes and deaf ears are found in Isa 6:9; 42:20; Jer 5:21; Mt 13:13; Jn 12:40.

Instructions
12:3-7

A. General Instructions (12:3)

As for you, son of man, prepare for yourself an exile's baggage. Go into exile by day before their eyes. You will go like an exile from your place unto another before their eyes. Perhaps they will see, for they are a rebellious house.

Ezekiel was told to prepare for himself the kind of articles that a person might be permitted to carry on a journey into exile. The barest necessities—a staff, knapsack, drinking cup—might be among the articles gathered. These preparations were to be made *by day* so as to call attention to them.

Ezekiel's strange behavior must have been the talk of the exilic community. No doubt he had no lack of spectators to watch and gossip about his every action. Having gained their attention Ezekiel was to imitate an exile by traveling from his *place* to an indefinite location outside his house. The object of this symbolic action was to attract the attention of the rebellious house. Though discouraged by his lack of visible results Ezekiel needed to be reminded that it was always possible that some might understand. *Perhaps* expresses doubt, but also hope.

B. Specific Instructions (12:4-7)

***Carry out your baggage like the baggage of an exile by day before their eyes. Go out in the evening before their eyes like those
who go out to exile. 5 Before their eyes dig for yourself in the wall,
then carry out through it. 6 Before their eyes carry it upon a shoulder. Carry it out at twilight. Cover your face so you cannot see the
ground because I have placed you as a sign to the house of Israel. 7
I did as I was commanded. My baggage I brought out like an exile's baggage by day. In the evening I dug for myself in the wall with my hand. At twilight I brought it out. Upon my shoulder I carried it before their eyes.***

Verses 4-6 set forth in more detail how Ezekiel was to carry out his fugitive parable. His pantomime consists of wordless gestures designed to attract attention and evoke questions.

Ezekiel was to take the necessary "props" out of his house and pile them up opposite his door. The baggage was to be assembled by day. The actual trek was to take place in the cool of the evening. At evening time he was to go forth like an exile seeking to evade the enemy. In this action Ezekiel was to assume the dejected demeanor and desperation of a man faced with the grim reality of exile.

He was to dig through *the wall* in plain view of the people. The reference probably is to the wall of the courtyard around his house,[289] not the wall of the city or of the house itself. Walls in Babylonia were built of sun-dried brick that could, with some exertion, be removed by hand. Through the hole in the wall, Ezekiel was to *carry out* his captive's baggage.

Once through the wall Ezekiel was to carry his exile's baggage upon his shoulder into the early evening darkness.[290] He was to wear a covering over his face. This had the effect of making it impossible for him to see the ground.

In all these actions Ezekiel was serving as a sign[291] to the house of Israel, i.e., a warning of the impending doom facing Jerusalem.

Ezekiel faithfully carried out his instructions. During the day he brought forth his "props." That evening he dug through the walls with his hands. Digging with the hands, rather than with a pick, suggests that the fugitive tries to avoid the sound of tools.

General Significance 12:8-11

The word of Yahweh came to me in the morning, saying, 9 Son of man, have not the house of Israel, the house of rebellion, said unto you, What are you doing? 10 Say unto them, Thus says Lord Yahweh: This burden concerns the prince in Jerusalem and all the house of Israel that are in the midst of them. 11 Say: I am your sign! As I have done so will it be done to them; with the captives they will go into captivity.

Following the night in which Ezekiel made his symbolic escape he received a revelation from God. Apparently not even Ezekiel was fully aware of the significance of the actions he had performed, except in the very general sense that it indicated the prospect of further

[289]The Hebrew is *qîr*, not *chōmāh*, which is used of a city wall. Tel Aviv probably did not have city walls at which Ezekiel might have demonstrated his message more accurately.

[290]The Hebrew *ʿălāṭāh* signifies the darkness that follows sunset. The word occurs elsewhere only in Gn 15:17.

[291]Isaiah (20:2) and Jeremiah (27:2) had also been "signs" to Israel.

exile for the Jews of Jerusalem. By means of a negative question God alludes to the fact that many people had been interrogating Ezekiel about his strange behavior.

Ezekiel was to inform the people that *the burden*—his prophetic message[292]—had to do with *the prince*,[293] i.e., King Zedekiah and *all the house of Israel* who still were *in the midst of them,* i.e., the arrogant apostates in Jerusalem. Some who belonged to the true Israel still remained in the condemned city.

To the exiles Ezekiel was a *sign* or an illustration or an object lesson. What he had done in symbolic parody will actually befall the inhabitants of Jerusalem—they will be driven from their homeland (*exile*) and forced to settle in areas set apart for them by their conquerors (*captivity*).

Escape Effort
12:12-15

A. Flight of the Prince (12:12)

The prince who is in the midst of them will bear upon his shoulder that he may go out. Through the wall they will dig to carry out through it. His face he will cover so that he will not be able to see the ground with the eye. 13 I will spread out my net over him, and he will be taken in my snare. I will bring him into Babylon, the land of the Chaldeans; yet he will not see it, though he will die there. 14 All who surround him to help and all his forces I will scatter to every wind. I will empty the sword after them, 15 that they may know that I am Yahweh when I scatter them among nations and disperse them in the countries.

In an attempt to avoid the fate of his people *the prince* (Zedekiah) will flee by night (cf. 2 Kgs 25:4). He will carry what meager belongings he could in a sack thrown over his shoulder. This exodus will be made through a hole which *they* (the royal servants) will be able hastily to dig through some palace wall. Zedekiah's face will be covered

---

[292]The word *burden* in the sense of "prophecy," so common in the pre-exilic prophets, is used in Ezekiel only here. Through constant use by false prophets (Jer 23:33-38), the term had fallen into discredit.

[293]Ezekiel seems to have regarded Jehoiachin, rather than Zedekiah, as legitimate king of Judah. He therefore refers to Zedekiah as *a prince* rather than a king.

for purposes of disguise and mourning so that he will not be able to see the ground.

Zedekiah's escape efforts will not be successful. The arm of God, as well as the armies of Nebuchadnezzar, will be against him. His flight will be arrested by an act of God. The soldiers of the Chaldean army will act as agents of God to ensnare the apostate king.[294] The king will be hauled off to Babylon; but he will never *see*[295] the land. This amazing prophecy was fulfilled when the Chaldeans blinded Zedekiah's eyes at Riblah (2 Kgs 25:7).

The royal bodyguard will desert their commander in the moment of crisis. They will flee for their lives with the Chaldean swordsmen in hot pursuit. When these gloomy prophecies were fulfilled, the remnant of God's people scattered through the nations will realize that Yahweh is God of justice as well as salvation.

Note of Hope
12:16

But I will spare a few men among them from sword, famine and pestilence in order that they may declare all their abominations among the nations where they come, that they may know that I am Yahweh.

A few will survive the overthrow of Jerusalem—the sword, the famine, the pestilence. They will become truly converted. They will openly admit to their guilt in worshiping pagan abominations. They will realize for the first time the full significance of the name *Yahweh*. They will make known the name and claim of Yahweh among the heathen nations where they dwell. Through their testimony heathen nations will recognize the justice of the exile and the righteous character of Yahweh who engineered it.

---

[294]The picture of a net trap is used also in 17:20; and 19:8. Also see Lam 1:13 and Hos 7:12.

[295]Josephus (*Ant.* 10:7.2; 8.2) relates a tradition that Ezekiel sent this prophecy to Jerusalem. Finding a discrepancy in the words that he should not *see* Babylon, and those of Jeremiah (32:4; 34:13), Zedekiah hardened himself in unbelief.

SIEGE HARDSHIP PARABLE 12:17-20

And the word of Yahweh came unto me, saying, 18 son of man, eat your bread with quaking, and drink your water with trembling and fear. 19 Say unto the people of the land, Thus says Yahweh to the inhabitants of Jerusalem, unto the land of Israel: They will eat their bread with fear, and their water they will drink with astonishment that her land may be desolate from its fullness because of the violence of all those who dwell in her. 20 The inhabited cities will become desolate. The land will be an astonishment, that you may know that I am Yahweh.

After an interval of silence another command came to Ezekiel. He was to set forth symbolically the conditions that will exist in Jerusalem during the Babylonian siege. Meager rations of bread and water were to be consumed in a state of fear and anxiety. Earlier Ezekiel had symbolized vividly the starvation diet of the besieged city (4:9-17). Here the focus is upon the acute terror that will grip the populace when the enemy besieged Jerusalem. The word *trembling* in v 18 is elsewhere used only of earthquakes. Thus the term connotes the idea of violent shaking.

So that there will be no misunderstanding of his actions Ezekiel adds a *thus says Yahweh* directed to *the people of the land* (his fellow exiles). It concerned those who still lived in Jerusalem. Much of what Ezekiel had said was directed to the national leaders; but here he includes the working classes from the farms and villages. The days were coming when they will consume their meager provisions of bread and water with fear and astonishment. Ezekiel cowered in a corner like one hunted down and dreading pursuit. He thereby portrayed the terror that will haunt the lives of the besieged in Jerusalem.

Her land, i.e., Jerusalem's land, was to become desolate from its fullness. The land was to be stripped of its possessions. The punishment, though severe, will be just *because of the violence*—the oppression and rebellion—of the inhabitants.

POPULAR SAYINGS CORRECTED 12:21-28

"The Days are Prolonged" 12:21-25

A. Current Proverb (12:21-22)

And the word of Yahweh came unto me, saying, 22 Son of man, what is this proverb that your people have concerning the land of Israel, saying, The days are prolonged and every vision has perished?

Still another revelation came to the prophet in order to instruct him about how to deal with a perverse attitude that was current among those who were in Israel. The same attitude was current among the Jews in Babylon. This attitude had crystallized into a clever, pithy, four-word Hebrew proverb (*māšāl*) that was wielding tremendous influence among the Jews. Prophet after prophet had come in the name of God predicting national doom. Yet *the days are prolonged*, i.e., time passes, and the visions of doom and destruction never materialize. Throughout history such has been the cry of those with little or no faith.[296] In effect this proverb sneers at the prophet because his threats had not immediately and dramatically become reality. Perhaps the people had the notion that with the passage of time the power of the prophetic word became ineffective.

B. Counter-proverb (12:23)

Therefore say unto them, Thus says Lord Yahweh: I have made this proverb to cease, and they will not make use of it any more in Israel; but speak unto them: The days draw near and the word of every vision. 24 For there will no longer be any lying vision or flattering divination in the midst of the house of Israel. 25 For I Yahweh will speak, and the word that I will speak will come to pass. It will not be prolonged anymore; for in your days, O rebellious house, I will speak, and I will perform it (oracle of Lord Yahweh).

God had an answer for the careless unconcern and unbelief of his people. The perverse proverb will not be used much longer in the

[296]Amos 6:3; Isa 5:19; Jer 17:15; Mt 24:48; 2 Pet 3:4.

land. In a four-word counter-proverb Ezekiel underscored the fact that his prophecies of doom were not for some distant age. *The days are at hand*[297] when every word[298] of every ominous vision will come to pass.

The devastating flow of events will stop the mouths of charlatans who were specialists in *lying vision* and *flattering divination.*[299] Optimistic promises of last-minute divine rescue for the holy city will be discredited. False slogans, however catchy, will die.

While false prophecy ceases God will speak.[300] Whatever he speaks will assuredly come to pass. As an evidence of grace execution of divine wrath had in the past been delayed. That will no longer be the case. The grace period was over. The present rebellious generation had heard the prophets preach God's word. They will witness the Lord of history perform that word in their land and city.

"For Distant Days"
12:26-28

The word of Yahweh came unto me, saying, 27 Son of man, Behold the house of Israel is saying, The vision that he sees is for distant days; of far off times he prophesies. 28 Therefore say unto them, Thus says Lord Yahweh: All my words will not be prolonged any longer, because I speak a word that it may be done (oracle of Yahweh).

Some had grudgingly recognized an element of truth in the predictions of Ezekiel. They did not say that his vision had failed. Rather they were content with throwing the fulfillment into the distant future. To those who transferred the divine threats to distant times God reaffirmed that his judgment was both absolute and imminent. The destruction of the temple and the holy city, and the departure of the divine presence from the sanctuary were already drawing near.

---

[297]Compare the language of John the Baptist (Mt 3:21), Jesus (Mt 4:17) and Paul (Rom 13:11).

[298]The Hebrew word *dābhār* means an effective word, a word that has lasting power (Isa 55:11). In this context it is equivalent to *fulfillment.*

[299]Divination originally meant the use of external devices such as stars, birds, sticks or the entrails of animals to predict the future. It is impossible to be sure whether some of the false prophets in Babylon resorted to such techniques, or whether Ezekiel simply used the term *divination* to underscore the worthlessness of their predictions.

[300]The pronoun *I* is emphatic in Hebrew.

EZEKIEL 13
SCATHING ORACLES

In ch 13 Ezekiel directs his attack against those who spawned the blasphemous proverbs that he has just refuted in 12:21-28. Ezekiel denounces these prophet-types for undermining the stability of the nation at a time when it needed to be built up. He speaks first of the condemnation of the prophets (vv 1-16), and then of the prophetesses (vv 17-23). In order to grasp the magnitude of the problem faced by the faithful herald of God's word in this period, Jer 29 should be read in connection with these denunciations.

CONDEMNATION OF PROPHETS[301]
13:1-16

Two charges are leveled against the national prophets: they had undermined the nation (vv 1-7); and they had encouraged false security (vv 8-16).

Authorization
13:1-2

The word of Yahweh came unto me, saying, 2 Son of man, prophesy against the prophets of Israel who prophesy, and say to those who prophesy from their own heart, Hear the word of Yahweh.

Surely it must have been with sarcasm that Ezekiel referred to his opponents as *the prophets of Israel.* These were the spiritual leaders preferred by the rebellious nation. Their messages had no higher authority than their own heart. Ezekiel had a genuine word from Yahweh for these deceivers.

---

[301]G.I. Davies, "An Archaeological Commentary on Ezekiel 13," in M.D. Coogan, et al. eds. *Scripture and Other Artifacts: Essays in Honor of Philip J. King* (Louisville: Westminster, 1994), 108-25.

Initial Indictment
13:3-7

Thus says Lord Yahweh: Woe unto the foolish prophets who walk after their own spirit and have seen nothing! 4 Like the foxes among the ruins are your prophets, O Israel! 5 You did not go up into the gaps, nor did you put up a fence around the house of Israel to stand in the battle in the day of Yahweh. 6 They have seen vanity and lying divination who say, Oracle of Yahweh, when Yahweh has not sent them, and they expect that this word will be confirmed. 7 Have you not seen a vain vision, and spoken a lying divination when you continually say, Oracle of Yahweh, even though I did not speak?

Three concepts characterize Ezekiel's word to the false prophets. First, their message was characterized by emptiness. Ezekiel pronounced a woe upon those foolish prophets (lit., "the prophets, the fools"). The Hebrew for *foolish* (*nᵉbhālîm*)[302] denotes more than stupidity. The fool was a person who was arrogant, blasphemous, and devoid of ethical and religious scruples.[303] Such were the prophets who followed *their own spirit* rather than the leading of God's Spirit. Their message was grounded in self-deception. The spiritual progeny of those prophetic pretenders are those today who present human wisdom as though it were from above.

Second, the work of false prophets was characterized by *destructiveness.* Israel's prophets—they are not God's prophets—are compared to *foxes among the ruins*. Like foxes they were cunning and destructive. Foxes found a natural habitation among the ruins of cities. Their presence only increased the devastation. So the false prophets had infiltrated the nation that was crumbling to destruction. They burrowed about among the foundations without any concern for the welfare of the place. They intended only to make dens for themselves. In an atmosphere of uncertainty and insecurity charlatans could easily gain a hearing for dogmatic optimism. Their pious platitudes and perverted theology, however, served to further undermine the already precarious position of the nation.

---

[302]A deliberate word play between the word for *prophet* (*nābhî'*) and *fool* (*nābhāl*) is probably intended.

[303]The *fool* was inclined to blasphemy (Ps 74:18), atheism (Ps 14:1), and immorality (2 Sam 13:13).

Third, the lifestyle of the false prophets was characterized by laziness. The evidence of the falsity of the popular prophets was the fact that they did not grasp the serious situation that confronted the nation. In the hour of peril those characters had made no contribution to the national defenses. The great need of the hour was for spiritual leaders to go up into the breaches[304] in the moral walls that protected Israel from destruction. The figure is that of warfare. When a wall was breached the defenders had to go up into the gap, i.e., quickly repair the break. The work of the true prophets was to preach on the great moral themes—to point out transgression—and call for repentance so that a protective hedge could be erected about the nation.[305]

As long as Israel followed the law of God the nation was untouchable. Because of unfaithfulness, however, Israel faced the judgment of *the day of Yahweh.*[306] The popular prophets[307] had done nothing to prepare the nation for this ordeal. When the storm of judgment broke forth in 586 BC, most of the Judeans were spiritually (as well as militarily) unprepared.

The false prophets had seen only vanity. Their visions were the fancy of their deluded minds. Their predictions about the future were *lying divination.* Divination was the pseudo-science of foretelling the future by human devices rather than by divinely inspired oracles.

True prophets never made use of divination. False prophets blatantly used the standard prophetic formula *oracle of Yahweh*;[308] but God had nothing to do with their mission. He had not *sent* them (cf. Jer 23:21). So self-deluded were those prophets that they actually believed that their words would be fulfilled. In attempting to deceive others they actually had deceived themselves.

In an abrupt change of person not uncommon in biblical style Ezekiel directed a rhetorical question to the pretenders. Perhaps he could shame them into confessing the falsity of their claims and methods.

---

[304]Cf. Isa 58:12; Ps 106:23.

[305]Lind (*Ezekiel*, 107) takes the metaphor of plugging the gaps in the wall to refer to intercessory prayer. He cites Ps 106:23 in support.

[306]The *day of Yahweh* in Scripture is always future and consists of the next great judgmental act of God.

[307]The pronouns referring to the prophets alternate between third person *they* (13:2-4, 6, 9) and second person plural *you* (13:5, 7-8). This is good Hebrew style. It is also characteristic of other ancient Near Eastern writings. Cf. Greenberg, *Anchor Bible*, 242-43.

[308] Cf. Jer 14:14; 23:21.

First Judgment Threat
13:8-9

Therefore thus says Lord Yahweh, Because you have spoken vanity and seen lies, therefore behold I am against you (oracle of Lord Yahweh). 9 My hand will be against the prophets who see vanity and lying divination. They will not be in the assembly of my people, nor will they be written in the register of the house of Israel, nor will they come unto the land of Israel, that you may know that I am Lord Yahweh.

Those who perverted the divine word are declared to be the enemies of God. In a formula that possibly originated in the days of hand-to-hand combat God declared his implacable hostility toward these prophets: *Behold I am against you.* The *hand* of God that had meant such strength and encouragement to Ezekiel will be raised against those prophets in anger. The very hand that had destroyed Israel's oppressors (Ex 15:12) now will destroy the false prophets.

The presently influential prophets will be discredited as counselors and leaders. In the future they will have no place *in the assembly of my people*, i.e., those who were full citizens. Presently their names were high on the national register;[309] but in the future they will not *be written in the register of the house of Israel.* Such an act is tantamount to losing full citizenship. There is no specific mention of a name being struck from the register in Old Testament times. It is probable therefore that Ezekiel contemplates a new register in which their names will never appear.

These prophetic pretenders will not even have a place in the land of Israel. The fulfillment of these threats will force the false prophets to admit that the Yahweh of Ezekiel, not their nationalistic Yahweh, was the God who controlled history.

Additional Indictment
13:10-12

Because, even because, they have caused my people to err, saying, Peace, when there is no peace. One builds up a wall, and be-

[309]Cf. Isa 4:3. Ezra 2 and Neh 7 are examples of such a register that had civil and religious significance.

hold others coat it with whitewash. 11 Say unto those who coat it with whitewash that it will fall. There will be a torrential shower. You, O hailstones, will fall; and a stormy wind will rend it. 12 Behold when the wall has fallen will it not be said unto you, Where is the coating with which you coated it?

In the initial indictment of the prophets Ezekiel focused on the false prophets in Babylon. Now he turns to the Jerusalem prophets. This indictment is introduced by the repetition of the conjunction *because*. Even as impending calamity closed in on the inhabitants of Judah the Jerusalem prophets were assuring their constituents that all was well. The Hebrew noun translated *peace* (*šālōm*) in this context refers to national prosperity. Such optimistic assessments are likened to the building of a wall.[310] The word for *wall—chāyits*—signifies a wall of stones heaped one upon another with no mortar to hold them together. A coat of whitewash (*tāphēl*) in no way added to the strength of such a wall; it only served to conceal its dangerous character.

The wall represents the false hopes that the people were erecting for themselves. The false prophets were indorsing this wall by their "lying lullabies" (Taylor). How tragic that some spiritual leaders cater to the desires of their auditors. They yield to the temptation to speak pleasant words to their people. Disaster is inevitable when religious leaders encourage people in unbiblical ways. The false prophets indorsed revolt against Babylon and promised divine deliverance from the inevitable confrontation with that power. They had created a spirit of complacency. The wall of theological and political promises that they had built will collapse at a touch. The population will be left exposed and vulnerable.

God had a word for the prophetic whitewash crew. Torrential rains, hailstones[311] and wind will put their deceitful wall to the test.

When that wall fell—and fall it surely will—angry citizens who had been deceived will hold the prophets up to derision: *where is the coating?*, i.e., the lies with which they sought to establish national security.

---

[310]Alexander (*Expositor's Bible Commentary*, 801) envisions the false prophets reinforcing their optimistic forecasts by literally plastering walls and helping people decorate the thin partitions of their homes.

[311]The hailstones are addressed as God's agents for the destruction of the wall. Some re-point the Hebrew to get the meaning, "and I will cause great hailstones to fall." The meaning is the same in either case.

Second Judgment Threat
13:13-16

Therefore thus says Lord Yahweh: I will rend it with a stormy wind in my fury. There will be a torrential shower in my anger, and hailstones in fury to consume it. 14 So I will smash the wall that you have daubed with whitewash, and bring it to the ground. Its foundations will be uncovered, and it will fall. You will be destroyed in its midst, that you may know that I am Yahweh. 15 Thus I will exhaust my wrath on the wall, and on those who daubed it with whitewash. I will say to you, The wall is no more, and those who coated it are no more, 16 the prophets of Israel who prophesy unto Jerusalem, and who see visions of peace for her when there is no peace (oracle of Lord Yahweh).

The stormy wind, hailstones and torrential rain of military assault will demonstrate the fury of God against his people. The fall of the whitewashed wall of imaginary security will be God's doing. In that day even the very foundations of those walls—the false theological notions about God's relationship to Judah—will be exposed to plain view. The use of whitewash instead of mortar is what made the false prophet a criminal. The prophets will be destroyed by the collapse of their wall[312] of words. They will be overwhelmed in the disaster that will befall the people they had deceived. In that day the prophets will know that Yahweh is faithful to his word of judgment as well as to his word of promise.

When his fury had been completely poured out both the metaphorical wall and those who built it will no longer exist. The nation did not enjoy peace, either with God or with the superpower of that day. Those who claimed to have received revelations to the contrary were clearly worthy of the heavenly judgment just announced.

---

[312]Lind (*Ezekiel*, 110) points out a subtle change in 13:14 that is not apparent in the English. The first two pronouns are masculine, referring to *wall*, a masculine noun; the last two are feminine, referring to *Jerusalem,* a feminine noun.

CONDEMNATION OF PROPHETESSES 13:17-23

Indictment 13:17-19

As for you, son of man, set your face against the daughters of your people who are prophesying out of their own heart. Prophesy against them. 18 You will say, Thus says Lord Yahweh: Woe to those who sew bands for every joint of the arm, and make veils for the head of every height to lie in wait for souls. Will you lie in wait for my people but save your own lives? 19 Will you profane me among my people in exchange for handfuls of barley and pieces of bread to slay souls who should not die, and to save souls who should not live by your lying to my people who hear (your) lies?

When it came to condemnation the Old Testament prophets were not respecters of persons. They condemned wayward women as well as wayward men.[313] The women Ezekiel condemns are not called prophetesses,[314] but women who play the role of prophet. The description of their activities suggests that they were more like witches. They mixed magical[315] practices with their prophecies. It is not surprising that in the turbulent first decade of the sixth century such leeches had appeared. The ways of Babylon, where necromancy and divination abounded, had been adopted by the Jews.

The prophetesses, as well as their male counterparts, were aggravating the spiritual and political problems of Judah. Like the prophets these women prophesied *out of their own heart*. Their message was of human rather than of divine origin.

The women employed magical arts by which they pretended to foretell the future. Magic bands—perhaps cases containing incanta-

---

[313]Besides the present section, the following passages are critical of women: Amos 4:1-3; Isa 3:16-4:1; 32:9-13.

[314]The title *prophetess* is bestowed on Deborah (Jud 4:4ff.), Huldah (2 Kgs 22:14): Miriam (Ex 15:20); Noadiah (Neh 6:14) and Isaiah's wife (Isa 8:1). Cf. Lk 236ff; Acts 21:9; Rev 2:20; 1 Cor 11:5. Cf. Nancy Brown, "The Daughters of Your People: Female Prophets in Ezekiel 13:17-23," *JBL* 118 (1999): 417-33.

[315]Magic is an attempt to manipulate divinity to achieve one's own goals. Magical practices are forbidden in Dt 18:9-22.

tions and charms were sewn on their wrists.[316] This seems to be similar to a Babylonian custom in which a sorcerer binds the wrist of a client to symbolize the binding power of the spell that was pronounced.[317] The sorceresses also draped their clients with full-length veils or shawls. They possessed a whole wardrobe of such veils adapted to persons of various heights so that in all cases it shrouded their whole form. Just what the purpose of these veils was cannot now be determined. Some spoken spell must have accompanied the use of these objects (cf. v 17).

The sorceresses were not harmless cranks. Their object was to *lie in wait* for the *souls* (i.e., the lives) of God's people. They were determined to capture the attention and control the minds of those who were still trying to be faithful to Yahweh.[318] Ezekiel seems to think of those magical veils as nets cast over victims. They were a snare from which they could not escape.

The prophetesses could care less about the fate of God's people; but they were determined to save their own lives.[319] This probably means that they were driven by the profit motive. Their sole concern was to receive the fees by which they could sustain their lives. By means of a variety of spells and incantations the prophetesses claimed the power to keep clients alive on payment of certain fees.

The prophetesses had profaned Yahweh among his people. Their actions caused people to deny their faith in Yahweh. They trusted in deceitful divinations. Thus the name of God was profaned by those who turned their backs on him.

The deceitful oracles of the prophetesses were cranked out with the aid of *handfuls of barley and crumbs of bread*. These materials probably were used as auguries to be examined to see whether a sick man would live or die.[320]

---

[316]Lit., "joints of my hands." This expression has been taken to refer to the knuckles, armpits and elbows as well as the wrists. The first person possessive suffix on the word is most difficult to explain. Perhaps the meaning is that the sorceresses were trying to bind or restrict the power of God by means of these magical paraphernalia. That the wrists of the sorceress, rather than the client, were bound is suggested by v 20.

[317]Taylor, *Ezekiel*, 124.

[318]Wevers, (*Ezekiel*, 109) thinks that hunting souls is a technical term for harming opponents by magical means.

[319]The Hebrew literally reads: "and save souls alive for yourselves."

[320]Taylor, *Ezekiel*, 125. Older scholars take the sense to be that the sorceresses put forth their spells for a mere pittance of reward.

The prophetesses slay *souls that should not die*, i.e., foretell the death for the righteous.[321] At the same time they save the souls alive that should not live, i.e., they promised life to the wicked. They were *lying* to God's people who were inclined to listen to untruth more than truth.

Punishment 13:20-23

Therefore thus says Lord Yahweh: Behold I am against your bands by which you lie in wait for souls there to make them like birds. I will rend them from upon your arms. I will send forth the souls, the souls for whom you have been lying in wait to make them fly. 21 I will rend your coverings. I will deliver my people from your hands. They will not again be in your hand to be hunted down, that you may know that I am Yahweh. 22 Because you have made sad the heart of the righteous with lies when I did not make him sad. You have strengthened the hands of the wicked that he should not turn from his evil way to cause him to live. 23 Therefore you will see no more vanity or engage in divination again; for I will deliver my people from your hand, that you may know that I am Yahweh.

Compared to the condemnation of the prophets in the preceding section these women were treated quite lightly. They will not suffer more than the loss of their influence and livelihood.

God declared his absolute opposition to the pagan paraphernalia employed by these women. On *bands* (or cushions), see on v 18. The bands (or cushions) will be ripped from the arms of these women. Their *veils* will be torn away.[322] Implied in the judgment is that the magic bands and veils in some way imprisoned the lives of the people.

The souls held captive by the magic spells will be liberated, set free like birds from a cage. God's people will no longer be in the *hands*, i.e., under the power of these prophetesses. As God once delivered his people from ruthless Pharaoh so he now will deliver them from their own oppressive leaders.

---

[321]Others take the expression to mean that they led on to destruction the souls that were meant for life, while they saved their own souls that were worthy of death.

[322]The suffix *your* on the words *bands* and *veils* is masculine. The use of the masculine form when speaking of women is not uncommon in the Old Testament. The feminine is resumed in *your hand* in v 21.

The prophetesses had caused the righteous to be disheartened. At the same time they had given encouragement to the wicked. The result of this was that the wicked had no inclination to *turn*, i.e., repent.

Because of their detrimental influence on society the profession of which these women were a part will be abolished. No more will they make claims to see visions or employ divination to ascertain the future. In the day of judgment, when all the magical schemes of these women fail, they will comprehend that the God who had spoken these things is Yahweh. They will understand that he is faithful to perform his word of judgment as well as his word of promise.

EZEKIEL 14
OBJECTIONS ANSWERED

In ch 14 Ezekiel deals with three theoretical objections that might be raised against the announcement of Jerusalem's judgment. The first is: we are sincerely seeking God's will (vv 1-8). The second is: we are only listening to our prophets (vv 9-11). The third objection raises the question of how God can destroy the holy city when there were still some righteous people within it (vv 12-23).

OBJECTION #1
"We are Seeking God's Will"
14:1-8

The exiles were coming to Ezekiel to inquire of Yahweh. In so doing, however, they were playing the role of hypocrites. Three times they are charged with setting up idols in their hearts. This fact is first revealed privately to Ezekiel (vv 1-3). He then exposes publicly the hypocrisy of the elders (v 4) and the entire house of Israel (v 7).

Private Revelation
14:1-3

Certain men of the elders of Israel came unto me, and sat before me. 2 The word of Yahweh came unto me, saying, 3 Son of man, these men have set up their idols in their hearts. The stum-

bling block of their iniquity they have placed before their face. Should I ever permit them to make inquiry of me?

During the period of the exile the *elders* were supposed to be the spiritual leaders of the nation. The *elders of Israel*[323] came to Ezekiel to seek a message from Yahweh. They probably were anxious to be enlightened about the future of their homeland. In *sitting* before the prophet the elders were acknowledging him as a genuine teacher from God.

In response to the inquiry of the elders Ezekiel received a revelation. God revealed to the prophet the heart condition of the elders. They were guilty of setting up their idols in their hearts. This does not necessarily mean that these elders were actually worshiping idols. They were longing after the old pagan practices that they had observed prior to the exile. Their thoughts were influenced by magic spells, divination and the like.

The elders in exile may have been contemplating acquiring idols like their counterparts back in Jerusalem (cf. 8:10). Certainly they were dreaming them up in their hearts. The elders were in grave danger of tripping over this obstacle to true devotion and overtly violating the first two commandments. The internalized idolatry was a *stumbling block* that these elders willfully had set before themselves.[324]

No special divine direction will be forthcoming for men who do not exclusively devote their hearts to Yahweh. To express this fact God used a rhetorical question couched in the most emphatic terms. Should God allow himself to be petitioned by hypocrites? A strong negation is implied.

Hypocrisy Exposed
14:4-5

Therefore speak unto them and say to them, Thus says Lord Yahweh: Any man of the house of Israel who sets up his idols in his heart, and places the stumbling block of his iniquity before his face,

---

[323]Blackwood (*Ezekiel*, 99) thinks these elders of Israel are the same as the elders of Judah mentioned in 8:1. Plumptre (*Pulpit Commentary*, 247) thinks these elders were a deputation from the earlier group of exiles taken captive by the Assyrians.

[324]The phrase *the stumbling block of their iniquity* is peculiar to Ezekiel (7:19; 14:3, 4, 7; 18:30: 44:12). It usually refers to idols. At this stage of history, idols were the chief occasion of sin for God's people.

and comes unto the prophet—I Yahweh will respond to him that comes according to the multitude of his idols 5 in order that I may take the house of Israel in their heart, because all of them have been turned aside from me through their idols.

Ezekiel now reveals to the elders what God had revealed to him privately. He sets forth the message in the form of a legal principle addressed to *any man* (person) *of the house of Israel.*[325] Because idolatry was so firmly rooted in their hearts these elders need not expect an oral answer to their inquiry from Yahweh. Rather, Yahweh himself will come to answer,[326] i.e., he will answer personally, not through an intermediary. He will answer them by deeds—by acts of judgment. Furthermore, the judgment that he metes out to each individual will be according to the multitude of his idols. God responds to their hypocrisy rather than their inquiry.[327]

God's great priority was to win complete allegiance from his people.[328] All of them, like the hypocritical elders, had divided hearts—hearts still estranged from God because of idolatry. Yahweh had exposed the pagan inclinations of the elders. He had announced judgment upon them for their lack of full commitment to him. Thereby Yahweh will force all members of the house of Israel to acknowledge him alone as God.[329]

Call for Repentance
14:6-8

Therefore say unto the house of Israel, Thus says Lord Yahweh: Return, and turn away yourselves[330] from your idols. From all your abominations turn away your face; 7 because any man of the

---

[325]Lind (*Ezekiel*, 117) points out that the beginning of Ezekiel's threat is identical with that of four Levitical laws: Lv 17:3, 8, 10, 13.
[326]The verb is Niphal or reflexive.
[327]Alexander (*Expositor's Bible Commentary*, 805) takes the v to mean that God will give them over to the many idols in their hearts (v 4). God knew that satiation with idolatry was the only way for Israel to become nauseated with the emptiness and perversion of idolatry.
[328]Brownlee (*Word Biblical Commentary*, 202) understands the verb *take* in judicial terms, i.e., to take in judgment.
[329]Others interpret the verb *take* in v 5 to be equivalent to "expose" or "hold responsible." Still others see v 5 simply as a threat that the hypocrites of the nation will be caught in a snare of their own making.
[330]Lit., "turn them," i.e., *your faces* referred to in the next clause.

house of Israel and of the alien who dwells in Israel who has turned aside from me, and erected his idols in his heart, and has set the stumbling block of his iniquity before his face, and comes unto the prophet to inquire by him of me—I Yahweh will respond to him by myself. 8 I will set my face against that man, and I will make him a sign and proverb. I will cut him off from the midst of my people, that you may know that I am Yahweh.

Ezekiel now addresses the people at large on the issue of divided allegiance. As always in the economy of God a call for repentance precedes the execution of judgment. The Hebrew verb *return/turn* (*šūbh*) is used 3x in one v. Ezekiel calls on them to *return* to God. He wants them to force themselves (Hiphil) to *turn away* from *idols* and *all abominations*, i.e., all the paraphernalia of idolatry.

Yahweh next addresses all who reject his call for repentance. Ezekiel expands the legal threat of v 4 to include *the alien who dwells in Israel*. Foreigners who lived in the Israelite theocracy were as much bound by the laws against idolatry as native-born citizens.[331] Ezekiel has in mind those aliens who had attached themselves to the Israelite community in Babylon.

Those who play the role of the hypocrite, who harbor idolatrous inclinations in their hearts, will receive a message from God when they appear before a prophet; but it will not be the kind of message they expect. Instead of a spoken answer by the mouth of the prophet there will be an answer in the discipline of life.

In fulfillment of the "curse" stipulations of the Mosaic covenant God will inflict four penalties on those whose hearts were divided regarding him. First, Yahweh will *set* his *face against* that man, i.e., he will assume a posture of hostility toward that hypocrite (cf. 13:9; Lv 20:3, 5-6). Second, God will make that man a *sign and proverb*, i.e., he will inflict upon that man an exemplary punishment that becomes proverbial. He thereby acts as a deterrent to others inclined toward idolatry (cf. Dt 28:37). Third, God will *cut off* that man from the midst of his people, i.e., excommunicate him (Lv 17:10; 20:3, 5, 6).[332] Fourth, when men witnessed this righteous judgment they will recognize that Yahweh is the only God.[333]

---

[331]Cf. Lv 17:10; 20:1-2.

[332]Another interpretation is *cut them off* by early death.

[333]The Mosaic material abounds in the recognition formula attached to Yahweh's deeds of deliverance and/or judgment.

OBJECTION #2
"We are only Listening to our Prophets"
14:9-11

As for the prophet, when he is enticed, and speaks a word, I Yahweh have enticed that prophet. I will stretch out my hand against him. I will destroy him from the midst of my people Israel. 10 They will bear their iniquity. The iniquity of the prophet will be like that of the one who inquires, 11 that the house of Israel might not again go astray from me, or defile themselves with all their transgressions; but they will be my people, and I will be their God (oracle of Lord Yahweh).

Some so-called prophets did give responsive oracles to hypocritical inquirers. Such men, however, were false prophets. The hypocrites sitting before Ezekiel knew their own hearts. They knew that inwardly they had not surrendered their idols. Since God will not give guiding counsel to such people the "prophet" who pretended to do so was not inspired of God.

The prophets who were causing such confusion in Jerusalem and Babylon had been *enticed*. God declares that he had enticed that prophet, i.e., he had permitted the enticement to take place (cf. 1 Kgs 22:19-23). This does not mean that the prophet who spoke falsely was divinely compelled to do so. He bore complete responsibility for his actions. The idea is that men who reject the truth of God have opened their mind for such judicial enticement to false thinking.[334]

One must distinguish between the permissive and active will of God. Part of the punishment that God metes out to sinners is that he permits them to be led into ever greater sin. When men obstinately refuse the truth God gives them over to falsehood.

The prophets had been enticed to falsehood. Shortly they will experience divine judgment. God will stretch out his hand against them. They will be destroyed from the midst of Israel.[335] God is no respecter of persons when it comes to judgment. Both the prophets and the citi-

---

[334]For Yahweh as a deceiver of prophets, see 2 Kgs 22:19-23 and Dt 13:1-5. Cf. 2 Thess 2:11. Secondary causation here has been eliminated as in Isa 45:7; Amos 3:6.

[335]Some think that *destroyed from the midst of my people* (v 9) is synonymous with *cut off from the midst of my people* (v 8). It seems, however, that the former refers to death, and the latter to excommunication.

zens who came to seek their counsel will have to bear their iniquity, i.e., suffer the same punishment.

The deceivers, and those who cried out to be deceived, will alike experience the judgment of God. The purpose of this divine judgment was not so much revenge as it was correction. The punishment was to serve as a deterrent so that God's people will no longer *go astray* from him to serve idols. The people defiled themselves by such transgressions.[336] By discouraging defilement by idolatry God was doing what was necessary to promote his relationship with his people. Free from the taint of idolatry they could be his people and he could be their God.

At this point hope shines through the otherwise gloomy discourse of Ezekiel. The prophet is a realistic optimist. He cannot deny the divine forecast of stormy judgment. He sees, however, a silver lining in those dark clouds. Some ultimate good will come of it. God's eternal purpose will not be frustrated by the collapse of earthly Jerusalem.

OBJECTION #3
"Righteous Men Live Among us."
14:12-23

General Principle
14:12-20

A. Illustration: Famine (14:12-14)

The word of Yahweh came unto me, saying, 13 Son of man, when a land sins against me by trespassing grievously, and I stretch out my hand against it, and break its staff of bread, and send against it a famine, and cut off from it man and beast; 14 though these three men—Noah, Daniel, and Job—were in its midst, they would deliver only their own lives through their righteousness (oracle of Lord Yahweh).

Famine is frequently mentioned in Scripture as a means by which God punished his people. When God will *break the staff of bread*[337] (i.e., bring about a famine) innocent beasts, as well as sinful men, are

[336]The priestly interest of Ezekiel is evident from the statement that transgressions (conscious rebellion against divine law) rendered one unclean, i.e., defiled one.

[337]Man's life is sustained by bread even as his weight is sustained by a staff.

thereby *cut off,* i.e., die. Yet there was no deliverance for the sinful land merely because innocent animals suffered.

Will the presence of righteous men in Jerusalem spare that city from the threatened destruction? In his mighty intercessory prayer (Gn 18:23ff) Abraham had used this as a ground to plead for the deliverance of Sodom and Gomorrah. Israel, however, was beyond the help of any human mediation. The presence of a righteous soul here or there cannot be a lucky religious charm, a community insurance policy that guarantees, if not immunity from judgment, at least a softened blow. So grievously had the land of Judah transgressed against God that not even the presence of super-saints like *Noah, Daniel, and Job*[338] would be able to deliver the land. The doctrine of personal responsibility here is carried to its logical conclusion. Judgment for unrepentant sinners is inevitable.

Noah and his family escaped the universal destruction by the great flood because he was a righteous man. Daniel[339] survived deportation to Babylon because of his steadfast loyalty to God. He saved his friends from an edict to slay the royal magicians. Eventually he was elevated to high office in the Babylonian government. Daniel already had established himself as a pious man of God and a folk hero in the eyes of the Jewish captives. Yet he had not been able to use his influence with Nebuchadnezzar to spare the people of Judah. Job was spared while his wayward children met with fatal accidents. In none of these cases did the righteousness of these godly men induce God to spare the wicked.[340] So it is that Noah, Daniel and Job will only be able to save their own lives through their righteousness.

B. Illustration: Beasts (14:15-16)

If I cause evil beasts to pass through the land and they bereave it, and it becomes so desolate that no man passes through her be-

---

[338]Feinberg (*Ezekiel*, 81) suggests that the order of the names is climactic rather than chronological: Noah delivered his family with himself; Daniel his friends; but Job, not even his own children.

[339]The notion that Ezekiel refers to a fifteenth century Phoenician hero named Daniel, rather than the famous biblical personage of the same name, is common among those who do not accept the authenticity of the Book of Daniel. John Day, "The Daniel of Ugarit and Ezekiel and the Hero of the Book of Daniel," *VT* 30 (1980): 174-184; Harold Dressler, "the Identification of the Ugaritic Dnil with the Daniel of Ezekiel," *VT* 29 (1979): 152-161; [reply by Baruch Margalit, "Interpreting the Story of Aqht," *VT* 30 (1980): 361-65].

[340]A similar argument is used by Jeremiah (15:1).

cause of the beasts; 16 though these three men were in its midst, as I live (oracle of Lord Yahweh), they will not deliver sons or daughters. They alone will be delivered, but the land will become a desolation.

Resorting to emphasis by repetition Ezekiel pounded home his point that Noah, Daniel and Job will not be able to deliver the land. In vv 15-20 he enumerates three more types of judgment that God might on occasion send against his people. These are punishments threatened in the Mosaic covenant (Lv 26:22-26).

Beasts (chayyāh)[341] might be brought against the land. These are probably rabid animals, not simply predatory beasts.[342] Rabies passes quickly from one animal to another. An infested rat might bring the disease into a city under siege with devastating effects on both humans and livestock. Out of fear the land will be deserted and become *desolate*. Men of other countries will loathe passing through. Still there will be no deliverance for the sinful land. Sons and daughters of the sinful inhabitants will die (vv 16, 18, 20). The combined goodness of all three men could not save Israel from divine destruction. *As I live* (vv 16, 18, 20) is a familiar oath formula in the Old Testament. God swears that under no condition can the righteousness of the most righteous men avert the destruction of a sinful nation.

C. Illustration: Sword (14:17-18)

Or if I bring a sword against that land, and I say, Let a sword pass through the land, so that I cut off from it man and beast; 18 though these three men were in its midst, as I live (oracle of Lord Yahweh), they will deliver neither sons nor daughters, for they alone will be delivered.

The *sword* (i.e., military invasion) might be used against the land. Such action will involve the indiscriminate slaughter of man and beast. From such slaughter there will be no deliverance.

D. Illustration: Plague (14:19-20)

Or if I sent a plague against that land, and I poured out my wrath upon it in blood to cut off from it man and beast; 20 though

---

[341]Some interpret the beasts to be Gentile invaders. There is, however, no reason these cannot be literal beasts.

[342]Brownlee, *Word Biblical Commentary*, 207. There are other expressions for "wild animals" such as "beasts of the field" (e.g., Lv 26:22) or "beasts of the earth/land" (e.g., 1 Sam 17:46).

Noah, Daniel and Job were in its midst, as I live (oracle of Lord Yahweh) they will not be able to deliver son or daughter; they will deliver only their own lives by their righteousness.

Plague (diseases) might be the means of punishment. God's fury poured out upon the land will manifest itself in blood, i.e., a high death rate. Still there will be no deliverance.

Pointed Application
14:21-23

Because thus says Lord Yahweh: How much more when I send my four calamitous judgments against Jerusalem—sword, famine, wild beasts, and plague—to cut off from it man and beast. 22 If a remnant is left in it who are brought forth—sons and daughters—behold they will come forth unto you. You will see their way and their deeds. You will be comforted concerning the calamity that I have brought against Jerusalem all that I have brought against her. 23 They will comfort you when you see their way and their deeds, that you may know that I have not done all that I did against her without cause (oracle of Lord Yahweh).

Ezekiel has set forth in vv 12-20 the general principle that the presence of even the godliest men cannot save a land—any land—from divine judgment. In v 21 the prophet makes the application to Jerusalem. If when only *one* of the above mentioned punishments is inflicted upon a land the righteous are unable to save the wicked, how much more true will this be in the case of Jerusalem that must suffer all four. The number four conveys the idea of completeness and universality because it reflects the notion of the four points of the compass.

A remnant will survive the fourfold catastrophe that befalls Jerusalem. The remnant will be *brought forth*, i.e., carried into exile. Their survival should not be interpreted as indicating their righteousness. Far from it! These escapees will serve as an object lesson. When the earlier exiles observed the character and conduct of those who later joined them, they will be *comforted concerning the calamity* that Jerusalem experienced. They will realize that God had no alternative but to destroy that city. His punishments had not been arbitrary or excessive. The preservation of a remnant from Jerusalem was an act of pure grace.

Indirectly the future captives will comfort[343] those who were already in Babylon. The kind of comfort referred to here is that which comes about when a person learns new facts that throw new light on what was perceived to be a disastrous situation.

EZEKIEL 15
A USELESS VINE

The justification of God's judgment against Judah continues in chs 15-17, but the nature of the defense changes. Here Ezekiel employs parables or allegories to paint a rather gruesome word picture of the ingratitude, sin and rebellion of God's people. He describes the useless vine (15:1-8); the faithless wife (16:1-43); the fallen sister (16:44-63); and the lowly vine (17:1-21). The section closes with a brief and optimistic parable of the stately cedar (17:22-24).

The earlier prophets frequently spoke of Israel as the vine of God.[344] That figure, while beautiful to contemplate, can lend itself to gross distortion in the minds of hypocrites. People might think that because of the accident of birth they were branches of the true vine that could never be destroyed. In ch 15 Ezekiel sets forth a parable, as later the greater Son of Man will do (Jn 15), to expose the groundlessness of such a notion.

ILLUSTRATION
15:1-5

The word of Yahweh came unto me, saying, 2 Son of man, what is the vine tree more than any other tree, the vine branch that is among the trees of the forest? 3 Is wood taken from it to make any work? or will men take a peg from it to hang any vessel thereon? 4 Behold it is cast to the fire for fuel. The fire has devoured both ends of it while the middle is singed. Is it profitable for any work? 5 Behold when it is whole it is not suitable for work; how much less when the fire consumes it and it is singed will it yet be suitable for work?

---

[343]The r. *nchm* does not mean comfort *in* sorrow, but comfort *out of* sorrow.

[344]Gn 49:22; Ps 80:9; Hos 10:1; Isa 5; Dt 32:32; Jer 2:21.

Five rhetorical questions make up this unit. The first question establishes the main point. The next two questions support that point with specific illustrations. The last two questions carry the main point forward to a different level.

Yahweh directed Ezekiel's attention to the *vine tree*—the wild vine of the woods. The *trees of the forest* represent the community of nations (cf. Isa 10:33-34). Compared to the nations of the world Israel was only a vine.

The vine was worthless. It was a fruitless vine. Its wood was useless as timber. No one would think of using that wood as material for making furniture. The wood of the vine was even too thin and pliable to be fashioned into a wall peg. The wild vine was fit only for kindling for the fire.

Should the vine be snatched from the fire before being completely consumed it would still be good for nothing. Before it was cast into the fire it was good for nothing; how much less after it had been charred and burned.

APPLICATION 15:6-8

Therefore thus says Lord Yahweh: Like the vine tree among the trees of the forest that I have appointed for fuel for the fire thus I have appointed the inhabitants of Jerusalem. 7 I will set my face against them. From the fire they have come forth, and the fire will consume them. You will know that I am Yahweh when I set my face against them. 8 I will make the land a desolation because they have grievously transgressed (oracle of Lord Yahweh).

The purpose of the vine is fruit bearing. If a vine bears no fruit, or sour fruit, it is, in comparison to other trees, of no value. So it was with Israel. If Israel bore no fruit—did not fulfill its mission—then it was poorer and weaker than the heathen nations round it. The inhabitants of Jerusalem were like that vine tree—good for nothing except destruction by fire.

God had set his face (cf. 4:3) against the inhabitants of Jerusalem. The city had passed through the fire of earlier Babylonian invasions—in 605 BC and 597 BC--and had been charred, but not consumed. That was no guarantee, however, that the city was inviolable. In the next fire the city will be consumed. When that happened, the inhabitants will know that the destruction was no chance occurrence.

They will realize that the destruction of Jerusalem resulted from the decree of the Almighty.

The concluding v summarizes the meaning of the parable: the judgment and its cause. It is not their inherent worthlessness, but their faithlessness in respect to their national calling that brings on the judgment. Their land will become a desolation because of grievous transgression.

EZEKIEL 16 FAITHLESS WIFE/ FALLEN SISTERS[345]

The word of Yahweh came unto me, saying, 2 Son of man, make known to Jerusalem her abominations.

To demonstrate that his parable of the worthless vine was no exaggeration Ezekiel surveys Jerusalem's history from the city's birth to his own day. The prophet is almost indelicately realistic in his description. He meant it that way. Sin is ugly. If the prophet is going to "tell it like it is" he must resort from time to time to ugly words. Hardened hearts sometimes respond to shock therapy. So the prophet is commissioned by God to cause Jerusalem to know *her abominations*. He does this by means of two parables—the parable of the faithless wife (vv 3-43) and the parable of the three sisters.

PARABLE OF THE FAITHLESS WIFE 16:3-43

In four paragraphs Ezekiel reviews the past and future dealings between God and his people. In unfolding this allegory Ezekiel discusses the circumstances of Jerusalem's birth (vv 1-7), the marriage

[345]Marvin Pope, "Mixed Marriage Metaphor in Ezekiel 16," in A.B. Beck, et al. eds. *Fortunate the Eyes that See; Essays in Honor of David Noel Freedman* (Grand Rapids: Eerdmans, 1995), 384-99; M.G. Swanepoel, "Ezekiel 16; Abandoned Child, Bride Adorned or Unfaithful Wife?" in Philip Davies and David Clines, eds. *Among the Prophets* (Sheffeld, JSOT, 1993), 84-104.

and adornment of Jerusalem (vv 8-14), the infidelity of the bride (vv 15-34), and the punishment of the harlot (vv 35-43).

Abandoned Child
16:3-7

A. Her Plight (16:3-5)

Say unto them, Thus says Lord Yahweh to Jerusalem: Your origin and birth are of the land of the Canaanite; your father was the Amorite, and your mother the Hittite. 4 As for your birth, on your birthday your navel was not cut. You were not washed in water for cleansing. You were not salted or wrapped at all. 5 No eye had pity upon you to do any of these things to you to have compassion upon you; but you were cast out upon the surface of the ground when you were regarded as loathsome in the day of your birth.

Jerusalem is specifically addressed, though much of what is said applies to the whole nation. Jerusalem's *origin and birth* took place on the soil of Canaan. The city was conceived by the Amorite[346] and the Hittite,[347] i.e., it was founded by the heathen peoples of Canaan.[348] At the time of the conquest Jerusalem was a Jebusite city (Josh 15:8, 63) and a member of the southern coalition of city states that opposed Joshua.

Like many female infants[349] Jerusalem was abandoned after birth, left exposed in a field to die. She had not received the customary treatment afforded newborn babies.

Normally after the navel was cut a baby was rubbed all over with salt water. The salt served as an antiseptic. It also strengthened the baby's skin.[350] The baby was then wrapped tightly in bands of cloth.

---

[346]Amorites were a west-Semitic people who began filtering into the Fertile Crescent from the desert about 2000 BC. At the time of Moses they were firmly entrenched in the mountains of Palestine, and in the Transjordan region as well.

[347]The Hittites were an Indo-European people whose center was in Asia Minor and, during some periods, Syria.

[348]When the hill country of Judah is particularly in view, Canaan was known as the land of the Amorites and the land of the Hittites. See Gn 10:16; 15:16; Nm 13:29; Josh 1:4; 5:1 7:7; 24:15, 18.

[349]Cf. *ANET*, 119.

[350]Brownlee (*Word Biblical Commentary*, 223) offers another explanation: the salt retarded the growth of bacteria in the swaddling material. That reduced the need for the heavy work of laundering, which was done by treading out or beating out the clothes against the rocks.

Every seven days through day forty the dirty clothes were removed, the baby washed, anointed with oil, and rewrapped.[351] None of these customary treatments, however, was applied to this child. Instead, she had been regarded as loathsome. She had been exposed to death by neglect.

The neglected baby is a picture of Jerusalem in her earliest years. The people of Canaan did not care about the place. Likewise the Israelites overlooked Jerusalem throughout the settlement period.

B. Her Rescue (16:6-7)

When I passed by you and saw you wallowing in your blood, I said to you: Though bloody, live; yes, I said to you, though bloody, live. 7 An increase like the sprout of the field I appointed you. You increased, and grew up, and came to excellent beauty. Your breasts were formed, and your hair was grown; yet you were naked and bare.

God *passed by* the ugly and unwanted child. *Though bloody* is lit., "in your blood." Although the child was repulsive to look upon, squirming about in her blood, i.e., unwashed, still God decreed that the child should *live*. This probably refers to David's capture of Jerusalem from the Jebusites (2 Sam 5:6-10).

To grow like *the sprout of the field* is a beautiful metaphor for what thrives through the blessing of God alone. The female infant grew to maturity. She possessed the physical attributes of a beautifully formed woman, viz. a full bust and long hair. Yet she was still *naked and bare*. The Hebrew terms usually mean "insufficiently clad." Jerusalem was like a poor shepherd girl inadequately clothed. The reference is to the earliest years of Israelite occupation of the city.

---

[351]The obstetrics of the v are best explained by the present-day customs of Arabs described by Mastermann in Cooke, *Ezekiel*, 162 and Brownlee, *Word Biblical Commentary*, 223.

Glorious Bride
16:8-14

A. Marriage (16:8-9)

Now when I passed by you and saw you, behold your time was the time of love. I spread my skirt over you, and covered your nakedness. I swore to you, and entered into a covenant with you (oracle of Lord Yahweh), and you became mine. 9 I washed you with water, cleansed your blood from upon you, and I anointed you with oil.

God *passed by* Jerusalem a second time. The relationship between God and Israel is frequently depicted under the metaphor of marriage. So it is here that the divine rescuer noticed that the Jerusalem had reached *the time of love* (*'ēt dōdîm*) or love-making,[352] i.e., marriageable age.

Yahweh *spread* his skirt over her, a gesture that was, apparently, part of the ancient marriage ceremony[353] (cf. Ruth 3:9). God thereby covered the nakedness of his bride, i.e., he provided for Jerusalem's needs. He entered into a marriage covenant with Jerusalem. God chose Jerusalem for a special relationship when David brought the ark of the covenant there (2 Sam 6). Later David purchased a threshing floor in Jerusalem that became the site for God's temple (2 Sam 24).

God treated his young bride most tenderly. He first washed her with water. The *blood* that is washed from the bride is surely not the blood of childbirth mentioned in v 4, or menstrual blood (Cooke).[354] It is probably the blood of virginal bleeding caused by initial coitus.[355] He then anointed her with oil.

---

[352]The *time of love* was not just when the girl was sexually mature, but when she became psychologically capable of responding to the love of her suitor.

[353]Brownlee (*Word Biblical Commentary*, 225) takes the expression to mean: "I opened my robe to you." "Such an act belonged to the consummation of marriage.... This is traditional, not indecent language."

[354]Marriage could not take place at the time of the menses (Lv 15:19-24; Ezek 18:6).

[355]Brownlee (*Word Biblical Commentary*, 225). The bride (or her father) saved the blood-stained garment or bed sheet as a cherished proof of her virginity at the time of her marriage (Dt 22:13-21).

B. Adornment (16:10-13a)

I clothed you with woven work. I shod you with sealskin. I bound you with fine linen. I covered you with silk. 11 I adorned you with ornaments. I put bracelets upon your hands, and a chain upon your neck. 12 I put a ring upon your nose and earrings upon your ears and a beautiful turban upon your head. 13 And you were decked with gold and silver, and your garments were of fine linen, silk, and woven work. You ate fine flour, honey and oil.

God clothed his bride with the finest garments from head to toe. He placed jewelry upon her wrists, neck, nose and ears. As befitting her queenly position a beautiful crown was placed on her head. She ate the finest foods.

C. Reputation (16:13b-14)

You became more and more beautiful until you achieved royal rank. 14 Your reputation went forth among the nations for your beauty, for it was perfect through my splendor that I put upon you (oracle of Lord Yahweh).

Jerusalem became ever more beautiful until she finally *achieved royal rank*, i.e., became the Queen City of the Near East during the days of Solomon. The *beauty*—the power and prosperity—of the nation was spoken of among other nations. Whatever greatness was achieved by Jerusalem, however, was not self-earned. It was bestowed by her divine husband. She reflected the splendor of God.

Ungrateful Wife
16:15-19

But you trusted in your beauty and committed harlotry because of your reputation. You poured out your harlotries upon all who passed by; it belonged to him. 16 You took from your garments, and made for yourself high places decked with different colors. You committed harlotry upon them. They are not coming, and it will not lie. 17 You took your fair jewels of my gold and my silver that I had given to you. You made for yourself images of men, and committed harlotry with them. 18 You took your woven garments and you covered them. My oil and my incense you placed before them. 19 My bread that I gave to you—fine flour, oil and honey that I fed you—you set before them for a sweet savor. Thus it was (oracle of Lord Yahweh).

Ezekiel points out three ways in which the beautiful bride had fallen out of favor with her divine husband. First, Jerusalem had misplaced trust. The beautiful bride proved unfaithful to the marriage covenant with God. Instead of trusting him she began to *trust* in her beauty, i.e., her material prosperity. She thought she could follow her instincts without regard to the moral demands of her divine husband. Self-trust is the first step in committing iniquity (cf. 33:13). Jerusalem *committed harlotry*[356] with foreign nations and their gods.

Jerusalem committed harlotry because of her *reputation.* She found herself popular. The eyes of the nations were cast on Jerusalem because of her material prosperity and strategic location. In response to Yahweh's gracious passing by (cf. vv 6, 8) Jerusalem lavished her harlotry on all who *passed by*. She readily responded to every proffer of love, i.e., she took up with every form of idolatry. *It belonged to him* refers to the beauty or devotion of Jerusalem belonging to the one who passed by. The reference is probably to the glory of Solomon's era, that king's entanglement in foreign alliances, and toleration of the pagan practices of his many wives.

Second, Jerusalem became guilty of misplaced wealth. The garments given to her by her divine Husband (i.e., material blessings) were used to make and decorate high places. There Jerusalem pursued her idolatrous lust. The repetition of *you took* (vv 16, 17, 18, 20) stresses that Jerusalem's involvement in idolatry was an act of free choice. The last expression in v 16 is difficult: *they* (feminine) *are not coming and it* (masculine) *will not be*. Perhaps these words express disgust at the lewdness of Jerusalem.

Jewelry of gold and silver had been melted down and fashioned into idols (cf. Hos 2:10)—*images of men* with whom the adulterous wife might commit her harlotry. The images were dressed with the rich garb that God had given his bride.

Third, Jerusalem was guilty of misplaced worship. Oil and incense, God's gifts to his people, were given as offerings to the lifeless idols. The rich foods God had given his bride were set before these idols in various pagan rituals to serve as a *sweet savor*, i.e., something to satisfy the appetite of the gods. *Thus it was*, God says; it cannot be denied.

---

[356]The metaphor of harlotry, in its noun and verb forms, is used 21x in Ezek 16. It highlights Israel's unfaithfulness to the covenant relationship, violating the first two commandments of the Decalogue. Lind, *Ezekiel*, 132.

Adulteress
16:20-34

A. Child Sacrifice (16:20-22)

You took your sons and your daughters whom you bore unto me, and you sacrificed them to them to be devoured. Were your harlotries a small matter, 21 that you slaughtered my children, and gave them up, in causing them to pass (through the fire) to them? 22 In all of your abominations and harlotries you did not remember the days of your youth when you were naked and bare, and you were wallowing in your blood.

As God's wife Jerusalem had a responsibility to rear her children in the fear of Yahweh. Some of these precious little ones, however, had been slaughtered and *devoured* (lit., "eaten"),[357] i.e., immolated in the worship of the god Molech.[358] Not satisfied with the lewd rites of Canaanite worship Jerusalem went the whole way even to the horrible extreme[359] of slaughtering children. These children belonged to God in a special way. Parents do not have absolute rights over the lives of their children.

The bride of God had sunk to this extreme because she failed to remember the days of her youth when she was *naked* (*'ērōm*) and *bare* (*'eryāh*). If from time to time she had called to mind her humble origins she surely would not have been guilty of these abominations.

B. Canaanite Shrines (16:23-25)

It came to pass after all your evil—woe, woe to you (oracle of Lord Yahweh)—24 that you built for yourself a platform, and you made for yourself a high place in every street. 25 At every head of the way you have built your lofty place, and you have made your beauty an abomination. You have opened your feet to everyone that passed by. You have multiplied your harlotries.

---

[357]Eating is commonly used in Hebrew to express a devouring fire. Hence it also means "to be burned up" or immolated.

[358]Warnings against this practice are found in Lv 18:21, 24 and Dt 18:9f. Ahaz of Judah seems to have introduced the practice (2 Kgs 16:3). During the reign of Manasseh the practice was widespread (2 Kgs 21:6).

[359]Verse 21 suggests that the children were first slain then burnt. *Pass through the fire* appears to be a euphemism for child immolation.

As the prophet contemplates the fate in store for Jerusalem as a result of her wickedness he bursts forth in a lament—*Woe, Woe unto you!* He then expands upon the theme of the wickedness of Jerusalem.

Jerusalem built a *platform* (*gebh*)[360] in every street, obviously some accommodation for the practice of idolatry. The term *high place* (*rāmāh*) seems to refer to a lofty shrine (NIV), perhaps a roof-top chamber of some kind. *At every head of the way*, i.e., intersection of every thoroughfare, the idols were conspicuous. The bride of God had put her beauty to an abominable use. She had spread her feet, i.e., committed prostitution, with *everyone who passed by*. She had taken up with every pagan cult with which she had come in contact

C. Egyptian Influence (16:26-27)

You committed harlotry with the Egyptians, your neighbors, great of flesh. You multiplied your harlotry to provoke me. 27 Behold I have stretched out my hand against you. I have diminished your allowance. I have delivered you into the will of those who hate you, the daughters of the Philistines, who are ashamed of your lewd way.

Jerusalem did not even confine her spiritual harlotries to Canaanite worship ways. Through foreign alliances she became involved with the gods of more distant powers. Spiritual harlotry with the sensuous (*great of flesh*[361]) Egyptians,[362] whose worship was characterized by obscene idolatries, was perhaps the climax of Jerusalem's degeneration. The tendency to worship so many foreign gods was motivated not so much by lust for forbidden forms of worship as by a subconscious desire to provoke and defy Yahweh.

Because of these acts of infidelity God stretched out his hand over Jerusalem for the purpose of inflicting punishment. As a betrayed husband might withdraw or reduce an unfaithful wife's maintenance (cf. Hos 2:11) so God reduced the portion he originally had

---

[360]So NRSV. Other translations render "mound" (NIV; JB); "vaulted place/chamber" (ASV; BV); "couch" (NEB); "shrine" (NASB). The LXX understood the word to refer to a brothel, and Brownlee (*Word Biblical Commentary,* 232) has adopted this view.

[361]So ASV. English versions struggle with this striking metaphor: "lustful neighbors" (NIV; BV; NASB; NRSV); "gross neighbors" (NEB); "big-membered neighbors" (JB). The distended male organ is a figure for the overly extended ambitions of the Egyptians who dreamed of restoring their ancient empire.

[362]Political involvement with Egypt was condemned by Hosea of Israel (12:1) and Isaiah of Judah (ch 20; 30:1-7; 31:1-3; 36:6-9).

assigned to Jerusalem. The reference here is probably to the territorial incursions by foreign nations against Israel from the days of Solomon to the time of Ezekiel. At the time the prophet spoke these words tiny Judah occupied only a fraction of the territory that God had given to Jerusalem of old. So weak were the people of God that their ancient archenemies the Philistines[363] were now able to satisfy their desire for revenge.[364] Ezekiel adds sarcastically that even the ruthless Philistines were ashamed of the disgraceful conduct of Jerusalem.

D. Mesopotamian Influence (16:28-29)

You committed harlotry with the Assyrians without having enough. You committed harlotry with them, and yet you were not satisfied. 29 You multiplied your harlotries with the land of merchants—Chaldea--but yet you were not satisfied.

Assyria and Chaldea,[365] the two great commercial centers, were among Jerusalem's lovers; but still the unfaithful wife could not find spiritual satisfaction.

E. Utter Degradation (16:30-34)

How weak is your heart (oracle of Lord Yahweh) when you do all these things, the work of a wanton harlot. 31 When you built your platforms at the head of every way, and have made your lofty place in every street, and you were not like the harlot who seeks more pay. 32 O woman that commits adultery who takes strangers instead of her husband! 33 To all harlots gifts are given; but you have given your gifts to all your lovers. You have bribed them to come unto you from round about in your harlotries. 34 You are different from other women in that you solicited to harlotry, and you were not solicited. In that you paid the wages of prostitution rather than the wages of prostitution being given to you, so you were different.

How morally weak and degenerate was the heart of God's once lovely wife! She had become a *wanton* (lit., "domineering") *harlot*, virtually a nymphomaniac whose promiscuous lust has caused her to

---

[363]It is generally understood that *daughters* of the Philistines refers to Philistine cities.
[364]Lind (*Ezekiel*, 133) takes the reference to be to the Philistine threat to Israel in the days of Samuel and Saul.
[365]Judah's association with Assyria began in the reign of King Ahaz during the Syro-Ephraimite war in 734-732 BC (2 Kgs 16:5-18). Flirtation with Chaldea probably dates to Hezekiah's reception of the envoys from Babylon. The envoys were attempting to stir up revolt against Assyria (2 Kgs 20:12-19).

reverse the usual order in prostitution. Unlike the ordinary harlot the profit motive did not figure in Jerusalem's spiritual liaison. Jerusalem prostituted herself not for gain, but to satisfy her unbridled lust.

The picture is pathetic. Jerusalem was unwilling to be a wife to her husband, but anxious for intimate association with strange gods and foreign lands. Rather than receiving gifts as is common with women of the street Jerusalem actually bribed lovers, i.e., she solicited alliances with foreign nations.

Punishment
16:35-43

:

The verdict of the judge is introduced by a double *therefore* (vv 35, 37). The first *therefore* is followed by *because* and then a reiteration of the charge of harlotry. The second *therefore* introduces the actual sentence.

A. Reason for Judgment (16:35-38)

Therefore O harlot, hear the word of Yahweh! 36 Thus says Lord Yahweh: Because your filthiness was poured out, and your nakedness revealed through your harlotry with your lovers, and because of all the idols of your abominations, and for the blood of your sons that you gave to them, 37 therefore behold I am about to gather your lovers unto whom you have been pleasant, and all whom you have loved along with all whom you hate; I will gather them against you round about, and I will reveal your nakedness unto them that they may see all your nakedness. 38 I will judge you with the judgments accorded adulteresses and those who shed blood. I will bring upon you the blood of fury and jealousy.

Because of all her spiritual adultery with foreign nations, her abominable idols and her revolting sacrifice of little children to those idols God will bring judgment upon Judah. Jerusalem's *lovers* are nations with whom she had a treaty and those other nations with whom treaties had been broken. These nations will be used by God to bring national humiliation upon his people. The land will be stripped bare by these forces. Jerusalem's nakedness thus will be exposed to public view.

The punishment of Jerusalem is described in terms of the punishment of an adulteress. An adulteress was executed publicly. Accusers started the bloody work. Others then joined in (cf. Dt 13:10).

So Jerusalem's *lovers* (nations with whom she had political ties) will summon other nations to join in the attack upon her.

Adulteresses and child murderers were judged most harshly under the Law of Moses. The same severe judgment was now about to be brought against Jerusalem. Only the blood of the guilty could assuage the divine fury and jealousy.

B. Result of Judgment (16:39-42)

I will give you into their hand. They will throw down your eminent places, and break down your lofty places. They will strip you of your garments and take your fair jewels. They will leave you naked and bare. 40 They will bring up an assembly against you. They will pelt you with stones, and will thrust you through with swords. 41 They will burn your daughters with fire. They will execute judgments against you in the sight of many women. I will cause you to cease from being a harlot. Also the wages of prostitution you will not give anymore. 42 So I will cause my wrath against you to rest. My jealousy will turn from you. I will be quiet, and will no more be vexed.

To accomplish that judgment God will use foreign nations, those who once were Jerusalem's lovers. This ruthless force will destroy the *eminent places* used in idolatrous rites. Enemy soldiers will strip the adulterous wife of clothing and jewels. They will leave her naked, i.e., Jerusalem will see her buildings destroyed and her wealth carried away.

Stoning was the penalty for adultery (Lv 20:10). Jerusalem will be bombarded by the missiles of the enemies as well as thrust through by their swords. Houses and public buildings will be burned. Many women, i.e., neighboring nations, will witness the execution. Hopefully they will learn a lesson from it.[366]

With the destruction of Jerusalem God will bring the harlotry of the nation to an abrupt end. No longer will Jerusalem be in a position to bribe neighbors for their friendship. Divine justice must punish such unfaithfulness as Jerusalem manifested. Only after the wrath and jealousy (zeal) of God had been satisfied could there be hope of reconciliation.

[366]It seems to have been the practice to make other women witness the execution of an adulteress as a warning.

C. Reason for Judgment (16:43)

Because you have not remembered the days of your youth, and you have made me angry with all of these things; therefore also, behold I will bring your way on your head (oracle of Lord Yahweh); or have you not done this lewdness above all your abominations?

The calamities outlined in the previous vv will befall Jerusalem because she had forgotten her past; she was ungrateful for what God had done for her.

PARABLE OF THREE SISTERS 16:44-52

Introduction of the Sisters 16:44-47

A. Observation (16:44-45a)

Behold everyone who employs proverbs will use this proverb against you, saying, As the mother, so the daughter. 45 You are the daughter of your mother who loathes her husband and her sons. You are the sister of your sisters who loathe their husbands and their children.

When the judgment fell no one will be able to say that it was unjust. In years to come those who specialized in proverbs will say concerning sinful Jerusalem, *as the mother, so the daughter*.

B. Accusation (16:45b-47)

Your mother was a Hittite and your father was an Amorite. 46 Your older sister is Samaria—she and her daughters—who dwell on your left hand. Your younger sister on your right side is Sodom and her daughters. 47 Yet you did not walk in their ways. You have not done after their abominations. But in a very little while you acted more corruptly than they in all your ways.

Jerusalem was unfaithful in marriage and as a mother. The *children* are literal children, as in vv 20-22. Likewise the *husbands* here are not gods or Yahweh (as in ch 23), but the human fathers of the children in these cities. Jerusalem and her sisters personify the married female population of Jerusalem, Samaria, and Sodom; the married men collectively are the husbands of these mothers. The point is that in sacrificing their children the mothers have condemned the fathers of the children as well.[367]

Jerusalem learned her ways from her mother and father, the *Hittite* and the *Amorite*. She had followed in the path of her older sister Samaria and her younger sister Sodom. Samaria is Judah's *elder sister*[368] because she was larger in size and more numerous in population. She is on the *left*, i.e., north of Judah. The *younger sister* on the right side (south) of Judah is *Sodom*. The *daughters* of Samaria and Sodom are subordinate towns.

For only *a very little while* after the fall of Samaria—during the reign of Hezekiah—Judah did not walk in the abominations of Samaria and Sodom. After that short pause in her ugly history, however, Judah acted more corruptly than either of her sinful sisters.

Sins of the Sisters
16:48-52

A. Sodom (16:48-50)

As I live (oracle of Lord Yahweh) Sodom your sister—she and her daughters—has not done as you have done, you and your daughters. 49 Behold this was the iniquity of Sodom your sister: pride, fullness of bread and careless ease were in her and in her daughters. She did not strengthen the hand of the poor and the needy. 50 They became haughty and committed abomination before me. Therefore I removed them when I saw it.

In vv 48-52 the comparison between the sins of the three sisters—Sodom, Samaria and Jerusalem—continues. Even sinful Sodom had not surpassed the sin of Jerusalem.

The root of Sodom's sin was *pride* that grew out of her security and prosperity. Genesis (18:20-21; 19:13) uses the word "outcry" to characterize the sin committed by Sodom. This word usually refers to the outcry of the oppressed. The outcry erupted because the Sodomites did not *strengthen the hand of the poor and needy*, i.e., they did not offer material assistance nor did they give any encouragement.

The Sodomites became so *haughty* that they *committed abomination* in the sight of God. He, therefore, *removed* (i.e., abolished) *them* after their sins came under his judicial inspection. The words *I saw it*

---

[367]Brownlee, *Word Biblical Commentary*, 246.

[368]The *sister* image may have been influenced by Jer 3:6-14.

hark back to Gn 18:20. They allude to what Yahweh saw in Sodom in Gn 19:1-9. The homosexual attack by the Sodomites was the ultimate manifestation of the haughty oppression that characterized the men of that place. [369]

B. Samaria and Jerusalem (16:51-52)

As for Samaria, she did not sin half as much as you. Actually you increased your abominations more than they while you vindicated your sisters in all the abominations that you did. 52 You also bear your own shame in which you have judged your sister. Through your sins in which you have been more abominable than they; they have been more righteous than you, yes, you! Be ashamed! Bear your guilt in your vindication of your sisters.

Samaria had not committed even half the sins committed by Jerusalem. In fact, in comparison to Jerusalem's guilt Sodom and Samaria appeared almost righteous (cf. Amos 3:9-10). Sins committed in Jerusalem were worse than those committed in Samaria and Sodom. The greater guilt results from greater revelation. Ezekiel commands Jerusalem to *bear your own shame*, i.e., she must accept as just the punishment that she is already experiencing.

How ashamed Jerusalem ought to be of her gross sin that will cause men to render a favorable judgment with regard to Samaria and Sodom. Jerusalem has been more *abominable* than her sisters. In suffering for her sin Jerusalem would bring *vindication* to her sisters. God had merciful long-range intentions for Jerusalem. His justice requires that he must show the same kindness to the lesser offenders.

Future of the Sisters
16:53-63

A. Future of Sodom and Samaria (16:53-55)

And I will turn their captivity, the captivity of Sodom and her daughters, and the captivity of Samaria and her daughters, and the captivity of your captives in the midst of them. 54 [This I will do] in order that you may bear your own shame, and may be ashamed because of all that you have done in comforting them. 55 And your sisters—Sodom and her daughters—will return to their former

---

[369]Following Brownlee, *Word Biblical Commentary*, 248.

state. Samaria and her daughters will return to their former state. You and your daughters will return to your former slate.

Sodom and Samaria have a future.[370] God will *turn their captivity* (i.e., restore their fortunes) and that of Jerusalem as well *in the midst of them*, i.e., between Samaria to the north and Sodom to the south. Sodom and Samaria represent the peoples who once lived in those cities. Samaria represents the old northern kingdom of Israel, the survivors of which were known as Samaritans in New Testament times. Sodom represents the Gentile population that had not been fully assimilated into the political structure of Israel. Many of these "Canaanites" worshiped Yahweh along with other gods. Ezekiel envisioned the day when such aliens, cleansed and converted (cf. Jer 12:16), will have equal standing as part of the people of God (cf. 47:22-23).

The purpose in changing the fortunes of Samaria and Sodom is so that Jerusalem may experience shame for past sin. The Jews (represented by Jerusalem) will come to see the depth of sin that brought on the destruction of the temple and the exile to Babylon. The thought of the v is similar to the thought in Rom 11:11-12.

If God restores Jerusalem he must also restore the two sisters for they had sinned less. The three sister cities are depicted returning to their *former state*, i.e., their former situation in their heyday. Ezekiel is speaking of spiritual transformation under images of physical reconstruction.

B. Immediate Future of Jerusalem (16:56-58)

For Sodom your sister was not mentioned by your mouth in the day of your pride; 57 before your wickedness was uncovered, as at the time of the reproach of the daughters of Aram and all that are round about her, the daughters of the Philistines who despise you round about. 58 You have borne your lewdness and your abominations (oracle of Yahweh).

In hypocritical self-righteousness Judah in former days would not so much as mention the name of Sodom. *In the day of your pride* recalls the heyday of Jerusalem. That pride led to Jerusalem's overthrow.

Judah's own wickedness was *uncovered*, i.e., made public, through divine judgment. Humbled Judah became the object of disdain by the singers in Aram and Philistia. The particular occasion

---

[370]This is the first of two restorations of Gentile peoples in Ezekiel. Cf. 29:13-16.

here mentioned is probably the humiliating and devastating Syro-Ephraimite invasion of Judah in the days of Ahaz.[371]

Judah already had suffered, and will yet suffer, for her infidelity. *Lewdness* (*zimmāh*) and *abominations* (*tō*[a]*bhōt*) hark back to the catalogue of crimes mentioned in vv 2-43.

C. Long-range Future of God's People (16:59-63)

For thus says Lord Yahweh: I will deal with you as you have done, you who has despised the oath to break the covenant. 60 Nevertheless, I will remember my covenant with you in the days of your youth. I will establish for you an everlasting covenant. 61 You will remember your ways. You will be ashamed when you receive your sisters, the older and the younger. I will give them to you for daughters, but not because of your covenant. 62 I will establish my covenant with you. You will know that I am Yahweh. 63 [This I will do] in order that you might remember and be ashamed, and never again open your mouth because of your shame when I have forgiven you of all which you have done (oracle of Lord Yahweh).

Words of comfort follow the condemnation and threat of the preceding vv. God could not ignore the adulterous behavior of his wife Jerusalem. She had broken the marriage *covenant*; she must suffer the consequences.

God will *remember* that covenant[372] that he had made with Jerusalem in the *youth* of the city, i.e., in the days of David. God remembers this covenant, not because he is bound by law to do so, but because he yearns for that relationship. After judgment God will enter into a new covenant—an *everlasting covenant*—with his people.[373] This covenant can be everlasting because of the new heart and the new spirit that are associated with this covenant (11:19-20; 36:25-28).

How ashamed Judah will be of her sordid past in that new day. God's grace in overlooking past sin, making a new covenant with his people, and even bestowing upon them Sodom and Samaria, will arouse in them a deep sense of remorse. This reinstatement of Jerusalem has nothing to do with the old Sinai covenant. That covenant had been broken. The new covenant will be with converted sinners, whether Jew, Samaritan or Gentile (Sodom). Samaria and Sodom be-

---

[371]See 2 Chr 28:5, 18.

[372]Jerusalem did not *remember* the days of her youth (16:22), but God will *remember* his covenant with Israel.

[373]Cf. Ezek 37:26; Jer 31:30ff.

come *daughters* of the new Jerusalem, i.e., all three are part of a unified land or kingdom (cf. 37:15-22).

The establishment of a new covenant is a sovereign act of God. This is emphasized by the pronoun *I* (emphatic in the Hebrew). Through the gracious provisions for the Jerusalem of the new covenant (Heb 12:22) men will learn about the nature of the God of the Bible.[374]

The unfathomable grace of God in forgiving past sin will forever silence any self-justification.

Special Study
RESTORATION OF SODOM

Ezekiel's allusion to *turning the captivity* of Samaria and Sodom (16:53, 55) has occasioned commentators great difficulty. The prophet seems to be saying that Sodom, which was destroyed in the days of Abraham, and Samaria, which had been carried away into captivity in 722 BC, will be restored as well as Jerusalem. There is no parallel in Scripture to the restoration of Sodom; but the Bible does point to the restoration of other evil nations surrounding Israel (cf. Jer 12:14-17). But how could Sodom that was obliterated without survivor be restored? Six different answers to this question have been given:

1. Currey and Ellicott deny that the passage contains any promise of restoration for Sodom. These commentators understand 16:53 to be underscoring the hopelessness of Jerusalem's punishment. Only when Sodom was restored—something manifestly impossible—will Jerusalem be restored. Yet it does appear in this passage that some kind of restoration is promised, or at least implied, for Sodom. Besides, if the prophet is saying that Jerusalem will never be restored he will be contradicting, not only other prophets, but his own predictions as well.

2. Feinberg sees here a prediction of a literal rebuilding of Sodom and the cities of the plain. During the Millennium these cities will be restored. But how can Sodom and her daughters be restored when all the inhabitants of that area have been swept off the face of

[374] This is the third time in the book that the recognition formula is the result of grace rather than judgment (cf. 12:16; 14:22-23).

the earth? Feinberg limply replies: ". . . the restoration of Sodom will pose no difficulty for the omnipotence of God."[375]

3. The renowned German commentator Keil insists that the passage must refer to literal Sodom. Keil, however, does not see here an earthly restoration. He contends that ". . . the realization of the prophecy must be sought for beyond the present order of things, in one that extends into life everlasting."[376] Keil is thus ambiguous about the fulfillment. Surely this passage does not refer to those Sodomite sinners who endure eternal fire (Jude 7). Keil's proposed fulfillment of the passage borders on universalism.

4. Payne suggests that the postexilic occupation of the Dead Sea area by the Jews constitutes a reasonable fulfillment to the prediction.[377] It is difficult, however, to see how this could constitute a reversal of the fortunes of Sodom.

5. Still others regard Sodom as symbolic of the descendants of Sodom. Ammon and Moab were born to Lot's daughters who had escaped from the destruction of Sodom (Gn 19:29-30). The restoration of Sodom will in reality be the restoration of Moab and Ammon. Jeremiah 20:16 refers to the cities of the plain as "the cities that Yahweh overthrew and repented not." This statement seems to preclude a literal, physical restoration of Sodom. Jeremiah, however, does predict the restoration of Ammon and Moab (48:47; 49:6). A.R. Fausset develops this view as follows:

> Probably Ammon and Moab were in part restored under Cyrus; but the full realization of the restoration is yet future; the heathen nations to be brought to Christ being typified by "Sodom," whose sins they now reproduce.[378]

6. Perhaps Sodom represents the heathen in general—all that survived of the Canaanites and their culture. The thrust of the passage is not the restoration of *cities*, but of rightful *inhabitants*. Ellison[379] points out that Samaria never actually ceased to be a city. Sargon, the conqueror of Samaria, immediately rebuilt and repopulated the place.

---

[375]Feinberg, *Ezekiel*, 91.
[376]Keil, *Biblical Commentary*, 1:228.
[377]Barton Payne, *Encyclopedia of Biblical Prophecy* (New York: Harper and Row, 1973), 359.
[378]A.R. Fausset, "Ezekiel" in *A Commentary: Critical, Experimental, and Practical* (Hartford, Conn.: S.S. Scranton), 1877), 4:257.
[379]Ellison, *Ezekiel*, 66.

Thus the prophecy must be talking about changing the fortunes of the *inhabitants* of Jerusalem, Samaria, and Sodom. God must punish wicked men; but his mercy is such that he must provide for the deliverance of even the greatest sinners.

Ezekiel is filled with the thought of the *spiritual conversion* of wicked people like Sodom. He expresses this thought concretely in terms of a reversal of the fortunes for Sodom (i.e., gross sinners). Sodom and Samaria will be given to Jerusalem as daughters (v 61). Citizens of the former northern kingdom and heathen in general will become part of that new covenant Jerusalem (Heb 12:22).

EZEKIEL 17
LOWLY VINE AND STATELY CEDAR

In ch 17 Ezekiel contrasts the current ruler in Jerusalem with the future son of David who will lead God's people. The former is compared to a lowly vine (vv 1-21), the latter to a stately cedar (vv 22-24). This ch consists of two parables separated by an announcement of judgment (vv 16-21).

EAGLE PARABLE
17:1-15

King Zedekiah committed an act of treachery against Nebuchadnezzar by breaking his solemn oath of allegiance to Babylon. He sought military aid from Egypt. In this oracle, delivered shortly before 586 BC, Ezekiel predicts the removal of Zedekiah's dynasty and the fall of Jerusalem. He first presents his parable (vv 1-10) and then makes an application of what he has said (vv 11-21).

Parable Presented
17:1-10

A. Introduction (17:1-2)

The word of Yahweh came unto me, saying, 2 Son of man, put forth a riddle and speak a parable unto the house of Israel...

A *riddle* (*chîdāh*) is a dark utterance, something put indirectly and in need of interpretation. A *parable* (*māšāl*) or allegory is the presentation of spiritual truths through physical forms. Here the two words are essentially synonymous. Riddles were used in international politics in the Near East. A king might lose his independence (or even his life) if he could not solve the riddle posed to him by another king. Here the heavenly king puts forth the riddle. King Zedekiah must solve it. If he does not he will lose his independence to the agents of Yahweh.[380]

B. First Great Eagle (17:3-6)

And say, Thus says Lord Yahweh: A great eagle with great wings and long pinions, full of feathers of various colors came unto Lebanon and took the top of the cedar. 4 He broke off the topmost of its twigs, and carried it unto a land of commerce. He set it in a city of merchants. 5 Moreover he took from the seed of the land and set it in a fruitful field. He set it as a stalk[381] alongside many waters as a willow. 6 It sprouted and became a spreading vine of low stature whose tendrils turned toward him, and whose roots were under him. So it became a vine. It brought forth branches and put forth sprigs.

The *great eagle*[382] is the mighty King Nebuchadnezzar who is king of kings, even as the eagle is the king of birds. Like the eagle Nebuchadnezzar swooped down upon his prey to plunder and destroy.[383] His *great wings* enabled him to fly long distances, and extend his influence over vast territories. The various colors of this great bird may represent the many different nations that were subject to Nebuchadnezzar. These nations contributed to his military might.

---

[380]Harry Torczyner, "The Riddle in the Bible," *HUCA* 1 (1924): 125-49.

[381]The Hebrew is difficult. The rabbinic understanding of the v has been followed here.

[382]Use of the eagle/vulture to symbolize God's judgment can be traced to Dt 28:49. This bird points to the swiftness of a conquering army (Isa 46:11; Jer 48:40; 49:22).

[383]Cf. Isa 46:11; Jer 48:40; Hos 8:1.

Lebanon represents the land of Israel, and especially the kingdom of Judah. The *cedar* represents Jerusalem. The *top of the cedar* stands for the nobility of the city, especially the princes of the house of David.

Nebuchadnezzar broke off the *topmost* of the twigs of the cedar. This twig clearly represents the youthful King Jehoiachin who was carried off by Nebuchadnezzar in 597 BC. Jehoiachin was taken to *a land of commerce,* i.e., Chaldea, and *a city of merchants*, i.e., Babylon.

Nebuchadnezzar set up the *seed of the land*, i.e., a member of the royal family. In place of Jehoiachin Nebuchadnezzar appointed Zedekiah as king of Judah. The *fruitful field* in which the seed was planted must be Judah. Beside *many waters* is probably a reference to Babylon (cf. Jer 51:13). Although Nebuchadnezzar put Zedekiah on the throne he was dependent on Babylon, like a stalk is dependent on the moisture of a near-by stream.

The *spreading vine of low stature* must depict the Judean vassal state administered by Zedekiah. The tendrils of this vine turned toward (and the roots were under) the eagle (Nebuchadnezzar). Zedekiah was given only limited authority. As long as the vine maintained this posture it prospered, at least in a measure.

C. Second Great Eagle (17:7-8)

There was another great eagle with great wings and many feathers. Behold this vine bent its roots unto him, and put forth its tendrils toward him to water it from the beds of its plantation. 8 In a good field by many waters it was planted that it might produce branches and bear fruit, that it might be a glorious vine.

The second *great eagle* is Pharaoh. To Pharaoh Hophra the vine (Zedekiah) turned for military aid in an attempt to free itself from the influence of the first eagle (Nebuchadnezzar). This spreading toward the direction of the second eagle (Egypt) was unnatural and unnecessary. The vine should have prospered and even could have produced *fruit*—children of Zedekiah—to carry on the royal succession.

D. Fate of the Vine (17:9-10)

Say, Thus says Lord Yahweh: Will it prosper? Will he not pull up its roots, and cut off its fruit that it wither, that it wither in all its sprouting leaves? Neither will great power nor many people be at hand when it is plucked up by its roots. 10 Behold being planted,

will it prosper? When the east wind touches it will it not utterly wither? In the beds where it sprouted it will wither.

The allegory concludes with four rhetorical questions. The repetition underscores the futility of Zedekiah's duplicity. How could the vine (Zedekiah) prosper when it had tried to spread beyond its prescribed domain? The first great eagle will uproot the vine. He will cut off its fruit so that it will completely wither and die. Zedekiah's reign will be terminated. All the heirs to the throne will be killed. The nobles of Judah will perish. No great power or army of soldiers will be at hand to thwart the great eagle in its vengeful attack. That Judean vine will utterly wither right in the spot where it was planted when the scorching *east wind* (Babylonian Empire) began to blow against it.

Parable Explained
17:11-15

Moreover the word of Yahweh came unto me, saying, 12 Say now to the rebellious house, Do you not know what these things mean? Say: The king of Babylon came to Jerusalem and took its king and its princes. He brought them to him in Babylon. 13 He took of the royal seed and made a covenant with him. He brought him under an oath; but the mighty of the land he took away. 14 He made it a lowly kingdom that it might not lift itself up, but that by keeping his covenant it might stand. 15 But he rebelled against him in sending his ambassadors to Egypt that he might give to him horses and much people. Will he prosper? Will the one who does these things escape? Will he break the covenant and escape?

So that the meaning of his parable will be absolutely clear Ezekiel was commanded to offer an interpretation of it to that rebellious house (the kingdom of Judah). He begins with a rhetorical question that is designed to rebuke the spiritual obtuseness of his hearers. He asked, Do you not know what these things mean? Nebuchadnezzar had carried away the princes of Judah (top of the cedar) and King Jehoiachin (the topmost of the twigs) to Babylon in 597 BC.

After deposing the youthful Jehoiachin Nebuchadnezzar took the seed royal, i.e., Zedekiah the son of Josiah and uncle of Jehoiachin, and placed him upon the throne in Jerusalem. Zedekiah was placed under a solemn oath taken in the name of God to be loyal to Nebuchadnezzar. The mighty of the land, i.e., influential leaders, were carried to Babylon as hostages so as to guarantee Zedekiah's compliance to the terms of his oath or covenant. Nebuchadnezzar's purpose was to keep Judah weak and subservient.

Disregarding his sacred oath Zedekiah rebelled against Nebuchadnezzar by making overtures to Egypt (the second eagle). He sought military aid from Pharaoh. Three rhetorical questions in v 15 underscore the futility of such a course.

ANNOUNCEMENT OF JUDGMENT 17:16-21

First Divine Oath 17:16-18

As I live (oracle of Lord Yahweh) surely in the place where the king caused him to reign, whose oath he despised and whose covenant he broke, with him in the midst of Babylon he will die. 17 Neither will Pharaoh with mighty army and great company assist him in the war, when they cast up mounds and build siege forts to cut off many lives. 18 Because he despised an oath by breaking a covenant (and behold he gave his hand), and has done all these things, he will not escape.

Under oath (*as I live*) Yahweh answers his own three questions (cf. v 15) with three statements. One could not break a sacred oath taken in the name of God and then expect any divine aid. The king against whom Zedekiah had committed treachery will haul him off to die in the midst of Babylon. Aid from Pharaoh will not be forthcoming when the Babylonians build their siege mounds and forts at Jerusalem. Egypt's reputation as an unreliable ally is based on Isa 36:6; cf. Jer 37:5-10).

Zedekiah *will not escape*. He had been required to take an oath by a heathen king. Therefore Zedekiah *despised* that oath and regarded it as non-binding. Nevertheless, he *gave his hand* as a pledge of faithful compliance with the terms of that oath.

Second Divine Oath 17:19-21

Therefore thus says Lord Yahweh: As I live surely my oath that he despised, and my covenant that he broke, I will even bring it upon his head. 20 I will spread my net over him. He will be taken in my snare. I will bring him to Babylon. I will plead with him there because of his treachery that he committed against me. 21 All his mighty men[384] in all his bands will fall by the sword. The rest will be scattered toward every wind; and you will know that I Yahweh have spoken it.

Zedekiah had taken his oath to Babylon in the name of God. It was, therefore, God's oath that he broke. So God takes an oath (*as I live* is an oath formula) for the second time that he will bring down on the head of Zedekiah the punishment for this treachery.

The rebellious king will be caught in the net of divine retribution. He will be carried off to Babylon. There God will *plead with him*, i.e., make him conscious of the serious crime he had committed against God.

The royal bodyguard that might try to protect Zedekiah from this fate will be slain or scattered by the Babylonians. When all these specific predictions came to pass all the Jews will realize that it was truly God who had spoken through the mouth of the prophet to oppose the rebellion against Babylon.

CEDAR TWIG PARABLE 17:22-24

Thus says Lord Yahweh: Moreover I, even I, will take of the top of the lofty cedar, and set it. I will break off from the topmost of its young twigs, a tender one. I will plant it upon a high and eminent mountain. 23 In the mountain of the height of Israel will I plant it. It will bring forth boughs and produce fruit. It will be a glorious cedar. Under it will dwell every bird of every wing. In the shadow of its branches will they dwell. 24 And all the trees of the field will know that I am Yahweh; I bring down the high tree, exalt the low

[384]This reading is supported by many Hebrew manuscripts. The standard (Masoretic) text reads "hid fugitives."

tree, dry up the green tree, and make the dry tree flourish. I am Yahweh; I have spoken, and I will perform it.

The message of doom in the preceding parable and application is tempered by a word of hope in vv 22-24. God in his sovereign grace is about to act.

Nebuchadnezzar had cut a twig from the cedar. He had removed it to far off Babylon (cf. vv 3f). God, however, will now cut a twig from that same royal cedar tree and plant it upon a high mountain. The basic idea is that the Davidic dynasty will be reinstated and will achieve a prominence that it had not heretofore enjoyed. The messianic king of the house of David is in view here.[385] Jesus of Nazareth now occupies the throne of God and rules over the new Israel of God.

The messianic twig will be prominent. It will be planted in the high mountain of Israel (cf. Isa 2:2). The cedar—messianic Jerusalem, the church of Christ—will be stately, i.e., dignified. It will bear fruit. Messiah heads a royal family of kings and priests (1 Pet 2:9). Many birds (different nations) will place themselves under the protection of this messianic monarch.

Looking back over God's dealings with Judah *the trees of the field* (Gentile nations) will come to recognize the sovereignty of Yahweh. He brings down *the high tree* and *green* (the Davidic dynasty and eventually Nebuchadnezzar). He exalts *the low* and *dry* tree (the Davidic dynasty after Zedekiah). They will recognize that what God announces he most certainly will perform.

EZEKIEL 18
BASIC DOCTRINES

In chs 18-19 Ezekiel brings to a close the long section of his book that began in ch 12. Two important doctrines are discussed in this ch. In vv 1-20 Ezekiel develops at length the doctrine of individual responsibility, and in vv 21-29 he implicitly affirms the doctrine of freedom of the will or self-determination.

---

[385]Some interpret this as a reference to the restoration under Zerubbabel, a descendant of Jehoiachin. Zerubbabel, however, was never a king.

PERSONAL RESPONSIBILITY
18:1-20

Ezekiel teaches that every individual is responsible for his own conduct before God. A person's fate is not determined by the goodness or wickedness of others, even his nearest of kin. The righteous are blessed by God. The wicked live under his curse.

General Principle
18:1-4

The word of Yahweh came unto me, saying, 2 What do you [pl] mean by making this proverb concerning the land of Israel, saying, The fathers have eaten sour grapes, but the teeth of the children have been set on edge? 3 As I live (oracle of Lord Yahweh) you will not make use of this parable any more in Israel. 4 Behold all souls are mine; as the soul of the father so also the soul of the son is mine. The soul that sins, it will die.

The sinners in Israel countered Ezekiel's parable (*māšāl*) by *making* (lit., "proverbing") a *proverb* (*mešālîm*) of their own. Sinful men always tend to underestimate their own wickedness. They blame their tribulations on others. So it was with the men of Israel. They attributed their suffering to the sins of their fathers. The *proverb* that was once current in Jerusalem (Jer 31:28) was now being heard in Babylon: *The fathers have eaten sour grapes*[386] (i.e., have sinned) *but the teeth of the children have been set on edge* (i.e., they were being punished).

Where did such an idea arise? Possibly from a misunderstanding of passages in the Law of Moses such as Ex 20:5 where God is said to visit the sins of the fathers on the children to the third and fourth generation. Or possibly the proverb arose out of the prophetic teaching that because of the sins of Manasseh the nation will be destroyed (2 Kgs 21:10-12). The former passage actually teaches that sin, even though forgiven, often has unavoidable repercussions in the lives of one's children. The latter passage indicates that the origin of Judah's sin was Manasseh. The following generation will be destroyed be-

---

[386]According to the Talmud, eating sour or unripe grapes was a widespread practice even though the results were less than appealing. Cf. Greenberg, *Anchor Bible*, 328.

cause it still practiced the grotesque idolatry introduced during Manasseh's reign.

The perverse proverb that in effect challenged the justice of God will no longer be employed. Experiences will prove it to be untrue.

God created all individuals. Though physically related the father and son are separate entities in his sight. Each must give account of himself to his Creator. The individual who sins will die. More than premature death is intended here. The sinner is dead in sin during his physical life. Eventually he experiences the second death.

Righteous Man
18:5-9

But if a man is righteous and practices justice and righteousness, 6 then he has not eaten upon the mountains, or lifted up his eyes to the idols of the house of Israel. He has not defiled the wife of his neighbor, or come near unto a menstruous woman. 7 He has not wronged any man, but has restored his pledge for a debt. He has seized nothing by robbery, and has given his bread to the hungry. He has covered the naked with a garment. 8 He has not given on interest, or taken increase. He has withdrawn his hand from iniquity, and executed true justice between man and man. 9 He has walked in my statutes, and kept my judgments to deal truly. He is righteous. He will surely live (oracle of Lord Yahweh).

The man who practices justice and righteousness lives under the blessing of God. This person is described in some detail in vv 5-9. The characteristics of a righteous person fall into four legal areas. First, in the cultic area the righteous man has not participated in the pagan rituals at the "high places." These rites normally involved eating of sacrificial meals (cf. Dt 12:2-4). *He has not lifted up his eyes to the idols*, i.e., offered prayer to them in expectation of aid. Baal is particularly in mind.

Second, in the area of sexual ethics the righteous man has not committed adultery in violation of the seventh commandment. He has *not come near,* i.e., sexually, *a menstruous woman.*[387] He has observed the sexual taboos of the Law of Moses (cf. Lv 18:19; 20:18; Dt

---

[387]Lind (*Ezekiel*, 150) points out the position of this demand to respect a woman's fertility cycle is placed between the law against adultery, that protects family structure, and the law against oppression, that protects equality. God's law protected certain sexual rights of women within the family.

22:22). Third, in the area of social ethics the righteous man has not engaged in any fraudulent dealings with his fellowman. He has complied with the law of Ex 22:25f. This law compelled creditors to return to borrowers any item of collateral that might be necessary to their well-being (cf. Dt 24:6; Amos 2:8). He has never resorted to violent robbery in order to enhance his wealth (cf. Ex 20:15; Lv 19:13). He has fed the hungry and clothed the naked (cf. Dt 15:7-11; 24:19-22; Isa 58:7).

Finally, in the area of business ethics the righteous man has not lent money on the express condition of receiving interest, nor has he accepted interest offered to him voluntarily by the debtor.[388] The laws on money lending are found in Ex 22:24; Lv 25:35ff; Dt 23:20. He has *withdrawn his hand from iniquity*. The sin probably intended here is giving false weight or measure (cf. Lv 19:35). As an arbiter of disputes he has been scrupulously fair.

In summary, the righteous person has *walked in my statutes* rather than in his own way, or in the ordinances of the nations. To the best of his ability he has observed the divine laws. He deals *truly*, i.e., his observance of God's law is motivated by love for the truth, not by any personal motive.

Wicked Son
18:10-13

If he begets a son who is a man of violence, who sheds blood, and who does to a brother any of these things 11 (whereas he himself had not done any of these things) for he has even eaten upon the mountains, and defiled his neighbor's wife. 12 He has wronged the poor and needy, and seized things by robbery. He has failed to return objects taken in pledge, lifted up his eyes to idols, and committed abomination. 13 He has made loans on interest, and has taken increase. Will he live? He will not live! He has done all these abominations. He will surely die. His blood will be on him.

The prophet describes a son who is the exact opposite of the righteous man described above. He is a man of violence who even commits murder. He is not beneath practicing any of the sins that his father so carefully avoided.

---

[388]Interest could be charged foreigners in commercial dealings, but Israelites were not to take advantage of a poor brother by charging interest on charitable loans.

Should such a wicked man escape divine retribution? Certainly not! The law required the death penalty for such crimes as murder, idolatry, and adultery.[389] The righteousness of his father could not save him. *His blood will be on him*, i.e., he alone bears responsibility for his life of sin. The executioner (Nebuchadnezzar?) will not be held guilty.

Penitent Son 18:14-19

Then behold he begets a son who sees all the sins his father has done. He considers and does not do any such thing. 15 He does not eat upon the mountains or lift up his eyes unto the idols of the house of Israel. He does not defile his neighbor's wife 16 or wrong a man. He does not he take a pledge or seize by robbery. He gives his bread to the hungry, and covers the naked with a garment. 17 He has withdrawn his hand from the poor, and has not taken interest or increase. He has executed my judgments, and walked in my statutes. He will not die in the iniquity of his father. He will surely live. 18 As for his father, because he cruelly oppressed, committed robbery against a brother, and did what is not good in the midst of his people, behold he will die in his iniquity. 19 But you say, Why does not the son bear the iniquity of the father? When the son has done what is just and righteous, has kept all my statutes, and has done them, he will surely live.

The third specific case cited by Ezekiel is that of a son who reflects upon the consequences of his father's sin. He resolves to abandon that sort of behavior.[390] The son does not participate in any of the activities that brought his father under civil and divine judgment. The son shows positive good will toward the less fortunate.

The son is not executed because of his father's sin. The father dies for his blatant iniquity, but the son is spared. This teaching absolutely refutes the notion current in Ezekiel's day that innocent children were punished for the sins of their fathers.

---

[389]Cf. Nm 35:16; Dt 17:5; Lv 20:10.

[390]Ezekiel's anonymous illustrations may have been triggered by the circumstances of good King Hezekiah, his wicked son, Manasseh, and his righteous great-grandson, Josiah.

Conclusion
18:20

The soul that sins it will die. The son will not bear the iniquity of the father, nor will the father bear the iniquity of the son. The righteousness of the righteous will be upon him, and the wickedness of the wicked will be upon him.

The lengthy treatise on personal responsibility reaches its climax in the crystal clear assertion of v 20. Wicked men bear the responsibility for themselves. They suffer the consequences of their wickedness. Neither iniquity nor righteousness is inherited. The individual's righteousness or wickedness will be upon him, i.e., he will bear the responsibility of his own conduct.

PERSONAL REPENTANCE
18:21-32

Ezekiel carries his subject one step further. Men are not locked in to a life of sin either genetically or environmentally. By the grace of God, and the assertion of their own free will, men can change their character, conduct and destiny. In these vv the basic thesis is that men are not punished for sins after they repent of them.

Penitent Sinner
18:21-23

But if the wicked one turns from all his sins that he has done, and keeps all my statutes, and deals justly and righteously, he will surely live. He will not die. 22 All of his transgressions that he has done will not be remembered against him. In his righteousness that he has done he will live. 23 Do I have delight in the death of the wicked? (oracle of Lord Yahweh); Is it not when he turns from his way and lives?

In genuine repentance there are two clearly defined steps, viz. turning from sin, and keeping the law of God. The Jewish rabbis speak of the essential elements of repentance being remorse and amendment. If a wicked man genuinely repents he will escape the divine death sentence.

Why does the penitent sinner escape judgment? The answer is simple: None of his former transgressions will be remembered against him. Sins not remembered are forgiven. Because of his present righteousness *he will live,* i.e., in communion with God and as a member of Yahweh's people.

God takes no delight in the fact that sinners must die for their sins. He is not willing that any should perish, but that all should come to repentance (2 Pet 3:9). The repentance of the wicked causes no change in the will of God since his will is that all men should have life eternal.

Backslider
18:24

But when a righteous man turns from his righteousness, and does iniquity according to all the abominations that the wicked have done, will he live? All his righteousness that he has done will not be remembered for his trespass that he committed, and for his sin that he has sinned; in them he will die.

A righteous man is one who is in the right relationship with God. Such a person can backslide to the point of being lost. He can choose to follow in the path of iniquity. He can become involved in all the abominations of the wicked. He will die in his transgressions. One must be faithful until death in order to receive the crown of life.

The former righteous acts of the backslider are not credited to his account. Such a backslider has committed a *trespass* and a *sin*. He has rebelled against God in casting aside his former way of life. He willfully has adopted a sinful life. For this twofold transgression he must die the death of a sinner.

Objection Answered
18:25-29

And you say, The way of Yahweh is not even! Hear now, O house of Israel: Is it my way that is not even? Is it not your ways that are not even? 26 When a righteous man turns from his righteousness, and does iniquity, he will die because of them; for his iniquity that he has done he will die. 27 And when the wicked man turns from his wickedness that he has done, and executes justice

and righteousness, he will cause his soul to live. 28 Because he considers and turns from all his transgressions that he has done, he will surely live; he will not die. 29 Yet the house of Israel has said, The way of Yahweh is not even. Is it my ways that are uneven, O house of Israel? Is it not your ways that are uneven?

The justice of God is frequently called into question by perverse and ignorant men. The Jews in Jerusalem and Babylon were saying (or at least thinking) that God's manner of ruling the universe was inconsistent. God is unchanging in his nature. He is absolutely righteous. He must therefore punish sin. At the same time he is merciful and gracious. He is, therefore, inclined to recognize the feeble efforts of his children to walk in his way.

God does not change; but men constantly change in relationship to God. The rays of the sun are constant; but in the course of the earth's rotation darkness falls upon a portion of the planet. The righteous man who turns away from the warmth of God's love faces inevitably the darkness of death.

By the same token the wicked man, by an act of his own free will, may decide to walk in the light of God's word. He will do those things that are lawful in the eyes of men and right in the sight of God. Thus he will save his life. His consideration of the fate of the wicked causes him to make this about face.

In view of the facts presented above how can the house of Israel continue perversely to charge God with inconsistency? If they have experienced the wrath of God it is because *they* have changed in relationship to him.

Warning and Exhortation 18:30-32

Therefore I will judge you, O house of Israel (oracle of Lord Yahweh), each according to his ways. Return, and cause others to turn from your transgressions that iniquity might not be a stumbling block to you. 31 Cast away from you all your transgressions that you have committed. Make for yourself a new heart and a new spirit; for why will you die, O house of Israel? 32 For I do not delight in the death of the one who dies (oracle of Lord Yahweh). Wherefore turn yourselves and live.

God judges each individual separately on the basis of his current spiritual standing. Ezekiel pleads with his hearers to repent and to seek to get others to repent. Otherwise iniquity will be a stumbling block that will ultimately mean their doom. All transgression must be *cast away* like an unclean and loathsome thing. The idea is once again of distancing oneself from sin.

The sinners must make for themselves *a new heart and a new spirit*, i.e., they must have a firm resolve to be faithful and obedient. Failing to make the negative and positive adjustments for which Ezekiel pleads exposes one to God's wrath. Those who do not repent will die a tragic and unnecessary death.[391]

God does not desire to punish sinners. Therefore repentance is urgent. Wise men will avail themselves of his grace.

EZEKIEL 19
BITTER DIRGES
19:1-14

In ch 19 Ezekiel becomes a sympathetic mourner. God is grieved over the impending fate of Jerusalem. Ezekiel is told to give vent to his emotions as a means of illustrating the divine agony. This ch contains two of the most beautiful allegories in all literature. Here Ezekiel abandons his tedious and repetitious prose and soars as a poet. In the first dirge the nation is portrayed as a lioness; in the second, as a grapevine. The combination of these two figures may be based on the portrayal of Judah as both a lion and as a vine in the blessing of Jacob (Gn 49:9, 11).

---

[391]In 11:19 God gives the new heart and spirit. Here they must make it for themselves.

DIRGE OVER JUDAH'S KINGS 19:1-9

As for you, take up a lamentation concerning the princes of Israel *(19:1).*

Some may have trusted in the wisdom of their national leaders to extricate Judah from iron grip of Babylon. Ezekiel responded to such misplaced trust with a lament (*qînāh*), i.e., funeral dirge, for the *princes* (i.e., kings) of Israel.[392] The first dirge speaks of the fate of two young kings—Jehoahaz and Jehoiachin—both of whom reigned but three months or so, and both of whom were deported to foreign lands. Some expected the one or the other of these two young men to return to Jerusalem to reclaim the throne and liberate Judah. Ezekiel, however, indicates that such hopes were sheer fantasy. With biting sarcasm the prophet refers to these young rulers as powerful young lions.

First Whelp 19:2-4

And say, How your mother was a lioness! Among the lions she crouched; in the midst of the young lions she reared her whelps! 3 She brought up one of her whelps. He became a young lion. He learned to tear the prey. He devoured men. 4 Then nations listened unto him. He was taken in their pit. They brought him by hooks into the land of Egypt.

The possessive *your* either views the princes collectively, or else Ezekiel is addressing the lament to the current prince or king. The house of David is the *mother* of these princes. She is compared to a *lioness*[393] because the tribe of Judah in general (cf. Gn 49:9), and the family of David in particular, were symbolized by a lion. As long as Judah remained faithful to Yahweh she dwelt securely and fearlessly

---

[392]This is the first of six laments in the book, the others being over Tyre (26:17-18; 27:2-36; 27:32-36), the king of Tyre (28:12-19), and Pharaoh (32:2-16).

[393]Panc Beentjes, "What a Lioness was your Mother: Reflections on Ezekiel 19," in Bob Becking and M. Dijkstra eds. *On Reading Prophetic Texts* (Leiden: Brill, 1996), 21-35.

among the *young lions*, i.e., surrounding nations. The period of King Josiah is in view. Tiny Judah was independent and prosperous during the reign of this godly king.

The royal lioness (house of David) reared up one of her whelps to become a *young lion*. The reference here is to Jehoahaz who became king of Judah at the age of twenty-three when his father was slain by Pharaoh Neco in the battle of Megiddo (cf. 2 Kgs 23:31ff). As a young lion Jehoahaz *learned to tear the prey*, i.e., to have hostile relations with other nations. He *devoured men*, i.e., he ventured to war. The implication is that Jehoahaz was hostile to Neco of Egypt.

The *nations*, i.e., Egypt and her vassal states, *listened unto him*, i.e., took up the challenge that he hurled at them. The young lion was lured to the pit and captured therein. He was bound in fetters and taken to Egypt. The allusion is to the capture of Jehoahaz by Pharaoh Neco in 609 BC (2 Kgs 23:33).

Second Whelp
19:5-9

A. His Power (19:5-7)

Now when she saw that, she was disappointed. Her hope was lost. Then she took one of her whelps and made him a young lion. 6 He went to and fro in the midst of the lions. He became a young lion. He learned to tear prey, he devoured men. 7 He knew their widows. He wasted their cities. The land and its fullness were desolate because of the noise of his roaring.

When the lioness (Davidic dynasty) saw that Jehoahaz had been deported she was *disappointed*.[394] She took another of her whelps and trained him to be a *young lion*. He took his place among the other lions (kings). He quickly learned the ruthless conduct that oriental kings manifested.

Because of his misrule he *knew their widows*,[395] i.e., he caused many women to lose their husbands and sons.[396] Because of his bois-

[394]The Hebrew r. *ychl* in the Niphal stem means "to wait expectantly." In certain contexts Hebrew verbs take on the opposite of their usual meaning. This appears to be the case here.

[395]Some think the Hebrew word is an unusual form of the word meaning "castles" or citadels.

[396]Another interpretation: He took as his wives the widows of the men he killed.

terousness (*noise of his roaring*) he brought destruction and desolation upon his land.

Ezekiel is not trying to give an allegory of all the last kings of Judah. Assuming that he meant to do so has led modern commentators to think that the second whelp represents Jehoiakim who ruled Judah from 605-598 BC or perhaps even Zedekiah.[397] More likely the second lion whelp was Jehoiakim's son Jehoiachin who ruled Judah for three plus months early in 597 BC.

B. His Capture (19:8-9)

Then the nations cried out against him roundabout from provinces. They spread their net over him. He was taken in their pit. 9 They put him in a cage with hooks. They brought him unto the king of Babylon. They brought him into strongholds so that his voice might not be heard again upon the mountains of Israel.

The *nations* led by Nebuchadnezzar attacked the kingdom of Jehoiachin in 597 BC. The young king was taken captive. He was brought before the king of Babylon. Thus did his rule over Judah come to an end. The growl of this young lion was no longer heard in the land.

DIRGE OVER JUDAH'S COLLAPSE 19:10-14

The second dirge in ch 19 is botanical, as in ch 17 where Jehoiachin is portrayed as *the top of the cedar* and Zedekiah is symbolized as a grapevine.

Glory of the Vine 19:10-11

Your mother was like a vine in your blood planted by waters. She was fruitful and full of branches because of much water. 11 She had strong rods to be scepters for rulers. Her height was exalted

[397]W.H. Brownlee, "Two Elegies on the Fall of Judah (Ezekiel 19)," in *Ex Orbe Religionum: Studia Geo Widengren* ed. J. Bergman et al (Leiden: Brill, 1972), 93-103.

among the branches. She was in her height in the multitude of her tendrils.

The figure changes in v 10. The *mother* is now the state of Judah.[398] She is compared to a *vine* rather than a lioness.[399] On the possessive *your,* see on v 2. *Your blood* is difficult. Two MSS read "your vineyard." This reading has been followed by NASB, NIV, and NRSV. This reading implies that Ezekiel had a personal vineyard. The standard Hebrew text, however, reads *your blood* or "your bloodline" (NKJV). The vine had its *blood*, i.e., sap, and was full of vigor. So *blood* may be a technical term for a luxuriant vineyard. The vine was fruitful because it was planted near abundant water. The allusion is to former days when the nation prospered under the rule of righteous kings.

The vine put forth strong rods—strong and resolute kings who ruled over the nation. Among the other thick branches (prosperous nations) Judah had a position of honor. The height of the vine may be figurative for national arrogance. Such human arrogance must be brought down by God.

Fate of the Vine
19:12-14

But she was plucked up in fury. She was cast down to the ground. The east wind dried up her fruit. Her strong rod was broken and withered. The fire consumed her. 13 Now she is planted in the wilderness, in a dry and thirsty land. 14 Fire has gone out from the rod of her branches. It has consumed her fruit so that she does not have a strong rod as a scepter to rule. This is a lamentation, and it became a lamentation.

Judah the exalted vine was *plucked up* and *cast down to the ground.* The present lowly position of the nation could only be due to divine determination. The *east wind* refers to the hot wind blowing into Palestine from northern Arabia. It was called the *hamsin* or *sirocco*. In this context the east wind is a symbol for Nebuchadnezzar

[398]Some commentators argue that the *mother* in vv 2 and 10 is Hammutal, the human mother of Zedekiah and Jehoahaz. Those who hold this view take the second whelp to represent Zedekiah rather than Jehoiachin.

[399]Alexander (*Expositor's Bible Commentary,* 830) suggests that the imagery changes from the Davidic figure of a lion to the figure of a vine because Zedekiah was not the legitimate legal king of Judah, as were Jehoahaz and Jehoiachin.

and his armies. To protect vines in Palestine from the east wind the vines were forced to grow low to the ground. In ch 17 it is said that Zedekiah at first sprouted and became a low spreading vine. Soon thereafter, however, the same vine decided to grow toward the high soaring eagle of Egypt. The vine of Ezekiel's allegory violated this most important principle of Palestinian viticulture. Instead of being low and sprawling it became high climbing. The arrogance of Zedekiah brings upon the vine the ultimate calamity.

The east wind *dried up the fruit* of that ignoble vine. Enormous tribute to Babylon over several years drained the royal coffers of Judah. The *strong rod* of that branch—the last king of Judah—had been broken off and withered by the mighty king from the east. The *fire* of war and divine judgment had consumed Zedekiah. He lost his crown and his eyesight before being carried away in humiliation to Babylon.

The once luxuriant vine planted by many waters was now forcibly transplanted to the wilderness. Planted by water in v 10 symbolizes a time of prosperity. Drought in this v symbolizes poverty. After the destruction of Jerusalem in 586 BC the vine was in a miserable condition. Most surviving Jews were in Babylon. A pitiful remnant remained briefly in Judah.

The fire that will ultimately destroy the nation had *gone out from the rod.* Zedekiah's rebellion against Babylon was the cause of the ruin that engulfed the nation of Judah. With the deportation of Zedekiah the royal house of David was reduced to insignificance *so that she does not have a strong rod* to assume the rule.[400]

Chapter 19 is a prophetic lamentation spoken before the final calamity took place. What is here recorded as prophecy became the general theme of the national lamentation after the disaster had transpired.

---

[400]Brownlee ("Two Elegies" op. cit., 101) thinks the fire that came forth from the stem of the vine is Ishmael, who was of royal descent. He assassinated the Judean governor that had been appointed by the Babylonians after the fall of Jerusalem.

EZEKIEL 20
ISRAEL: PAST AND FUTURE

Eleven months intervene between Ezekiel's last series of oracles and the present utterances. He effectively had shattered Judah's insane hope that judgment would never fall on Jerusalem. Every argument put forth in objection to his dogmatic assertion of imminent judgment had been rebutted. Ezekiel may have spent the past eleven months in silence.

Late in the summer of 591 BC news of Egyptian military victories in Africa spawned new delusions of deliverance among the Jews in Judah and in Babylon. King Zedekiah was now looking to Egypt for assistance against Babylon. Sometime between the end of 591 BC and the summer of 589 BC Zedekiah formally severed his allegiance to Nebuchadnezzar. The question uppermost in the minds of the captives was: what bearing will this political realignment have on the fortunes of Judah? In response to this unasked question Ezekiel speaks of the past corruption of the nation (20:1-29); the future restoration of Israel (20:30-44); and the imminent judgment on Jerusalem (20:45-21:32).

ISRAEL'S PAST CORRUPTION[401]
20:1-29

After a brief introduction to this section (vv 1-4) Ezekiel traces Israel's waywardness through the period of Egyptian bondage (vv 5-9), wilderness wandering (vv 10-26), and settlement in the land of Canaan (vv 27-29).

Introduction
20:1-4

It came to pass in the seventh year, the fifth month, the tenth day of the month that certain men of the elders of Israel came to inquire of Yahweh. They sat before me. 2 The word of Yahweh

[401]Cf. Leslie Allen, "The Structuring of Ezekiel's Revisionist History Lesson (Ezekiel 20:3-31)," *CBQ* 54 (1992): 448-62; Corrine Patton, "'I Myself Gave Him Laws That Were Not Good': Ezekiel 20 and the Exodus Traditions," *JSOT* 69 (1996): 73-90.

came unto me, saying, 3 Son of man, Speak unto the elders of Israel and say to them, Thus says Lord Yahweh: Are you coming to inquire of me? As I live, I will not be inquired of by you (oracle of Yahweh). 4 Will you judge them? Will you judge them, O son of man? Cause them to know the abominations of their fathers.

This section begins with a new date that apparently includes all the material in chs 20-23. Ezekiel has now functioned in his prophetic office for two years, one month and five days. Converted into terms of the modern calendar the date of this section is August 14, 591 BC.

Certain elders of Israel[402] approached Ezekiel in order *to inquire* of Yahweh through him, i.e., seek the interpretation of a current event.[403] This is now the third time that these elders have come to Ezekiel (cf. 8:1; 14:1). On this occasion they may have been seeking a prediction on the outcome of Zedekiah's overtures to Egypt.

In the presence of his guests Ezekiel received a new revelation. The characteristic address of the prophet as *son of man*, i.e., mortal man, stands in stark contrast to the transcendent Yahweh. The double use of the personal name Yahweh in v 3 underscores this point. Ezekiel had an answer for the inquirers, but it was not what they expected.

Whatever their specific query was God regarded it as impertinent and irrelevant. God through Ezekiel already had made it abundantly clear that Jerusalem was doomed for destruction. He was not interested in hearing their requests. God wanted to see their repentance! What sinful men want to hear from Yahweh is not always what they need to hear. The divine oath formula (*as I live*) stresses that the request of the elders ran counter to Yahweh's very being.

Yahweh's objection to the elder's third inquiry is essentially the same as in 14:4. By means of a double question God commissioned Ezekiel to sit as a judge in the trial of his people Israel. He is to recount to the elders all the *abominations of their fathers*. He was not to use parables as in ch 16. He was to reveal their sin in a straight forward manner. The plight of the nation and the necessity of the impending doom will become clear to his auditors through this sad survey of Israel's history.

---

[402]The elders in 8:1 were said to have been "of Judah." Ezekiel seems to use the terms Israel and Judah interchangeably.

[403]On the significance of the expression, *inquire of Yahweh*, see 1 Kgs 14:5-18; 22:7-28; 2 Kgs 8:8-15; 22:13-20; Jer 21:2-14; 37:7-10.

Israel in Egypt
20:5-9

Instead of indulging the elders' curiosity regarding the "times and the seasons" of future divine activity Ezekiel launched into a stern sermon. The theme of this sermon is the persistent rebellion of Israel against leadership of Yahweh.

A. Pledge to Israel (20:5-6)

Say unto them, Thus says Lord Yahweh: In the day when I chose Israel I lifted up my hand to the seed of the house of Jacob. I made myself known to them in the land of Egypt when I lifted up my hand to them, saying, I am Yahweh your God. 6 In that day I lifted up my hand to them to bring them from the land of Egypt unto the land that I sought out for them, flowing with milk and honey, that is the beauty of all lands.

Ironically Israel's case history began in Egypt, the same country to which she was now appealing for aid. There God *chose* Israel to be his very own people.[404] It was there that God bound himself by an oath to the *seed of the house of Jacob*, i.e., he confirmed the covenant made with Jacob, and with Isaac and Abraham before him. The process of selection began with his self-revelation to Moses at the burning bush (cf. Ex 6:2, 7). Then God swore with an oath (*lifted up my hand*) that he was Israel's God.

Yahweh further swore to bring Israel out of Egyptian bondage and into a very special land—a land *flowing with milk and honey*. This language was first used by God to describe Canaan in Ex 3:8. This is the land that Yahweh *sought out* for Israel.[405] The comparative fertility of Canaan, its geographical features and climate, made this land *the beauty of all lands* (cf. Jer 3:19). The double mention in vv 5-6 of the physical gesture associated with swearing an oath enhances the impression of Yahweh's commitment to Israel's welfare.

B. Rebellion of Israel (20:7-8)

I said unto them, Let each man cast away the detestable things of his eyes. Do not defile yourselves with the idols of Egypt. I am

---

[404] The word *chose* appears only here in Ezekiel, but it is used at least 6x in Deuteronomy.

[405] Ezekiel takes up the term *tûr* ("seek out, spy out, explore") that is used of the reconnoitering of the spies in Nm 13-14. He reapplies that term to Yahweh.

Yahweh your God. 8 But they rebelled against me. They did not want to listen to me. Every man did not cast away the detestable things of his eyes. They did not forsake the idols of Egypt. Then I thought to pour out my wrath upon them, to exhaust my anger on them in the midst of the land of Egypt.

Yahweh made one single requirement of those he chose as his people, viz. that they cast aside the *detestable things* (idols). They must not defile themselves with idolatrous practices. They must recognize Yahweh alone as God.

Even this basic commandment was totally ignored. The Pentateuch says nothing about the religious life of the Hebrews during the Egyptian period. Joshua, however, alluded to the gods the Israelites served in Egypt (Josh 24:14).[406] On the strict principle of justice Israel should have perished in Egypt.

C. Yahweh's Response (20:9)

But I took action for the sake of my name, that it might not be profaned before the nations among whom they lived, to whom I made myself known so as to bring them out from the land of Egypt.

Had the Israelites perished in Egypt the heathen would not have attributed it to divine retribution. They would have concluded that Yahweh lacked power to redeem his people. God did not, however, allow his great name to be thus *profaned before the nations*.[407]

God had revealed himself to Israel. Publicly through Moses he had announced his intention to bring them out of Egypt. The Egyptians knew all this. Had no redemption taken place Israel's God would forever have been held in contempt in the land of Egypt. Therefore in bringing Israel out of Egypt God was acting in his own self-interest. He acted for his name's sake.[408] To misunderstand God's nature—to regard him less highly than he ought to be regarded—is to profane his name. "It is the duty of the new Israel, as it was of the old

---

[406]The episode of the golden calf at the foot of Sinai (Ex 32:4) shows to what extent heathenism had influenced the thinking of Israel.

[407]Ezekiel uses the concept of the profanation of Yahweh's name to describe the lowering of his prestige outside Israel. Such profanation retards the realization of God's long-range goal of bringing all nations to recognize that he alone is God. See S.H. Blank, "Isaiah 52:5 and the Profanation of the Name, *HUCA*, 25 (1954): 1-8.

[408]*For the sake of my name* appears three other times in this ch: vv 14, 22, 44. Cf. Jer 14:7; Ps 106:8. In contrast to Hosea (3:1) and Jeremiah (31:3), Ezekiel never uses *love* as the motivation for God's salvation of Israel.

Israel, to see that God's name is not profaned through inadequate witness to his nature and his truth."[409]

Wilderness: First Generation 20:10-17

A. God's Gracious Gifts (20:10-12)

I brought them out from the land of Egypt, and brought them unto the wilderness. 11 I gave to them my statutes, and my ordinances I made known to them, which if a man do them, he will live by them. 12 Also my sabbaths I gave to them to become a sign between me and them, that they might know that I am Yahweh who sanctified them.

God's concern for his name prevailed over his desire to rid himself of his rebellious people. He brought them out of Egypt and into the wilderness. At Mount Sinai God graciously gave to Israel his law. In keeping this law one could find the key to life, i.e., he could prosper materially and spiritually. National faithfulness to that law would have resulted in social happiness and political stability. As further evidence of his gracious concern God ordained the Sabbath[410] as an outward sign of his covenant with Israel. Every observance of the Sabbath was an affirmation of their relationship to him (cf. Ex 31:17).

B. Sin of the First Generation (20:13-17)

But the house of Israel rebelled against me in the wilderness. They did not walk in my statutes and they spurned my ordinances, which if a man does them, he will live by them. My sabbaths they profaned exceedingly. I intended to pour out my wrath upon them in the wilderness to consume them. 14 But I took action for the sake of my name, that it might not be defiled before the nations before whom I brought them out. 15 And also I lifted up my hand to them in the wilderness, that I would not bring them unto the land that I had given them, flowing with milk and honey, the beauty of all the lands; 16 because they rejected my judgments. In my statutes they did not walk. They defiled my sabbaths, for after their idols their

---

[409]Taylor, *Ezekiel*, 158.

[410]The text reads *sabbaths* and may include the various festivals as well as the weekly Sabbath.

heart did go. 17 But my eye had pity upon them from destroying them. I did not make a complete end of them in the wilderness.

Within days of the gracious giving of the law Israel rebelled against Yahweh in the incident of the golden calf. The Book of Numbers contains numerous examples of the times when Israel murmured against Yahweh. Direct violation of the Sabbath is recorded on two occasions (Ex 16:27; Nm 15:32), but that sacred day was defiled by attitude again and again.

Because Israel had spurned God's gracious wilderness gifts to his people he was fully prepared to destroy them there and then. Again for the sake of his name—his reputation among the heathen nations—he refrained from executing his wrath. God, however, did swear that the guilty generation that showed such lack of faith at Kadesh-barnea (Nm 13-14) could not enter the land of promise. God sentenced that generation to wander in the wilderness for forty years because they had defiled the law of God and secretly had craved for their idols in their heart.

Because of his mercy God did not make a full end of Israel at that time. Those under the age of twenty survived the disciplinary death march.

Wilderness: Second Generation 20:18-22

I said unto their sons in the wilderness: Do not walk in the statutes of your fathers. Do not observe their ordinances. With their idols do not defile yourselves. 19 I am Yahweh your God. Walk in my statutes. Keep my ordinances and do them. 20 Sanctify my sabbaths that they may be signs between me and you, that you may know that I am Yahweh your God. 21 But the children rebelled against me. They did not walk in my statutes. They did not keep my ordinances to do them, which if a man will do them, he will live by them. They profaned my sabbaths. 22 I intended to pour out my wrath on them to finish my fury on them in the wilderness. 22 I withdrew my hand. I took action for the sake of my name, that it should not be defiled in the sight of the nations before whom I brought them out.

God warned the new generation not to follow in the sinful paths of their fathers, but rather to recognize his absolute divinity. He earnestly pled with them through Moses to obey the divine law and faithfully to observe the sabbaths as an outward sign and reminder that they were indeed God's people.

Unfortunately the new generation was every bit as bad as the previous one. At Baal-peor, in their very first exposure to Canaanite Baal worship, the men of that new generation rushed headlong into the vilest form of degrading worship (Nm 25:1-9; Hos 9:10).

God was of a mind to destroy the nation entirely. Again, however, for the sake of his own self-interest—for the sake of his reputation among surrounding nations—God relented (*withdrew my hand*).

Consequences of Rebellion 20:23-26

Moreover I lifted up my hand to them in the wilderness to scatter them among the nations and to disperse them in the lands; 24 because my ordinances they did not perform, and my statutes they rejected, and my sabbaths they profaned, and their eyes were after the gods of their fathers. 25 Moreover I gave to them statutes that were not good, and ordinances whereby they could not live. 26 I defiled them with their gifts, in that they consecrated all that opened the womb, that I might destroy them, that they might know that I am Yahweh.

Although God chose not to destroy Israel, the national rebellion had two serious consequences, each introduced by *moreover*. First, God swore on oath (*lifted up my hand*) that he would scatter them to various lands. The time and manner of that dispersion was not specified. The long periods of oppression during the period of the judges probably were the first step in the fulfillment of this threat. Attacks by neighboring nations during the monarchy period resulted in God's people being deported far and wide (cf. Amos 1:6, 9; Joel 3:1-8). The culmination of this threatened dispersion was the deportation of the northern tribes by the Assyrian kings,[411] and the removal of captives from Judah by Nebuchadnezzar.[412]

---

[411]The two main Assyrian deportations occurred in 745 BC by Tiglath-pileser III, and in 722 BC by Sargon.

[412]Four deportations by Nebuchadnezzar are recorded in Scripture: The first was in 605/604 BC and the last in 582 BC. See Jer 52:30. Lind (*Ezekiel*, 169) thinks that for Ezekiel the exile was a predetermined conclusion of the salvation story even before Israel entered the land. The Mosaic covenant stipulated exile as the punishment for disobedience. Cf. Lv 26:33; Dt 28:36, 64; Ps 106:26-27.

The exile was a just punishment because the generation that was brought into Canaan also rejected God's holy law and went after idols.

Second, God punished Israel's national rebellion by giving them over to the consequences of their own sinful desire. Yahweh punished their sin by means of their sin. He gave them *statutes that were not good, and ordinances whereby they could not live.* As they went ever deeper into the baser forms of idolatry they brought themselves under statutes and judgments of a different sort. The pagan religious code that they adopted as their own did not contribute to health, happiness and well being (life). That code became a vicious and demanding taskmaster. Stephen describes this situation when he says, "God turned and gave them up to worship the host of heaven" (Acts 7:42).

God punished his people by permitting them to do what they really wanted to do. All the material gifts that God bestowed upon his people were permitted by him to be defiled in the debasing worship of Baal. Israel rejected God's law of dedicating their firstborn to Yahweh (Ex 13:2). They replaced it with the horrible practice of child sacrifice (cf. Ezek 16:21). The ultimate end of such perverse pagan practices was national destruction. Only then would Israel realize that Yahweh is the only God.

Israel in Canaan
20:27-29

Therefore speak unto the house of Israel, son of man, and say to them, Thus says Lord Yahweh: Yet in this your fathers have blasphemed me in that they have dealt treacherously with me. 28 For when I brought them to the land that I lifted up my hand to give unto them, then they saw every high hill, and every leafy tree, and they made sacrifices there. They gave there the provocation of their offering. They placed there their sweet savor, and they poured out their drink offerings. 29 Then I said unto them: What is the high place to which you are going? So its name is called Bamah (high place) unto this day.

In addition to their wickedness in Egypt and in the wilderness the fathers had continued their sinning when they were in the land of Canaan. In fact *they blasphemed*, i.e., committed a cardinal sin against Yahweh; they *dealt treacherously* with him, i.e., broke the most solemn kind of commitment.

As soon as they, by God's mercy, had entered the land of Canaan they appropriated to themselves the heathen hill-top shrines. They adopted the Canaanite ways of worship. The leafy trees were desirable for the sinful orgies that accompanied sacrifices to Baal. Their offerings, which should have been a sweet savor to Yahweh, were in reality provocation that only engendered the divine anger.

Someday the Jews will have to give an account of their worship conduct. *What is the high place to which you are going?* Ezekiel asks. Who authorized you to go there? What business do you have there? In spite of the repeated condemnation of high place worship still those shrines existed throughout the land. The *bāmāh* or high place was still very much a part of the worship scene in Judah.

ISRAEL'S FUTURE RESTORATION 20:30-44

Hypocrisy of Leaders 20:30-32

Therefore say unto the house of Israel, Thus says Lord Yahweh: In the way of your fathers you have defiled yourselves. You are whoring after their abominations. 31 When you offer your gifts in making your sons to pass through the fire, you defile yourselves with all your idols unto this day. Will I allow you to inquire of me, O house of Israel? As I live (oracle of Lord Yahweh) I will not allow you to inquire of me. 32 What goes up on your spirit will not be, because you are saying, We will be like the nations, as the families of the lands, to serve wood and stone.

Ezekiel replied to the request of the visiting elders by reviewing the past corruption of Israel; now he applies this teaching to the present and future of the nation. How can these representatives of the nation expect to receive encouraging divine responses to their inquiries when the abominable practices of idolatry continued to that very day? The present generation had defiled itself after the manner of their fathers by offering gifts to Baal. They even caused their children to *pass through the fire*, i.e., offered them as burnt offerings to Molech.[413]

How could God suspend or cancel the threat of judgment when they continued to defile themselves by such degrading religious practices? Their defilement drove a wedge between them and their God. Under present circumstances he refused to *be inquired of* by them, i.e., he will grant them no special insight into the immediate future beyond the threats that he had already announced through his prophet.

The attitude among the exiles was reprehensible. Ezekiel reads the hearts of the inquirers.[414] Being humiliated, subject to foreign domination, and driven from their homeland they now felt free to join in the worship of their neighbors. How was it possible for them to continue to render homage to Yahweh when his temple was so far away, and when all public acts of worship to him were restricted to that temple? Were the temple to be destroyed, they thought, then the one restraint on their idolatries would be removed, and that by God himself. According to their perverse logic if God wanted their continued allegiance he would have to preserve the temple and quickly restore them to Canaan. God, however, will not allow this perverse purpose to stand.

Gathering of Israel
20:33-34

As I live (oracle of Lord Yahweh) surely with a mighty hand, with an outstretched arm, and with fury poured out I will reign over you. 34 I will bring you out from the peoples, and I will gather you from the lands where you were scattered with a mighty hand, and with an outstretched arm, and with fury poured out.

God was about to intervene in Israel's history with the same *mighty hand* and *outstretched arm* that saved them at the exodus (Dt 4:34; 5:15). He will show himself again to be king over this people by leading them from judgment into another wilderness experience (cf. Hos 2:14f; 12:9). The Babylonian exile was Israel's second wilder-

---

[413]That immolation of the children is intended, and not just ritual purification, is made clear by Jer 19:5.

[414]J. Lust, "Ezekiel Salutes Isaiah: Ezekiel 20,32-44" in J. van Ruiten and M. Vervenne eds. *Studies in the Book of Isaiah: Festscrift Willem A. M. Beuken* (Leuven: Leuven University Press, 1997), 367-82.

ness period.[415] When the discipline is over God will gather his people. Israel will by no means lose her identity among the nations!

Purpose of Exile
20:35-38

I will bring you unto the wilderness of the peoples. I will plead with you there face to face. 36 As I pleaded with your fathers in the wilderness of the land of Egypt, thus will I plead with you (oracle of Lord Yahweh). 37 I will cause you to pass under the rod. I will bring you into the bond of the covenant. 38 I will purge out from you the rebels and those who transgress against me. I will bring them out from the land of their sojourn. Unto the land of Israel they will not come. You will know that I am Yahweh.

The exact prophetic import of vv 35-38 is in dispute. Some commentators understand these vv to be predicting that after the Babylonian exile, Israel will be brought into another dispersion. It is better, however, to regard the *wilderness of peoples* as yet another reference to the Babylonian captivity. In v 34 God states the general principle that he will, in his own good time, gather his people. Verses 35-38 tell how that will come about. In the wilderness of Egypt God constituted Israel as a nation. In the Babylonian wilderness he will reconstitute them as a nation. There they will come *face to face* with God. He will *plead* with them, i.e., remonstrate and reason with them, through those harsh circumstances, through the voice of conscience, and through the stern preaching of men like Ezekiel.

Not all those who were carried off to the wilderness of exile will be coming home. The captives will be scrutinized by the Good Shepherd. They will pass under the rod. The allusion is to Lv 27:32 where every tenth sheep that passed *under the rod* of the shepherd was to be consecrated to Yahweh. The select sheep of Israel will be brought into *the bond of the covenant*. The apostasy had cancelled the blessings set forth in the Sinai covenant. The chastisement of exile, for those who will accept it, will serve the purpose of restoring that broken relationship with God.

The land of restored Israel will be a land of righteousness. Those who had rebelled against God's authority, and who had transgressed

---

[415]Another view is that the wilderness of the peoples is the great Arabian Desert, surrounded by the peoples of the Fertile Crescent (Lind, *Ezekiel*, 172).

against him, will be purged from the nation. They will not be allowed to re-enter the land of Canaan. God might bring them out of the land where they were presently sojourning; but he will by no means allow them to re-enter Canaan. When he brought them back the chastened remnant will know that he truly was Yahweh, the God of covenant faithfulness.

Restoration to the Land
20:39-41

As for you, O house of Israel, thus says Lord Yahweh: Go, serve each his idols, even because you have not hearkened unto me; but my holy name you will not profane again with your gifts and with your idols. 40 For in my holy mountain, in the mountain of the height of Israel (oracle of Lord Yahweh) there all the house of Israel, all of them, will serve me in the land. There I will accept them. There I will require your heave offerings, and the first of your gifts with all your holy things. 41 With your sweet savor I will accept you when I bring you out from the peoples, and gather you from the lands where you were scattered. I will be sanctified in the sight of the nations.

In prophetic irony Ezekiel now called upon the house of Israel to go ahead with their idolatry. They cannot thereby frustrate God's ultimate purpose for a holy people. The day will come when God's holy name[416] no longer will be profaned by idolatrous practices.

Ezekiel passes on from the earlier stages of the restoration to speak of its consummation. He sees Israel as a mighty mountain (*mountain of the height of Israel*) or nation of the world (cf. Mic 4:1-2; Isa 2:2-3). He sees a united nation (*all of them*)—Israel and Judah—worshiping on Mount Zion (*my holy mountain*). He sees a holy people rendering acceptable service and sacrifice to their God. Gone forever are the heathen influences that marred the worship of his day. *Heave offerings*,[417] *offerings of firstlings*,[418] and other gifts will be willingly offered by the redeemed people.

---

[416]Alex Luc, "A Theology of Ezekiel: God's Name and Israel's History," *JETS* 26 (1983): 137-143.

[417]*Heave offerings* (*terūmōt*) are mentioned in Ex 24:27; Lv 7:14 and many other places.

Ezekiel foresees several positive consequences of the new relationship between God and his people. First, the sacrifices that Israel offers to God are considered a *sweet savor* by Yahweh, i.e., will be pleasant in his sight. Second, God *accepts* Israel, i.e., acknowledges them as his own. Third, through that restored remnant God's name is *sanctified*, i.e., respected and revered, by surrounding nations. God's name is sanctified when he is recognized as holy (Lv 10:3; Nm 20:13). Even the heathen come to recognize that God's dealings with Israel had been holy and just.

Spiritual Enlightenment 20:42-44

You will know that I am Yahweh when I bring you unto the land of Israel, unto the land that I lifted up my hand to give to your fathers. 43 And there you will remember your ways and all your deeds by which you were defiled. You will loathe yourself in your eyes for all your evils that you have done. 44 You will know that I am Yahweh when I deal with you for the sake of my name, not according to your evil deeds or according to your corrupt ways, O house of Israel (oracle of Lord Yahweh).

Because of the positive experiences of the preceding vv Israel is spiritually enlightened. The recognition formula (*you will know*) at the beginning and end of this unit forms an envelope full of encouraging developments. Remnant Israel will realize without a doubt that they have been restored to Canaan through the might of God. They willingly acknowledge that he, and none other, is God.

Remnant Israel recognizes that God keeps his word. He had sworn to give to their fathers the land of Canaan. Through sin Israel forfeited the right to live in that holy land. Now God will give them a second chance in Canaan.

Remnant Israel remembers past failings. They *loathe* themselves for the abominations that they had committed prior to the captivity. In spite of repentance and forgiveness the redeemed man can never forget that he is a sinner saved by grace.

---

[418]The *first of your gifts* includes the first-ripe grain (Dt 26:2ff), the firstborn of the cattle, the redemption fee for firstborn male children (Ex 13:2, 12ff), and the first portion of the dough (Nm 15:20f).

Remnant Israel realizes that their change in fortunes was not due to their own merits. They deserved to perish. For the sake of his name, however, the gracious God had ransomed the house of Israel.

PARABLE OF THE FOREST FIRE 20:45-49

The word of Yahweh came unto me, saying, 46 Son of man, set your face toward the south; preach unto the south. Prophesy unto the forest of the field of the south. 47 Say to the forest of the south, Hear the word of Yahweh. Thus says Lord Yahweh: Behold I am about to kindle against you a fire. It will consume every green tree in you and every dry tree. It will not be quenched, a flaming flame. All faces from the south to the north will be seared by it. 48 All flesh will see that I am Yahweh when I burn it. It will not be quenched. 49 Then I said, Ah Lord Yahweh! They are saying to me, Is he not a maker of parables?

In the Hebrew Bible v 45 becomes the first v of ch 21. Clearly this is a better arrangement than that adopted by the King James Version and subsequent English translations. What is said in 20:45-49 has no connection with what immediately precedes; but these vv do the stage for what follows in ch 21.

In another revelation from Yahweh Ezekiel was told *set your face toward the south*. This prophetic formula was previously used in 6:2 and 13:17. Ezekiel was to direct his attention verbally and perhaps physically as well toward *the south*.[419] He was to preach[420] the word of Yahweh in that direction. These instructions are given to Ezekiel from the perspective of the Babylonian army that will approach Jerusalem from the north. The whole of Judah is *the forest of the south* that Ezekiel was to address in this utterance.

The entire forest will be consumed by an unquenchable fire kindled by God. *Fire* is symbolic of the devastation wrought by the

---

[419]Ezekiel uses three Hebrew synonyms that may be translated *south*. The first (*tēmān*) and last (*negebh*) are also place names, and could be so rendered (cf. NASB). Ezekiel's interpretation, however, involves only Jerusalem. Hence it is best to regard the three words as synonyms for *south*.

[420]*Preach* is literally, "drop your word." This was a technical expression used to designate prophetic utterances. The same word is used in Amos 7:6 and Mic 2:6, 11.

Chaldean armies. What few righteous there might have been (*every green tree*), as well as the hardened sinners (*every dry tree*), will be affected by that conflagration. From one end of the land to the other every face will be seared by the hot flames of judgment. That destruction will be of such proportions that *all flesh,* i.e., the entire world, will recognize it as an act of divine judgment.

Ezekiel's audience was not so spiritually perceptive as to be able to grasp the significance of this parable and others like it (cf. chs 15-17). His auditors were holding Ezekiel up to ridicule because of his use of the parabolic method. He could hear them whispering to one another and referring to him as *a maker of parables* (lit., "riddler of riddles"). With sorrow, exasperation and perhaps indignation Ezekiel turned to God in a brief narrative prayer. No petition is directly stated; but Ezekiel is obliquely requesting that he be permitted to put his parable into plain language.

EZEKIEL 21
IMMINENT JUDGMENT

Chapter 21 opens with an explanation of the parable of the forest fire that was related in the closing vv of the preceding ch. To his parable Ezekiel adds a song about a sword (21:8-17). This song becomes the springboard for two oracles dealing with the words of the king of Babylon (21:18-27), and the sword that will one day fall upon Ammon (21:28-32).

PARABLE APPLIED
21:1-4

The word of Yahweh came unto me, saying, 2 Son of man, Set your face toward Jerusalem. Preach toward the sanctuaries. Prophesy unto the land of Israel. 3 Say to the land of Israel, Thus says Yahweh: Behold I am against you! I will bring out my sword from its sheath. I will cut off from you both righteous and wicked. 4 Because I will cut off from you righteous and wicked therefore my sword will go out from its sheath against all flesh from the south to the north. 5 All flesh will know that I Yahweh have brought out my sword from its sheath. It will not return any more.

After an interval of undetermined duration God granted the unspoken request of his prophet. Ezekiel was told to *set your face toward Jerusalem.* The formula is explained in the subsequent clauses by the verbs *preach* and *prophesy. The sanctuaries* (high places?) and the *land of Israel,* as well as Jerusalem, are to be the target of his discourse.

Ezekiel was to announce that God had assumed a posture of hostility toward the land of Israel. Yahweh hurls at the nation the same challenge formula that he used in 13:8. The divine *sword* of judgment (the fire in the parable) was about to come out of its *sheath.* Both wicked and righteous will be *cut off.*

Ezekiel already had taught that in the final judgment the righteous will not be destroyed with the wicked (ch 18). Of necessity, however, in temporal judgments the entire population of an area will be affected. Other peoples besides Israel will feel the effect of the sword of Yahweh that at this point was wielded by the Chaldeans.

Even the foreign nations will realize that they had experienced a divine judgment. The sword of Yahweh will not return unto its sheath until the destructive work assigned to it was complete.

PARABLE OF SIGHING
21:6-7

As for you, son of man, sigh. With the breaking of loins and with bitterness sigh before their eyes. 7 It will come to pass when they say unto you: Why are you sighing? Then say: Because of the report, for it comes. Every heart will melt and all hands will droop. Every spirit will faint. All knees will drip water. Behold it comes! It will be done (oracle of Lord Yahweh).

Ezekiel was deeply moved by this revelation. He was told not to hide his emotion. As in other instances (4:4; 5:1-4) he was to dramatize in his own person the coming calamity. He was to assume the role of a mourner whose sighs were so deep that they seem to *break his loins*, i.e., he is to bend double as though smitten with great pain in the abdomen. This agonizing sigh was to be done *before their eyes* so as to provoke questions.

When asked about his bitter sighing Ezekiel was to explain that this was but an example of what all the exiles will do when they get the message from Jerusalem that the temple had been destroyed. The prophet, because of his special relationship to God, already had heard those tidings through revelation. Five years later all the exiles will hear that same message from someone who barely had escaped the fallen city. With the loss of the temple all hope of return to Jerusalem will be smashed.

Four expressions set forth the physical and psychological reaction to the news of Jerusalem's destruction: 1) every heart will melt; 2) all hands will be slack; 3) every spirit will be faint; and 4) all knees will drip with water, i.e., kidney functions could not be controlled. Nonetheless that bad news was coming. When it came it will prove to be a true account of what had actually happened in Jerusalem.

SONG OF THE SWORD 21:8-17

What Ezekiel was to Say 21:8-11

The word of Yahweh came unto me, saying, 9 Son of man, prophesy, and say, Thus says Yahweh: Say: A sword, a sword is sharpened and also polished. 10 In order to make a great slaughter it is sharpened. In order that it might flash it is polished—or do we make mirth—the rod of my son who rejects everything of wood. 11 He gave it to be polished, to be seized by the hand. The sword, it is sharpened and it is polished to give it into the hand of the slayer.

The thought of the unsheathed sword in v 3 gives rise to these words. These lines may have been a common lament song sung in times of coming judgment. It is even possible that Ezekiel accompanied these words with some kind of sword-brandishing. The sword of Yahweh is ready for action. Its dazzling brightness is added to its sharpness as a fresh element of terror.[421]

Ezekiel quickly broke off his sword song as he noticed the smiles on the faces of his auditors. *Or do we make mirth?* means "Do you think I am joking about this whole matter?" This sharpened and glittering sword is *the rod of my son*, i.e., the rod with which God's son

---

[421]Samuel Terrien, "Ezekiel's Dance of the Sword and Prophetic Theonomy" in Richard Weis and David Carr, eds. *A Gift of God in Due Season: Essays on Scripture and Community in Honor of James A. Sanders* (Sheffeld: Sheffeld Academic Press, 1996), 119-32.

Israel must now be disciplined.[422] The nation had despised everything of wood, i.e., every former instrument of punishment (cf. Isa 10:5). God had given that sword to be polished. Then the sword was handed over to the executioner.

What Ezekiel was to Do
21:12-17

A. Gestures with the Sword (21:12-15)

Cry out and wail, son of man; for it is against my people, it is against all the princes of Israel, those who are thrust down to the sword with my people. Therefore smite upon the thigh. 13 For there is a trial! What if the despising scepter will be no more? (oracle of Lord Yahweh). 14 As for you, son of man, prophesy. Smite your hands together. Let the sword be doubled the third time, the sword of those to be slain, the sword of the great one who is to be slain that surrounds them. 15 In order that their heart may melt and their stumbling be multiplied I have set the point of the sword. Ah! it is made to flash, it is sharpened for slaughter.

God called upon the prophet to take up a lament over the impending doom. He was to slap his thigh as a gesture of grief and despair. Even the princes of Judah will be thrust down by the divine sword along with the common people. The *trial* of Judah had now come. During that trial the *scepter* (Zedekiah) that despised the word and warning of God *will be no more*. Judah will be left without a ruler.

God directed Ezekiel to perform yet another gesture. He was to slap his hands together. This action indicated either lamentation or the summons to the agent of destruction. Ezekiel was to brandish the sword with a double motion, backward and forward, three times.[423] That sword of divine justice will slay many, even *the great one*, i.e., the king. From that sword there will be no escape for it will surround them like a besieging army.

---

[422]Alexander (*Expositor's Bible Commentary*, 842) understands the v in a very different way: "Shall we rejoice in the scepter of my son Judah? The sword despises every such stick." They were clinging to the promise of Gn 49:9-10 of a scepter arising from the tribe of Judah, i.e., Messiah. There was no hope for contemporary Judah in the promises of Gn 49, for God's sword would devour every such scepter, viz. the rulers in Jerusalem.

[423]Perhaps the brandishing of the sword three times points to three times Nebuchadnezzar invaded the land of Judah—in 605/604, in 597 and finally in 586 BC.

The point of the sword of Yahweh will be set at every gate of the city. It will cause consternation within and stumbling as the citizens attempt to escape that sword that glittered because of sharpening and furbishing.

B. Address to the Sword (21:16-17)

Unite yourself, go right, set yourself, go left! Where is your face set? 17 I also will smite my hands together and cause my wrath to rest; I Yahweh have spoken it.

God now addresses the sword[424] (king of Babylon). This agent of divine judgment is urged to make a decision as to which direction he will move. He should get on with the judgment. It is, after all, Yahweh who had given that command with a gesture of supreme authority (*clap my hands together*). When the divine sentence had been executed against Judah God's anger will be appeased. God had spoken. What he had said must come to pass. With these words the song of the sword ended. There followed another interval of silence.

SWORD OF BABYLON'S KING 21:18-27

Diagram 21:18-20

The word of Yahweh came unto me, saying, 19 Now as for you, son of man, make for yourself two ways that the sword of the king of Babylon may come. The two of them will come forth out of one land. And make a signpost; make it at the head of the way to the city. 20 You will make a way that the sword may come to Rabbah of the children of Ammon, and to Judah in the fortress of Jerusalem.

Ezekiel received a new revelation in which he was commanded to sketch a road that, at a certain point, branched in two directions. The road *came forth out of one land*, i.e., out of the land of Babylon. That was the road that God's divinely appointed sword—the king of Babylon—will travel. At the crossroads the prophet was to draw, or perhaps cut out and place, a *signpost* (literally, "a hand") pointing *the*

[424]The verbs have the feminine form, indicating that the *sword* (a feminine noun in Hebrew) is being addressed rather than the prophet, as proposed by some.

way to the city, i.e., Jerusalem. The other branch in that road led to Rabbah Ammon.

Decision
21:21-23

For the king of Babylon stands at the parting of the way, at the head of the two ways, to employ divination. He shakes the arrows. He inquires of the teraphim. He observes the liver. 22 In his right hand is the divination of Jerusalem to set battering rams to open the mouth for the slaughter, to lift the voice in a battle cry, to set battering rams against the gates, to construct mounds, to build siege forts. 23 It will be unto them as false divination in their sight, who have sworn oaths unto them. But he brings iniquity to remembrance that they may be taken.

His props in place Ezekiel was to depict the king of Babylon standing at that crossroads. By means of pagan divination he was attempting to discover which of those two routes to travel. Three forms of divination are mentioned. Shaking the arrows involved writing the names of the two objectives on arrows, shaking them up in the quiver, and drawing forth one of them. The precise manner by which the small household gods called *t^erāphîm* were used to receive oracular direction is unknown. Examining the color and markings of a liver[425] from a sacrificial animal, however, is a well-known form of divination among the Babylonians. This is, however, the only place the custom is mentioned in the Scriptures.

Ezekiel depicts Nebuchadnezzar drawing forth from the quiver the arrow that had the name Jerusalem written on it. His pagan divination informed him that he was to employ every siege weapon to assault the city—battering rams to assault the walls and gates; mounds of earth and mobile forts from which to hurl missiles over the walls. As he attacked Jerusalem his men will *open the mouth for the slaughter*, i.e., lift up their voices in blood-curdling battle cries designed to terrify the inhabitants of the city.[426]

---

[425]Many clay models of livers have been found, some with inscriptions of omens and magical texts used by diviners. *IDB*, 1:856-58.

[426]On the siege tactics mentioned here, see Y. Yadin, *The Art of Warfare in Biblical Lands* (New York: McGraw-Hill, 1963), 313-17, 388-93.

To the men of Jerusalem what Nebuchadnezzar had done was but vain divination. They lulled themselves into a false sense of security. They had escaped the king's wrath in the past by swearing oaths of allegiance to him.[427] They were fully prepared to take such oaths again. This time, however, Nebuchadnezzar will come to settle the account with the rebels—*he will bring iniquity to remembrance.* This time they *will be taken*, i.e., seized by the invader. They will either be slain or be taken prisoners.

Humiliation of the King
21:24-27

Therefore thus says Lord Yahweh: Because you have caused your iniquity to be remembered in that your transgressions have been uncovered so that your sins appear in all your deeds; because you are remembered you will be seized with the hand. 25 You, O profane and wicked prince of Israel, whose day has come in the iniquity of the end; 26 thus says Lord Yahweh: The turban will be removed. The crown will be taken off. Things will be thrown into confusion. The lowly will be exalted. The high will be brought low. 27 A ruin, a ruin, a ruin I have made it. This also will not be until he comes whose right it is. I will give it to him.

The iniquity of Judah had forced both the king of Babylon and Yahweh himself to remember their iniquity. Their more recent transgressions had caused their former iniquities to be remembered before God. Because of their consistent record of willful disobedience they will fall into the hand of the God of judgment.

Zedekiah is addressed in v 25 as *a profane and wicked prince.* This weak-kneed monarch had shown himself to be unfaithful both to his overlord Nebuchadnezzar and to the God in whose name he had taken his vassal oath. Now his day had come. He had committed the iniquity that brought down punishment.

Zedekiah will lose the insignia of his rank.[428] Things will be *thrown into confusion.*[429] The rulers of Judah will be brought down

[427]The Hebrew reads literally, "oaths of oaths are theirs." Keil thinks the reference is to the oaths of Yahweh that he had sworn unto his people. They were trusting in divine promises of protection and deliverance. God, however, will bring to remembrance their iniquity.

[428]Alexander (*Expositor's Bible Commentary*, 844) thinks the *turban* points to the high priesthood, the *crown* to kingship. The thought is that kingship (and priesthood)

and abased. The humble citizens who heeded God's word will be exalted. The honors offered Jeremiah after the Babylonian conquest of Jerusalem might be an example of the exaltation of the humble (cf. Jer 40:5f).

Following the removal of Zedekiah Judah's monarchy will be in utter *ruin* (emphasized by the threefold repetition of the noun).[430] The monarchy will exist no more *until he comes whose right it is*. There can be little doubt that this is a messianic prediction and a clear reference to Gn 49:10.[431] The kingly line will be overthrown and God's people will remain without a king until that one arose who had been anticipated throughout Old Testament history. When Messiah finally comes the royal insignia is given to him. He will be "the culmination of everything to which the Davidic house and the messianic kingship in Israel always have pointed."[432]

SWORD AGAINST AMMON 21:28-32

Symbolic Action 21:28-30a

As for you, son of man, prophesy and say, Thus says Lord Yahweh concerning the children of Ammon and their taunt, and say: O sword, keen-edged, furbished to the uttermost for slaughter that it may flash. 29 While they see falsehood about you, while they divine lies regarding you to lay you upon the necks of the wicked who will be slain, whose day has come, in the time of the iniquity of the end. 30 Cause it to return to its sheath!

Apparently Ezekiel again takes up his sword. He turns it against the Ammonites. They might have thought that they would escape the

---

will be removed in judgment but returned ultimately in the Messiah's coming in accord with Gn 49:10.

429Literally the Hebrew reads, "this not this." The paraphrase of Lofthouse has been followed here.

430The term *ruin* (*'avvāh*) is a word play on the term *iniquity/guilt* (*'āvōn*) that is used 3x in vv 23-25. The punishment was to fit the crime.

431"Until Shiloh comes" in Gn 49:10 (NASB) shows that the rule (scepter) was to remain in the tribe of Judah till Messiah (Shiloh) came. Cf. James Smith, *The Promised Messiah* (Nashville, Nelson, 1993), 54-58.

432Taylor, *Ezekiel*, 165.

wrath of Nebuchadnezzar when Judah was invaded. The ones, however, who had mocked when Judah had experienced earlier invasions by Nebuchadnezzar should not imagine that they will escape a similar fate. The sword of divine judgment was sharpened and polished *to the uttermost*, i.e., as much as it could receive, so as to be a terrifying and effective instrument of punishment.

Ammonite soothsayers were envisioning peace and security for their kingdom. Such divination was false and unreliable. Ultimately Ammon will share the same fate as Jerusalem. Her slain will fall in heaps *upon the necks of the wicked who will be slain*, i.e., upon the bodies of the Jews previously slain by Nebuchadnezzar. For them divine punishment has been decreed. That punishment must certainly come. At this point Ezekiel is commanded to return his symbolic sword to its sheath.

God's Anger on Ammon 21:30b-32

In the place where you were created, in the land of your origin, I will judge you. 31 I will pour out my wrath upon you. I will blow you with the fire of my wrath. I will give you into the hand of ruthless men, skillful destroyers. 32 You will become fuel for the fire. Your blood will be in the midst of the land. You will not be remembered; for I Yahweh have spoken it.

The symbolic action performed by Ezekiel came to an end. The execution of the judgment shortly will follow. God will judge Ammon[433] on its own soil—*the place where you were created.* God's anger against Ammon will grow ever more intense as does a flame blown by bellows. Ammonites could expect no mercy from the ruthless Babylonians into whose hands they were about to fall.

Judah will be carried into exile; but Ammon will be destroyed in the midst of its land. For Ammon there was no hope of restoration like that which Ezekiel portrays as Israel's future. Ammon will pass into oblivion. Such was the final decree of the sovereign ruler of all nations.

---

[433]Allen (*Word Biblical Commentary*, 28) understands vv 30-32 to refer to a threat against the sword, i.e., Babylon. The "sword" becomes Yahweh's victim. Babylon too was doomed to fall.

EZEKIEL 22
SINFUL NATION

In chs 22-24 Ezekiel continues to hammer away at the theme of Israel's defilement. Again his underlying premise is that Judah deserves the forthcoming judgment. By means of three oracles, two parables and a symbolic action the prophet underscores the defilement of the land of Israel in the past and in the present. Each ch in this section forms a distinct unit.

Chapter 22 contains three separate oracles, each of which begins with the phrase *the word of Yahweh came to me* (vv 1, 17, 23). These messages originally may have been uttered on separate occasions. There is logic, however, in the grouping of these three messages here. They share the common theme of the defilement of Israel. One might suggest the following titles for these three sermons: "Bloody City" (vv 1-16); "Smelting Furnace" (vv 17-32); and "Corrupt Land" (vv 23-31).

BLOODY CITY
22:1-16

As in chs 16 and 20 Ezekiel sets forth Jerusalem's *abominations*. Here, however, the prophet exposes present, rather than past sins.

Introduction
22:1-2

The word of Yahweh came unto me, saying, 2 As for you, son of man, will you judge, will you judge the bloody city? Then make known to her all her abominations.

Again Ezekiel is asked if he will judge Jerusalem (cf. 20:4). Before he can pronounce such judgment Ezekiel must inform the inhabitants of *the bloody city*[434] of the charges against them. Therefore he lists for them their crimes.

[434]The phrase is used of Nineveh in Nah 3:1.

Initial Indictment 22:3-5

Say: Thus says Lord Yahweh: O city that sheds blood in her midst that her time may come, and that makes idols unto her to defile herself. 4 You are guilty in the blood that you have shed. You are defiled by the idols that you have made. You have caused your days to draw near. You have come unto your years. Therefore I have made you a reproach to the nations and a mockery to all lands! 5 Those that are near and those that are far from you will mock you, O you defiled of name and great of tumult.

Jerusalem's abominable deeds are essentially two. First, the city *sheds blood in her midst*. This brazen disregard for life indicates the terrible moral debasement of the place. Second, the Jerusalemites had made idols for themselves. Thus they had committed the ultimate sin on the vertical as well as the horizontal dimension of covenant obligation.

The abominations of Jerusalem have five terrible results. First, the citizens had become judicially guilty, hence deserving of punishment. Second, they had become religiously defiled, i.e., contaminated by something foreign to Jerusalem's very nature. Third, they were now politically in jeopardy. Jerusalem's *days,* i.e., days of retribution, were drawing near. The years of dispersion and exile that commenced in 597 BC continued until the fall of Babylon in 539 BC.

Fourth, in the eternal counsels of God Jerusalem already had been made a reproach and an object of mockery to all neighboring lands. The judgment is certain. Finally, the people of God will be despised far and near. They will be *defiled of name*, i.e., have a bad reputation derived from the fact that their land was full of *tumult*, i.e., turmoil and confusion caused by war and natural calamity.

Detailed Indictment 22:6-12

A. Sins of Oppression (22:6-7)

Behold the princes of Israel, each according to his strength, have been in you in order to shed blood. 7 In you they have made light of father and mother. In the midst of you they have dealt with

the stranger by oppression. In you they have wronged the orphan and widow.

Behold introduces the shocking crimes of the princes or leaders of Judah who had abused their power even to the point of bloodshed. *His strength* is lit., "his arm." The strong arm of government was used to oppress rather than uplift people.[435] In open defiance of the fifth commandment the people of Judah had ridiculed and mocked their elderly fathers and mothers. Furthermore, oppression of the helpless—the strangers or sojourners, the orphans and widows—was common throughout the land.

B. Religious Sins (22:8-9a)

You have despised my holy things. You have profaned my sabbaths. 9 Talebearers have been in you to shed blood. In you they have eaten upon the mountains.

The Jerusalemites had despised the holy things of God by the disrespectful way in which they conducted themselves in the temple. The weekly Sabbath and the special festival days designated as sabbaths had been profaned by the hypocritical conduct of the worshipers.

Involvement in idolatrous worship had caused a general decline in commitment to truth. Disregarding the prohibition against bearing false witness talebearers or slanderers had sent many innocent persons to face the death penalty. Many participated in the idolatrous worship exercises upon the hills.

C. Sexual Sins (22:9b-11)

In the midst of you they have committed lewdness. 10 In you a father's nakedness has been uncovered. In you they have humbled the woman who was unclean in her impurity. 11 One has committed an abomination with the wife of his neighbor, while another has defiled his daughter-in-law with lewdness. Still another in you has humbled his sister, his father's daughter.

Lewdness or unchastity was an integral part of pagan rituals. Unlike his contemporary Jeremiah who says virtually nothing about sexual sins, Ezekiel expands on the general charge of lewdness with five sexual crimes.

First, Ezekiel accuses the Jews of having *uncovered a father's nakedness*, i.e., engaged in an incestuous relationship with a step-

---

[435]A recent example of abuse of royal power is that of King Jehoiakim who built an new palace with forced labor (Jer 22:13-19).

mother (cf. Lv 18:7f.).[436] Second, the men had *humbled the woman*, i.e., forced sexual relations with a spouse during her monthly flow. The law forbade intercourse with a menstruous woman (cf. Lv 18:19; 20:18). Third, the Judeans had committed the abomination of *adultery* with a neighbor's wife. Fourth, they had committed incest with a daughter-in-law. Marriage made a woman a sister to every other male in the family. Though not blood kin sex with a daughter-in-law was equivalent to incest. Finally, the Judeans had *humbled*, i.e., raped, their half-sisters (cf. Lv 18:9, 15).

D. Sins of Avarice (22:12)

In you they have taken gifts in order to shed blood. Interest and increase you have taken. You have gotten illicit gain from your neighbor by oppression. You have forgotten me (oracle of Lord Yahweh).

Bribery of judicial officials leading to the execution of the innocent was common in Judah. In violation of the laws against usury (cf. Lv 25:36f) the wealthy had taken undue interest. Thus they had enhanced their personal wealth through greed and oppression. All of the above sins grew out of one fundamental transgression: Judah had forgotten God. To remember God is to respond to his gracious acts by covenant faithfulness.

Punishment
22:13-16

Behold I have smitten my hand at your illicit gain that you have made, and against your blood that exists in your midst. 14 Can your heart endure? Can your hands be strong for the days when I will deal with you? I Yahweh have spoken and will do it. 15 I will scatter you among the nations, and spread you in the lands. I will consume your uncleanness from you. 16 You will be profaned in yourself in the sight of the nations. You will know that I am Yahweh.

Behold introduces the shocking response of God to the sin of Judah. In a gesture of anger God is said to smite his hands, i.e., to clap his hands to summon the agents of judgment. By means of a rhetorical question Ezekiel drives home the point that the Jews will not have

[436]According to a rabbinic tradition, this v refers to King Amon who is said to have had intercourse with his mother.

have the fortitude or the physical strength to stand against the enemies by which God will bring judgment upon them. With God the very pronouncement of judgment is tantamount to the act of judgment. What he decrees he will surely bring to pass.

As far as Judah was concerned judgment involved (ultimately) exile to foreign lands. Those who had escaped the deportation of 597 BC were soon to experience that fate. This exile, however, will have a positive benefit. The people of God will be purged of their *uncleanness*, i.e., their sin and iniquity. They then will realize that Yahweh who knows the end from the beginning had brought this calamity to pass; but however beneficial the ultimate results the exile will not be a pleasant experience. In the sight of the nations Judah will be *profaned*, i.e., humiliated and debased. This will generate feelings of shame and remorse. In a certain sense this profanation will also affect Yahweh himself, as 36:20 will explain.

SMELTING FURNACE
22:17-22

The word of Yahweh came unto me, saying, 18 Son of man, the house of Israel has become to me dross. All of them are bronze, tin, iron and lead in the midst of a furnace. They are the dross of silver. 19 Therefore thus says Lord Yahweh: Because all of you have become dross, therefore behold I am about to gather you into the midst of Jerusalem. 20 As they gather silver, bronze, iron, lead and tin into the midst of a furnace to blow the fire upon it to melt it, thus I will gather you in my wrath and fury. I will cast you into [the fire] and melt you. 21 I will gather you. I will breathe upon you with the fire of my wrath. You will be melted in the midst of it. 22 As silver is melted in the midst of the furnace thus you will be melted in the midst of it. You will know that I Yahweh have poured out my wrath upon you.

The thought in v 15 that the exile will purge the filthiness from Judah is amplified in this paragraph. The *house of Israel*, i.e., Judah, has become like a metallic ore, a mixture of various minerals and impurities that must undergo a smelting process.[437] They once were silver; now they are dross, i.e., worthless.

[437]Numerous ancient smelting furnaces have been found, along the Arabah, south of the Dead Sea. *IDB*, 3:366.

Jerusalem, where the inhabitants will gather to make their last stand, will serve as the symbolic furnace in which the refining process will begin. The *wrath* and *fury* of Yahweh will be the fire that will heat that furnace. Through the holocaust the precious silver—the spiritual remnant—will become evident. All the inhabitants of Jerusalem will know that they had experienced the judgmental fury of the one true and living God.

CORRUPT LAND 22:23-31

Corruption of the Religious Leaders 22:23-26

A. Prophets (22:23-25)

The word of Yahweh came unto me, saying, 24 Son of man, say to her: You are a land not cleansed or rained upon in the day of indignation. 25 There is a conspiracy of her prophets in her midst, like a roaring lion tearing the prey. They have devoured souls. They have taken treasure and precious things. They have multiplied her widows in the midst of her.

Yahweh regarded Judah as defiled (*a land not cleansed*), spiritually desolate (*or rained upon*) and deserving of judgment. This condition existed primarily because of the actions of her national leaders. The *prophets* had entered into a *conspiracy*, a solemn pact that they will predict only peace and security for the nation. Their loud oratory, like the roar of a lion, was only the prelude to national disaster. The character of these men was indicated by their greed. In exchange for treasure and precious things they will paint the future in the most optimistic hues. The results of this kind of prognostication, however, were disastrous. Lives will be lost and widows made numerous by the ruinous national policy that they encouraged.

B. Priests (22:26)

Her priests have done violence to my law. They have profaned my holy things. They have not distinguished between the holy and the common. They have not taught the difference between the un-

clean and clean. They have hidden their eyes from my sabbaths. I am profaned among them.

The *priests* were no better than the prophets. They failed to teach God's law. They violated its teaching. They *profaned the holy things* of God by not adhering to the regulations that served to underscore the sanctity of the temple. They failed both in their private lives and in their public teaching to differentiate between *holy* and *common*, i.e., they allowed holy things to be used in profane ways (cf. Lv 10:10f). Likewise the Mosaic distinction between *clean* and *unclean* was ignored both in regard to meat fit for food and in regard to the ritual purity of worshipers. They hid their eyes from the sabbaths of God, i.e., they looked on indifferently as God's people desecrated those sacred days. By means of all the above named transgressions the priests had *done violence* to God's law.[438] They had *profaned*, i.e., treated disrespectfully, Yahweh God.

Corruption of Societal Leaders 22:27-29

Her princes in her midst are like wolves tearing the prey: to shed blood and to destroy souls in order to acquire illicit gain. 28 Her prophets have daubed for them with white plaster, seeing falsehood and divining lies to them, saying, Thus says Lord Yahweh, when Yahweh has not spoken. 29 The people of this land have engaged in oppression. They have been involved in theft. They have wronged the poor and needy. They have oppressed the stranger unlawfully.

The *princes*, like fierce wolves, shed blood and destroyed lives so as to enrich themselves. Probably these men used legal machinery to achieve their ends.

Prophets were supposed to rebuke wicked men, expose national corruption and warn of impending disaster. Judah's prophets, however, had whitewashed the leadership. They supported their dangerous international policy by proclaiming falsehood. They used pagan

[438]The connotation of the verb is that of "violence" done against persons, not property. Since the law reflects God's nature, violation of his law is a personal attack against him. See P.J. Harland, "What Kind of 'Violence' in Ezekiel 22?" *ET* 108 (1996): 111-14.

divination to conjure up some of their lies. Yet they brazenly announced their prophecies with *thus says Yahweh* (cf. 13:10).

The *people of the land*, i.e., the wealthy landholders, unlawfully had resorted to robbery and oppression against the helpless element of society and the *stranger* (foreigner) who sojourned in the land.

Total Corruption 22:30-31

I sought for a man among them to build up the wall, one to stand in the breach before me for the land that I should not destroy it. I found none. 31 Therefore I have poured out upon them my wrath. In the fire of my anger I have consumed them. Their way I have placed upon their head (oracle of Lord Yahweh).

The population was thoroughly corrupt. God could find no moral leader to *stand in the breach* in the moral wall that protected Judah from judgment (cf. 13:5). Morality is like a wall that shields a people from divine wrath. Where that wall breaks down judgment enters. Judah needed a national leader of the highest quality to use his influence for good to repair that broken wall. None was available.

The moral collapse of a nation is inevitably followed by its physical destruction. So certain was the judgment that God used the past tense to describe what will yet befall Judah. There was no escape!

EZEKIEL 23 A SAD HISTORY

In ch 23 Ezekiel vividly portrays the history of the sister kingdoms of Israel and Judah.[439] In ch 16 God likened Jerusalem to a prostitute. The same figure is used of the entire nation here. The emphasis in the previous allegory was on spiritual fornication with Canaanite cults. Here the emphasis is on Israel's political adultery, i.e., political alliances with foreign powers. Chapter 16 stressed the beginnings of Israel's history whereas ch 23 places more emphasis on her later history.[440]

---

[439]This is the third of Ezekiel's surveys of Israel's history (cf. chs 16, 20). Inspiration for the present allegory may have come from Jer 3:6-10.

[440]Alexander, *Expositor's Bible Commentary*, 851.

SISTERS INTRODUCED 23:1-4

The word of Yahweh came unto me, saying, 2 Son of man, there were two women, the daughters of the same mother. 3 They committed harlotry in Egypt. They committed harlotry in their youth. There their breasts were pressed, yes there their virgin breasts were fondled. 4 Their names were Oholah the elder, and Oholibah her sister. They became mine. They bore sons and daughters. As for their names, Samaria is Oholah, and Jerusalem is Oholibah.

The allegory begins with the introduction of two women, daughters of one mother. The kingdoms of Israel and Judah had their origin in the united nation of Israel that existed from the time of Egypt to the days of Solomon.

The tribes of Judah (represented by Jerusalem) and Ephraim (represented by Samaria) had experienced the Egyptian bondage. Even in that formative period of Israel's history the sisters had shown inclinations toward idolatry. Using the figure of sexual license—the fondling of the breasts—Ezekiel describes how God's people lost their virgin chastity even before leaving Egypt.

The sisters are given similar names. Samaria is Oholah (*she who has a tent*). The significance of this name is not clear. It may refer to Samaria's propensity for heathen tent-shrines.[441] Jerusalem is Oholibah (*my tent is in her*). Perhaps this name has reference to the tent that David erected in Jerusalem to house the ark of God.[442]

God says that both cities *became mine*, i.e., they belonged to Yahweh as his possession. This is usually taken to indicate marriage, although the text does not make this clear.[443] Both cities bore *sons and daughters*. These children most likely refer to their inhabitants and satellite towns.

---

[441]Alexander (*ibid*) references a recently excavated platform for a tent-shrine on Mount Gerizim.

[442]Cf. 2 Sam 6:17; 1 Kgs 8:4; 1 Chr 15:1; 16:1 et al. Another view is that Ezekiel is thinking of a nomadic tent, i.e., God's people were only camping out down in Egypt.

[443]Under the Mosaic Law, marriage to two sisters was forbidden (Lv 18:18). If Ezekiel uses an illegal marriage arrangement to illustrate God's relationship to Israel and Judah, he may be hinting that he regarded the schism of 931 BC as illegal. On the other hand, the language *they became mine* may refer to adoption (Gn 48:5).

SAMARIA'S PROSTITUTION 23:5-10

Description of the Harlotry 23:5-8

Oholah committed harlotry under me. She threw herself on her lovers, on the Assyrians. [They were] warriors 6 clothed with blue, governors and rulers, all of them handsome young men, horsemen riding on horses. 7 She bestowed her harlotries upon them, the choicest men of Assyria all of them. On whomsoever she threw herself with all their idols she defiled herself. 8 She did not forsake her Egyptian harlotries; for they lay with her in her youth, and they bruised her virgin breasts. They poured out their lust upon her.

For the purposes of this allegory Samaria is called the elder sister because she had experienced the judgment of God prior to Jerusalem. Oholah (Samaria) committed harlotry from *under* God, i.e., from under his authority. She threw herself at various lovers among whom the Assyrians were most notable.[444] The Assyrian warriors, dressed in handsome uniforms and led by men of note, attracted the inhabitants of Samaria.[445]

Israel plunged headlong into political alliance with Assyria. She willingly paid the price demanded of all allies, viz. homage to the Assyrian deities. Thus did Samaria defile herself *with all their idols*.

The corrupt Oholah (Samaria) did not forsake her earlier harlotries when she took up with the Assyrians. She had committed spiritual adultery in Egypt. She had prostituted herself before Egyptian idols. Throughout her history she had continued to engage in those pagan cultic practices. Samaria was fascinated by military powers and the gods worshiped by those powers.

---

[444]Ezekiel is echoing Hosea in condemning the northern kingdom's involvement with Assyria. Cf. Hos 5:13; 8:9; 14:3.

[445]The first king of Israel to render tribute to Assyria was Jehu in 841 BC. The Black Obelisk of Shalmaneser depicts and describes the scene. Another example of involvement with Assyria is found in 2 Kgs 15:19-20. Hosea had opposed military alliance with Assyria (Hos 5:13-6:6).

Punishment of the Harlotry
23:9-10

Therefore I gave her into the hand of her lovers, into the hand of the Assyrians upon whom she threw herself. 10 They uncovered her nakedness. They took her sons and daughters, and slew her with the sword. She became a byword to women, for judgments were made against her.

Because of her harlotries Oholah (Samaria) was delivered by God into the hands of her lovers, the Assyrians. What irony to be destroyed by the nation that was one of her *lovers*, i.e., allies.

The Assyrians stripped Oholah—ravished her land, removed her wealth. The sons and daughters of Samaria were carried away into captivity. Oholah herself was slain with the sword, i.e., Samaria was destroyed by military action. Oholah became a name—a byword or warning—to all other women (nations) who might contemplate unfaithfulness to Yahweh. What happened to Samaria should have been a warning to Jerusalem.

JERUSALEM'S PROSTITUTION
23:11-21

Harlotry with the Assyrians
23:11-13

Her sister Oholibah saw this. She became corrupt in her doting more than she, and in harlotries more than the harlotries of her sister. 12 She threw herself upon the Assyrians. [They were] governors and rulers, warriors, clothed handsomely, horsemen riding horses, all of them handsome young men. 13 I saw that she was defiled. They both went the same way.

Oholibah (Jerusalem) learned nothing from the experience of her elder sister. She became yet more corrupt, adopting the same policy of political and religious flirtation with foreign powers, but intensifying it. She too fell for the Assyrians with their handsomely clad officers and warriors (cf. vv 5-6).

Judah derived much advantage from the alliance with Assyria.[446] From the religious point of view, however, the association was disastrous. God saw immediately that Judah had defiled herself with the Mesopotamian practices. Both sisters—Samaria and Jerusalem—had pursued the same corrupt way.

Lust for the Chaldeans
23:14-16

She added to her harlotries; for she saw men depicted upon the
wall. [She saw] the images of Chaldeans depicted in red color, 15
girded with girdles upon their loins, with flowing turbans upon their
heads, all of them with the appearance of captains, the likeness of
the sons of Babylon, the Chaldeans, the land of their captivity. 16
When she saw them she threw herself upon them. She sent messen-
gers to them to Chaldea.

The *harlotries*—pagan practices—of Jerusalem were more extensive than those of Samaria. Oholibah saw paintings depicting the glories of a people who lived beyond Assyria. Oholibah's lust for political liaison was kindled by the sight of the martial Chaldeans girded in native dress. The waist-belt and turban with dangling fillets was the garb that set the sons of Babylon apart as a distinct people in the ancient world. Oholibah (Jerusalem) was unable to resist the lure to associate with this strange and exotic people. She threw herself upon them by sending messengers there to negotiate the alliance.

Harlotries with the Babylonians
23:17-18

The Babylonians came to her to the bed of love. They defiled
her with their harlotries. She was defiled by them. Then her soul
was alienated from them. 18 So she uncovered her harlotries. She
uncovered her nakedness. Then my soul was alienated from her as
my soul was alienated from her sister.

The Babylonians were quick to take advantage of Judah's thoughtless infatuation. They *came to her into the bed of love*, i.e., they entered eagerly into the alliance with Judah. The result was in-

[446]The reference may be to King Ahaz's appeal to Tiglath-pileser for help (2 Kgs 16:7). Isaiah opposed the policy of reliance on Assyria.

evitable. Judah was further defiled by the Babylonian cults that were transplanted there. Eventually Judah felt revulsion at this alliance. She tried several times unsuccessfully to disengage herself from this entanglement.[447]

One step remained before Oholibah (Jerusalem) reached the depth of corruption. In the process of trying to pry herself loose from the clutches of Babylon Oholibah had *uncovered her nakedness* in an effort to attract other lovers who might rescue her. Such degrading national conduct was revolting to God. He now felt toward Judah the same antagonism that he had felt towards Samaria over a century earlier. Yahweh was alienated from his people.

Further Harlotries
23:19-21

Yet she multiplied her harlotries, remembering the days of her youth when she played the harlot in the land of Egypt. 20 She threw herself upon their concubinage whose flesh is as the flesh of donkeys, and whose sexual potency is like that of horses. 21 So you relived the lewdness of your youth when in Egypt your breasts were bruised because of the breasts of your youth.

Oholibah seemed undismayed at the accusation of God's prophets that she was alienating herself from God. She *multiplied her harlotries*. Recalling her ancient association with Egypt she made overtures in that direction.

To break her ties to Babylon Oholibah *threw herself upon their concubinage*, i.e., Judah was willing to become one of the numerous vassal states of Egypt. The harlot Oholibah was attracted by the sexual potency of Egypt that is likened to that of a donkey or horse. *Flesh* is a euphemism for male genitals (cf. NIV). *Sexual potency* refers to emission of semen. Oholibah was drawn toward bestiality! Ezekiel uses this astonishing figure to underscore the vulgarity of power politics.[448]

---

[447]The reference is to efforts of Jehoiakim and later Zedekiah to free themselves from Babylonian domination.

[448]At the same time, Ezekiel may be warning that the mismatch of such an unequal sexual liaison will result in painful death (cf. Lind, *Ezekiel*, 197).

Egyptian customs and cults long forgotten were called to remembrance. Judah plunged headlong into spiritual harlotry and political alliance with the ancient enemy to the south.

JERUSALEM'S JUDGMENT 23:22-35

Ezekiel now utters five threats against Oholibah (Jerusalem). Four of the five threats begin with *thus says Lord Yahweh.*

First Threat 23:22-24

Therefore O Oholibah, thus says Lord Yahweh: Behold I am about to stir up your lovers against you, those from whom your soul is alienated. I will bring them against you round about: 23 the Babylonians and all the Chaldeans, Pekod and Shea and Koa, and all the Assyrians with them, handsome young men, governors and rulers all of them. [They are] captains and counselors, all of them riding upon horses. 24 They will come against you with hosts,[449] ***chariots, wheels, and with an assembly of peoples. With shield, buckler, and helmet they will set themselves against you round about. I will commit judgment to them. They will judge you according to their judgment.***

The first threat focuses on the coming of Babylon. Ezekiel makes four points. First, the Babylonians come at God's summons. As time went on Judah became *alienated* from her lovers. She wished to be free of all foreign entanglements. Morally and spiritually, however, the damage already had been done. Ironically God will use Judah's *lovers* as the instrument by which to punish his people.

Second, the Babylonians come as a vast throng. Ezekiel names the various racial and linguistic groups that made up the empire of Nebuchadnezzar.[450] What a handsome sight that will be when those troops from far-off Mesopotamia come against Jerusalem! The de-

---

[449]The word is of uncertain meaning.

[450]Pekod, Shea, and Koa are now known to be races inhabiting the land east of the Tigris and bordering on Elam or Persia. See Fisch, *Ezekiel*, 154.

scription of the military personnel is virtually repeated from vv 6 and 12.

Third, the Babylonians come for war. The host from Mesopotamia is armed to the teeth with the finest military equipment. This great force will be deployed against Jerusalem in siege operations. Ezekiel is underscoring Yahweh's opposition to Israel's involvement in the military culture of the day.

Finally, the Babylonians come for judgment. God had commissioned those troops to execute his judgment upon Jerusalem. They will fulfill that commission *according to their judgment*, i.e., in their own ruthless fashion.

Second Threat
23:25-27

I will set my jealousy against you. They will deal with you in wrath. They will remove your nose and your ears. The rest of you will fall with the sword. They will take your sons and daughters. The rest of you will be consumed with fire. 26 They will strip off your garments and take away your fair jewels. 27 I will cause your lewdness to cease from you and your Egyptian harlotry, so that you will not lift up your eyes unto them, or remember Egypt anymore.

The second threat focuses on deportation to Babylon. Ezekiel makes three points. First, the Judeans will either be deported or killed. Yahweh is a jealous God. He will not tolerate his people engaging in flirtations with other deities and trusting in human might. God will set his *jealousy* against Judah, i.e., he will bring divine retribution upon them. The *I/they* interchange underscores that God will use foreigners as the agents of his wrath. The attacking forces will deal ruthlessly with Jerusalem. The *nose* and *ears* of the adulterous Oholibah will be removed. The reference probably is to be taken figuratively of the execution or deportation of the leading citizens of the nation.[451] Other citizens will *fall by the sword* or be taken as slaves.

Second, the houses and property of the Jerusalem will be put to the torch after being plundered.

Third, the fall of Judah and subsequent exile will cure the Jews of their *lewdness*, i.e., fascination with political power. Pagan practices learned in Egypt will be abandoned and forgotten. To *lift up your eyes*

[451]In ancient times disfigurement was inflicted on women caught in adultery.

to them indicates trust and devotion. The expression is usually used of idols. Trusting in earthly powers is akin to idolatry. History records that God's judgment of Jerusalem did have this purging and purifying effect.

Third Threat
23:28-31

For thus says Lord Yahweh: Behold I am about to give you into the hand of the one you hate, into the hand of the one from whom your soul is alienated. 29 They will deal with you in hatred. They will take away all your labor. They will leave you naked and bare. The nakedness of your harlotries will be uncovered, both your lewdness and your harlotries. 30 These things will be done to you because you have whored after nations, and because you were defiled by their idols. 31 You walked in the way of your sister. Therefore I will place her cup in your hand.

The Jews will be delivered into the hand of their hated enemy, the Babylonians. The Babylonians will deal with the Jews in hatred. They will take away all the *labor*, i.e., fruit of the labors, of the Jerusalemites. The land will be stripped of all its wealth and left *naked and bare*. By the drastic extremes of the punishment the magnitude of the *harlotries* of Jerusalem, i.e., idolatrous sins, will be revealed.

Again the prophet pounds home his point that the judgment will fall upon Jerusalem because the Jews had entered into alliances with foreign nations instead of trusting in Yahweh. Consequently they had been corrupted by the practices of these nations.

Oholibah (Jerusalem) had followed the example of her sister Oholah (Samaria). The bitter *cup* of divine judgment had been drunk by the northern kingdom in the days of the great Assyrian kings. Now that cup will pass into the hands of Judah.

Fourth Threat
23:32-34

Thus says Lord Yahweh: You will drink the cup of your sister that is deep and large. It will be for scorn and derision. It is full to the uttermost. 33 You will be filled with drunkenness and sorrow, with the cup of astonishment and desolation, the cup of your sister

Samaria. 34 You will drink it, drain it, and gnaw its shards. You will tear your breasts, for I have spoken (oracle of Lord Yahweh).

The cup of judgment was deep, large and full to the brim with bitter brew. Consuming the contents of that cup of judgment will bring scorn and derision to Judah. The nation will manifest the characteristics of a drunken man.

The cup will be drained to the last drop. The vessel itself will be chewed up so that the beverage that had soaked into the pottery could be consumed. In drunken madness the inebriated Oholibah will tear at her breasts in anguish. This figure conveys the thought that the complete measure of divine judgment must be endured.

Fifth Threat
23:35

Therefore thus says Lord Yahweh: Because you have forgotten me and cast me behind your back; therefore bear also your lewdness and your harlotries.

The fifth threat repeats the word *therefore*. The first *therefore* identifies the root cause of Jerusalem's dalliance with power politics and the associated idolatry. Jerusalem had *forgotten* God. To *cast me behind your back* is a metaphor depicting a deliberate and violent act. To forget God is to deny his saving acts and to choose the path of trusting in self or others rather than in God. The second *therefore* indicates that such *lewdness* and *harlotries* (i.e., faithlessness exhibited on numerous occasions) must be punished.

ADDITIONAL INDICTMENT
23:36-44

Apostasy Literally Depicted
23:36-39

Yahweh said unto me, Son of man, will you judge Oholah and Oholibah? Then declare to them their abominations. 37 For they have committed adultery. Blood is on their hands. With their idols they have committed adultery. Also their sons whom they bore to me they offered up to them to be devoured. 38 This also they have done

unto me: they have defiled my sanctuary in the same day. They have profaned my sabbaths. 39 For when they had slain their sons to their idols, then they came unto my sanctuary the same day to profane it. Behold thus they did in the midst of my house.

To correctly judge the guilty sisters Ezekiel must declare to them the abominations that they had committed. What a record! Adultery—both literal and spiritual—bloodshed, idolatry! Children who had been committed to God in the rite of circumcision were later set apart to be devoured by (i.e., sacrificed to) the god Molech.

Such gross pagan rites were deliberately scheduled for a Sabbath. Human sacrifice at the high place of Molech was followed by a trip to the temple of Yahweh. Was this brazen hypocrisy, or evidence of seared conscience? In either case their presence in the temple was an affront to God.

Apostasy Figuratively Depicted 23:40-44

Furthermore you have sent for men that come from afar to whom a messenger was sent. Behold they came, [these] for whom you washed, painted your eyes, and decked yourself with ornaments. 41 You sat upon a stately bed with a table arranged before it upon which you set my incense and my oil. 42 The voice of a multitude at ease was in it. With men of the common sort were brought drunkards from the wilderness. They put bracelets upon their hands, and beautiful crowns upon their heads. 43 Then I said to her worn out by adulteries: Still they commit harlotries with her, even her. 44 For one went in unto her as one goes unto a harlot. So they went in unto Oholah and unto Oholibah, the lewd women.

Judah actively pursued idolatry. Messengers were sent to far places to invite idolaters to come and teach them pagan rites. Like a harlot attempting to lure men into her house Judah prepared for her lovers. She washed herself, put make-up about her eyes, and bedecked herself with ornaments.

The harlot sat on a beautiful bed or couch[452] at a sumptuous table. It was the custom at meals to burn incense and to rub oneself with scented oils after the meal. The adulterous Judah took the luxuries

[452]The allusion is to the ancient custom of reclining on couches during a meal.

that God had bestowed on her and used them to advance the cause of idolatry.

Sounds of careless revelry were heard in Jerusalem. Thus were alliances formed with various nations, even with common men and drunkards from the wilderness, i.e., men of the most degraded kind. With bracelets and crowns Oholibah sought to attract these worthless neighbors.

The two nations (Judah and Israel) never seemed to tire of this profligacy. They persisted in their imported idolatries. The immoral sisters had relations with any idolatrous cult that made any effort to enter the country. Oholah and Oholibah became like a harlot who is indiscriminate in her immoral conduct.

DEPICTION OF JUDGMENT 23:45-49

But righteous men will judge them with the judgment of women who commit adultery, and with the judgment of those who shed blood; for they are adulteresses and blood is on their hands. 46 For thus says Lord Yahweh: An assembly will be brought up against them. They will be made a horror and a spoil. 47 The assembly will stone them with stones. They will be cut down by their swords. Their sons and their daughters they will slay. They will burn their houses. 48 I will cause lewdness to cease from the land that all the women might be taught that they might not do according to your lewdness. Your lewdness will be placed upon you. You will bear the sins of your idols. 49 You will know that I am Lord Yahweh.

Compared to Jerusalem and Samaria the Babylonians and Assyrians were *righteous men*. These "righteous men" were God's appointed judges over the adulterous sisters. Oholah and Oholibah were adulteresses and murderesses. They were to be judged accordingly. The blood that stained the hands of the sisters was mainly that of innocent children slain in pagan rites.

God was about to bring a great assembly of nations against Jerusalem. The holy city will be treated so mercilessly that it will become an object of horror and spoliation. As under the Law of Moses the adulteress (Jerusalem) will be stoned (cf. Dt 13:10). The sons and daughters of Jerusalem will be thrust through with swords. The houses of the city will be burned.

A fourfold purpose in God's judgment is indicated in vv 48-49. First, judgment will bring an end to lewdness (idolatry) in the Promised Land. Second, other women (surrounding nations) will take warning from the fate of Oholibah. Third, it was necessary that Jerusalem received the recompense for her idolatrous harlotry. Finally, God must execute this punishment in order to bring his people into a proper knowledge of himself.

EZEKIEL 24
JUDGMENT HAS ARRIVED

Chapter 24 begins with an important chronological note. Three things of importance happened in the ministry of Ezekiel on that date. Ezekiel delivered a judgment parable (vv 1-14), received word concerning two judgment signs (vv 15-27), and uttered four oracles condemning neighboring nations (25:1-17).

INTRODUCTION
24:1-2

The word of Yahweh came unto me in the ninth year, the tenth month, the tenth day of the month, saying, 2 Son of man, write for yourself the name of the day, this very day. This very day the king of Babylon has leaned upon Jerusalem.

Nebuchadnezzar began his attack against Jerusalem in the ninth year (of Zedekiah), the tenth day of the tenth month.[453] The Jews commemorated this date for centuries by fasting (Zech 8:19). Ezekiel was told to write the name of the day of the week and the day of the month (*this very day*). This written record was to be made so that later when the news filtered back to the captives in Babylon the genuine prophetic foresight of Ezekiel would be authenticated.

---

[453]The same date is given in 2 Kgs 25:1; and Jer 52:4. In terms of the modern calendar, the date is Dec 29, 588 BC. Only here does Ezekiel depart from his usual practice of giving dates according to the captivity of Jehoiachin. The importance of this date caused him to use the reign of Zedekiah, in order to bring his listing of the date into harmony with that of 2 Kgs 25:1 and Jer 52:4.

PARABLE OF THE COOKING POT 24:3-14

Parable Introduced 24:3-5

Utter a parable against this rebellious house and say unto them: Thus says Lord Yahweh: Set on the pot. Set it on. Pour water into it. 4 Gather into it the pieces belonging to it, every good piece—the thigh and the shoulder. Fill it with the choice bones. 5 Take the choice of the flock, and also pile the bones under it. Boil it well that its bones may boil in the midst of it.

On that fateful day Ezekiel set forth a parable concerning Jerusalem. For the third time he expresses his thoughts in a song.[454] The inhabitants of Jerusalem previously had used the image of a caldron to support their delusion of invincibility (cf. 11:3). Now Ezekiel gives the true interpretation to that image. A pot is filled with water and placed on the stove. This symbolizes the first stage of the siege of Jerusalem.

The chunks of meat placed in the pot symbolize the inhabitants of Jerusalem and the fugitives from other towns who sought refuge there. The good pieces of meat and *choice bones* represent the civil and military leaders who come from the *choice of the flock*, i.e., the upper classes. Bones as well as meat—the total population—were to be placed in that pot, with the bones under the meat.

Ezekiel is then to bring the pot to a boil until even the bones—the toughest members of society—are brought to a boil. The boiling water points to the destructive turbulence of the Babylonian siege.

First Woe 24:6-8

Therefore thus says Lord Yahweh: Woe to the bloody city, to the pot whose filth is in it, and whose filth has not gone out of it! Bring

[454]This "cooking pot song" is comparable to the "sword song" of 21:8-17 and the "cup song" of 23:32-34.

it out piece by piece. No lot is fallen upon it. 7 For her blood is in the midst of her. Upon the bare rock she set it. She did not pour it out upon the ground to cover it with dust, 8 to cause fury to go up, that vengeance might be taken. I have set the blood upon a bare rock that it should not be covered.

The prophet drops the symbolism in v 6 and sets his message in plain prose. He pronounces a *woe* on the *bloody city*[455] of Jerusalem, *the pot whose filth* had never been removed. The reference is to the bloodstains of the innocent who had been murdered in Jerusalem. *Piece by piece* the chunks of meat in that pot will be removed. By this the prophet means that the destruction of the city and the deportation of the inhabitants will take place in stages. *No lot is fallen* on the content of that pot, i.e., the deportation will be indiscriminate.

Openly and unashamedly crimes had been committed in Jerusalem. Evidence of bloodshed could be seen throughout the place. It was as though Jerusalem had smeared blood on a bare rock that was in plain view. The law required animal blood to be poured to the ground and covered with dust (cf. Lv 17:13). No similar effort, however, had been made to conceal the blood of humankind unjustly slain. God will preserve those bloodstains in plain view so that he might execute divine wrath on those responsible.

Second Woe
24:9-12

Therefore thus says Lord Yahweh. Woe to the bloody city. I also will make the pile great, 10 heaping on the wood, kindling the fire, that the flesh may be consumed; and preparing the mixture that the bones may be burned. 11 Then I will set it empty upon its coals that it may be hot, and the bottom of it burn that its impurity may be melted in it, that its filth may be consumed. 12 She has wearied (me) with toil. Yet its great filth will not go out from it. Its filth will be in the fire.

A second time the sentence against Jerusalem is pronounced. They had piled one sin on top of another. God will now *make the pile great*, i.e., he will heap up the fuel for their punishment. God will gather the wood, kindle the fire, and prepare *the mixture* of spices to

---

[455]For similar indictment of Jerusalem as a *bloody city*, see 22:2. Cf. 7:23; 9:9; 22:6-13.

be added when the meat had been sufficiently cooked. It was God's purpose to consume the meat (population of Jerusalem) and burn the bones (leaders, especially military leaders) in that pot.

After the contents of that pot (Jerusalem) had been consumed God will see to it that the pot itself is melted down thereby removing the *filth*. Thus Jerusalem will be purified by the conflagration. God had attempted from time to time to purge Jerusalem. The effort was to no avail. This may be an allusion to the deportations of 604 BC and 597 BC. The uncleanness of the city could only be removed by the drastic process of melting down the caldron, i.e., destroying Jerusalem.

Conclusion
24:13-14

Because of your filthy lewdness, because I purged you and you were not purged from your uncleanness, you will not be purged from your uncleanness anymore until I have satisfied my wrath on you. 14 I Yahweh have spoken it. It will come to pass. I will do it. I will not go back. I will not have pity. I will not repent. According to your ways and according to your deeds they will judge you (oracle of Lord Yahweh).

The prose conclusion to the Song of the Pot uses the first-person singular pronoun 7x. All efforts to reform the nation through prophetic admonition had failed. No further effort in that direction will be attempted. All that remained was for God to pour out his wrath and purge the place by total destruction. *Lewdness* in Ezekiel is used in a figurative sense for negotiating military treaties and idolatry.[456]

Yahweh will hand the Judeans over to the Chaldeans who will execute a judgment upon Jerusalem that was appropriate to her sins. Such is the irrevocable divine decree.[457]

---

[456]See Ezek 16:27, 43, 58; 22:9; 23:21, 27, 29, 35, 48-49.
[457]The Hebrew uses the prophetic perfect, viewing the action as so certain it could be described as already completed.

FIRST JUDGMENT SIGN 24:15-24

Instructions 24:15-19

The word of Yahweh came unto me, saying, 16 Son of man, behold I am about to take from you the desire of your eyes with a stroke. Yet you will not lament or weep, nor will your tears come down. 17 Sigh silently. Make no mourning for the dead. Your headdress bind upon you. Your sandals put upon your feet. Do not cover your lip. Do not eat the bread of men. 18 So I spoke unto the people in the morning. My wife died in the evening. I did in the morning as I was commanded. 19 The people said unto me: Will you not declare to us what these things are to us that you are doing?

A shocking announcement was made to the prophet on that day when Jerusalem came under siege. It was an announcement that caused Ezekiel much grief. *The desire of your eyes*—your wife—will die *with a stroke*, i.e., she will die suddenly without having been previously sick. The prophet was commanded to refrain from any lamentation or mourning rites.

Ezekiel was to *sigh in silence*, i.e., to internalize his agony (cf. Jer 16:5-7). He was not to resort to the customary loud cries of lamentation. He was not to loosen his headgear to let his hair hang down covering his upper lip. He was not to remove his sandals nor *eat ... the bread of men*, i.e., the mourner's meal supplied by friends and relatives. What a difficult burden Yahweh laid on his prophet. Ezekiel's silent grief was to symbolize the stupefying effect that the fall of Jerusalem will have on the Jews at home and abroad. They will be too stunned for customary expressions of grief. Even though he knew his wife might die at any moment Ezekiel continued his ministry of preaching. That evening his wife died. The next morning Ezekiel carried out Yahweh's command to sigh in silence. Perplexed by his strange behavior the people sensed that the prophet was trying to convey some symbolic meaning to them. Thus they inquired concerning his conduct.

Explanations
24:20-24

I said unto them, The word of Yahweh came unto me, saying, 21 Say to the house of Israel, Thus says Lord Yahweh: Behold I am about to profane my sanctuary, the pride of your power, the desire of your eyes, and the longing of your soul. Your sons and your daughters whom you have left behind will fall by the sword. 22 You will do as I have done. You will not cover your lip. You will not eat the bread of men. 23 Your headdress will be upon your heads, and your sandals upon your feet. You will not lament or weep; but you will waste away in your iniquities and moan one to another. 24 Ezekiel will be to you a sign. According to all that he has done you will do. When it comes to pass you will know that I am Lord Yahweh.

In response to the inquiry of his fellow exiles Ezekiel first indicated that what he had been doing and what he was about to say came from God.

Ezekiel explained that he had just suffered the loss of the desire of his eyes, the one he held most precious. The Jews were about to lose their temple. The loss thus incurred is indicated in the text by three expressions that underscore the prominent place that sacred structure occupied in the hearts of the Jews. The temple was *the pride of your power*, i.e., what guaranteed, so they thought, the invincibility of Jerusalem and permanence of their national existence; *the desire of your eyes*, i.e., what they held to be most precious; and the *longing of your soul*, i.e., what they most missed by being exiled to Babylon. That sacred spot was about to be profaned by being delivered into the hands of heathen men. Along with the loss of the temple the exiles will lose their *sons and daughters* who had been left behind in the doomed city.

News of the destruction of the temple and the loss of their children will throw the exiles into shock. They will be unable to observe the conventional mourning customs. Added to the news of the unthinkable disaster in Jerusalem will be the pangs of guilty conscience. During that period of grief the once proud exiles will waste away in their iniquities. In almost inaudible expressions they will moan one to another.

In his manner of mourning Yahweh had appointed Ezekiel as a *sign* to the exiles. As the prophet had abstained from outward display of mourning so also will the exiles. When all this came to pass—the news that Jerusalem had fallen and the temple had been destroyed—they will know that the event had been decreed by Yahweh.

SECOND JUDGMENT SIGN
24:25-27

As for you, son of man, will it not be in the day I take from them their stronghold, the joy of their glory, the desire of their eyes, the yearning of their soul, their sons and their daughters, 26 that the one who escapes in that day will come unto you to cause you to hear it with your ears? 27 In that day your mouth will be open, together with the one who escaped. You will speak, and will no more be dumb. You will be a sign to them. They will know that I am Yahweh.

The love that a Jew had for the temple is difficult for westerners to understand. The temple was their *stronghold* upon which they based their confidence of national permanence. It was the *joy of their glory*, the magnificent edifice of which they were so proud. It was *the desire of their eyes*,[458] what they loved dearly. It was the *yearning of their soul*, what above all they longed to see again. When that structure fell along with their sons and daughters, a fugitive of the slaughter will hasten to Babylon to bear the sad tidings.

In the day the news of Jerusalem's fall was announced Ezekiel will no longer be dumb.[459] The message he had been preaching for so many years will thus be authenticated. His mission as a messenger of God will then be accepted by his fellow exiles. The sign of his wife's death portends judgment and death; this second sign will trumpet salvation and life.

---

[458]Some commentators take the phrase *desire of their eyes* to refer to the sons and daughters rather than the temple.

[459]The previous discussion of the dumbness of Ezekiel in 3:25-27 should be reviewed at this point.

EZEKIEL 25
WARNING TO NEIGHBORS

Ezekiel devotes eight chs of his book to oracles against foreign nations. Jerusalem had fallen. Yet before Ezekiel related this fact to his readers he recorded the revelation that God will someday judge the heathen nations and cities around Judah.

Ezekiel speaks of seven different nations in all.[460] He first warned four small neighbors (25:1-17). He then denounced the two commercial centers of the day, Tyre and Sidon (26:1-28:26). The final blast is directed against Egypt (29:1-32:32).

Some commentators express surprise that Babylon is not singled out in this section for condemnation. Ezekiel deliberately refrained from announcing the destruction of that nation. To do so would have been too glaring a provocation. It did not demand great intelligence, however, to conclude that if God was going to pour out his judgment upon these nations Babylon surely could not altogether escape. Jeremiah already had written a lengthy condemnation of Babylon; onc from Ezekiel was unnecessary. Furthermore, an anti-Babylon oracle by Ezekiel could have stirred up the exiles to foolish resistance to the Babylonian government.

Throughout history Israel experienced the hostility of the neighboring states of Ammon, Moab, Edom and Philistia. In the time of Jerusalem's dying agony these countries tormented and mocked God's people. Their attitude toward Israel was also their attitude toward Israel's God. Jeremiah already had announced that God's agent was to unleash his wrath upon these four neighbors.[461] They were to come under the fist of Babylon for seventy years (Jer 25:11).

The four brief oracles in ch 25 serve the double purpose of declaring God's wrath on all arrogant people who mock him; and indicating to the penitent exiles that God was still concerned for his people in that he was punishing their enemies.

---

[460] John Geyer, "Mythology and Culture in the Oracles against the Nations," *VT* 36 (1986): 129-145.

[461] Jer 9:25-26; 25:1-26; 27:1-11; 48:1-49:22.

WORD AGAINST AMMON 25:1-7

The Ammonites had been vicious enemies of Israel since the time of the judges (Judg 10:9). Their ruthlessness is clearly indicated in the account of the siege of Jabesh-gilead (1 Sam 11). When the territories east of Jordan had fallen to Assyria the Israelite tribes there had been deported. The Ammonites then took over the unoccupied area.

First Judgment Announcement 25:1-5

The word of Yahweh came unto me, saying, 2 Son of man, set your face against the children of Ammon. Prophesy against them 3 and say to the children of Ammon, Hear the word of Lord Yahweh! Thus says Lord Yahweh: Because you have said, Aha! against my sanctuary when it was defiled, and against the land of Israel when it was made desolate, and against the house of Judah when they went into captivity; 4 therefore behold I am about to give you to the children of the east for a possession. They will set their encampments and make their dwelling places among you. They will eat your fruit and drink your milk. 5 I will make Rabbah a pasture for camels, and the children of Ammon for a resting place for flocks. Then you will know that I am Yahweh.

The Ammon oracle begins with the strongest possible declaration of inspiration. To this is added the directive for Ezekiel to set his face against Ammon and *prophesy against them*. This may have involved an actual facial expression, or it may simply indicate that the prophet was to deliver a negative prophecy. Ezekiel was to address the Ammonites as though he stood in their midst: *Hear the word of Lord Yahweh*. Yahweh alone was Lord, i.e., master (*ᵓᵃdōnāy*), not Chemosh, the god of Ammon. To further underscore the authority of what follows Ezekiel adds the traditional messenger formula: *Thus says Lord Yahweh.*

The Ammonites were gloating (*Aha!*) over three misfortunes of the Judeans: 1) God's *sanctuary* had been *defiled*. 2) *the land of Israel* had been made *desolate*; and 3) *the house of Judah* had gone into *captivity*. The Ammonites had cast covetous eyes on the now unoccupied land of Judah.

For their arrogant pride and blasphemous intentions God will bring swift judgment on Ammon. That nation will be delivered over to the *children of the east*, i.e., marauders from the Arabian Desert.[462] They will overrun the land, encamp within it, and build their permanent dwellings there. These strangers will forcibly take from the Ammonites the fruit of their labor.

As a result of God's judgment Rabbah, Ammon's capital city, will become a stable for the hoards of camels possessed by the desert invaders. The rest of the land will become grazing pasture for their flocks. The fulfillment of the predictions will vindicate Yahweh in the eyes of the Ammonites. They will learn by bitter experience that God is not mocked.[463]

Second Judgment Announcement 25:6-7

For thus says Lord Yahweh: Because you have clapped the hands and stamped with the feet, and have rejoiced with all contempt in (your) soul against the land of Israel, 7 therefore behold I have stretched forth my hand against you. I will give you for spoil to the nations. I will cut you off from the peoples. I will cause you to perish from the lands. I will destroy you. Then you will know that I am Yahweh.

The Ammonites had rejoiced with utmost glee over the fate of the land of Israel. Outwardly they manifested their joy by clapping the hands and stamping the feet.[464]

Because of their attitude God will stretch out his hand against them, i.e., take active measures to assure their downfall. In four awesome and essentially synonymous "I wills"[465] God declared that Ammon's national existence will come to an end.

---

[462]In 21:28-32 Ezekiel had predicted Nebuchadrezzar will turn his wrath against Ammon after he had destroyed Jerusalem. Some conclude that *the children from the east* here are the Babylonians. Cf. Grider, *Beacon Bible Commentary*, 579; Alexander, *Expositor's Bible Commentary*, 865.

[463]Cf. J. Strang, "Ezekiel's use of the Recognition Formula in his Oracles against the Nations," *PRS* 22 (1995): 115-33.

[464]Clapping the hands or stamping the feet can express scorn, anger or rejoicing. Cf. 6:11; 21:14, 17; 22:13; Isa 55:12.

[465]I will 1) deliver you for spoil; 2) cut you off; 3) cause you to perish; and 4) destroy you.

Josephus (*Ant.* 10.9.7) reports that Nebuchadnezzar campaigned against Ammon and Moab in his twenty-third year (582 BC). The area was largely depopulated before the middle of the sixth century BC until the third. At that time desert tribes came in to fill the vacuum.[466]

WORD AGAINST MOAB[467] 25:8-11

Thus says Lord Yahweh: Because Moab and Seir have said, Behold the house of Judah is like all the nations, 9 therefore behold I am about to open the flank[468] of Moab on the side of the cities, its cities from its frontier,[469] the glory of the land, Beth-jeshimoth, Baal-meon, and Kiriathaim. 10 I will give it to the children of the east, along with the children of Ammon, for a possession in order that the children of Ammon may not be remembered among the nations. 11 So in Moab I will execute judgments. They will know that I am Yahweh.

From the earliest times the Moabites had manifested hostility toward Israel. Balak, king of Moab, had attempted to curse the children of Israel just before the death of Moses (Nm 22-24). Legend has it that the Moabites slew the parents of David when he left them there for safety during his flight from Saul (cf. 1 Sam 22:3). The Moabites warred against Omri, Ahab,[470] and the combined army of Jehoram of Israel and Jehoshaphat of Judah (2 Kgs 3). The region of Seir,[471] jointly occupied by Moab and Edom, is included in the present oracle.

The sin of Moab and Seir was twofold: failing to recognize the distinctiveness of Israel and the uniqueness of Israel's God. Israel no longer enjoyed the miraculous protection she had enjoyed in the past. In their view Israel's God was no more able to protect her than were the gods of surrounding nations.

The fortress cities of Moab will pose no obstacle to the advancing forces of Yahweh. To make this point concrete Ezekiel names three

---

[466]G.M. Landes, *IDB*, 1:112-13.

[467]For background, see A.H. van Zyl, *The Moabites* (Leiden: Brill, 1960).

[468]Literally, "shoulder of Moab," i.e., the side of Moab exposed to invasion.

[469]Literally, "its end."

[470]The Moabite Stone records the boasts of the king of Moab in this respect.

[471]Seir is not found in the Greek text of Ezekiel. Due to the fact that Seir is usually associated with Edom, rather than Moab, the Greek translators apparently deliberately omitted the word.

such cities. *Beth-jeshimoth* ("the house of waters") was on the plain of Moab opposite Jericho, about a thousand feet below sea level. *Baal-meon* ("house of Baal's habitation") and *Kiriathaim* ("double city") were about ten miles to the southeast on the Moab plateau, about two thousand feet above sea level.[472]

On the eastern frontier Moab's fate is similar to Ammon's. *Children of the east*, i.e., desert raiders, will overthrow the land. These judgments will convince the Moabites that Yahweh of Israel was the powerful and almighty God.

WORD AGAINST EDOM[473] 25:12-14

Thus says Lord Yahweh: Because Edom's dealings with the house of Judah have been the result of vengeful conduct, he has incurred enormous guilt by executing vengeance against them. 13 Therefore thus says Lord Yahweh: I will stretch out my hand against Edom. I will cut off from it man and beast. I will make it a desolation. From Teman even toward Dedan they will fall by the sword. 14 I will put my vengeance in Edom by the hand of my people Israel. They will deal with Edom according to my wrath and according to my anger. Thus they will know my vengeance (oracle of Lord Yahweh).

The Edomites were descended from Esau. They occupied the territory south of the Dead Sea. Although the twins, Esau and Jacob, were reconciled during their lifetime (Gn 33) their descendants were involved in perpetual hostilities. The Edomites had not allowed the Israelites to pass through their land in the days of Moses (Nm 20:14-21). Amos (1:11-12), Obadiah[474] condemned the Edomites for hostile acts against Israel.[475] Jeremiah lashed out against them (Jer 49:7-11; Lam 4:21-22). Later Malachi will blast Edom as well (Mal 1:2-5).

Edom's sin was a vengeful spirit toward the people of God. Private vengeance is forbidden in both testaments (e.g., Lv 19:18; Rom

---

[472] *IDB*, 3:320.

[473] M.H. Woudstra, "Edom and Israel in Ezekiel," *CTJ* 3 (1968): 21-35.

[474] The date of Obadiah is in dispute among biblical scholars. Many consider Obadiah as one of the earliest of the writing prophets. He may have been active during the reign of Jehoram of Judah (848-841 BC).

[475] The historical record indicates that Israel had responded in kind to the viciousness of the Edomites (2 Sam 8:13; 1 Kgs 11:14-16; 2 Chr 25:11-12).

12:17-19). Even in international relations vengeance is a divine prerogative (cf. Dt 32:35; Heb 10:30). Apparently at the time of the Babylonian invasion of Judah the Edomites had seized the opportunity to get revenge against Judah. Thus they had committed a grave offense.

For the crimes committed against his people God will *stretch out* his hand against Edom. Man and beast will be *cut off* from the land. Even Teman, one of the leading cities of Edom, will become desolate. The slaughter will extend south of Edom as far as Dedan.[476] The devastation of Edom will be wrought by the hands of the Israelites. Acting as God's agents they will teach Edom the vengeance of Yahweh. God exercises vengeance to rectify wrong.

As in most of the prophecies against foreign nations the predicted demise of Edom occurred gradually. The process started with an attack by Nebuchadnezzar.[477] Edom fell into Arab hands in the fifth century BC. In the third century BC the area was overrun by the Nabateans. In the second pre-Christian century the remnant of the Edomites was conquered by the Jewish general Judas Maccabeus (1 Macc 5:65). The Edomites were finally forced to accept circumcision and the Jewish faith. In this amalgamation the Edomites disappeared from history.

WORD AGAINST PHILISTIA 25:15-17

Thus says Lord Yahweh: Because the Philistines have acted in revenge, they have taken vengeance with contempt in (their) soul to destroy with eternal enmity, 16 therefore thus says Yahweh: Behold I am about to stretch out my hand against the Philistine. I will cut off the Cherethites, and destroy the remnant of the seacoast. 17 I will execute great vengeance on them by acts of furious chastise-

---

[476]The Dedan most frequently mentioned in the Scripture was located in Arabia, about three hundred miles southeast of Teman. Dedan is elsewhere mentioned in connection with Edom only in Jer 49:8. Possibly Jeremiah and Ezekiel are referring to a settlement of Dedanites within the territory of Edom rather than the famous caravan city of that name. On the other hand, the two prophets may be suggesting that the disaster that will befall Edom will sweep southward even to Dedan.

[477]Jer 9:26; 25:21; 27:1-11. In some sense Ezek 32:29 and Mal 1:2-5 regard Edom's desolation as past.

ment. They will know that I am Yahweh when I execute my vengeance on them.

The Philistines invaded Palestine about 1200 BC in the days of the judges. They hailed from the island of Caphtor (Amos 9:7). Knowing the secret of smelting iron they immediately gained the advantage over the Israelites who still fought and farmed with bronze weapons and implements. Samson fought valiantly against them. Samuel inflicted upon them a stinging defeat (1 Sam 7:13). It was David, however, who broke their power. From that point on Israel dominated Philistia. In periods of Israelite weakness, however, the Philistines broke free. During these periods of independence the Philistines did all they could to harass the Judeans.

Ezekiel condemned the Philistines for their constant enmity against Judah. Filled with ruthless vengeance they were determined to destroy utterly the people of God.

God's mighty hand, so recently stretched out against Jerusalem, will now be turned against these neighbors who had aided and abetted the Babylonians. The Philistines and the Cherethites[478] who lived among them will be destroyed. In fact all the *remnant of the seacoast* will be destroyed.

God's vengeance against these people will take place in the form of "wrathful rebukes" (NASB) or acts of "furious chastisement" (BV). This suggests that the demise of the seacoast peoples will be the result of repeated blows.

The fulfillment of this prediction began in the sixth century BC during the lifetime of Ezekiel. Gaza was attacked and destroyed by Pharaoh Hophra. Later the Babylonians devastated the land. During the intertestamental period the Jewish armies made several campaigns into the area,[479] doing substantial damage.

Reading the four short oracles of ch 25 one cannot help but recall the promise made to Abraham: "I will bless them that bless you, and curse them that curse you" (Gn 12:3a).

People of the world are not in sympathy with God's program and plan. Ammonites who gloat over the misfortune of God's people are

---

[478]The Cherethites were probably a band of Cretan mercenaries brought to the southern coast of Palestine by the Egyptians. David hired them for his personal bodyguard. They proved intensely loyal to him. In this passage, as well as Zeph 2:5, Cherethites are condemned along with Philistines. The two peoples must have been closely related.

[479]1 Macc 5:68; 10:84; 13:47-48.

still in abundance. Modern Moabites secularize the people of God by refusing to acknowledge that he indeed has called out of the world a chosen people. The Edomites are illustrative of those who are vindictive and openly hostile toward God's people. The Philistines are those who act out their hatred and brutality toward God's people. The abiding message of this ch is that God defends the honor of his people Ultimately he overthrows all who oppose his people.

EZEKIEL 26
DESTRUCTION OF TYRE

The Phoenician seaport cities of Tyre and Sidon now come under the purview of the prophet. Tyre, the more important of the two cities, receives far more attention—seventy-six vv as compared to but four vv devoted to Sidon.

To appreciate the prophecies regarding Tyre one needs to be familiar with some of the geography of the place. Tyre is located a mere thirty-five miles as the crow flies from the Sea of Galilee, and only a hundred miles or so from Jerusalem. Ancient merchants traversed this distance by camel in a few days. Tyre was situated in a most advantageous location on the Mediterranean Sea coast. The city possessed two excellent harbors. One was on the mainland where a portion of the city was built. The other was on an off-shore island where the main fortress was located. It was this rocky island that gave the city its Hebrew name *tsōr*, "rock." The island city helped double the trading capacity of Tyre. It also provided a last refuge for the citizens in time of attack.

The Phoenicians were the merchants of antiquity. Export products included glassware and dyed materials. A beautiful purple dye was made from a shellfish native to the area. Tyre was a prize that conquerors desired above all others. Tyre seems to have suffered less damage than the other states of Syria-Palestine during the Assyrian era, although she had to pay heavy tribute to maintain her commercial freedom.

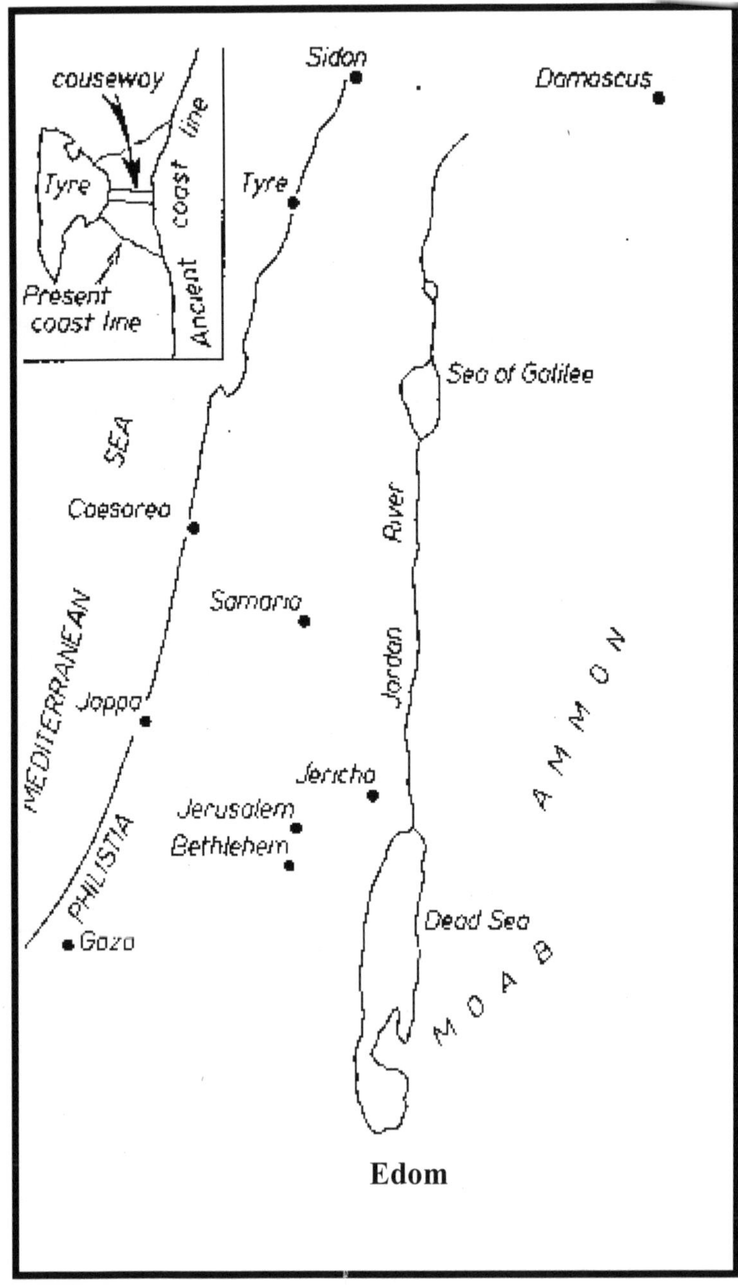
couseway
Tyre
Ancient coast line
Present coast line
Sidon
Domoscus
Tyre
Sea of Golilee
SEA
MEDITERRANEAN
Coesoreo
River
Jordan
Somorio
Joppo
AMMON
Jericho
Jerusolem
Bethlehem
PHILISTIA
Gozo
Dead Sea
MOAB
Edom

REASON FOR THE DESTRUCTION 26:1-6

Tyre's Gloating 26:2-3a

It came to pass in the eleventh year, in the first day of the month, that the word of Yahweh came unto me, saying, 2 Son of man, because Tyre has said concerning Jerusalem: Aha! She who was the gates of peoples is broken; it has turned unto me; I will be filled with the one who has been laid waste. 3 Therefore thus says Lord Yahweh: Behold I am against you, O Tyre.

The Tyre material is dated to the eleventh year of Jehoiachin's captivity. The month is not stated in the text, but it was likely the sixth month. If it was the first day of the sixth month on which the oracles against Tyre were composed the date would be September 18, 587 BC. About twenty months have elapsed since the last events and prophecies recorded in the book (cf. 24:1-2; 26:1). The siege of Jerusalem had been under way for about nine months at the time Ezekiel delivered his Tyre messages.

The first paragraph of the Tyre oracle is couched in the *because ... therefore* pattern of the previous ch. Tyre's offense was that she had gloated over the fall of Jerusalem. That brought down on her the wrath of Yahweh in fulfillment of Gn 12:3. Proverbs 17:5 declares: "whoever gloats over disaster will not go unpunished." Jerusalem had been *the gates of peoples*, a major trading center at the intersection of international trade-routes. The caravan tolls that once filled Jerusalem's coffers came to Tyre now that the capital of Judah had been laid waste. A bit of greed and selfishness is evidenced in the joyous exclamation *I will be filled*. Because of this greed and arrogant pride the God of Israel declared himself to be an adversary of Tyre.

Five Predictions
26:3b-6

I will bring up against you many nations as the sea causes its waves to come up. 4 They will destroy the walls of Tyre and break down her towers. I will scrape her dust from her and make her a bare rock. 5 She will become a place for the spreading of nets in the midst of the sea; for I have spoken it (oracle of Yahweh). She will become a spoil for the nations. 6 Her daughters who are in the field will be slain with the sword. They will know that I am Yahweh.

Five specific predictions concerning the future of Tyre are contained in vv 3b-6. Prediction #1: many nations will come against Tyre. Wave after wave of enemy soldiers will storm that place. Commencing with the attack of Nebuchadnezzar Tyre experienced at least five major assaults: Alexander the Great attacked the place in 332 BC. He succeeded in conquering the city after a siege of seven months. Antigonus besieged Tyre in 314 BC and conquered the city after a siege of fifteen months. The Arabs captured the city in AD 636. The place was retaken by the Crusaders in AD 1124. Finally, the Arabs recaptured Tyre in AD 1291.

Prediction #2: Tyre will be made a *bare rock*. The proud walls and towers will be broken down. Alexander the Great scraped the old mainland site of Tyre clean. With the debris and rubble he built a peninsula out into the sea. By means of this mole he was able to make a land assault on the island fortress.

Prediction #3: fisherman will spread their nets over the site of Tyre. The dry rocky island will be a suitable place for such activity. The presence of fishnets implies fishermen. Hence the prophet is not suggesting that the site of Tyre will be totally abandoned. A small fishing village exists upon the ancient ruins of Tyre today.[480]

Prediction #4: Tyre will become *spoil for the nations*. History records that each successive wave of attackers enriched itself at the expense of Tyre.

Prediction #5: satellite towns and villages (*her daughters*) on the mainland will be slain by the sword, i.e., destroyed by warfare. Nebuchadnezzar took the mainland city of Tyre and the surrounding towns and villages during his campaign in that region.

---

[480]Modern Tyre (Sur) is not the original city, but was built down the coast from the ancient site.

All of the five blows mentioned above will befall Tyre for two reasons: the God who cannot lie had so decreed it in a solemn oracle; and the God of Israel will thereby be vindicated in the eyes of the Phoenician peoples.

AGENTS OF DESTRUCTION 26:7-14

Nebuchadrezzar's Siege 26:7-9

For thus says Lord Yahweh: Behold I am about to bring Nebuchadrezzar against Tyre, king of Babylon, from the north, king of kings, with horses and chariots, horsemen, a company, even much people. 8 He will slay with the sword your daughters in the field. He will make movable towers against you, cast up a mound against you, and raise up shields against you. 9 He will set his battering rams against your walls. Your towers he will break down by his axes.

The successive waves of attack against Tyre are initiated by Babylon. Prediction #6: Nebuchadrezzar[481] will destroy the mainland city of Tyre. The Chaldean king is here called *king of kings* because he had dominion over dozens of vassal kingdoms (cf. Dan 2:37; 4:1). Nebuchadnezzar will approach Tyre *from the north* around the hump of the Fertile Crescent. Armed to the teeth Nebuchadrezzar's cavalry, chariots and innumerable infantry will approach Tyre.

First, the mainland towns and villages—Tyre's daughters—will fall. The attack on the island fortress was to follow the standard siege tactics of that day. Forts or *siege towers* will be erected to allow the attacking soldiers to be elevated to the level of the wall where they more easily could engage the defenders. *Mounds* of earth and rubble were heaped up about the city to accomplish the same purpose. Large shields linked together provided protection for the besiegers. *Battering rams* were used to attempt to penetrate the stone walls. Axe-like swords were used to destroy other fortifications.

---

[481]The name *Nebuchadrezzar*, a variant spelling of Nebuchadnezzar (Jer 27:8), appears 4x in the book (26:7; 29:18-19; 30:10). Ezekiel's spelling is closer to the Babylonian form of the name.

Nebuchadrezzar's Conquest 26:10-11

Because of the multitude of his horses their dust will cover you. At the noise of his horsemen, wheels, and chariots your walls will shake, when he enters into your gates as men enter a city through a breach. 11 With the hoofs of his horses he will tread down all your streets. He will slay your people with the sword. The pillars of your strength will go down to the ground.

In hyperbolic language typical of such battle scenes Ezekiel paints the picture of the coming conqueror. Clouds of dust generated by the approach of innumerable horses will billow up over the walls. The walls of the city will seem to shake from the pounding hoofs and speeding chariots. The hostile conqueror will enter into the *gates* of the trembling city *as men enter a city through a breach*, i.e., without resistance.

Within the captured city a merciless slaughter will take place. Cavalry units will be dispatched down every street to slay all who might be found there. The sacred and symbolic pillars that had been erected in honor of the national god Melqart[482] will come crashing to the ground.

Nebuchadrezzar's Successors 26:12-14

They will make spoil of your wealth and confiscate your merchandise. They will break down your walls and tear down your delightful houses. They will put your stones, your timber and your dust in the midst of the water. 13 I will cause the noise of your songs to cease. The sound of your harps will be heard no more. 14 I will make you a bare rock. You will become a place for the spreading of nets. You will be built no more; for I Yahweh have spoken (oracle of Lord Yahweh).

The destruction of Tyre was not to be accomplished by Nebuchadnezzar alone. Verse 3 already has alluded to the many nations that will be involved. This suggests that the destruction of Tyre will be spread over the centuries. Nebuchadnezzar did besiege Tyre. His

---

[482]Herodotus makes mention of two such pillars in the city of Tyre.

siege lasted thirteen years (587-574 BC).[483] While he appears to have conquered the mainland suburbs of Tyre, however, he was never able to conquer the island fortress.

Ezekiel was very much aware that Nebuchadnezzar would not be able to capture the entire city (29:17-20). For this reason God will give to him the land of Egypt. Nonetheless, the long struggle against the Babylonians exhausted the power and resources of Tyre.

Tyre's capitulation in 574 BC meant the end of Phoenician national life.[484] During the Persian period Tyre lost to Sidon its dominating position on the coast. She also lost her most important trading colonies. Tyre continued to survive, however, as a trading and shipping center throughout the Persian period.

An important shift in pronouns from *he* to *they* occurs in v 12. At this point the prophet begins to describe a second stage of Tyre's destruction. The first half of v 12 amplifies prediction #4 mentioned above; the latter half of the v expands on prediction #2. Verse 14a combines and repeats predictions #2 and #3.

The wealth of Tyre will fall into the hands of the enemy. The walls and luxurious houses will be torn down. The stone, timber and even the dust of the place will be pushed into the water of the Mediterranean Sea.

The allusion in vv 12-14a is likely to the armies of Alexander the Great. The Macedonian conqueror attacked the city in 332 BC. He easily conquered the mainland city, as Nebuchadnezzar had done 250 years earlier. Alexander utterly demolished the place. Then by means of an amazing engineering feat Alexander accomplished what Nebuchadnezzar had failed to accomplish, viz. he conquered the island fortress.

Using the debris from the mainland city Alexander constructed a causeway half a mile long and two hundred feet wide across the straits. The Tyrians resisted for a time heroically. They utilized fire ships to damage the construction work. Using catapults they flung on their attackers pots of burning naphtha, sulfur and red-hot sand. Alexander was forced quickly to assemble a fleet of over three hundred ships to protect the construction crews and blockade the city.

After about seven months the young general grew impatient with the entire operation. He finally ordered floating batteries to be con-

[483]Josephus, *Antiquities* 10.11, 1; *Against Apion* 1.21. No contemporary record of this siege remains.
[484]Kapelrud, *IDB*, 4:723.

structed upon which rams were mounted. His naval vessels were able thereby to force their way into the two island harbors. His troops quickly scaled the walls and captured the city. Eight thousand citizens of Tyre were slaughtered, thirty thousand were sold into slavery. Later two thousand more were hanged.[485] The mole that the armies of Alexander built partly from houses and monuments torn down on the mainland still remains. It connects what formerly was an island to the mainland.

The joyous sounds of once vibrant Tyre will be silenced. The island fortress will be nothing but a barren rock upon which fishermen will spread their nets.

Prediction #7: Tyre will never be rebuilt (v 14b). After the destruction by Alexander the Great several successive cities were built on at least part of the ground once occupied by ancient Tyre. After the *Phoenician* city of Tyre was conquered by the Moslems, however, it was never rebuilt. The Phoenicians disappeared from history. The insignificant villages built by the Moslems on the site can in no wise be equated with *Phoenician* Tyre any more than a modern American city could be considered the resurrection of some ancient Indian village that might have once occupied the site.

A further consideration is that a city in biblical days was not considered to be built (or rebuilt) until it had walls. A wall-less fishing village could not be considered a resurrection of ancient Tyre.[486]

RESULT OF TYRE'S DESTRUCTION 26:15-18

Effect on Trading Partners 26:15-16

Thus says Lord Yahweh to Tyre: Will not the islands shake at the sound of your fall, when the wounded groan, when the slaughter occurs in your midst? 16 Then all the princes of the sea will go down from upon their thrones. They will remove their robes and

---

[485]Fuller, *Encyclopedia Britannica*, 14th ed., 22:653.

[486]Hall (*Wesleyan Bible Commentary,* 437) interprets the prophecy to mean that subsequent cities built on the site will lack the greatness of Phoenician Tyre.

strip off their woven garments. They will clothe themselves with trembling. Upon the ground they will sit. They will tremble continually and be appalled over you.

A whole network of satellite trading colonies will be affected by the fall of Tyre. The coastal states along the Mediterranean will quake in consternation at the news of the fall of Tyre. Again using prophetic hyperbole the prophet describes the rulers of the trading partners removing their royal robes. They clothed themselves with *trembling*, i.e., they took on the demeanor of mourners. They will sit on the ground[487] trembling, visibly shaken by the news that such a powerful overlord had been destroyed.

Effect on Neighboring Princes 26:17-18

They will take up for you a lamentation and say to you: How sad that the one who was populated from the seas has been destroyed—the famous city that was strong in the sea, she and her inhabitants that caused their terror to be on all its inhabitants. 18 Now will the islands tremble in the day of your fall. The islands that are in the sea will be frightened because of your departure.

News of the demise of Tyre will evoke a lament from neighboring princes: *How sad* it is.[488] The most famous and most powerful of all the seafaring people had been destroyed! Tyre had fallen. Who will be next? The shipping communities on the islands and coastlands of the Mediterranean will tremble as they contemplated their own prospects for survival.

DOOM OF TYRE 26:19-21

For thus says Lord Yahweh: When I will make you a desolation like the cities that are not inhabited; when I will bring up the deep upon you, and the great waters will cover you; 20 then will I bring you down with them that go down to the pit to the people of old. I

[487]Alexander (*Expositor's Bible Commentary*, 872) thinks the language points to abdication, "perhaps in an act of surrender and submission to Babylonia before she attacked them."

[488]The Hebrew *ech* (elsewhere *echah*) introduces a dirge.

will make you dwell in the lower parts of the earth like the places that are desolate from of old with those who go down to the pit, in order that you may not be inhabited. But I will set glory in the land of the living. 21 I will make you a terror. You will be no more. Though you be sought for, you will never be found again (oracle of Lord Yahweh).

Tyre will become as desolate as an uninhabited city. The sea will wash over the bare rock that once was covered with the palaces of merchant princes. The prophet apparently thought of the sinking into the depth of the water as leading to the world of the dead that was beneath. Tyre will descend into the nether world—*the pit*—the abode of the dead. The idea is that Tyre will die. Descent into *the pit* is a frequent metaphor for death in Ezekiel and in other prophets.[489]

In the pit of death Tyre will join the *people of old*, the dead of former ages, and the inhabitants of other cities left desolate. From the time of its destruction the city will not be re-inhabited. Yahweh, however, will manifest his glory *in the land of the living*, i.e., in this present world. The everlasting kingdom of God in all of its power and glory will be established.

Prediction #8: Tyre will be depopulated. *You will not be inhabited.* Again the prediction applies to *Phoenician* Tyre, not subsequent villages that may have had the same name or partially occupied the same site.

God will use the destruction of Tyre to bring terror to the hearts of other pompous powers (*I will make you a terror*).[490] The once proud metropolis will leave no trace of her former glory. Tyre will be in the abode of the dead. No one will be able to find her in the land of the living.

Prediction #9: Tyre will never be found again. Does the prophet mean to say that the city will be so destroyed that its very location will be lost? It is difficult to believe that the actual location of the city could be lost when it formerly occupied an island completely. Probably the meaning is that *Phoenician* Tyre, once destroyed, will never be found. The glorious and glamorous city will disappear forever.

---

[489]Cf. Ezek 31:14-16; 32:18, 23-25; Isa 14:15; 38:18.

[490]NASB renders, "I will bring terrors upon you." This translation raises the question whether the terrors referred to what transpired prior to the destruction of Tyre, or after Tyre descended into the pit.

EZEKIEL 27
LAMENT OVER TYRE

Chapter 27 consists of an allegorical dirge song artistically interrupted by a prose section. Tyre is pictured as a beautiful ship superbly equipped and manned by a skilled crew (vv 3-11). In the prose section the ship is said to stop at various ports to collect her cargo (vv 12-25a). The ship becomes so laden with merchandise that she sinks into the depths of a stormy sea (vv 25b-36). This exquisite composition stresses the abiding truth that worldly wealth is transitory and ultimately self-defeating to those who worship it.

PREPARATION FOR SAILING[491]
27:1-11

Construction of the Ship
27:1-7

The word of Yahweh came unto me, saying, 2 Now as for you, son of man, take up a lamentation over Tyre. 3 Say to Tyre, who dwells beside the entrances of the sea, merchant of the peoples unto many coastlands: Thus says Lord Yahweh: O Tyre, you have said, I am perfect in beauty. 4 Your borders are in the heart of the sea. Your builders have perfected your beauty. 5 With fir trees from Senir they have constructed all the planks. Cedars from Lebanon they have taken to make the mast for you. 6 With oaks of Bashan they have fashioned your oars. Your deck they made of ivory inlaid in boxwood from the coastlands of Cypress. 7 Of exquisitely embroidered work from Egypt was your sail that served as your ensign. Purple and blue from the coastlands of Elishah was your awning.

[491]Cf. Edwin Good, "Ezekiel's Ship: Some Extended Metaphors in the Old Testament," *Semitics* 1 (1970): 79-103; John Geyer, "Ezekiel and the Cosmic Ship" in Philip Davies and David Clines, eds. *Among the Prophets* (Sheffeld, JSOT, 1993), 105-26; M. Diakonoff, "The Naval Power and Trade of Tyre," *IEJ* 42 (1992): 168-93.

The princes of the sea take up a lament over the fall of Tyre. Here Ezekiel is told to join them by lifting up[492] a lament. Two phrases describe Tyre, the object of this lament. Tyre is addressed first as she *who dwells beside the entrances of the sea.* The plural *entrances* probably refers to the two sections of the harbor that were known respectively as "the Sidonian" and "the Egyptian" because of the directions that they faced. The second address to Tyre refers to her as the *merchant of the people unto many coastlands.* The far-flung trading colonies of the Phoenician city-states are one of the marvels of ancient history.

Tyre was a proud city. She boasted of her perfect beauty. The boast was not without foundation. Such national arrogance, however, was the root of her downfall. Because of her situation on a Mediterranean island, and because of her sea-faring enterprises, Tyre is likened to a ship that roams the seas. Her *borders were in the heart of the sea.*[493] The builders had spared nothing to make that ship of state a magnificent vessel.

The construction of the ship Tyre was sound: planks of fir from Senir (Mount Hermon, Dt 3:9), masts of Lebanon cedar, oars of Bashan[494] oak. The decking material was made of boxwood (from Cyprus) inlaid with ivory. The sails were of the most costly Egyptian linen embroidered with distinctive colors so as to serve as an ensign for the ship. Her deck awning was of two shades of purple from Elishah.[495]

Crew of the Ship
27:8-11

A. Naval Personnel (27:8-9)

The inhabitants of Sidon and Arvad were your rowers. Your skilled men, O Tyre, were on board as pilots. 9 The elders of Gebal

---

[492]This verb is always used in connection with a lamentation because it was uttered in a loud voice.

[493]The Assyrians referred to the Tyrians as those who "dwelled in the midst of the sea." Prichard, *ANET*, 296f.

[494]Bashan was east of Jordan. The region was famous for its oaks (Isa 2:13; Zech 11:2).

[495]Opinions differ on the location of Elishah. Some argue for a site on Cyprus; others opt for a Syrian location.

and her skilled men were on board as repairmen.[496] All the ships of the sea with their sailors were on board in order to barter for your merchandise.

The crew on board the good ship Tyre were the finest in the world. The rowers hailed from Sidon and the island Arvad, a hundred miles north of Sidon. The wisest men of Tyre[497] were at the helm.[498] Skilled craftsmen from Gebal[499] served as ship-carpenters (lit., "repairers of the seams"). Furthermore, all the navies of the world assisted her in the transference of her cargo.

B. Military Personnel (27:10-11)

Persia, Lud and Put were in your army, your men of war. Shield and helmet they hung on you; they enhanced[500] your splendor. 11 The sons of Arvad and your army were upon your walls round about. The Gammadim were in your towers. They hung their shields upon your walls round about; they perfected your beauty.

The marines on board the ship were mercenaries from distant lands. They were attracted, no doubt, by the handsome wages offered by the wealthy merchants of Tyre. They came from *Persia*[501] to the east, *Lud* (Lydia) in Asia Minor, and *Put* (Punt) on the western coast of the Red Sea. The colorful shields and helmets of these soldiers were hung in awesome array along the sides of the good ship Tyre. Add to this the presence of yet other armed personnel—the men of Arvad (see on v 8), and the Gammadim, a people not elsewhere mentioned in the Bible. These soldiers, as well as the army[502] of Tyre itself, will hang their shields on the ship's sides to further enhance the splendor of the vessel.

---

[496]Lit., "the strengtheners of your breach."

[497]RSV has "corrected" the Hebrew text to read *Zemer*, a city associated with Arvad. Such arbitrary alterations of the text are unnecessary and unwarranted.

[498]*Pilots*, lit., "rope pullers" or sailors.

[499]Gebal (modern Byblos) supplied skilled craftsmen for work on Solomon's temple (cf. 1 Kgs 5:32).

[500]Lit., "gave forth."

[501]Persia is mentioned here for the first time in the Bible.

[502]*Your army* (NASB; KJV) is made a proper name in the RSV, "Helech," which is thought to be Cilicia. Such a rendering involves a change in the vowel points of the word in question.

PORTS OF CALL
27:12-25a

The cities that traded with Tyre are given in geographical order in three groupings.

Western "Ports"
27:12-15

Tarshish was your client because of the abundance of all kinds of wealth. Silver, iron, tin and lead they traded for your wares. 13 Javan, Tubal and Meshech were your trading partners. Persons of men and vessels of bronze they traded for your merchandise. 14 Those from Beth-togarmah traded horses—war horses and mules—for your wares. 15 The children of Dedan were your trading partners. Many coastlands were your market. Horns of ivory and ebony they brought as your gift.

The first group of trading cities consists of those that lie along the Mediterranean trade route. The list begins with *Tarshish* at the western end of the sea. Tarshish, a mining district in southern Spain,[503] was attracted by the wealth of Tyre to become one of her trading partners. They traded valuable metals for the export products of Tyre.

Javan is Greece; *Tubal* and *Meshech* were tribes in Asia Minor. With these regions Tyre trafficked in slaves (cf. Joel 3:6) and copper ore.[504] From *Beth-togarmah* (probably Armenia), Tyre secured horses, war horses,[505] and mules.

Dedan (island of Rhodes)[506] traded with Tyre too. Many other coastlands were part of Tyre's commercial network. Vessels of ivory and ebony were paid as tribute to Tyre for the privilege of belonging to this commercial community. These products will come from the

---

[503]Others suggest that Tarshish may have been the Phoenician name for the ancient city of Nora in Sardinia.

[504]The Hebrew *n^{e}chōšet* may refer to either copper, bronze (an alloy of copper and tin) or brass (alloy of copper and zinc). See *NBD*, 825.

[505]The term *pārāšîm* frequently means *horsemen.* In some passages the word refers to the horses used with war chariots. Cf. Isa 28:28; Jer 46:4; Joel 2:4.

[506]Dedan in v 15 obviously is not the same as the Arabian Dedan mentioned in v 20. The Septuagint (Greek version) preserves the tradition that this Dedan is the island of Rhodes in the Mediterranean. Some think that a port on the Persian Gulf is meant.

African interior via the Phoenician traders on the coast of North Africa.

Neighboring "Ports" 27:16-22

Aram was your client because of the abundance of your works. Emeralds, purple, embroidered work, fine linen, coral and rubies they traded for your wares. 17 Judah and the land of Israel were your trading partners. The wheat of Minnith, cakes[507] of honey, oil and balm they have traded for your merchandise. 18 Damascus was your client because of the multitude of your works, because of the abundance of all kinds of wealth, with the wine of Helbon and white wool. 19 Vedan and Javan traded for your wares from Uzal. Iron, cassia and calamus were among your merchandise. 20 Dedan was your trading partner in saddle-cloths for riding. 21 Arabia and all the princes of Kedar were your clients; in lambs, rams, and goats, for these were they your clients. 22 The traders of Sheba and Raamah were your trading partners. The best of all kinds of spices. All kinds of precious stones, and gold they traded for your wares.

Aram[508] (Syria) provided Tyre with precious stones and beautiful fabrics. *Judah* exported agricultural products to Tyre—wheat,[509] cakes,[510] honey, oil and balm. *Damascus* supplied Tyre with the finest wine, the wine of *Helbon*, and white[511] wool. *Vedan*[512] was probably an Arab city. *Javan* may refer to a Greek colony in Arabia. Both cities are said to export the trading merchandise from *Uzzal*[513]—*iron bars*,[514] perfume (*cassia*) and sweet cane (*calamus*).[515] Verse 19 is difficult to translate. Opinions differ widely on its meaning.

---

[507]The Hebrew is of uncertain meaning.

[508]Some Hebrew manuscripts and the Septuagint read "Edom." In Hebrew the difference between *Aram* and *Edom* is slight.

[509]*Minnith* was an Ammonite town (cf. Judg 11:33) that apparently sent wheat as tribute to Judah (cf. 2 Chr 27:5).

[510]The Hebrew word *pannag* occurs only here. It is of doubtful meaning. It has been rendered "early figs" (BV; RSV); and "cakes" (NASB). Some kind of foodstuff is intended.

[511]Exact translation is uncertain.

[512]Could also be translated *and Dan*. *Vedan* has conjecturally been identified with Waddan near the Arab city of Medina.

[513]Several Hebrew manuscripts and the Septuagint support this translation.

[514]Again the exact meaning is uncertain.

From Arabian *Dedan* Tyre received saddle cloths. The nomadic Arabs and the princes of *Kedar* were famous for their flocks (cf. Isa 60:7). They supplied Tyre with livestock. *Sheba* in southwest Arabia and *Raamah*, thought to be along the Persian Gulf, were famous trading people (cf. Job 6:19). Gold, precious stones and aromatics were among the items these traders bartered with Tyre.

Mesopotamian "Ports"
27:23-25

Haran, Canneh, Eden and the traders of Sheba, Assyria (and) Chilmad were your trading partners. 24 These were your trading partners in gorgeous fabrics, in cloth of blue and embroidered work and chests[516] of rich apparel, bound with cords and cedar-lined, among your merchandise 25. The ships of Tarshish were the carriers for your merchandise.

The next three "ports" mentioned were located in Mesopotamia. *Haran*, a stopping point in Abram's migration (Gn 12:4), was an important commercial center on the main trade route from Babylon to Syria. *Canneh* is probably to be identified as Calneh (Gn 10:10), otherwise called Calno (Isa 10:9), a city in Babylonia. *Eden* is known on Assyrian inscriptions as Bit-Adini, a city that occupies both sides of the Euphrates River due south of Haran. Through these trading centers, the merchandise of *Sheba* (see previous v), *Assyria* and *Chilmad* (location unknown) moved toward Tyre.

The Mesopotamian trading partners brought to Tyre *gorgeous fabrics* (lit., "things perfected"), cloaks of blue and richly woven work, and beautiful cedar chests containing other kinds of luxurious wearing apparel.

The list concludes with a reference to the ships of *Tarshish* (see v 12) that brought their dues to Tyre, the queen of the merchant marine.

---

[515]Cassia and calamus were ingredients of anointing oil (cf. Ex 30:23f).
[516]RSV, NASB and BV render "carpets."

SHIP SINKING
27:25b-36

Report of the Calamity
27:25b-27

So you became full and very heavy*[517] *in the heart of the seas. 26 Into great waters your rowers have brought you. The east wind has broken you in the heart of the seas. 27 Your wealth, your wares, your merchandise, your sailors, your pilots, your repairmen and your merchant men, all your men of war which were on board, with all your company that is in your midst, will fall into the heart of the seas in the day of your collapse.

Through all this commercial activity the good ship Tyre became overloaded in the midst of the sea, in the very place where she was thought to be supreme. Into the dangerous open sea the sailors have rowed the vessel. There she will meet disaster. The east wind (cf. Ps 48:7) stirred up the waves and battered the ship until it broke apart under the pressure. All was lost—the merchandise, and all the individuals associated with transporting and protecting it.

Reaction to the Calamity
27:28-31

At the sound of the cry of your pilots the countryside will shake. 29 All who handle the oar, the sailors, all the pilots of the sea will come down from their ships, and stand upon the land. 30 They will cause their voice to be heard over you. They will cry bitterly, cast dust upon their heads, and wallow in ashes. 31 They will make themselves bald because of you. They will gird themselves with sackcloth. They will weep over you in bitterness of soul, with bitter mourning.

The countryside[518] that had supplied so many of the personnel on board will shake at the desperate cries of Tyre's crew sinking beneath the waves. World-wide shipping will come to a halt as sailors pause on land to express sympathy for the departed Queen of the Seas. The

---

[517]NASB, "very glorious."
[518]Literally, " the open spaces."

lament will be bitter. It will be accompanied by all the outward signs of mourning that were customary in the ancient world—dust on the head, baldness, and sackcloth.

Lament over the Sunken Ship
27:32-36

Moreover in their wailing they will take up a lamentation for you. They will lament over you: Who is like Tyre, like she that is silent in the midst of the sea? 33 When your wares went out from the seas you satisfied many peoples. With the multitude of your wealth and your merchandise you enriched the kings of the earth. 34 Now you are broken by the seas in the depths of the waters. Your merchandise and all your company have fallen in your midst. 35 All the inhabitants of the coastlands are appalled over you. Their kings are horribly afraid. They are troubled in their countenance. 36 The merchants among the people whistle in astonishment over you. You have become a terror, and you will be no more.

Verse 32 introduces a rather unusual lament within a lament (cf. 27:2). What other city could be compared to Tyre that now lies silent in a watery grave? In their lament the sailors emphasize the benefits that Tyre had brought to the kings of the earth. Her exports along the shipping lanes had contributed to international wealth. Now, however, the sea had rebelled against her mistress. The good ship Tyre, with crew and cargo, had gone to the bottom.

Other seafaring peoples now feared for their own future. The outward signs of sympathy for Tyre were but a mask to conceal the selfish fears that they too might experience a similar fate. Merchants throughout the world express their astonishment by hissing, i.e., whistling.

EZEKIEL 28
PRINCE OF TYRE

The three chs dealing with Tyre conclude with a vigorous attack against the prince of Tyre for his claims to deity. This attack is not to be interpreted personally of any one Tyrian king.[519] Here the king of Tyre becomes an embodiment of the entire nation. The attitude of the prince was that of the city and vice versa. This section divides naturally into two parts: the death of the prince (vv 1-10); and the dirge over the prince (vv 11-19).

DEATH OF THE PRINCE[520] 28:1-10

Pride of the Prince 28:1-5

The word of Yahweh came unto me saying, 2 Son of man, say to the prince of Tyre: Thus says Lord Yahweh: Because your heart is lifted up, and you have said, I am God, I sit in the seat of God in the heart of the seas; yet you are a man and not God, even though you consider yourself as wise as God.[521] 3 Behold you are wiser than Daniel.[522] No secret can be hidden from you! 4 By your wisdom and understanding you have acquired for yourself wealth. You have amassed gold and silver in your treasuries. 5 By your great wisdom in your trading ventures, you have increased your wealth. Your heart is lifted up because of your wealth.

Obnoxious haughtiness and national arrogance were the besetting sins of Tyre. The prince of Tyre exalted himself to the position of God. The prince regarded his island fortress in the midst of the sea as a divine abode. The splendor of the place, combined with its richness and isolation, caused the proud monarch to regard his realm as not of this world—*the seat of God*.[523] In his *heart* (intellect) he considered

[519] Some conjecture that Ithobaal II was ruler of Tyre in the days of Ezekiel.

[520] Cf. Norman Habel, "Ezekiel 28 and the Fall of the First Man," *CTM* 38 (1967): 516-524.

[521] Literally, "you set your heart in the heart of God."

[522] NIV and NEB render as a question. The implied answer to the question is negative. Taken in this sense Ezekiel is saying that the prince did not know as much as Daniel, who at least revealed some secrets to Nebuchadnezzar.

[523] Alexander (*Expositor's Bible Commentary*, 880) thinks that Tyre's well-known, magnificent temple of Melqart, Tyre's patron deity, was in the prophet's mind. It was not uncommon for a city or a temple to be called the throne of a god. On ancient bas-relief's of Tyre the city and its temple are seen projecting high out of the surrounding sea.

himself as smart as God. Yet in reality this pompous ruler was only a man, subject to all the frailties and limitations of the flesh.

The prince's claim to wisdom is not denied by the prophet. Daniel was famous for his piety (14:14) and for his wisdom.[524] In the latter quality the prince of Tyre exceeded Daniel. Ezekiel is probably speaking sarcastically here. Like Daniel, who could understand the dark mysteries of dream revelations, no secret could elude the prince of Tyre. The prince's wisdom in commercial transactions had resulted in the amassing of wealth into the treasuries of Tyre. As is so often the case with those who know material success the prince's heart was lifted up because of those riches.

Punishment of the Prince
28:6-10

Therefore thus says Lord Yahweh: Because you considered yourself as wise as God, 7 therefore behold I am about to bring strangers upon you, the most ruthless of the nations. They will bring their swords against the beauty of your wisdom. They will defile your splendor. 8 They will thrust you down to the pit. You will die the death of the slain in the heart of the seas. 9 Will you still say before the one who slays you, I am God (although you are a man and not God) in the hand of those who wound you? 10 You will die the death of the uncircumcised by the hand of strangers; for I have spoken (oracle of Lord Yahweh).

The prince of Tyre regarded his intelligence as equal to that of God. For this reason he was destined to face the wrath of the God of Israel. Foreigners—the most ruthless of the nations—will come against Tyre. All that the prince of Tyre had acquired through his wisdom will fall to the invading forces. The splendor of the king, who considered himself to be God-like, will be profaned by the sword.

The prince himself will die in the attack. His island fortress will afford no protection. He will go down to the pit (grave) with all those slain in battle. Will the vainglorious, self-deified prince still proclaim his deity in the face of execution by the blade of the enemy? Obviously not! Gods do not bleed! The humanity of the prince will be perfectly obvious in that day.

---

[524]One can sense in Ezekiel's references to Daniel a humble respect. For Ezekiel, Daniel was the epitome of righteousness and wisdom.

In death all men realize their humanity. The once proud prince will be treated with the contempt reserved for uncircumcised men.[525] He will be dishonored and unlamented with no outward sign of reverence. What a way for a "god" to go!

LAMENT OVER THE PRINCE 28:11-19

Ezekiel 28:11-19 is one of the most obscure passages in the Old Testament. The text is notoriously difficult. God ordered Ezekiel to lament the death of the king of Tyre. Such prophetic laments are anticipatory of a calamity that will occur in the near future. In carrying out this command Ezekiel was partially fulfilling his ministerial commission (cf. 2:10).

The overall thrust of this passage is clear; the details are not. Ezekiel is comparing the fall of the king of Tyre to the fall of Adam.[526] Both fell from a position of prominence and privilege to death and disaster. The passage refers only to the king of Tyre, not to Satan.[527] The language is poetic, and highly figurative.

The lament has two distinct divisions of thought. In vv 12-14 the prophet describes the person and position of the king of Tyre; and in vv 15-19, his sin and sentence.

Person and Position of the King[528] 28:11 14

The word of Yahweh came unto me, saying, 12 Son of man, lift up a lamentation over the king of Tyre and say to him: Thus says Lord Yahweh: You had the seal of perfection, full of wisdom and

---

[525]It is unclear whether the treatment of the uncircumcised will be accorded the dead body of the prince in this world, or in Sheol, the realm of the dead. The Phoenicians practiced circumcision until their contact with the Greeks in the fourth century. The *death of the uncircumcised* is a threat of violent and ignominious death. See Hall, *Wesleyan Bible Commentary*, 441.

[526]It is not impossible that Ezekiel is alluding to a pagan version of the paradise story. This accounts for both the similarities and differences between this passage and Gn 2-3. No such Canaanite paradise account, however, has been found.

[527]Several of the early Church Fathers suggested that Satan is in view here. Among the modern scholars who embrace this position are Barnhouse, Chafer and Scofield.

[528]James Miller, "The *Melek* of Tyre," *ZAW* 105 (1993): 497-500.

perfect in beauty. 13 You were in Eden, the garden of God. Every precious stone was your covering: ruby, topaz, diamond, beryl, onyx, jasper, lapis lazuli, turquoise, and emerald. The gold, the workmanship of your settings and sockets, was in you. On the day you were created they were prepared. 14 You were an anointed guardian cherub. I placed you on the holy mountain of God. You walked about in the midst of the stones of fire.

The king of Tyre is likened to the first inhabitant of Paradise.[529] He is depicted as perfect in physical form (*you had the seal of perfection*[530]), intellectual capabilities (wisdom) and beauty. At least this was his self-estimate.

The king of Tyre occupied a paradise in Eden known as *the garden of God* (or *a garden of gods*). Ancient temples normally encompassed a large enclosure with a garden. The term *Eden* may be used metaphorically to describe the splendor of the temple complex of Tyre's main god Melqart with whom the king was seeking identity.[531]

This garden dweller was not naked as was Adam in the biblical Garden of Eden. He walks in his garden wearing a luxurious robe or breastplate on which were nine[532] precious stones displayed in the most exquisite settings of gold.[533] It seemed that his magnificent garb had been prepared especially for the garden dweller from the day of his creation, i.e., his enthronement.

---

[529]Cf. John McKenzie, "Mythological Allusions in Ezek 28:12-18," *JBL* 75 (1956): 322-27; Anthony Williams, "The Mythological Background of Ezekiel 28:12-19?" *BTB* 6 (1976): 46-61.

[530]The translation of the NASB has been followed. Literally the Hebrew reads, "the one sealing a plan." Alexander (*Expositor's Bible Commentary*, 882) takes this to mean that Tyre's king was the mastermind of the city's commercial sea traffic. The RSV gives another possible rendering: "the signet of perfection," i.e., a seal that everyone recognizes as the pattern for others.

[531]Alexander, *Expositor's Bible Commentary*, 882.

[532]The nine stones enumerated are identical with those that were set in three of the four rows of the breastplate of the high priest (Ex 28:17-20). The Septuagint adds three stones that are omitted in the Hebrew text to complete the set of twelve. The stones in the Hebrew text are not listed in the same order as they appeared on the high priest's breastplate. There is no reason to think that Ezekiel had the priestly breastplate in mind.

[533]Keil (*Biblical Commentary*, 1:409) renders "the service of your timbrels and of your women." He takes this to be a reference to the festivities when the king took over the harem of his predecessor.

The figure changes a bit in v 14. The king of Tyre is now likened to a *cherub*.[534] In the ancient Near East a cherub was depicted as a sphinx-like creature with an animal body, wings, and a human head. These statutory creatures normally guarded the entrances to pagan temples. Cherubim in the Old Testament are always depicted as guarding something. Cherubim guarded the entrance to the original garden (Gn 3:24). For this reason the king of Tyre is depicted guarding his paradise, the garden of his god Melqart.[535] He spread his wings over Tyre like the cherubim who guarded the ark of God in the tabernacle and temple.

The king is said to have been on *the holy mountain of God*.[536] The phrase is probably synonymous with *the garden of God*. This is a further description of Tyre situated on its rocky isle.

The garden dweller walked in the midst of *the stones of fire*. The most popular view is that the phrase refers to the lightning that issues forth from above the towering mountain of God[537] (cf. Ex 19:16; Ps 18:8, 12).

Sin and Sentence of the King 28:15-19

You were perfect in your ways from the day you were created, until iniquity was found in you. 16 By your many trading ventures you were filled with violence, and you sinned. Therefore I have cast you as a profane thing from the mountain of God. I have destroyed you, O guardian cherub, from the midst of the stones of fire. 17 Your heart was lifted up because of your beauty. You have cor-

---

[534]Most commentators follow the Septuagint in reading, "you were *with* the anointed cherub."

[535]Two other details support this interpretation of the text. First, the Phoenician cherub (sphinx) was normally bejeweled (as was the king of Tyre in the previous v) and sometimes had the head of the priest-king. Second, the sphinx was considered to be all-wise (Alexander, *Expositor's Bible Commentary*, 883).

[536]The mountain of the gods was important in ancient Near Eastern mythology. Pagans believed that the gods met in this mountain to determine the decrees of fate (cf. Isa 14:13). Another possibility mentioned by Alexander (*Expositor's Bible Commentary*, 883f) is that *the holy mount of God* is Zion. This means that the king of Tyre was walking *in* (not *on*) the city of Jerusalem after its fall to the Babylonians (cf. 26:1-6). The *stones of fire* were Jerusalem's stones which were still smoldering at the time.

[537]Cook (*Ezekiel*, 2:318) contends that the stones of fire are gems that give splendor and brilliance to the garden.

rupted your wisdom on account of your splendor. I have cast you to the ground before kings that they may gaze upon you. 18 By the multitude of your iniquities, in the unrighteousness of your trading ventures, you have profaned your sanctuaries. Therefore I have brought out a fire from your midst. It has consumed you. I have made you to become ashes upon the ground in the eyes of all who see you. 19 All who know you among the people will be appalled at you. You have become a terror. You will be no more.

Before his vast wealth filled his heart with pride the king of Tyre was *perfect,* i.e., no fault could be found with his conduct as a ruler. Eventually, however, *unrighteousness* was found in the character of this king. Increasing commerce led to increasing corruption. The midst of Tyre was filled with goods taken by *violence*, i.e., force of arms or fraudulent business tactics.

He who was *guardian cherub* over this city must bear the blame for what transpired there. The prince had profaned the garden spot in which God had placed him. Like Adam of old he must be thrust forth from paradise.

Holiness and purity are essential to those who aspire to dwell in *the mountain of God.* The fallen prince must be stripped of his royal rank and insignia. He will be removed from the midst of *the stones of fire,* the flashing thunders and lightings of divine majesty that had protected him. He will cease to be the protector of Tyre, the *guardian cherub*.

At the root of the fall of the king of Tyre was pride. The king's heart was lifted up because of his *beauty* and brightness, his splendor and magnificence. The *wisdom* with which the prince of Tyre had been endowed was corrupted by arrogance. "True wisdom cannot be exercised where there is a spirit of arrogance."[538]

The prince of Tyre will be humbled, *cast to the ground.* There on the ground the fallen prince will be the object of wonderment, sadness and perhaps even some gloating by the kings of the earth.

The multitude of iniquities committed through unrighteous business dealings had *profaned* the sanctuary,[539] the garden of God, the mountain of God, in which this king ruled.

---

[538]Fisch, *Ezekiel*, 192.

[539]The Hebrew text reads plural, "your sanctuaries;" but several manuscripts, the Syriac and Targum read singular. If the plural is original it is probably a plural of amplification, meaning something like sanctuary *par excellence*.

The evil in the midst of Tyre is like a fire that will reduce the place to a pile of ashes. The fall of the once proud city and its pompous prince will send shock waves throughout her commercial empire. Never again will Phoenician Tyre be rebuilt.

RIVAL OF TYRE
28:20-24

The word of Yahweh came unto me, saying, 21 Son of man, set your face against Sidon, and prophesy against her 22 and say, Thus says Lord Yahweh: Behold I am against you, O Sidon. I will be glorified in the midst of you. They will know that I am Yahweh when I execute judgments in her, and manifest my holiness in her; 23 for I will send into her pestilence and blood in her streets. The slain will fall in the midst of her by the sword upon her on every side. Then they will know that I am Yahweh. 24 And there will be no more for the house of Israel a pricking brier or a piercing thorn of any that are round about them who treated them with contempt. They will know that I am Lord Yahweh.

Tyre's rival to the north will also experience the wrath of the God of Israel. In early times Sidon was larger and more prestigious than Tyre. From the eleventh to the fourth century BC, however, Tyre controlled, almost without dispute on the part of Sidon, the affairs of Phoenicia. In biblical prophecy the two cities are closely connected (cf. Isa 23).

As far as the Hebrew prophets were concerned Tyre and Sidon were "seaside partners in sin."[540] Sidon, however, was sufficiently independent from Tyre to justify a separate oracle, sufficiently identified with Tyre not to call for any longer oracle. No indication of Sidon's offenses is given in this oracle; but it is assumed that her sins were the same as those of Tyre. Those sins required a similar punishment.

God declared that he was an adversary of Sidon as well as of Tyre. By dispensing a just judgment on this city God will be vindicated. He will manifest his *holiness*[541] in this judgment. He will receive glory. He will be sanctified (reverenced) as a result of such activity.

---

[540]Grider, *Beacon Bible Commentary*, 582.

[541]Ezekiel uses the word *holy* as a noun 49x, and the related verb 15x.

Sidon will experience the pestilence that usually accompanied ancient sieges. When the enemies breached the walls the blood will flow in her streets. The slain will fall in heaps.[542]

When all of predictions regarding Sidon are fulfilled men will acknowledge that the doom of Sidon had not occurred by chance. It was an act of God. Such judgments will serve the purpose of removing all sources of danger, opposition, and ridicule (*a pricking brier, a piercing thorn*)[543] to the people of God. In time past Israel had been wounded by those thorns and briers, i.e., had been tainted by the wicked worship and lascivious life of these Canaanite neighbors. In the future restoration, however, the corrupting Canaanite influence will be forever removed.

The bloody history of Sidon after the time of Ezekiel can be summarized as follows:

1. Sidon was devastated during Nebuchadnezzar's thirteen-year siege of Tyre (587-572 BC).
2. With the fall of Babylon Sidon regained some of its old importance. For a time the city served faithfully the new Persian world rulers. In 351 BC, however, the Sidonians revolted against Artaxerxes II Ochus. In the face of the siege of the Persian monarch the king of Sidon fled, leaving the city to its fate. The city fathers ordered all ships in the harbor to be destroyed to prevent any flight by the citizens. More than forty thousand are said to have lost their lives when the city was sacked and burned.
3. Sidon meekly surrendered to Alexander the Great in 332 BC.
4. Under the Seleucid rulers Sidon again attained a rather independent status.
5. In 64 BC Pompey imposed Roman rule throughout Phoenicia. Sidon still flourished; but its importance gradually declined.
6. In the days of the crusades Sidon was taken and retaken several times by opposing forces.
7. Under Turkish rule the site of Sidon continued to suffer tribulation. In 1840 Sidon was bombarded by the combined fleets of England, France and Turkey.

---

[542]A rare form of the verb *fall* is used in this v. It probably denotes intensity.

[543]The same words are used in Nm 33:55 of the Canaanite peoples. Ezekiel applies the terms to the Phoenician cities that were the last vestige of the old Canaanite culture.

8. The modern Arab city of Saeda (population, 50,000) that occupies the site of ancient Sidon did not escape the bloody religious warfare that erupted in Lebanon in 1976.

As a footnote to the Tyre and Sidon oracles it may be pointed out that Jesus once passed through the region (Mt 15:21). According to the best text of Mk 7:24 he probably trod the streets of Sidon. Some of the great multitude that heard him teach in Mk 3:8 came from Tyre and Sidon. Jesus remarked that it will be more tolerable in the day of judgment for Tyre and Sidon than for the faithless cities of Galilee (Mt 11:21; Lk 10:13). In this statement Jesus seems to be affirming that the day of judgment had not yet fully come to the two cities even though they had suffered much before his time. Jesus may be referring to the Roman campaigns in the region of Palestine in the latter part of the seventh decade AD Jerusalem was destroyed in that judgment; Tyre and Sidon survived.

FUTURE OF ISRAEL
28:25-26

Thus says Lord Yahweh: When I gather the house of Israel from the peoples among whom they are scattered, and I manifest my holiness in them in the eyes of the nations, then they will dwell upon their land that I gave to my servant Jacob. 26 They will dwell safely upon it. They will build houses and plant vineyards; yea, they will dwell safely when I have executed judgments on all those who treated them with contempt round about them. Then they will know that I am Yahweh their God.

In contrast to the bloody future of Sidon God's people will experience a glorious future. God will gather his people from the foreign lands where they had been scattered. God's servant Jacob (a name for the nation Israel) will again dwell on the land God had given him. The nation will be devoted to peaceful pursuits. Israel can live in peace and security because hostile neighbors have been removed.

All that God does for Israel is done with one grand purpose in view, viz. that all the world might acknowledge him as the one true and living God—that he might be sanctified (reverenced, revered) in the eyes of the nations.

The wonderful thoughts embraced in the last vv of ch 28 are developed at length in chs 33-48.

EZEKIEL 29
ECLIPSE OF EGYPT[544]

Egypt is the seventh and last nation to hear the words of divine judgment. In the four chs devoted to Egypt Ezekiel speaks seven "words" from Yahweh. The number seven is not likely accidental. In prophecy seven is the number of perfection or completeness. Hence God will completely and fully deal with the enemies of his people.

In chs 29-32 ninety-seven vv are devoted to the fall of Egypt. This is more vv than are contained in 1 Peter, more than 2 Timothy and more than are in Paul's letter to the Colossians. Why such a large section devoted to this one heathen power? Ezekiel agreed with Jeremiah that God had bestowed universal sovereignty temporarily on Nebuchadnezzar. Babylon's principal rival in the sixth century was Egypt. The other nations condemned in this section were minor irritations to Nebuchadnezzar; but Egypt had the potential of presenting a serious obstacle to Yahweh's will for Babylon.

Chart 7 SEQUENCE OF EZEKIEL'S EGYPT ORACLES		
Text	**Date (Yr/Mo/Da)**	**Modern Dating**
29:1	10/10/10	Dec 29, 588
30:20	11/1/7	Apr 30, 587
31:1	11/3/1	Jun 21, 587
32:1	12/12/1	Mar 4, 585
32:17	12/?/15	Mar 18, 585
29:17	27/1/1	Apr 26, 571

Egypt had been very much involved in encouraging Judah's final revolt against Babylon. The main point stressed by Ezekiel and the other Hebrew prophets is that the final destiny of Israel was in the hands of God, not the hands of human monarchs. Furthermore, the prophets dared to preach what was in their day a revolutionary doctrine: even the destiny of the superpowers was determined by God—

---

[544]See Lawrence Boardt, *Ezekiel's Oracles Against Egypt* (Rome: Biblical Institute Press, 1980).

and God was Yahweh! Tiny Israel appeared to be only a pawn in the hands of political strategists; but Israel's God was powerful. In reality those strategists were but pawns in his hand. Thus the oracles against Egypt—and others like them—were not merely designed to vent the frustrations and hostilities that Israel felt toward her neighbors. These oracles served to underscore vital points of theology—the sovereignty, omniscience and omnipotence of Israel's God.

The Egypt oracles are similar in structure: a general threat against Pharaoh under some allegorical designation; amplification of the general threat with regard to the instrument of punishment, the destruction of the country and the disposition of its inhabitants; a description of the effect that the fall of Egypt will have on other nations.

SINS OF EGYPT
29:1-16

The first oracle against Egypt is a composite of four separate oracles. Ezekiel condemns Egypt's pride (vv 1-6a), and unreliability (vv 6b-9a). He then announces Egypt's defeat (vv 9b-12) and restoration (vv 13-16).

Egypt's Pride
29:1-6a

In the tenth year, in the tenth month, in the twelfth day of the
month, the word of Yahweh came unto me, saying, 2 Son of man,
set your face against Pharaoh king of Egypt. Prophesy against him
and against all Egypt. 3 Speak and say, Thus says Lord Yahweh:
Behold I am against you Pharaoh king of Egypt, the great monster
that lies in the midst of his rivers, that has said, The river is mine,
and I myself made it. 4 I will put hooks in your jaws, and make the
fish of your rivers cling to your scales. I will bring you up from the
midst of your rivers. All the fish of your rivers will cling to your
scales. 5 I will cast you into the wilderness, you and all the fish of
your rivers. Upon the face of the open field you will fall. You will
not be gathered or brought together. To the beasts of the land and
the fowl of the heavens I have given you for food. 6 All the inhabi-
tants of Egypt will know that I am Yahweh.

The first word against Egypt is dated, according to the modern calendar, to December 29, 588 BC. This was about the time that the Babylonian siege of Jerusalem began (Jer 52:4; 39:1; cf. Ezek 24:1), and seven months earlier than the preceding oracle against Tyre. The first oracle emphasizes the pride of Egypt and the desolation that God brings on her for her arrogance.

Ezekiel was to *set his face against Pharaoh*[545] in a gesture of defiance. He was to announce God's hostility toward him.

Pharaoh is addressed with the challenge formula. This same formula also introduced the first Tyre oracle (26:3) and the oracle against Sidon (28:22). The *great monster* in the rivers is to the crocodile.[546] *Rivers* are the various branches of the Nile in northern Egypt. The wealth—and in fact the very existence of Egypt—depended upon the Nile River, which by metonymy stands for the entire country of Egypt.

Most kings in the ancient world represented themselves to their people as the source of their prosperity. Pharaoh went even further in his outrageous claims. Like the prince of Tyre Pharaoh regarded himself as the incarnation of a god. He thought of himself as the creator of all the wealth and prosperity of Egypt.

Pharaoh will fall prey to his enemies. Like a crocodile drug from the river by captors[547] Pharaoh will be removed from his domain by his enemies. Pharaoh's people, allies and mercenaries (*fish of the river* that *stick to your scales*) will accompany him. A battle with a crocodile stretched the limits of human power (Job 40:25f); but that Egyptian beast will be no challenge to the Creator. There on dry land—the *wilderness*—the crocodile and fish joined to it will die. No one will gather up the carcass of the crocodile for burial. The birds and beasts of prey will devour the remains.[548]

---

[545]The current Pharaoh was Hophra (Jer 44:30), fourth king of the twenty-sixth dynasty. His reign was 589-570 BC.

[546]The metaphor of Pharaoh resting confidently and indolently in the waters of the Nile was a favorite in Egyptian hymns and prayers. Pharaoh was also depicted as a ferocious crocodile to his enemies. Cf. *ANET*, 374. Ezekiel promised that Yahweh will treat Pharaoh like a crocodile. The crocodile god, Sebek, was very important to the Egyptians in the Nile delta area. He was considered Egypt's protector.

[547]Ancient accounts of crocodile hunts depict the beast pulled by means of hooks in its jaws out of its native element on to dry land where it was then slaughtered. Cf. Herodotus 2:70.

[548]The tombs and pyramids of Egypt demonstrate how important proper royal burial was to the Pharaoh's successful journey through the Egyptian afterlife. Lack of such burial was a horrible fate.

In the demise of Pharaoh the Egyptians will recognize Yahweh's judgment upon them for being an unreliable ally.[549]

Egypt's Unreliability 29:6b-9a

Because they have been a staff of reed to the house of Israel—7 when anyone took hold of you with the hand, you broke and tore every shoulder;[550] and when they leaned upon you, you broke and made all their loins stand up[551]—8 therefore thus says Lord Yahweh: Behold I bring upon you a sword. I will cut off from you man and beast. 9 The land of Egypt will become a desolation and a waste. Then will they know that I am Yahweh.

Egypt had proved itself to be *a staff of reed*[552] *to the house of Israel. Leaned* is part of the Old Testament vocabulary of faith. By turning to Egypt God's people were looking for the support they should have sought in Yahweh. Through bitter experience Israel discovered the truth of what the prophets had warned about reliance on Egypt. If one tried to make Egypt his crutch he was destined for a fall. That crutch will break causing those who were dependent upon it to fall and dislocate their shoulder. They will then have to stand erect (*make all their loins to stand up*) and carry their own weight. Egypt was the proverbial paper tiger.

A few months after these words were spoken in Babylon the Jews in Palestine lived through another episode of Egyptian failure. In Israel's moment of need, when Nebuchadnezzar was literally banging on the gates of Jerusalem, Egypt failed to send effective aid (cf. Jer 37:7). The Egyptian foray into Palestine brought only a temporary lull in the siege of the city.

Because of Egypt's arrogance God will bring a sword upon that land. Man and beast will be affected. The fertile land of Pharaoh will be left desolate and waste. The gods of Egypt will be discredited.

---

[549]The recognition formula is found 9x in the Egypt oracles: 29:6, 9, 16, 21; 30:8, 19, 25, 26; 32:15.

[550]Some manuscripts read "hand."

[551]NASB, "quake;" RSV, "shake."

[552]Just over a century earlier, an Assyrian officer gave Egypt a similar description—"a bruised reed ... which if a man lean, it will go into his hand and pierce it" (Isa 36:6).

Wise people will be forced to acknowledge the sovereignty of Yahweh.

Egypt's Desolation
29:9b-12

Because he has said, The river is mine, and I made it, 10 therefore behold I am against you and against your rivers. I will make the land of Egypt utterly waste and desolate from Migdol to Syene, even unto the border of Ethiopia. 11 No foot of man will pass through it, or foot of beast will pass through it. It will not be inhabited forty years. 12 I will make the land of Egypt desolate in the midst of lands that are desolate. Her cities in the midst of cities that are laid waste will be desolate forty years. I will scatter Egyptians among the nations and disperse them through the lands.

Pharaoh boasted that he owned and had created the Nile! God defies the arrogant claims of this king. Yahweh lays waste the land from north to south (*Migdol*[553] to *Syene*[554]), even as far as the border of Ethiopia (ancient Nubia) between the Nile's second and third cataracts. Then what will become of Pharaoh's boast. The desolation of Egypt is a result of an invading army. Even animals will desert the land owing to the lack of pasture.

Nebuchadrezzar made at least two invasions into Egypt. The Jewish historian Josephus tells of an invasion of Egypt by Nebuchadnezzar five years after the fall of Jerusalem (582 BC). In this invasion the king of Egypt was killed. A fragmentary inscription from the archives of Babylon tells of another invasion of Egypt in the thirty-seventh year of Nebuchadrezzar's reign (i.e., 568 BC). It appears that Nebuchadrezzar was aiming to cripple Egypt so as to prevent Pharaoh from ever again meddling in Syria-Palestine.

The reference to the forty years of Egypt's desolation has occasioned lengthy discussion among the commentators. The figure may be derived from Ezek 4:6 where Judah is depicted as suffering under the punishment of God for forty years. Keil regards the forty years as a symbolic period—the period denoted by God for punishment and

---

[553]Migdol (*Tower*) was a frontier fortress at the northeastern border of Egypt (cf. Ex 14:2; Jer 44:1). E.D. Oren may have found biblical Migdol when he uncovered a mud brick fort some twelve miles east of Daphne south of Pelusium. The ten acre site demonstrated that Migdol was a cosmopolitan city in the sixth century BC.

[554]Modern Aswan near the Ethiopian border.

penitence. It is best, however, to regard the forty years as a definite historical period. The forty years of Egypt's desolation may be said to fall between 568 BC when Nebuchadnezzar invaded the land and 530 BC. In the latter year the Persians entered the land. It may have been they who initiated the policy of reconstruction in Egypt even as they encouraged reconstruction in Judea.

In comparison to other countries ravished by war Egypt will stand out as a most unfortunate land (*desolate in the midst of lands that are desolate*). Egyptian cities will be *laid waste*, i.e., left a ruinous condition for *forty years*.

During the time of desolation the Egyptians will be scattered among the nations. No evidence of mass deportation of Egyptians subsequent to the time of Ezekiel has yet come to light. It is known, however, that deportation of captive peoples was a standard procedure employed by great empires of that time. One is certainly on safe ground in assuming that it was the Chaldean king who fulfilled the prediction that God will scatter the Egyptians among the nations. See above on v 11.

Egypt's Restoration
29:13-16

For thus says Lord Yahweh: At the end of forty years I will gather the Egyptians from the peoples among whom they were scattered. 14 I will turn the fortunes of Egypt, and cause them to return to the land of Pathros, to the land of their origin. They will be there a lowly people. 15 It will be the lowliest of all kingdoms. She will not lift herself up again over the nations. I will diminish them so that they will no more rule over the nations. 16 It will never again be the confidence of the house of Israel bringing to remembrance iniquity when they turned after them. They will know that I am Lord Yahweh.

Ezekiel, like Jeremiah (46:26; cf. Isa 19), envisioned restoration for Egypt. God said through Ezekiel that he would *turn the fortunes of Egypt*. After the forty years Egyptians will return into the *land of Pathros*, the southern part of the land, i.e., Upper Egypt. This was *the land of their origin*, i.e., the area in which the Egyptian government first rose to prominence. The restored Egypt, however, is only a shadow of the glorious kingdom that once graced the banks of the Nile.

Following her restoration Egypt will not be able to dominate other peoples. She will be inferior to all other nations. No more will Egypt allure Israel into disastrous alliances. Israel will not repeat the great mistake of her past, viz. trusting in Egypt rather than in God. Israel in that future day will know assuredly that Yahweh is God.

PRIZE OF EGYPT
29:17-21

The second Egypt oracle dates to New Year's day (April 26) 571 BC. It is the latest oracle in the entire book. The placement here is appropriate. The oracle connects the invasion of Egypt with the cessation of the Babylonian siege of Tyre that took place about 574 BC.

Compensation to Nebuchadrezzar
29:17-20

It came to pass in the twenty-seventh year, in the first month, in the first day of the month that the word of Yahweh came unto me, saying, 18 Son of man, Nebuchadrezzar king of Babylon caused his army to serve a great service against Tyre. Every head was made bald, and every shoulder was peeled. Yet neither he nor his army received any wages from Tyre for the service that he performed against it. 19 Therefore thus says Lord Yahweh: Behold I am about to give to Nebuchadnezzar king of Babylon the land of Egypt. He will carry off her abundance, take her spoil and seize her prey. She will be the wages for his army. 20 I have given him the land of Egypt as his hire for which he served because they worked for me (oracle of Lord Yahweh).

Nebuchadrezzar rendered a great service to God by besieging Tyre for thirteen years (Josephus, *Ant.*, 10.11.1). The siege perhaps was prolonged because of Egyptian support for Tyre. Nebuchadrezzar's soldiers were weary with that warfare. Bald spots worn by ill-fitting helmets scared the heads of the besiegers. The skin of their shoulders was raw from carrying heavy loads of timber and stone to construct the siege works. In spite of his determined effort to cross the narrow arm of the sea and reach the island fortress Nebuchadrezzar had been unsuccessful.[555] Neither he nor his troops had been enriched through the spoils of war that generally made a lengthy siege operation rewarding.[556]

To compensate him for the service he rendered at Tyre God decreed that Nebuchadrezzar should be given the land of Egypt.[557] The spoils of that great north African nation will fall into the hands of the Chaldeans. Nebuchadrezzar was entitled to this booty. All that he had done at Tyre he had done in the service of Yahweh (*they worked for me*).

A Babylonian force invaded Egypt in 568 BC. Owing to the damaged state of the inscription that alludes to this campaign it is impossible accurately to gauge the success of the effort. It is known that Pharaoh Ahmose II came to terms with the invaders.

Compensation for Israel
29:21

In that day I will cause a horn to shoot up unto the house of Israel. I will give you the opening of the mouth in the midst of them. They will know that I am Yahweh.

The decisive political events of the sixth century were orchestrated by God to accomplish his plan of salvation for his people Israel. Ezekiel indicates three results of Nebuchadrezzar's invasion of Egypt.

A *horn*, symbol of power and prosperity, will spring forth for the house of Israel.[558] This prophecy seems to be saying that Israel's restoration will correspond to Egypt's humiliation. Egypt's period of humiliation ended in 530 BC. Israel's period of restoration began some eight or nine years earlier when Cyrus allowed the Jews to return home.

---

[555]What exactly took place at Tyre is uncertain. Ezekiel does not actually say Nebuchadrezzar was unsuccessful there. He only indicates that the material reward for his siege efforts was not sufficient.

[556]Allen (*Word Biblical Commentary*, 110) points out that v 18 is a chiasmus with an ABCD/DCBA structure.

[557]Jeremiah also foretold Nebuchadrezzar's invasion of Egypt. Cf. Jer 43:8-13; 46:1-25.

[558]The expression *make a horn sprout* is found elsewhere only in Ps 132:17 in reference to the restoration of the Davidic dynasty. The reference here appears to be more general. It alludes to the coming deliverance of Israel. Vawter & Hoppe, *Ezekiel*, 139.

God will give to Ezekiel *opening of the mouth* at the time Nebuchadnezzar invades Egypt. The expression indicates a cheerful confidence in speaking.[559] The implication is that Ezekiel had come under reproach regarding his oracles against foreign nations and the related prediction of Israel's restoration. Ezekiel's prophetic ministry is vindicated anew. The Israelites will know that Yahweh is God and that he truly had revealed himself to Ezekiel.

EZEKIEL 30 FALL OF EGYPT

IMMINENT FALL OF EGYPT 30:1-19

The third oracle against Egypt is likely to be dated the same as the previous one (see 29:17). Ezekiel focuses on Egypt's gloom, destruction, adversary, cities and gods.

Egypt's Gloom 30:1-5

The word of Yahweh came unto me, saying, 2 Son of man, prophesy and say: Thus says Lord Yahweh: Wail, woe be the day! 3 For the day is near, yes the day of Yahweh is near! A cloudy day, it will be the time of the nations. 4 A sword will come upon Egypt. Consternation will be in Cush, when the slain fall in Egypt. They will take away her abundance. Her foundations will be broken down. 5 Ethiopia, Put, Lud, all the mingled peoples, Cub, and the children of the land that are in league[560] will fall with them by the sword.

The oracle begins with direct address to the Egyptians. They are urged rhetorically to wail over their fate. Egypt's day of reckoning looms on the horizon. The proclamation of the day of Yahweh is ex-

[559]It is better not to think here of the prophet's specific inability to speak, which is referred to in 3:26 (24:27; 33:22).

[560]NIV "covenant land." This is a possible reference to the Jews who fled to Egypt after the assassination of Gedaliah n (2 Kgs 25:23-26).

pressed in language familiar from Ezek 7. The day of Yahweh—a day of divine reckoning—will be a gloomy day for the Gentile nations.

Egypt experiences invasion in the day of Yahweh. Her satellite state Ethiopia will fear for her own safety when she sees what transpires across the border in Egypt. The *foundations* of Egypt—the allies and mercenaries—upon whom the Egyptian state rested will be broken down.

Six groups are mentioned who will fall by the sword: *Ethiopia* (Cush), Put, Lud (see on 27:10) and *Cub*, a people not as yet identified, had alliances with Egypt. The multi-racial character of the Egyptian army is indicated by the expression *all the mingled peoples.* Along with *the children of the land* (native Egyptians) these allies will fall by the sword of the invaders.

Egypt's Destruction
30:6-9

Thus says Yahweh: those who uphold Egypt will fall. The pride of her strength will come down. From Migdol to Syene they will fall in her by the sword (oracle of Lord Yahweh). 7 And they will be desolate in the midst of lands that are desolate. Her cities in the midst of cities will lie in ruins. 8 They will know that I am Yahweh when I place a fire in Egypt and all her helpers are shattered. 9 In that day messengers will go from before me in ships to terrify the secure Ethiopians. Confusion will come on them in the day of Egypt; for behold it comes.

Throughout the land, from Migdol to Syene (see on 29:10), the sword will cut down Egypt's inhabitants. The sword of divine retribution had raged in Judah (ch 21); now it rages in the much mightier kingdom of the pharaohs. Egypt's pride was in her military and economic power. This pride, however, will be humbled.

Desolation will follow invasion (cf. 29:12). The desolation caused by war, as frequently in the Bible, is likened to *fire.* The fulfillment of this prediction to bring conflagration to Egypt will be a demonstration of the sovereignty of the true God. Seldom had Egypt seen a foreign foe bring all the horrors of war within its borders.

In the day of Egypt's downfall *messengers* will be dispatched, as though by God himself. Traveling the waterways to every part of the land of Ethiopia the messengers will spread the alarming news of

Egypt's fall. *Confusion* will fill their land as they contemplate the possibility that their own country might be invaded.

Egypt's Adversary
30:10-12

Thus says Lord Yahweh: I will cause the multitude of Egypt to cease by the hand of Nebuchadnezzar king of Babylon. 11 He and his people with him, the most ruthless of the nations, will be brought in to destroy the land. They will empty their swords against Egypt. They will fill the land with the slain. 12 I will make the rivers dry. I will deliver the land into the hand of evil men. I will make the land and all that is in it desolate by the hand of strangers. I Yahweh have spoken.

Ezekiel emphasizes that the native population (*multitude of Egypt*), as well as the mercenary forces, will perish in the overthrow of Egypt. Nebuchadnezzar is specifically named as the conqueror (cf. 29:19). He and his ruthless warriors (cf. 28:7) leave a trail of corpses wherever they go.

The much heralded Egyptian irrigation system will be destroyed by the *evil men*, i.e., the pitiless and lawless troops that comprised Nebuchadnezzar's army. Without irrigation the land will become (temporarily) desolate.

Egypt's Cities
30:13-19

Thus says Lord Yahweh: I will destroy the idols and cause the non-entities to cease from Noph. There will no longer be a prince out of the land of Egypt. I will put a fear in the land of Egypt. 14 I will make Pathros desolate. I will set a fire in Zoan and execute judgments in No. 15 I will pour out my wrath upon Sin, the stronghold of Egypt. I will cut off the multitude of No. 16 I will set a fire in Egypt. Sin will be in great upheaval. No will be torn asunder. Against Noph adversaries will come by day. 17 The young men of Aven and of Pi-beseth will fall by the sword. These (cities) will go into captivity. 18 At Tehaphnehes the day will withdraw itself when I break there the yokes of Egypt. The pride of her strength will cease in her. As for her, a cloud will cover her. Her daughters will

go into captivity. 19 Thus will I execute judgments in Egypt. They will know that I am Yahweh.

Ezekiel again employs the technique of emphasis by enumeration. The complete collapse of Egypt is underscored by reference to the fate of the leading cities of the land.[561] Ezekiel did not stand in awe of the ancient and magnificent cities of Egypt. These vv reveal an amazing knowledge of Egyptian geography.[562] Seven different cities are named plus one district of ancient Egypt.

First, Ezekiel focuses on *Noph* (Memphis). The gods of Egypt prove worthless in the face of the mighty conqueror raised up by Yahweh. Noph was famous for its numerous gods and elaborate temples, especially those of Ptah and Apis. The *non-entities* (lit., "things of naught"), however, will be made to cease from Noph. So it has happened. An enormous, albeit prostrate, figure of Pharaoh Ramses is the only image of note to mark the spot where once stood the magnificent capital of Egypt. Wilbur Smith summarizes the situation well when he writes:

> The temples of Egypt and the elaborate carvings and drawings of her gods and goddesses are still the wonder of modern students; but her gods are gone. No temple to an Egyptian god or goddess has a priest in attendance today; no offering is presented to any of these once powerful deities representing the sun, the stellar bodies, the river Nile, and the underworld; no one bows the knee to any of these ancient images.[563]

The destruction of the gods at Noph will be implemented by *adversaries* that come *by day*, i.e., in broad daylight (v 16).

Following her destruction Egypt will never again be ruled by a native *prince* (v 13). So it has been. Persians, Greeks, Ptolemies, and Romans ruled Egypt in olden times. Since AD 638 Egypt has been ruled by Moslems. James Breasted summarizes the situation:

> With the fall of Psamtik III [to Cambyses in 525 BC], Egypt belonged to a new world, toward the development of which she had contributed much, but in which she could no longer play an active part. Her great work was done, and unable, like Nineveh and Babylon, to disap-

---

[561]Other examples of the listing of threatened cities in prophetic literature are Amos 1:3-5, 6-8; Mic 1:10-15.

[562]For other examples of geographical enumeration in a judgment context, see Isa 10:27-32; Mic 1:10-15; Zeph 2:4.

[563]Wilbur Smith, *Egypt in Biblical Prophecy* (Grand Rapids: Baker, 1957), 115.

> pear from the scene, she lived on her artificial life for a time under the Persians and the Ptolemies, ever sinking, till she became merely the granary of Rome, to be visited as a land of ancient marvels by wealthy Greeks and Romans, who have left their names scratched here and there upon her hoary monuments, just as the modern tourists, admiring the same marvels, still continue to do. But her unwarlike people, still making Egypt a garden of the world, show no signs of an awakening and the words of the Hebrew seer, 'There shall be no more a prince out of the land of Egypt.,' have been literally fulfilled.[564]

The one region mentioned in this unit is *Pathros*. This region is southern or Upper Egypt extending as far south as Aswan. Yahweh threatens to make this region *desolate* (v 14).

Second, *Zoan* (classical Tanis) was an important city in the eastern Nile delta. Yahweh threatens to *set fire* to Zoan, i.e., bring a military force against the city.

Third, *No* (or No-Amon) is classical Thebes (RSV), modern Karnak and Luxor, located about five hundred miles south of Cairo. *No* was capital of Egypt during much of Egyptian history. It was the worship center for the sun-god Amon. Yahweh will execute judgments in No (v 14). *The multitude of No will be cut off* (v 15), i.e., the place will be uninhabited. *Fire* is figurative for warfare. God will not use supernatural means to judge Egypt, but the destructive force of an invading army.

No (Thebes) will be *torn asunder*, i.e., breached and penetrated by an invading army (v 16). An insurrection at Thebes was ruthlessly quelled by the Persians in 335 BC. Alexander the Great next conquered Egypt (332 BC). In the first pre-Christian century Ptolemy IX completely destroyed Thebes in order to quell an uprising. No city walls are to be seen at the ancient site. Only gateways and pylons mark the places where walls once stood.

Fourth, *Sin* is probably Pelusium (RSV) on the Mediterranean coast. This *stronghold* guarded Egypt from attack from the north. Yahweh will *pour out* his *wrath* on Sin (v 15). The city will be in *great upheaval* (v 16).

Fifth, *Aven* is also called On in the Old Testament. The Greeks knew the town as Heliopolis, the city of the sun god. *The young men of Aven will fall by the sword* (v 17). The ruins[565] are found in the outskirts of modern Cairo.

---

[564]James H. Breasted, *A History of Egypt* (2nd. ed.; 1937 reprint), 595.

[565]Traces of an enclosure-wall and a temple obelisk still stand.

Sixth, *Pi-beseth* (modern Basta) about forty miles northeast of Cairo. Like the other cities mentioned in vv 13-18 Pi-beseth was a cultic center. The cat was particularly sacred there. Along with Aven, Pi-beseth will *go into captivity* (v 17). On deportation see discussion on 29:12b.

Seventh, *Tehaphnehes*—spelled Tahpanhes in Jeremiah—was known to the Greeks as Daphni. The modern Tel Defenneh on the Suez Canal is the spot to which Ezekiel refers. Jeremiah was taken there after the assassination of Gedaliah (Jer 43:7). *The day will withdraw itself at Tehaphnehes*, i.e., the Egyptian defeat at that place will plunge Egypt into dark despair (v 18).

The fall of the seven sister cities to an invader means that *the yokes of Egypt*—the tyranny that Egypt inflicted on other nations—will be broken. The *daughters of Egypt*, i.e., her various cities, will go into captivity.

The ultimate purpose of these judgments was the vindication of the sovereignty of Israel's God.

FALL OF PHARAOH
30:20-26

About four months before the fall of Jerusalem to Nebuchadnezzar (July 3, 586 BC) Ezekiel received another revelation against Egypt.

Pharaoh's Arms
Shattered
30:20-23

It came to pass in the eleventh year, in the first month, in the seventh day of the month that the word of Yahweh came unto me, saying, 21 Son of man, I have broken the arm of Pharaoh king of Egypt. Behold it has not been bound up to be healed, to put a bandage that it be bound up to become strong that it might hold a sword. 22 Therefore thus says Lord Yahweh: Behold I am against Pharaoh king of Egypt. I will break his arms, the strong, and the one that was broken. I will cause the sword to fall out of his hand. 23 I will scatter the Egyptians among the nations, and disperse them through countries.

Pharaoh's *arm* had been *broken*. The allusion is probably to the defeat of Pharaoh Hophra when he tried to come to the aid of beleaguered Jerusalem (cf. Jer 37:1-10). Nebuchadnezzar had inflicted irreparable damage upon the military machine of Egypt (cf. 2 Kgs 24:7). Pharaoh's *arm*—symbol of his military might—could not be mended.[566] Never again will he attempt to launch a military offensive against Nebuchadnezzar.

The defeat at the borders of Judah indicated that God was opposing Pharaoh. That setback signaled the beginning of a succession of defeats. Both of Pharaoh's arms—the good one and the bad one—will be broken. The sword will drop from his hand. Egypt will be rendered completely powerless. Egyptians will be scattered among the nations (cf. 29:12; 30:26).

Pharaoh's Adversary Strengthened 30:24-26

I will strengthen the arms of the king of Babylon. I will put my sword in his hand. But I will shatter the arms of Pharaoh. He will groan with the groanings of the slain before him. 25 I will uphold the arms of the king of Babylon, but the arms of Pharaoh will fall down. They will know that I am Yahweh when I put my sword in the hand of the king of Babylon. He will stretch it out against the land of Egypt. 26 I will scatter the Egyptians among the nations, and disperse them through the lands. They will know that I am Yahweh.

The king of Egypt will decrease while the king of Babylon will increase in power. Pharaoh will appear as helpless as a mortally wounded soldier before the advancing army of Nebuchadnezzar. The king of Babylon will wield the sword of divine judgment against the helpless land of Egypt. The dispersal of the Egyptians will establish the sole divinity of Israel's God.

---

[566]Pharaoh is often depicted with his arm flexed wielding a sword in battle. A king with great biceps was especially a popular concept under the Saite Dynasty of Ezekiel's day. Pharaoh Hophra took a second formal title that meant "possessed of a muscular arm" or "strong-armed." Alexander, *Expositor's Bible Commentary*, 897.

EZEKIEL 31
GREAT CEDAR TREE
31:1-18

In the first unit of this ch Egypt is likened to a cedar (vv 2-9). This poetic comparison is followed by two prose messages describing the downfall of the magnificent tree at the hands of foreigners (vv 10-14) and its descent into Sheol (vv 15-18).

DESCRIPTION OF THE CEDAR 31:1-9

Ezekiel uses the common ancient Near Eastern motif of the tree of life to underscore again the reason for Egypt's downfall. It was not Egypt's greatness that drew the prophet's fire. Egypt ignored God's sovereignty. Egypt promised to aid Judah to escape submission to Babylon. In so doing Egypt was contradicting the expressed will of God for his people. The audacity of Egypt in encouraging Judah to rebel against Babylon had to be addressed by Yahweh. Eichrodt calls this threatening poem "Ezekiel's most powerful piece of testimony against Egypt's world-power."[567]

Introduction 31:1-2

It came to pass in the eleventh year, in the third month, in the first day of the month that the word of Yahweh came unto me, saying, 2 Son of man, say unto Pharaoh king of Egypt and unto his multitude: Unto whom will you compare yourself in greatness?

The fifth Egyptian oracle follows the preceding one by two months. It is a prophecy of judgment in the form of an allegory. The date, according to the present calendar, is June 21, 587 BC.

---

[567]Eichrodt, *Ezekiel*, 429.

A rhetorical question sets the theme for the following poem. Pharaoh and his *multitude* (the Egyptian people) thought themselves to be incomparably great and powerful. Yet they will not escape the judgment of God. The rhetorical question introduces a poetic allegory.

Pictures of Assyrian Greatness 31:3-9

Behold Assyria was a cedar in Lebanon with beautiful branches, foliage that provided shade, and a high stature. Its top was among the thick boughs. 4 Waters nourished it, the deep made it grow. Her rivers ran around about her plantation. She sent forth her channels unto all the trees of the field. 5 Therefore its height was exalted above all the trees of the field, its boughs were multiplied, and its branches became long because of the many waters when it put them forth. 6 In its boughs all the birds of the heaven made their nests. Under its branches all the beasts of the field bring forth young. In its shadow all great nations dwell. 7 Thus it was fair in its greatness, in the length of its branches; for its root was by many waters. 8 The cedars could not hide it in the garden of God. The cypress trees could not compare to its boughs. The plane trees were not like its branches. No tree in the garden of God could compare to it in beauty. 9 I made it beautiful by the multitude of its branches. All the trees of Eden that were in the garden of God were jealous of it.

Assyria was once a lofty Lebanon cedar encircled at the top by leafy and thick boughs. The subterranean reservoir of waters (*the deep*) sent forth a river to nourish the cedar. Smaller rivulets watered the other trees. Perhaps this is an indirect reference to Assyria's great water sources in the Tigris and Euphrates rivers.

As a result of abundant watering the cedar (Assyria) grew taller, stronger and more luxurious than the other trees (nations). All the fowl of the heavens and beasts of the field passed under the control of Assyria. These birds and beasts represented the nations under Assyria's control.[568]

Receiving constant nourishment from many waters the Assyrian cedar continued to spread out its branches, i.e., to annex additional

---

[568]Cf. Dan 4:10-12, 19-22; Mt 13:31-32.

territories. None of the other great trees in *the garden of God*, i.e., the world could compare to that mighty Assyrian cedar. That tree attained its stature and beauty from the God of Israel. Assyria was an enemy of all the other trees that God had planted in his Eden, i.e., in the world.

DOWNFALL OF THE CEDAR 31:10-14

Reason for the Downfall 31:10-12

Therefore thus says Lord Yahweh: Because you were exalted in height, and he has set his top among the thick boughs, and his heart was lifted up in his height; 11 therefore I will give him into the hand of the mighty one of the nations. He will surely deal with him in the midst of his wickedness. I have driven him out. 12 And strangers—the most ruthless of the nations—have cut him down and have cast him down. Upon the mountains and in all the valleys his branches have fallen. His boughs are broken in all the channels of the land. All the peoples of the earth have gone down from his shadow. They have left him.

Assyria became *exalted in height*, i.e., proud of her greatness. Such pride precedes a fall (Prov 16:18). God delivered Assyria into the hand of *the mighty one of the nations*,[569] i.e., Nebuchadnezzar, to be treated as ruthlessly as she had treated other nations. The Assyrians were driven out of the garden of God as surely as Adam had been driven out of primeval Eden.

Assyria was cut down and cast off as worthless by the *most ruthless* of foreign invaders (cf. 28:7). The reference is to the Babylonians. They are compared to lumberjacks. The *boughs* and *branches* of that once glorious tree—the Assyrian armies—were broken and dispersed about the countryside. Those vassal states that had resided in the protective *shadow* of Assyria deserted their master.

---

[569]This phrase is frequently used in these chs to denote the Babylonians.

Result of the Downfall
31:13-14

Upon his carcass all the birds of the heavens dwell, and upon his boughs every beast of the field. 14 The results will be that no tree by the waters will exalt itself in its height, nor set its top among the thick boughs. Their mighty ones will not stand up in their height, even all who drink water; for they are all given over to death, unto the lower parts of the earth, in the midst of the children of men, with those who go down to the pit.

The birds and beasts feed upon the dead bodies of the Assyrian soldiers. The idea is that all remnants of the Assyrian Empire disappeared from the scene. All of this befell Assyria so that other trees (nations) in the world will not be tempted to follow her example. Nations, like men, are mortal; they die. They depart the scene of history to descend, as it were, into Sheol—the pit—the abode of the dead.

DESCENT OF THE CEDAR
31:15-17

Thus says Lord Yahweh: In the day he went down to Sheol I caused the deep to mourn and cover over him. I held back her rivers, and the great waters were stayed. I caused Lebanon to mourn over him. All the trees of the field fainted for him. 16 At the sound of his fall, I caused the nations to shake when I brought him down to Sheol with those who go down to the pit. All the trees of Eden, the choice and best of Lebanon, all that drink water, were comforted in the lower parts of the earth. 17 They also went down with him to Sheol unto those who were slain by the sword, even they who were his arm, who dwelt in his shadow, in the midst of nations.

The fall of Assyria caused a great upheaval in the world. Even *the deep*, from which all the nations of the earth were watered, was plunged into mourning.[570] The rivers, that formerly nourished the great tree (cf. v 4), now had dried up, i.e., the sources of her wealth were gone. All the trees of Lebanon—other notable nations of the time—fainted in fear for their own safety.

---

[570]Cf. 32:7 where the sun is plunged into mourning.

Previous world powers (*all the trees of Eden, the choice and best of Lebanon*) were comforted by the thought that now Assyria had joined them in the lower parts of the earth—in Sheol, the realm of the departed. The five uses of the first-person pronoun of divinity in vv 15-16 indicate that Yahweh is in complete control of the community of nations.

The allies of Assyria (*they who were his arm*) were destroyed once their protector was gone. They too joined their once proud master in the most disgraceful of deaths (*those who were slain by the sword*).

APPLICATION TO PHARAOH 31:18

To whom are you like in glory and greatness among the trees of Eden? Yet you will be brought down with the trees of Eden unto the lower parts of the earth. You will lie in the midst of the uncircumcised, with those who are slain by the sword. This is Pharaoh and all his multitude (oracle of Lord Yahweh).

In the final v of ch 31 Ezekiel drives home the application of his lengthy allegory. If the giant Assyrian cedar had been cut down how can Egypt hope to escape? Pharaoh and his people will be brought down to a humiliating defeat and death. He will lie among the *uncircumcised.* The term is not to be taken literally. It refers to an uncircumcised foreigner who does not receive a decent burial. To the Israelites the uncircumcised were those excluded from the community. Hence, in Sheol Pharaoh will lie with the excluded, dishonorable dead. Some think the reference is to those who suffer death by the sword and whose bodies lie unburied on the ground. This is a bitter pill to swallow for one who cherished opulent burial and despised foreigners.

EZEKIEL 32
SNAPSHOTS OF EGYPT'S DEMISE

DIRGE OVER PHARAOH 32:1-16

Captured Crocodile 32:1-6

It came to pass in the twelfth year, in the twelfth month, in the first day of the month that the word of Yahweh came unto me, saying, 2 Son of man, lift up a lamentation over Pharaoh king of Egypt. Say unto him, You likened yourself to a young lion of the nations, but you are like a crocodile in the seas. You burst forth in your rivers. You troubled the waters with your feet. You polluted their rivers. 3 Thus says Lord Yahweh: I will spread out over you my net with a company of many peoples. They will bring you up in my net. 4 I will leave you in the land. Upon the field I will cast you forth. I will cause all the birds of the heaven to remain upon you, and fill the beasts of all the earth with you. 5 I will put your flesh upon the mountains, and fill the valleys with your height. 6 I will water the land where you swim with your blood, even to the mountains. The rivers will be full of you.

The last oracle against Egypt is dated about a year-and-a-half after the fall of Jerusalem. The date, according to the modern calendar, is March 4, 585 BC.[571] The prophet is told to take up a *lamentation*—a prophetic doom-song—over Pharaoh. This lament recapitulates the previous judgment messages. Ezekiel emphasizes Egypt's false pride. He bewails the fate of judgment.

Pharaoh fancied himself to be like a lion roaming among the nations. He struck fear into all who saw him. In reality Pharaoh was

[571]Some confusion exists in the ancient versions on the date of this oracle. Some ancient scribes, determined to keep the oracles in Ezekiel in chronological order, emended the Hebrew text to read *eleventh year* and *twelfth month.* Others retained the reading *twelfth year*, but altered the month to read *tenth month.* The reading of the standard Hebrew text is not to be surrendered.

more like a crocodile (see on 29:3) whose movement was restricted to the waters. Occasionally Egypt's army burst forth from his waters, i.e., ventured forth beyond the national frontiers. Moving into yet other rivers, the Egyptian crocodile will thrash about churning up the waters and befouling them.

God had decreed the end of the disruptive crocodile. He will spread out his net to capture and immobilize the vicious beast. A company of many people—Babylon and her allies—will assist in drawing up that divine net.

The crocodile will be cast upon dry land out of his natural habitat. Thus his doom is sealed. The birds of prey and beasts of the field take their fill of him. The carnage is great. The mountains and valleys are filled with the long carcass of the crocodile. The blood of the beast saturates the land and fills the rivulets.

Darkened Luminaries
32:7-10

When you are extinguished I will cover the heavens, make their stars dark, and cover the sun with a cloud. The moon will not give its light. 8 All the light-bearing bodies in the heavens I will make dark over you. I will set darkness over your land (oracle of Lord Yahweh). 9 I will provoke the heart of many people when I bring your destruction among the nations, unto countries that you have not known. 10 I will make many people astonished concerning you. Their kings will be horrified on account of you when I unsheathe my sword before them. They will tremble at every moment, each man for his life, in the day of your fall.

A second figure depicts the demise of Egypt. The once bright star (Egypt) will be extinguished. This day of divine judgment is depicted as a day of darkness. The sun, moon and stars will refuse to give their light. Earth-shaking events are heralded by cosmic calamity. Such passages are not to be interpreted literally, but rather are the traditional way of depicting the fall of a great nation.[572]

Many other nations, including some unknown to Egypt, will be terrified by the news of the destruction of that empire. Other kings will tremble before the sword of God—the agent of God's judgment upon the world.

---

[572]Cf. Isa 13:10; Joel 2:10; Amos 8:9.

Explanation of Pharaoh's Fall
32:11-16

For thus says Lord Yahweh: The sword of the king of Babylon will come upon you. 12 By the swords of the mighty, I will cause your multitude to fall. The most ruthless of the nations are all of them. They will spoil the pride of Egypt. All her multitude will be destroyed. 13 I will destroy all her cattle from beside many waters. The foot of man will not trouble them anymore, nor will the hoofs of cattle trouble them. 14 Then I will make their waters to settle. Their rivers I will cause to go as oil (oracle of Lord Yahweh). 15 When I make the land of Egypt a desolation and waste, a land devoid of fullness, when I smite all the inhabitants in it, then will they know that I am Yahweh. 16 With this lamentation will they lament over it. The daughters of the nations will lament over her. On account of Egypt and all her multitude, they will lament her (oracle of Lord Yahweh).

Like Jeremiah, Ezekiel regarded Nebuchadnezzar as Yahweh's servant (cf. 30:24). The Babylonians are called *the mighty, the ruthless of the nations* (cf. 28:7). The *pride of Egypt*—all the multitude of her population—will be spoiled by the northern invaders.

Even the cattle that fed along the banks of the Nile and its canals will be destroyed. Neither man nor beast will befoul the waters of the land anymore.[573] The land will be temporarily desolate. The undisturbed waters will flow as smoothly as a river of olive oil. By smiting Egypt with desolation God will cause men to recognize His sovereignty.

The oracle closes as it began (32:1) with a reminder that it is a lamentation. The *daughters of the nations*—the professional mourners—will take up this lamentation over Egypt.[574]

---

[573]Clearly Ezekiel knows something of the slimy brown appearance of the Nile at the time when it floods. Walther Zimmerli, *A Commentary on the Book of the Prophet Ezekiel* in "Hermeneia" (2 vols.; Philadelphia: Fortress, 1979, 1983) 2:161.

[574]In Ezekiel's foreign nation oracles, lamentations are chanted by *princes of the sea* (26:16-17), the prophet (27:2; 28:12), *sailors* and *pilots of the sea* (27:29-32), and by *daughters of the nations* (32:16). The lament over Egypt's demise is an international one befitting the fall of a great empire.

DESCENT INTO SHEOL 32:17-32

Lofthouse calls the sixteen vv of the final Egyptian oracle "the death song of the world in which Israel had grown up." The language is highly poetical and one must be careful not to press it too far in formulating the biblical doctrine of the afterlife. In this ch Sheol is envisioned as consisting of compartments where nations lie together in graves gathered about their kings. Warriors who experienced proper burial are thought of as occupying a higher status than those who did not.

Introduction 32:17-18

And it came to pass in the twelfth year, in the fifteenth day of the month the word of Yahweh came unto me, saying, 18 Son of man, wail for the multitude of Egypt. Cast them down, even her and the daughters of the mighty nations, unto the lower parts of the earth, with those who go down to the pit.

The month is missing in the Hebrew text of v 17. The Greek version supplies *the first month*. It is more likely, however, that this oracle should be dated to the same month as the preceding one, viz. *the twelfth month*. That being the case, it was composed two weeks after the oracle contained in vv 1-16. According to the modern calendar the date is March 18, 585 BC.

Ezekiel was told to wail over Egypt. A prophetic lament had the power to actually set in motion the wheels of judgment. In this sense Ezekiel is to *cast down* the multitude of Egypt into *the lower parts of the earth*. This is Sheol, the abode of the dead, in which the once powerful nations on earth are thought of as continuing their collective identity. The *daughters of the mighty nations* are the countries that share the fate of Egypt in going down to Sheol. The *pit* is still another designation for Sheol.

Death of Egypt
32:19-21

Who do you surpass in beauty? Go down and be laid with the uncircumcised. 20 They will fall in the midst of those who fall with the sword. To the sword she is given. Draw her down and all her multitude. 21 The strong ones among the mighty will speak to him from the midst of Sheol with his helpers: They have gone down. They lie still, even the uncircumcised, those slain by the sword!

The rhetorical question cuts Egypt down to size. Egypt is in no way superior to the other powers of that day. Though it is a beautiful land Egypt is not exempt from national death. She will go down in defeat. She will lie with the *uncircumcised*, those who have experienced the most dishonorable death.

Egyptian soldiers will fall by the sword. Their corpses are abandoned on the field of battle. Nations already in Sheol are exhorted to drag the slain Egyptian forces on down into their midst (*draw her down and all her multitude*).

The irony here is obvious. No nation in history put more emphasis on life after death—the elaborate pyramids and subterranean burial vaults; the art of embalming; the amassing of enormous wealth and every conceivable provision for abundant life in the world to come. None of this, however, will prevent the mighty Pharaohs from being brought down in shame to the pit.

The leaders of nations already in Sheol are represented as greeting Pharaoh and his allies with mocking words upon their arrival in the pit. The mighty Egyptians have died an ignominious death—the death of the uncircumcised—by the sword.

Occupants of Sheol
32:22-30

Ezekiel names three great nations that lie in the place of dishonorable burial (vv 22-28). He then depicts the fate of some of the lesser nations of his day (vv. 29-30).

A. Assyria (32:22-23)

Assyria is there and all her company. Round about them are their graves, all of them slain, fallen by the sword, 23 whose graves

are in the uttermost parts of the pit. Her company is round about her grave, all of them slain, fallen by the sword who caused terror in the land of the living.

Egypt has joined Assyria and her allies in Sheol. The Egyptian graves lie scattered about those of the Assyrians in the *uttermost part of the pit.*[575] This expression may point to degrees of ignominy in the afterlife.

The great nations that terrorized the earth have been permanently and totally removed from the world of the living. They are now only a bad memory. The graves of satellite nations surround that of Egypt itself in those inaccessible regions. In vv 23-32 the prophet repeats the charge that these nations *caused terror in the land of the living* 7x. The ancients bragged about their brutality.

B. Elam (32:24-25)

There is Elam and all her multitude round about her grave, all of them slain, fallen by the sword, who have gone down uncircumcised unto the lower parts of the earth, who caused terror in the land of the living. Yet they have borne their shame with those who go down to the pit. 25 They have put for her a bed in the midst of the slain with all her multitude. Her graves are round about them, all of them uncircumcised, slain by the sword, because they caused terror in the land of the living. Yet they have borne their shame, with those who go down to the pit. They are put in the midst of the slain.

Other once powerful nations lie quietly in Sheol far removed from the land of the living where once they spread terror. *Elam* rests in shame there after having spread terror in the land of the living. Furthermore, Elam had gone *uncircumcised* to its grave. The capital of Elam was Susa. During the last half of the seventh century BC there was a great struggle for power between Assyria and Elam. The Assyrian Ashurbanipal delivered the death blow to Elam in 640 BC.[576]

C. Meshech and Tubal (32:26-28)

There is Meshech, Tubal and all her multitude. Her graves are round about them, all of them are uncircumcised, slain by the

---

[575]Lind suggests that the meaning is "the lowest place in hell" (*Ezekiel,* 255). Cf. JB.

[576]Jeremiah uttered an oracle against Elam (49:34-39) that is dated to the beginning of Zedekiah's reign. Apparently some Jews expected a rebellion in Elam to lead to the fall of the hated neo-Babylonian empire.

sword; because they caused their terror in the land of the living. 27 The ones who are inferior to the uncircumcised will not lie down with the mighty ones who went down to Sheol with all their war weapons, with their swords laid under their heads, and their iniquities upon their bones; because the terror of the mighty ones was in the land of the living. 28 But you, in the midst of the uncircumcised will be broken. They will lie with those slain by the sword.

Meshech and *Tubal* were once powerful kingdoms located south and southeast of the Black Sea. Other warlike powers descended into Sheol with their military equipment. Meshech and Tubal, however, met with an even more humiliating end. They rest among those who had been stripped of their arms and who were uncircumcised. Ezekiel does not specify the particular crimes that justified this more severe humiliation of Tubal and Meshech.

Apparently Pharaoh will experience still a worse fate. He will lie among those slain by the sword, but not, apparently, with the mighty ones mentioned in the preceding vv.

D. Other Nations (32:29-30)

There was Edom, her kings and all her princes who in their might are put with those slain by the sword. They, with the uncircumcised, will lie with those who go down to the pit. 30 There are the princes of the north, all of them, and all the Sidonians who went down with the slain, ashamed for the terror that was caused by their might. They lie down uncircumcised with those slain by the sword. They bear their shame with those that go down to the pit.

Pharaoh will lie among the leaders of Edom, the princes of the north (Babylonian satellite kings) and the Sidonians (Phoenicians). These all lie uncircumcised, i.e., they have experienced the ignominious death of those slain in battle and left unburied.

Conclusion 32:31-32

Pharaoh will see them and will be comforted concerning all his multitude, even Pharaoh and all his army, slain by the sword, (oracle of Yahweh). 32 For I have put my terror in the land of the living. He will be laid in the midst of the uncircumcised, with those slain by the sword, even Pharaoh and all his multitude (oracle of Lord Yahweh).

Pharaoh, unmentioned since 32:2, is named 3x in these vv which ooze irony. Pharaoh will take some measure of comfort in the fact that others have shared Egypt's fate. All the mighty powers that terrorize *the land of the living* will be brought to naught. Ultimately God's power prevails on earth. The fall of Pharaoh and his host will be another indication of this grand truth.

Special Study
NEBUCHADNEZZAR'S INVASION OF EGYPT

The Old Testament prophets devote more vv to Nebuchadnezzar's invasion of Egypt than to that king's conquest of Jerusalem.[577] Whereas, however, Nebuchadnezzar's conquest of Jerusalem is recorded in various documents dating to the sixth century, his invasion of Egypt has been ignored by the ancient historians. Consequently, most biblical critics before 1900, and a few since that date, have pointed to the prophecy of Nebuchadnezzar's invasion of Egypt as an example of error in prophetic anticipation. In the first edition of the *Cambridge Ancient History*, H.R. Hall categorically asserted:

> We have no warrant to suppose that the Babylonian king ever carried out great warlike operations against Amasis [Pharaoh of Egypt], far less that he conquered or even entered Egypt either personally or by proxy.[578]

The first biblical prophecy of the fall of Egypt to Nebuchadnezzar is found in Jer 46. Here Nebuchadnezzar is mentioned by name (v 13), as is also the Pharaoh he will defeat, viz. Pharaoh Neco (609-593 BC). Four Egyptian cities are mentioned here: Migdol, Noph (Memphis) and Tahpanhes in northern Egypt, and No (Thebes) in southern Egypt.

Some twenty years after the destruction of Jerusalem Jeremiah again alluded to the invasion of Egypt by Nebuchadnezzar (Jer 43:12-13). This oracle emphasizes the destruction of the gods of Egypt. Two Egyptian cities are specifically mentioned—Tahpanhes and Beth-shemesh (also called On or Heliopolis).

---

[577]Op. cit., 108.
[578]*Cambridge Ancient History*, 1925, 3:299.

In his second and third prophecies against Egypt (571 BC) Ezekiel named Nebuchadnezzar as the agent of God's judgment on the land of the Nile. The destruction of the idols of Egypt is specifically mentioned (Ezek 29:17-21; 30:10-12).

The evidence that Nebuchadnezzar did in fact invade Egypt is threefold:

1. Josephus[579] relates that in the fifth year after the destruction of Jerusalem (582 BC) Nebuchadnezzar fell upon Egypt, slew their king and set up another in his place. Some of the Jewish refugees in Egypt were taken captive back to Babylon.

2. A small fragment of a Babylonian chronicle first published by Pinches shows that Nebuchadnezzar launched an attack against Egypt in his thirty-seventh year, 568 BC. This text can be found in *Ancient Near Eastern Texts* edited by James Pritchard, p. 308.

3. Driver pointed out a statue in the Louvre representing Nes-Hor, governor of Southern Egypt under Pharaoh Hophra (589-664 BC). The inscription thereon seems to state that an army of Asiatics and northern peoples, that apparently had invaded Egypt, intended to advance up the Nile valley into Ethiopia. This invasion of southern Egypt, however, was averted by the favor of the gods. So states Nes-Hor.[580]

EZEKIEL 33
COMMISSION RENEWED

Ezekiel's predictions of the destruction of Jerusalem had become a tragic reality. No more does the prophet sound forth the threatening blast against the inhabitants of Judah, for Judah no longer existed. It was time for consolation. Hope had to be rekindled. A remnant had to be prepared for the restoration[581] and rebirth of the nation.

Ezekiel opens this section of the book with an oracle underscoring individual responsibility[582] and the power and potential of repentance (ch 33). Then the prophet predicts the removal of the corrupt leadership of the nation (ch 34) and the national enemies of Judah (ch

---

[579] *Antiquities* 10.9.7.

[580] Cited in Smith, *Egypt*, 122.

[581] Cf. Lawrence Boadt, "The Function of the Salvation Oracles in Ezekiel 33 to 37," *HAR* 12 (1990): 1-21.

[582] Barnabas Lindars, "Ezekiel and Individual Responsibility," *VT* 15 (1965): 452-467.

35). By so doing he sets the stage for his later prophecies of restoration.

EZEKIEL AS A WATCHMAN
33:1-9

Watchman Parable[583] Presented
33:1-6

The word of Yahweh came unto me, saying, 2 Son of man, speak to the children of my people. Say to them: When I bring the sword upon a land, and the people of the land take a man from their midst, and set him as their watchman; 3 if he sees the sword come against the land, and he blows the horn, and warns the people; 4 then whoever hears the sound of the horn, and does not take warning, if the sword come and take him away, his blood will be upon his own head. 5 He heard the sound of the horn, but did not take warning, so his blood will be upon him; for if he had taken warning he will have delivered his soul. 6 But if the watchman sees the sword come and does not blow the trumpet, and the people are not warned, and the sword come and take a person from them, he is taken away in his iniquity, but his blood I will require at the hand of the watchman.

Following the interlude in which Ezekiel spoke to foreign nations, the prophet is again instructed to devote his attention to *the children of my people*. When God in his sovereign will determined to bring *a sword*, i.e., war, upon *a land*,[584] normally that land tried to protect itself as best it could. A responsible person was appointed as watchman. He was charged with the task of sounding the alarm as the enemy approached.

A watchman can do nothing to prevent the coming of or the taking away by the sword. He can only sound the alarm. Normally the watchman will warn his neighbors by means of a (ram's) *horn*[585] (cf.

---

[583]William Brownlee, "Ezekiel's Parable of the Watchman and the Editing of Ezekiel," *VT* 28 (1978): 392-408.

[584]The warning, directed not simply to Israel but also to *a land* (i.e., any land), is appropriate since it follows the oracles against the nations.

[585]The ram's horn (*šōphār*) was used to signal the Jubilee year (Lv 25:13), celebrate the ark processional (1 Chr 15:28), announce a new reign (2 Sam 15:10), and call up

Amos 3:6). Those who failed to heed the warning blast were responsible for their own death. If they had taken refuge or had fled the doomed land, they would have saved their lives. No blame can be attached to the watchman in such a case. He did his job. *His blood will be upon his own head* reflects the oriental custom of carrying one's burdens on the head. In this case the burden of guilt comes down on the head of the one who refuses to heed the warning. He thus forfeits his life.

If the watchman sees the danger and fails to sound the alarm he is responsible for the death of those who are slain. Even if those who died were worthy of death because of their iniquity still the watchman is held accountable by God. That unfaithful watchman will someday pay for his negligence.

Watchman Parable Applied 33:7-9

As for you, son of man, I have set you as a watchman to the house of Israel. Therefore when you hear from my mouth a word, then you will warn them from me. 8 When I say to the wicked: O wicked man, you will surely die, and you do not speak to warn the wicked of his way that wicked one will die in his iniquity; but his blood I will seek from your hand. 9 But if you warn the wicked one of his way to turn from it, and he does not turn from his way, he will die in his iniquity, but you have delivered your own soul.

The long section of judgment oracles (chs 4-32) concludes as it began (3:17-21), with Ezekiel's commission as Israel's watchman.[586] The fundamental responsibility of an Old Testament prophet was to convey to God's people any threatening word that he might have heard from the mouth of God. If he fails to warn the wicked man of the consequences of his way the blood of that wicked man will be upon the hands of the prophet.

You will surely die is the announcement of a death sentence. The sentence may be spoken by God (e.g., Gn 2:17), the king (e.g., 1 Sam 14:44), the prophet (e.g., 2 Kgs 1:4) or temple officials (Jer 26:8).

---

the militia (Judg 3:27). It is used metaphorically by Jeremiah of the prophet's warning (Jer 4:5).

[586]The watchman metaphor is found already in the eighth century prophets Isaiah (e.g., 21:11) and Hosea (9:8). Ezekiel's contemporary Jeremiah also employed this metaphor (Jer 6:17).

Always it is the response to disobedience to a specific command. In every case this formula applies to a sentence passed on an individual.[587] So the prophet had the responsibility of warning the nation as a whole; but he also had the task of warning individuals about the consequences of their disobedience. Implicit in the death sentence is the promise of "life" to those who heed the warning.

The prophet can only clear himself before God by the faithful discharge of his duty of sounding the alarm. Whether or not the sinner heeds the prophet's call to repentance the watchman has saved his own life.

POSSIBILITIES OF REPENTANCE 33:10-20

Appeal for Repentance 33:10-11

As for you, son of man, say unto the house of Israel, Thus you have said: Our transgressions and our sins are upon us. We waste away in them. How then can we live? 11 Say unto them, As I live (oracle of Lord Yahweh) surely I do not delight in the death of the wicked one, but rather when the wicked one turns from his way and lives. Turn, turn from your evil ways; for why will you die, O house of Israel?

Despair engulfed the exilic community after the fall of Jerusalem. For the first time the captives faced up to the enormity of their sin. There could be no other explanation for the disastrous overthrow of their holy city and temple. The words *upon us* suggest the picture of a people crushed under the heaviest burden. That crushing burden consists of *transgressions* (rebellious disobedience) and *sins*. The punishment for that enormous burden is described under the image of wasting away, i.e., slow but irreversible deterioration.[588] *How can we live?* they asked in desperation.

---

[587]Zimmerli, *Ezekiel*, 2:186.

[588]Ezekiel also uses this figure in 4:17 and 24:23. The figure may have been derived from Lv 26:39 where the remnant is scattered in exile among the nations.

The Jewish nation seemed doomed to extinction. Life more abundant and life eternal seemed remote for such sinners. God had good news for those captives as he always does for those who honestly face up to the sin problem in their lives. He underscores this good news by an oath (*as I live*). God is not vindictive. He does not desire to see his enemies die in their sins. Divine chastisement is designed to move wicked people to repentance so that they might escape the ultimate consequences of their sin.

The prophet responded to the despairing question of the preceding v with a question of his own: *Why will you die?* The judgments prophesied in chs 4-32 could have been averted. The death sentence on wicked individuals also can be averted by repentance. In fact, it is God's *delight*, i.e., pleasure, hidden will, desire, that individuals escape death (cf. 2 Pet 3:9). This hopeful note was underscored by a divine oath. Ezekiel urged his hearers to turn from their evil ways. That is always the key to life.

Here the watchman metaphor is transformed. What Ezekiel saw in the distance was not the approach of another enemy. The watchman saw God coming with forgiveness for all who will accept it through repentance.[589]

Need for Repentance
33:12-13

Now as for you, son of man, say unto the children of your people: The righteousness of the righteous man will not deliver him in the day of his transgression. As for the wickedness of the wicked man, he will not be brought down by it in the day he turns from his wickedness; neither will the righteous man be able to live thereby in the day of his sin. 13 When I say to the righteous man that he will surely live; if he trusts in his righteousness and commits iniquity all his righteousness will not be remembered, but he will die in his iniquity that he has done.

A person's past does not of itself determine future relations with Yahweh. A backslider who formerly lived by the righteous law of God will not *live*, i.e., escape punishment, when he casts his lot with the wicked. By the same token, a penitent sinner will not suffer punishment or recrimination, because of his past. The life/death contrast

[589]Vawter and Hoppe, *Ezekiel*, 149.

of the preceding vv here becomes the contrast between *deliver* and *brought down.*

God's promises to the righteous are conditional. The righteous man must continue to trust in God, not in his own goodness. Should he deliberately commit iniquity he will die for that iniquity.

Description of Repentance 33:14-16

When I say to the wicked man: You will surely die! and he turns from his sin and does what is just and right; 15 if the wicked man returns what has been taken in pledge, if he restores what has been seized by robbery, walks in the statutes of life, so that he does not do iniquity; be will surely live, he will not die. 16 None of his sins that he has committed will be remembered against him. He has done what is just and right; he will surely live.

The threats made to the wicked are not absolute. God has decreed that death—physical, spiritual, eternal—is the penalty for wickedness. If the wicked man, however, turns from sin to pursue a righteous and lawful life that death threat is cancelled.

The repentance envisioned here is more than contrition for sin. The penitent person must 1) restore pawned articles that he had illegally retained; 2) restore what had been taken by violence; and 3) walk *in the statutes of life*, i.e., those laws of God that lead to life more abundant and ultimately life eternal.

If the former sinner manifests genuine repentance God will not hold his past against him. He will live.

Objection Answered 33:17-20

Yet the children of my people say: The way of Yahweh is not equal; but as for them, their way is not equal. 18 When the righteous man turns from his righteousness, and commits iniquity, he will die in them. 19 When the wicked man turns from his wickedness and does what is just and right, he will live on account of them. 20 But you say, The way of Yahweh is not equal. I will judge each man according to his ways, O house of Israel.

Some Jews argued that Ezekiel's teaching portrayed God as inconsistent. The *way of Yahweh is not equal*, they said. To this reasoning, however, the prophet replies that it is not God who makes the change but man.

Righteous men do in fact turn from righteousness and pay the consequences. Wicked men sometimes do repent and reap the reward. God deals with men as they are in the present, not as they were in the past.

ISRAEL AND THE PROMISED LAND 33:21-33

Ezekiel's Mouth Opened 33:21-22

It came to pass in the twelfth year of our captivity, the tenth month, the fifth day of the month, the fugitive from Jerusalem came, saying, The city has been smitten! 22 Now the hand of Yahweh was upon me in the evening, before the fugitive came. He had opened my mouth until he came unto me in the morning. My mouth was opened, and I was dumb no more.

In fulfillment of the prophecy of 24:26-27 a *fugitive* escaped Jerusalem's destruction. He arrived in Babylon to report the city's fall to the exiles. The term *fugitive* (*pālîṭ*)—one who escaped from battle (Josh 8:22)—becomes in Ezekiel a technical term for the Jerusalem exiles (cf. 24:26-27). The person who came to Ezekiel was one of the many exiles recently brought from Jerusalem.[590] He may even have been a disciple of Jeremiah.

Jerusalem fell to Nebuchadnezzar in the fourth month of the eleventh year of Zedekiah's reign, i.e., Tammuz 586 = July 3, 586 BC (Jer 39:2). The news arrived in Babylon in the tenth month of the twelfth year of Jehoiachin's captivity (Jan 4, 585). Six months elapsed between the event and the report of it among the captives.

For Ezekiel's ministry, Jan 4, 585 BC was the continental divide. It closes out seven and a half years of "sentinel ministry" in which Ezekiel sounded the warning of God's judgment to Jerusalem and the

[590]Lind, *Ezekiel*, 266.

nations as well. The news of Jerusalem's fall opened the mouth of the prophet to a pastoral ministry of hope and comfort.[591]

On the evening before the arrival of the messenger Ezekiel again experienced *the hand of Yahweh* upon him. Each time this expression appears in the book it refers to an extraordinary experience.[592] In this case the speech restriction imposed upon the prophet seven-and-one-half years earlier[593] was removed,[594] as predicted in 24:26f. God opened Ezekiel's mouth to speak messages of encouragement to the exiles immediately prior to their reception of the tragic news of Jerusalem's fall.

Audacity of the Judeans 33:23-26

Then the word of Yahweh came, saying, 24 Son of man, those who are living in these waste places in the land of Israel are saying, Abraham was one man, but he inherited the land; but we are many. The land has been given to us for a possession. 25 Therefore say unto them, Thus says Lord Yahweh: You eat along with blood. You lift up your eyes unto your idols. You shed blood. Will you possess the land? 26 You stand upon your sword. You do abominations. Each of you defiles the wife of his neighbor. Will you possess the land?

Again Ezekiel received revelation from Yahweh. It pertained to those pitiful survivors who remained among the ruins of Judah under the governorship of Gedaliah.[595] Once the initial shock of seeing their homeland ravished had passed that ragtag band began to imagine that they were the favored of Yahweh. They apparently believed that they constituted the nucleus of a new nation. They consoled themselves by the thought that originally Canaan had been given to a solitary individual, the patriarch Abraham. How much greater their claim to that land! They were many, and they were actually occupying that land.

---

[591]Lind, *Ezekiel*, 263.

[592]The expression *the hand of Yahweh* appears also in 1:3; 8:1; 37:1 and 40:1.

[593]For a discussion of the problem of Ezekiel's muteness, see comments on 3:24-27.

[594]Zimmerli (*Ezekiel*, 2:193) understands the hand of Yahweh to have imposed silence in the evening. This silence left him in the morning when the eyewitness arrived with his message.

[595]William Brownlee, "The Aftermath of the Fall of Judah according to Ezekiel," *JBL* 89 (1970): 393-404.

They will be able to recoup their losses and rebuild that land in no time.

By the words *the land has been given to us* the survivors were appropriating the property of the exiles. The Judean survivors have derived a right from the fact of their having been spared in 586 BC. "What should have been understood only as grace here becomes a claim."[596]

Even the fall of Jerusalem did not cure the Jews of their rebellious conduct. The hopes of those few survivors to rebuild Judah were doomed to failure so long as they persisted in the very crimes that caused God to destroy their city in the first place.[597] Six such crimes are listed. They 1) violated the Mosaic dietary regulations;[598] 2) prayed to idols; 3) *shed blood*, i.e., persisted in child sacrifice; 4) *stand upon the sword*, i.e., live by violence; 5) worked abomination, i.e., participated in immoral pagan practices; and 6) committed adultery. Clearly law and order had broken down in Judah following the capture of Jerusalem.

Prediction of Further Disaster 33:27-29

Thus you will say unto them: Thus says Lord Yahweh: As I live, surely the ones who are in the waste places will fall by the sword. The ones who are upon the open field I have given to the beasts to be devoured. The ones who are in the fortresses and in the caves will die of the pestilence. 28 I will make the land desolate and waste. The pride of her strength will cease. The mountains of Israel will be desolate so that no one will pass through. 29 They will know that I am Yahweh when I make the land a desolation and a waste because of all their abominations that they have done.

Further disaster awaited those ungodly survivors who inhabited the ruins of Judah. They will yet face the *sword* of divine judgment as wielded by the Babylonians or their agents. *Beasts* of the field will devour those who might escape the sword. Those holed up in caves

---

[596]Zimmerli, *Ezekiel*, 2:199.

[597]Cf. Lind (*Ezekiel*, 267): "The text challenges the notion that Abraham's covenant is unconditional."

[598]The specific regulation they violated was eating meat from which the blood had not been properly drained (cf. Lv 3:17; 17:10).

and other natural strongholds will face the *pestilence* that resulted from overcrowding, and lack of food and sanitation.

Those sinful survivors of Jerusalem's fall will not be the ones to rebuild Judah. God will make that land so desolate that no one will even want to make a trip through it. The stubborn *pride of her strength*, i.e., pride in her position as a favored nation, will cease. Then they will recognize that the God from whom they expected deliverance actually had brought desolation to their land because of their idolatrous abominations.

Ezekiel's Standing
33:30-33

As for you, son of man, the children of your people talk about you beside the walls and in the doors of the houses. They speak one to another saying, Come, I pray you, and hear the word that comes forth from Yahweh. 31 They come unto you as the people come. They sit before you as my people. They hear your words, but do not do them. With their mouth they show much love, but their heart goes after their covetousness. 32 Behold you are to them a love song of one who has a beautiful voice, and who can play an instrument well. So they hear your words, but they do them not. 33 When this comes to pass (behold, it will come), then will they know that a prophet has been in their midst.

When the news of Jerusalem's fall reached Babylon Ezekiel and his prophecies became the topic of general conversation. Now for the first time in his ministry the exiles were anxious to hear the word of Yahweh from the lips of God's accredited prophet.

While they were now eager to hear Ezekiel's word, however, they still had not surrendered their hearts to follow the commandments of Yahweh. With their mouths they were very complimentary to the prophet; but their hearts were full of covetousness, i.e., their own selfish concerns.

Ezekiel must not be deceived by the expressions of appreciation for his teaching. To those unspiritual souls Ezekiel was like a musical entertainer—the crooner of love songs. They enjoyed listening to him, but were unmoved by his passionate exhortations. When all his predictions came to pass—and they surely will come to pass—they will know that a true prophet had been among them.

EZEKIEL 34
CORRUPT LEADERS REPLACED

Israel's past sin and punishment stemmed largely from corrupt and selfish leadership. The first step in Ezekiel's program of reconstruction for the nation was the replacement of those worthless leaders by rulers of a different kind. God will place at the head of his restored people a scion of the house of David. Under his rule God's people will enjoy peace, safety and prosperity.

EVIL SHEPHERDS OF THE PAST
34:1-10

Indictment of the Shepherds
34:1-6

The word of Yahweh came unto me, saying, 2 Son of man, prophesy against the shepherds of Israel. Prophesy, and say unto the shepherds: Thus says Lord Yahweh: Woe unto the shepherds of Israel who were feeding themselves! Should not the shepherds feed the flock? 3 You eat the fat. With the wool you cloth yourselves. You slaughter the fatlings. But you do not feed the flock. 4 The weak you have not strengthened. The sick you have not healed. You have not bound up the broken. You have not brought back those that strayed away. You have not sought those that are lost. With force and rigor you have ruled them. 5 So they were scattered because there was no shepherd. They became food for every beast of the field. They were scattered. 6 My sheep wandered through all the mountains and upon every high hill. Over the face of the land my sheep were scattered, and none did search and seek.

The *shepherds*[599] against whom Ezekiel is told to prophesy were the kings, princes and other leaders of the now defunct nation of Judah.[600] The nobility and dignity of the office of shepherd reside in the fact that the shepherd works wholeheartedly for the flock (cf. Jn 10:11). The leadership of Israel, however, stands under a divine *woe* because they had been concerned only about their own welfare, not that of the sheep that had been committed to their guardianship. They lived sumptuously at the expense of the flock. Even so they did not *feed*, i.e., care for the needs of, the masses.

From the sins of commission by the leaders Ezekiel turned to sins of omission. Ezekiel arranged the sheep that need special care into five groups: the weak, sick, broken, straying, and lost sheep. These are the poor and defenseless among the population. They had been ruled with force, not with consideration and justice (cf. Mt 9:36).

Unprotected by their national rulers God's people became a prey to surrounding nations. Attacked by these beasts of prey the sheep scattered in all directions. They wandered through strange hills and valleys all over the face of the land[601] in their efforts to escape the invaders. None of their leaders made any efforts to regroup the flock or avert the flight. The flock was simply abandoned.

Judgment on the Shepherds 34:7-10

Therefore, O shepherds, hear the word of Yahweh: 8 As I live (oracle of Lord Yahweh), surely in as much as my sheep became a prey, and my sheep became food to every beast of the field because they had no shepherd, nor did my shepherds search for my sheep, but the shepherds fed themselves, and did not feed my sheep; therefore, O shepherds, hear the word of Yahweh. 10 Thus says Lord Yahweh: Behold I am against the shepherds. I will require my sheep at their hand. I will cause them to cease from feeding the sheep. The shepherds will not feed themselves anymore. I will deliver my sheep from their mouth that they may not be food for them.

---

[599]The Hebrew noun occurs in Ezek 34 15x: 11x as a metaphor of Israel's kings, 2x of God, and 2x of the future David.

[600]Kings in the ancient Near East frequently refer to themselves as *shepherds*.

[601]Zimmerli thinks the reference is to the whole earth. The charge is that the exile is the bitter fruit of bad shepherding (*Ezekiel*, 2:215).

Concerning those worthless leaders God had a word. He refers to the national leaders as *my shepherds*[602] because they were answerable to him. God's people had suffered immensely because of these greedy shepherds. God bound himself by an oath (*as I live*) that he was implacably opposed to those leaders. He will hold the under-shepherds responsible for all losses sustained by the flock. He will deprive them of the privilege of leadership. No more will they be able to further their personal aims and ambitions at the expense of the flock.

Judah's "shepherds" virtually had become beasts of prey. God eventually will liberate his people from their leadership. From one point of view at least the Babylonian exile was a liberating experience.

DIVINE SHEPHERD 34:11-22

Good Shepherd's Mission 34:11-12

For thus says Lord Yahweh: Behold I am here. I will search for my sheep, and seek them out. 12 As a shepherd seeks out his flock in the day he is in the midst of his flock that are separated thus I will seek out my sheep. I will deliver them from all the places where they have been scattered in the day of clouds and thick darkness.

God's people were not left without a shepherd. Having removed the hirelings from office the Good Shepherd[603] himself took over direct responsibility. He began his task by searching out his *sheep*, viz. those who hear and respond to his word (Jn 10:27). So the searching process was that of proclaiming the prophetic word among the exiles.

What a beautiful picture! The Lord God takes the initiative in reclaiming his own. Wherever they have been scattered the Faithful Shepherd finds them. The *day of clouds and thick darkness*, i.e., calamity, is past. The age of re-gathering and restoration had begun.

---

[602]The shepherd image for Israel's rulers is frequent in the book of Jeremiah, and is also found in Zech 11. Jer 23 has many affinities with Ezek 34.

[603]Yahweh is addressed as the "shepherd of Israel" (Ps 80:1; cf. Gn 49:24). His caring activity toward his people collectively (Ps 77:20; Isa 40:11) and individually (Ps 23) is described in the shepherd metaphor.

Good Shepherd's Provision
34:13-16

I will bring them out from the peoples, and gather them from the lands. I will bring them into their land. I will feed them upon the mountains of Israel, by the streams, and in all the habitable portions of the land. 14 In a good pasture I will feed them. Upon the high mountains of Israel will their fold be. There will they lie down in a good fold. In a lush pasture will they graze upon the mountains of Israel. 15 I will feed my sheep, and make them to lie down (oracle of Lord Yahweh). 16 The one that is lost I will seek. The one that has strayed I will bring back. The broken I will bind up, the sick strengthen. The fat and the strong I will destroy. I will feed them in justice.

God first gathers the dispersed sheep into an identifiable and dedicated band. Then he delivers them from the lands of captivity. The Good Shepherd restores the sheep to Canaan, the Promised Land. There God feeds his flock *upon the mountains* and *by the streams*. Israel occupies all the land that was capable of supporting population.[604] Lush pasture and secure fold await the flock of God in Canaan.

The flock, torn and driven about by beasts of prey (adversary nations), at last lies down under the watchful care of the Good Shepherd.

Unlike the faithless shepherds of the pre-exilic era the Good Shepherd devotes special attention to the weak and vulnerable members of the flock. Those that were lost through foolish straying will be retrieved. Those hurt and sick as a result of the neglect of their shepherds and the attacks of adversaries will be nursed back to health. On the other hand, those that were *fat and strong*—the wealthy landowners—will be destroyed. Previous shepherds had shown favoritism to these powerful persons, but God will feed them in justice. He will care for them, but they will receive no more than is due them. Thus, as a class within the flock *the fat and the strong* will be eliminated.

---

[604]Lind (*Ezekiel*, 275) calls attention to the progression in the verbs of vv 12-13: *search, seek, rescue, bring out, bring into, feed.*

Good Shepherd's Judgment 34:17-22

As for you, O my sheep, thus says Lord Yahweh: Behold I am about to judge between stock and stock, between ram and he-goats.18 Is it a small matter to you to have fed upon the good pasture that you must trample the rest of your pastures with your feet? and have drunk of the settled water, but you must stir up the rest with your feet? 19 As for my sheep, they eat what you have trampled with your feet, and they drink what you have stirred up with your feet. 20 Therefore thus says Lord Yahweh unto them: Behold I, even I, will judge between the fat cattle and lean cattle. 21 Because you push with side and shoulder, and with your horns you shove about all the weak, till you have scattered them abroad; 22 therefore I will save my sheep. They will no more be a prey. I will judge between cattle and cattle.

Judah's political leadership was not the only problem that needed to be addressed. There was a problem in the flock itself. Great injustices were the result of Judah's stratified society. Powerful citizens mistreated other members of the flock. Ezekiel "regards the unpropertied and unprivileged classes with the same sympathy as Amos or Micah."[605] God was about to *judge* between members of the flock, i.e., between the oppressed poor and their rich oppressors. The latter are referred to here as *the rams and the he-goats*, those that ruthlessly shove the others aside during grazing time.

The leaders among the flock by force had appropriated for themselves all the good pasture and clear water. They also had spoiled the rest of the pasture and muddied the rest of the water with their feet. The powerful deprived the weak among the flock of adequate sustenance.

God repeats his intention to judge between fat and lean cattle—the prosperous and the poor among the people. By the exercise of brute force, the fat and strong animals had scattered the others. The fat cattle had been responsible for the dispersion of Israel. God will save his flock from the bullying of such tyrants. Class distinctions will disappear from the flock as the Good Shepherd *judges between cattle*, i.e., treats all the flock with absolute equity.

---

[605]Eichrodt, *Ezekiel*, 473.

FUTURE SHEPHERD
34:23-31

His Davidic Roots
34:23-24

I will raise up over them one shepherd. He will feed them, even my servant David. He will feed them. He will be their shepherd. 24 I Yahweh will be their God. My servant David will be prince among them. I Yahweh have spoken it.

After the return from exile and the period of direct divine supervision of the flock God will set up a shepherd over his people. The Davidic dynasty will be restored. The responsibility of feeding and tending the flock of God will be committed to him. Yahweh will still be their God; but his servant David[606] will be *prince*[607] among them. The reference is to the Messiah who was to come from the line of David. He is the second David. What a marvelous fore-gleam of the New Testament doctrine of the Father and the Son.

New Covenant
34:25-27

I will make a covenant of peace for them. I will cause the evil beasts to cease from the land. They will dwell safely in the wilderness, and sleep in the woods. 26 I will make them and the areas surrounding my hill a blessing. I will cause the rain to come in its season. There will be showers of blessing. 27 The tree of the field will give its fruit, and the land will give its increase. They will be safe upon their land. They will know that I am Yahweh when I have broken the bars of their yoke, and I have delivered them from the hand of those who made them bondmen.

---

[606]Two other passages speak of the future David who will rule over God's people: Hosea 3:5 and Jer 30:9f.

[607]Zimmerli (*Ezekiel*, 2:218) thinks Ezekiel uses the archaic and honorific title *prince* (*nāśî'*), rather than *king* (*melek*), so as to avoid an outworn everyday word current in the politics of that day. The future ruler will be a true servant, not a king in the mold of the kings who reigned in Ezekiel's world.

The blessings enumerated in vv 25-29 find parallels at every point in the future hope of earlier prophets.[608] A new covenant is a prominent feature of the messianic age (cf. Jer 31:31; Ezek 16:60). Here it is called a *covenant of peace* because it will establish a relationship of well-being between the partners of the covenant, viz. Yahweh and his people.[609] Under the supervision of the messianic David the flock will have freedom from fear. *Evil beasts*, i.e., bad rulers,[610] will not be part of his domain. Even those most dangerous areas—the wilderness and woods—will be free from the ravenous beasts (cf. Hos 2:18).[611]

The entire region around God's *hill* (Zion) will be blessed of God, along with those who inhabit that region. *Showers of blessing* will descend upon them thus assuring abundant harvest (cf. Hos 2:21f). The inhabitants of that blessed land will all know by personal experience that Yahweh had delivered them from captivity—*the bars of their yoke*. No longer will they be slaves to political overlords who have enslaved them as the Egyptians had done at the beginning of Israel's history.

New Security
34:28-31

They will not again be a prey to the nations, nor will the wild beasts of the earth devour them; but they will dwell safely. None will make them afraid. 29 I will raise up unto them a famous plantation. They will not again be consumed by hunger in the land. They will not bear the shame of the nations anymore. 30 They will know that I Yahweh their God am with them, and that they, the house of Israel, are my people (oracle of Lord Yahweh). 31 You my sheep, the sheep of my pasture, are Adam, and I am your God (oracle of Lord Yahweh).

The messianic flock will never fall victim to the *beasts of the earth*. Adversary nations will not be able to carry them off as prey. In their divinely provided security they will manifest boldness uncharacteristic of sheep.

---

[608]Eichrodt, *Ezekiel*, 479.

[609]Cf. Gregory Polan, "Ezekiel's Covenant of Peace," *TBT* 37 (1999): 18-23.

[610]Alexander (*Expositor's Bible Commentary*, 914) holds that the evil or wild beasts that are removed are foreign nations.

[611]Ezekiel uses the traditional language of blessing (cf. Lv 26:4-6) to help his people grasp his vision of their future (Vawter and Hoppe, *Ezekiel*, 157).

Because of the amazing fertility of the land Israel will be known far and wide. Famine, so common in biblical days, will be a thing of the past. The inhabitants of God's land will never have to suffer the humiliation of having to look to other nations for material assistance (cf. Isa 32:15-18).

The blessings described above will cause the new Israel to realize that God is with them and that they are in fact God's special people. Ezekiel has saved this promise of spiritual restoration, the greatest blessing of the messianic age, until last.

God's flock is more than mere sheep; they are *Adam*, i.e., a special creation of God. The entire passage relates to the new Israel of God—God's present-day chosen people (Gal 6:16). The spiritual blessings that God in this messianic age showers down upon his people are here portrayed in terms of agricultural prosperity.

EZEKIEL 35 NATIONAL ENEMIES REMOVED

Ezekiel's auditors must have been wondering how the Messiah could be their shepherd when their land was desolate and dominated by hostile forces. The prophet now addresses that issue. Edom's complicity in Judah's conquest by the Babylonians already has triggered two oracles of judgment (cf. 25:12-14)[612] The purpose here is to establish a backdrop of judgment and desolation against which to highlight Judah's salvation and restoration depicted in the following ch.

ANNOUNCEMENT OF EDOM'S DOOM 35:1-4

The word of Yahweh came unto me, saying, 2 Son of man, set your face against Mount Seir, and prophesy against it. 3 Say unto it: Thus says Lord Yahweh: Behold I am against you, O Mount Seir. I will stretch out my hand against you. I will make you an utter

[612]Marten Woudstra, "Edom and Israel in Ezekiel," *CTJ* 3 (1968): 21-35.

desolation. 4 I will lay waste your cities. You will be desolate; and you will know that I am Yahweh.

The first obstruction to restoration has now been dealt with, viz. the problem of corrupt leadership. Now Ezekiel deals with the second obstruction to Israel's golden age. All nations that oppressed God's people must be judged and destroyed. Mount Seir,[613] i.e., Edom, the ancient archenemy of Israel is singled out for special condemnation here.

Edom is symbolic of every nation that had oppressed Israel.[614] Only when all the enemies of Yahweh are destroyed is the deliverance of God's people complete. In this oracle God immediately declares himself to be in an adversarial relationship to Edom. He will stretch out his hand against Edom, i.e., smite that country. God's outstretched hand results in the undoing and ultimate desolation of Edom.

The once proud cities of Edom will be laid waste. In this calamity the Edomites detect the operation of God.

EXPLANATION OF EDOM'S DOOM 35:5-15

Yahweh's control over the nations is not exercised capriciously, but according to strict principles of justice. Ezekiel offers three justifications for Edom's doom.

Edom's Hatred 35:5-9

You have had an ancient hatred, and you have given over the children of Israel to the power of the sword in the time of their calamity, in the time of the iniquity of the end. 6 Therefore, as I live (oracle of Lord Yahweh), surely I will prepare you for blood. Blood will pursue you. Surely you hate blood, but blood will pursue you. 7

---

[613]The original home of Edom was the mountainous country of Seir east of the Arabah. Here Mount Seir is used of the entire territory occupied by the Edomites.

[614]In other passages Edom also figures as the symbol of all Israel's enemies (e.g., Isa 63).

I will make Mount Seir an utter desolation. I will cut off from it travelers.[615] 8 I will fill its mountains with its slain. In your hills, your valleys and your streams those slain by the sword will fall. 9 I will make you desolations forever. You will not inhabit your cities; and you will know that I am Yahweh.

The divine judgment is a recompense for the ancient hatred of the Edomites[616] toward the people of God. This bitter animosity most recently had been manifested in the aid that the Edomites had rendered to the Babylonian conquerors of Jerusalem.[617] Captured Israelites were handed over to the invaders for execution. Thus the Edomites, no less than the Chaldeans, participated in *the time of their* (Judah's) *calamity, in the time of the iniquity of the end*, i.e., the iniquity that brought about their destruction.

God had prepared Edom *for blood*, i.e., Edom will die a bloody death. Twice the prophet emphasizes that *blood* will *pursue* Edom. The bloodshed by Edom now becomes the active pursuer of the guilty. Edom had *hated blood*, i.e., Israel—those to whom Edom had blood-ties.[618] The blood of slain Israelites was now demanding retribution. The dead bodies lie everywhere—hills, valleys, and streams.

Those slain in the anticipated attack will be so numerous that Mount Seir (Edom) becomes desolate. No man survives to traverse that land. Edom remains desolate forever. Such as might escape to neighboring lands gradually realize that the hand of the great God of Israel had been against them.

Edom's Blasphemies
35:10-13

You have said: These two nations and these two lands will be mine, and I will possess it; while Yahweh was there. 11 Therefore, as I live (oracle of Lord Yahweh), I will do according to your anger, and according to your jealousy that you have done out of your hatred against them. I will make myself known among them when I

---

[615]Literally, "he that passes through and he that returns."
[616]Philistia is also said to have had "eternal enmity" toward God's people (25:15). Amos (1:11) said that Edom's anger toward his brother "raged continually" (NIV).
[617]Obadiah condemns the similar behavior of the Edomites during an earlier sack of Jerusalem.
[618]Esau, ancestor of the Edomites, was the twin brother of Jacob, the ancestor of Israel (Gn 25:25).

judge you. 12 You will know that I Yahweh have heard all of your blasphemies that you have said against the mountains of Israel, saying, They are desolate; they have been given to us to devour. 13 You have magnified yourself against me with your mouth. You have multiplied your words against me; I have heard it.

As the motivation of the judgment two quotations are attributed to the Edomites. In the first Edom bluntly claims ownership of the entire land once occupied by *two nations*, i.e., Judah and Israel (cf. 37:22). Edom harbored intentions of seizing Yahweh's property.[619] Even though the two apostate nations had been ejected from the territory that had been assigned to them, yet Yahweh was still there. True, his divine and holy presence had been seen earlier in a vision to depart from the land (cf. 11:23). He was still there, however, in the sense that the land was his. He alone had the right to determine who will occupy that land.

God must recompense Edom for his anger and envy toward Israel. By punishing Edom God will make himself known in Israel, i.e., he will show himself still to be their protector and guardian.

The second quotation attributes to the Edomites the intention to *devour the mountains of Israel* like some beast of prey. Twice in vv. 12-13 Yahweh emphatically declares that he has *heard*, i.e., was aware of, the *blasphemies* spoken by the children of Edom. They were saying that since those mountains were now *desolate*, i.e., uninhabited, they had been given (by God?) to Edom.

Edom's attitude constituted an affront to God. They had misunderstood the implications of God's judgment on his people. They had failed to recognize the uniqueness of the land of Israel. Yahweh owned the territory that Israel had formerly occupied. To plan seizure of that territory was a manifestation of sinful pride that lifts itself up against God. Yahweh had heard Edom's proud boasts.

Edom's Gloating
35:14-15

Thus says Lord Yahweh: As the whole earth rejoices I will make you a desolation. 15 Because you rejoiced over the inheritance of the house of Israel when it was desolate so will I do to you. You will

[619]Ezekiel may have learned of the arrogant claims of the Edomites from the fugitive who recently had arrived with the report of Jerusalem's fall.

become a desolation, O Mount Seir, and all of Edom, even all of it; and they will know that I am Yahweh.

The whole earth rejoices when Edom becomes desolate. Edom had gloated when Israel's inheritance—God's gift to his people—had been destroyed. Therefore Edom's punishment will correspond to the transgression. With the destruction of Edom, the enemy of God's people, the whole earth realizes that Yahweh is just and mighty in the defense of his honor and his people.

EZEKIEL 36 RESTORATION OF THE LAND[620]

Thus far Ezekiel has expressed his hope for the future in terms of the establishment of new leadership for the people of God, and the punishment of those who previously had opposed his people. He now proceeds to speak of the restoration of the land of Israel (ch 36); and the rebirth of the nation (ch 37).

In the judgment message to Mount Seir (ch 35) the deliverance of Israel was implicit. Ezekiel now is commanded to make that deliverance explicit in an address to *the mountains of Israel*. Mount Seir had no future; the mountains of Israel do. Here Ezekiel speaks of the material and spiritual aspects of the restoration of Israel. Chapter 36 may be the brightest ch in the entire book. Four units of thought can be observed, each of which is related to the land. Ezekiel speaks of the redemption (vv 1-7), repopulation (vv 8-15), purification (vv 16-21), and return to the land (vv 22-38).

[620]Moshe Greenberg, "The Design and Themes of Ezekiel's Program of Restoration," *Inter* 38 (1984): 181-208.

REDEMPTION OF THE LAND 36:1-7

First Address to the Mountains 36:1-3

And as for you, son of man, prophesy unto the mountains of Israel, and say, O mountains of Israel, hear the word of Yahweh. 2 Thus says Lord Yahweh: Because the enemy has said against you: Aha! even the ancient high places are our possession. 3 Therefore prophesy and say, Thus says Lord Yahweh: because, even because they have made you desolate and swallowed you up on every side that you might be a possession to the rest of the nations, and you are the object of conversation by talkers and the evil report of people.

As motivation for the positive word to Israel, the words of the opponents are again cited (cf. 35:10). The scornful *Aha!* (*he'āh*) echoes the mockery of the Ammonites (25:3) and Tyrians (26:2). The *ancient high places* are the mountains of Israel. The enemies who had cast a covetous eye on the hilly terrain of Canaan had underestimated the power and intention of the God of Israel. God had wonderful plans for his people. On the other hand, the enemies have to pay for their crimes against Israel.

Three crimes had been committed against the land of Israel: they (the Babylonians) had made the land desolate; *the rest of the nations*, i.e., the neighbors of Israel, had cast covetous eyes upon that vacant land; and they had spoken of the defeated Judeans with contempt.

Second Address to the Mountains 36:4-5

Therefore, O mountains of Israel, hear the word of Lord Yahweh: Thus says Lord Yahweh to the mountains and to the hills, to the streams and to the valleys, and to the desolate wastes, and to the cities that have been forsaken which have become a prey and a deri-

sion to the rest of the nations that are round about; 5 therefore thus says Lord Yahweh: Surely in the fire of my jealousy I have spoken against the rest of the nations and against Edom, that have appointed my land as a possession for themselves with the joy of all their heart, with disdain of soul, in order that its open country should be for spoil.

God had good news for the forsaken cities and desolate wastes that neighboring nations were attempting to seize. In the form of an oath God confirms his word of judgment on *the rest of the nations*. He was moved by *jealousy*, i.e., zeal, for his people.[621] The *fire* of that jealousy was burning against those nations—especially Edom—that desired to possess Canaan for themselves. Four crimes of these nations are recapitulated: unjustified claim to ownership of the land, gloating over the misfortune of the land, disdain for the people who once occupied that land, and greedy desire to make spoil of that land.

Third Address to the Mountains 36:6-7

Therefore prophesy concerning the land of Israel, and say to the mountains and to the hills, to the streams and to the valleys; Thus says Lord Yahweh: Behold I, in my jealousy and in my fury, have spoken because you have borne the reproach of the nations; 7 therefore thus says Lord Yahweh: I have lifted up my hand. Surely the nations that are round about you will bear their reproach.

Because the land of Judah had borne the shame of invasion and derision by neighbors, God had spoken in his jealous fury against those nations. To suffer *reproach,* i.e., disgrace or shame, is a frequent theme in Ezekiel.[622] God had *lifted up* His hand[623] in a formal oath that those nations will eventually bear their own shame. They will experience the humiliation that they had inflicted upon the Judeans.

---

[621]Ezekiel speaks of Yahweh's *jealousy* (*qin'āh*) 6x (36:5, 6; 5:13; 23:25; 38:19; 39:25), 4x in favor of Israel and 2x against Israel. When used in the positive sense the term is often rendered *zealous*.

[622]Cf. Ezek 16:52, 54; 32:24f, 30; 34:29; 36:6f. 39:26; 44:13.

[623]Swearing with an uplifted hand is found also in Ezek 20:5f, 15, 23, 28, 42; 44:12.

REPOPULATION OF THE LAND 36:8-15

Yahweh's word now focuses on what will happen on the mountains of Israel once the reproach of desolation is removed from them.

Inhabitants Multiplied 36:8-12

But as for you, O mountains of Israel, you will put forth your branches. Your fruit you will bear for my people Israel; for they are near to come. 9 For, behold, I am for you! I will turn to you. You will be tilled and sown. 10 I will multiply men upon you, all the house of Israel, even all of it. The cities will be inhabited, and the waste places will be built up. 11 I will multiply men upon you and cattle. They will increase and be fruitful. I will cause you to be inhabited as in former times. I will make it better than your beginnings. You will know that I am Yahweh. 12 I will cause men to walk upon you, even my people Israel. They will possess you. You will be an inheritance for them. You will no more bereave them of their children.

The mountains of Canaan will become once again Israel's mountains. The fertile hills of Canaan will yet yield their fruit to God's people, not to strangers. Israel's return is *near to come*, lit., "at hand to come."[624] The end of the exile was not far off.

The divine *I am against you* that God uttered against Mount Seir (35:3) is reversed as regards the mountains of Israel. God is not only *for* the mountains of Israel,[625] he is about to *turn* unto them, i.e., take an active interest in them. As a result, those hills and valleys will once again be cultivated. Divine turning to them with resultant agricultural abundance is a restatement of the Mosaic prediction of Lv 26:9.

Men multiply in the land as former citizens of both kingdoms unite to rebuild their ruined land. The promise of multiplication of

---

[624]Statements of proximity, as Zimmerli calls them, appeared earlier in the announcements of the day of Yahweh (7:7; 30:3) and days of judgment (12:23).

[625]The challenge or approach formula here is literally, "Behold I am unto you." The formula appears in the Old Testament only here in a positive sense.

population is repeated in the exact words of the previous v for emphasis. Beasts as well as men will increase. The numbers of both will be equivalent to their former strength in pre-exilic times. In fact, God will bless restored Israel beyond anything experienced in bygone days.

The feet of God's people will yet walk over the mountains of Canaan. They will again possess those hills as their national inheritance. No more will those hills rob God's people of their children through war, pestilence and famine that in former days had occurred there.

Reproach Removed
36:13-15

Thus says Lord Yahweh: Because they are saying to you: You devour men, and bereave your nations; 14 therefore you will not devour men anymore, and your nations you will not again bereave (oracle of Lord Yahweh); 15 I will not allow the insults of the nations to be heard against you anymore. You will not bear the reproach of peoples anymore. You will not bereave your nations anymore (oracle of Lord Yahweh).

One of the derogatory allegations hurled at the land of Canaan was that the land devoured its inhabitants. The land that ought to be the mother and bearer of children seems to resemble the wild ravening beast seeking to devour its victims. The original inhabitants—the Canaanites—had been destroyed; now Israel had undergone a similar fate.[626] It seemed that every nation that had occupied that land had been bereaved. The latter part of this quote may be translated, and "you have aborted your nations." The Hebrew term (*m^e^šakkelet*) is used in this sense (Ex 23:26; 2 Kgs 2:19). The land once spewed out its Canaanite population (Lv 18:25, 28). It also devoured Israelites in the invasions of 732, 722, 597 and 586 BC.

Once Israel returns to that land things will be different. God's people will neither be devoured nor bereaved. No more will God's people have to endure the derision of the nations because of what occurred to them in that land. The land of Canaan will no more be a stumbling block to the people who live in it. They will dwell safely and securely in that land.

---

[626]Cf. Nm 17:32 where the spies reported that Canaan was "a land that eats up the inhabitants thereof."

The promises of this ch are conditional. As long as the returnees are faithful to God he will bless them in the ways Ezekiel predicted. History records that even after their return to the land the Jews failed to live up to their commitment to Yahweh.

PURIFICATION OF THE LAND 36:16-21

Defilement of the Land 36:16-18

The word of Yahweh came unto me, saying, 17 Son of man, when the house of Israel dwelled upon their land, they defiled it by their way and by their deeds. Like the uncleanness of a menstruous woman was their way before me. 18 I poured out my fury upon them because of the blood that they poured out upon the land, and because they had defiled it with their idols.

Ezekiel intends to set forth clearly the magnificent grace of God in bringing Israel back to her land. To accomplish this purpose he reviews the circumstances that brought about Israel's dispersion among the nations. Israel, the wife of God, had *defiled* the land by her general *way*, i.e., course of conduct, and by her specific *deeds*. The divine Husband temporarily avoided the impure wife just as any ancient Israelite male was required to avoid intimacy with his wife during her monthly period.

God *poured out*[627] his wrath upon his people because of their inexcusable impurity manifested especially in bloodshed and idolatry.

Profanation of God's Name 36:19-20

I scattered them among the nations. They were dispersed through lands. According to their way and according to their deeds, I judged them. 20 When they came unto the nations where they

[627]Yahweh also pours out his wrath in Ezek 7:8; 9:8; 14:19; 20:8, 13, 21; 22:22; 30:15.

came, they profaned my holy name. Men said of them: These are the people of Yahweh. From his land they have gone forth. 21 But I had pity upon my holy name that the house of Israel had profaned among the nations where they had come.

The wayward people were judged according to their deeds. God scattered them (cf. 12:15; 20:23) among the nations. He judged them *according to their deeds* as in 24:14.

In the foreign lands Israel *profaned* the name of Yahweh, not by what they did, but by just being there. What a dilemma for God! First the holy people, then the holy land, and most importantly the holy name had been profaned. The nations did not realize that Israel's punishment was just retribution for moral and religious shortcomings. Seeing the condition of Yahweh's people they concluded that the God of Israel was unable to protect his own devotees. The fears expressed by Moses in intercessory prayers (Ex 32:12; Nm 14:16) had become a reality. According to pagan logic the gods of Babylon had to be superior to Yahweh since the Babylonians had made the land of Israel desolate and dispersed the people of Yahweh. Thus the divine name had suffered indignity without cause.

God took pity upon his holy name—his reputation—that was being unjustly attacked. God is motivated to intervene on behalf of Israel because of his great concern that all mankind come to know him as Creator and Redeemer. The exiles must have been pondering how the holy Yahweh could ever again forgive his sinful people whom he had been forced to drive out of Canaan on account of his holiness. The present oracle is Ezekiel's answer to this despair.

RETURN TO THE LAND
36:22-38

God's Name Sanctified
36:22-23

Therefore say unto the house of Israel, Thus says Lord Yahweh: I am not doing this for your sake, O house of Israel, but for my holy name that you have defiled among the nations where you came. 23 I will sanctify my great name that has been profaned in their midst; and the nations will know that I am Yahweh (oracle of Lord Yahweh) when I am sanctified in you before their eyes.

Israel did not merit salvation from exile and restoration to the homeland. It was necessary, however, as part of God's long-range plan to re-establish the divine reputation. Since his *name* was inseparably connected with the fortunes of Israel positive divine action on behalf of his people was imperative. God's *name* is all that he has revealed about himself, all that can be known of him. For the sake of this revelation Yahweh will not abandon his people.

By restoring Israel to the land of Canaan God will *sanctify* his name, i.e., set it apart for awe and reverence. The restoration of Israel will prove that the Babylonian captivity was not due to God's weakness. The nations will come to know the God of Israel as truly the great I AM, Yahweh, when they witnessed the sudden reversal of the fortunes of his devoted followers.

Relationship with God Restored
36:24-28

For I will take you from the nations. I will gather you from all the lands. I will bring you unto your own land. 25 I will sprinkle upon you clean water. You will be clean from all your uncleanness. From all your idols I will cleanse you. 26 I will give to you a new heart. A new spirit will I place within you. I will remove the heart of stone from your flesh, and give you a new heart. 27 My Spirit I will put within you. I will bring it about that you will walk in my statutes, and that you will keep and do my ordinances. 28 You will dwell in the land that I gave to your fathers. You will be my people, and I will be your God.

The thesis of this unit is that Yahweh will now act to sanctify his name in a way that far surpasses his activity as described in 20:9, 14, 22. He will create something fundamentally new.[628] Israel will be reconstituted along lines that will make possible uninterrupted fellowship with Yahweh. This takes place in five stages.

First, Yahweh will bring his people back from among the nations (cf. 34:13). The ridicule of the nations in v 20 is silenced when Yahweh's people and land are reunited.

Second, Yahweh will purify Israel from *uncleanness*. The verb *sprinkle* (r. *zrq*) is most used in connection with the application of

[628]Zimmerli, *Ezekiel*, 2:248.

blood (e.g., Ex 24:6; Lv 1:5). The verb points to a priestly ministry.[629] The agent of the sprinkling is God himself. This passage clearly forms part of the background for the New Testament teaching on the priestly ministry of Christ. The reference to *clean* water sets this passage apart from the ritual purification by the water of purification (Nm 19:9-22). The *uncleanness* here is not physical and cultic, but moral and spiritual. The cleansing is *from idols*, i.e., idolatry and violent deeds (cf. v 18), actions from which cleansing was impossible by Mosaic rituals.[630] This promise may be built upon the ritual consecration of Levites[631] (Nm 8:7), suggesting the priestly nature of the messianic Israel. Only a holy people can live in a holy land. The writer of Hebrews probably had this passage in mind when he spoke of Christians who have their hearts sprinkled by Priest Jesus and their bodies washed with water[632] (Heb 10:32).

Third, Yahweh effects an inner transformation of penitent[633] Israel. As a result of the cleansing those delivered from exile receive a *new heart*—a tender and responsive heart of flesh—to replace the stony heart that so long had been impervious to divine pleas and warnings (cf. 11:19).[634] In the Bible the heart is not so much the center of emotion as of thought and will. The *new spirit* is even more inclusive. It points to the whole inner life or disposition of a person.

Fourth, Yahweh empowers through his Spirit those who have turned to him. The Holy Spirit in the Old Testament provides power to accomplish what would not be possible without his presence (e.g., 1 Sam 10:6f.). In this case the indwelling Spirit enables God's people

---

[629]The verb *zrq,* meaning "to toss, throw, scatter in abundance" appears 35x; its synonym *nzh* appears 24x. Both are translated "sprinkle" with but few exceptions. The subject of these verbs is almost always a priestly figure.

[630]It is God himself, not a priest, who performs the sprinkling. Ezekiel is using a symbol immediately intelligible to every Israelite. Elsewhere cultic actions are similarly used as symbols. E.g., Ps 141:2 compares prayer to an offering of incense and an evening sacrifice.

[631]Moses was commanded to *sprinkle* (r. *nzh*) upon the Levites the *water of cleansing* (lit., "water of sin").

[632]In priestly consecration the bodies of the priests were washed (Ex 40:12).

[633]Ezekiel says nothing here about repentance as a preface to God's gift of the new heart and transformed life. Lind (*Ezekiel*, 292) points out that here "remembrance and reflection come not first but last." One could argue, however, that the necessity for repentance, argued so powerfully in ch 18, is here assumed.

[634]The assurance of the new heart corresponds to Jeremiah's promise of a new covenant that messianic Israel willingly obeys (Jer 31:31-34). Elsewhere Ezekiel speaks of the *stout of heart* (2:4), *hard of heart* (3:7) and the *adulterous heart* (6:9).

to walk the path of obedience (cf. 11:20). Ezekiel goes beyond the expectation of Jer 31:31ff that announces that God will put his law within the human heart.

Fifth, glorious consequences follow upon the spiritual regeneration of Israel—God's people: 1) they dwell in the land that God had given to the Patriarchs. The obedience mentioned in the previous v is the precondition for remaining in the land. As long, however, as they follow the direction of God's Spirit they are secure in that land. Here, as is frequent in prophecy, the land of Canaan is a type of Christ's kingdom. 2) They belong to God as his special possession. 3) Yahweh is their God in the special sense in which he is the God of all who love and obey him.

Blessings Dispensed 36:29-32

I will save you from all your uncleanness. I will call unto the grain, and increase it. I will not bring famine upon you. 30 I will increase the fruit of the tree, and the increase of the field, in order that you may no longer receive the reproach of famine among the nations. 31 Then you will remember your evil ways and your deeds that were not good. You will loathe yourselves in your sight on account of your iniquities and your abominations. 32 Not for your sake will I do this (oracle of Lord Yahweh), be it known to you. Be ashamed and confounded because of your ways, O house of Israel.

Changes in the external life of the nation accompany the inward changes described in the previous vv.[635] By the power of the indwelling Spirit God *saves*[636] them from uncleanness, i.e., he helps them to overcome their tendency to lapse into sin. God summons, as if miraculously, the grain. He restores the fertility of the land. Fruit trees, as well as grain fields, yield their abundant harvests. Famines, which periodically had plagued the Canaan of old, are a thing of the past (cf.

[635]The connection between obedience to God's commands and the external condition of the country is stressed in the Book of Haggai.

[636]The important verb *save* (r. *yš'*) appears only 3x in Ezekiel. In 34:22 it is used in the usual sense of redemption from external enemies or troubles. Here, and possibly in 37:23 (cf. NIV), the word is used of redemption from the internal enemy, i.e., impurities and disloyalties. Ezekiel's usage prepares the way for the New Testament emphasis: "You shall call his name Jesus, for he will *save* his people from their *sins*" (Mt 1:21).

34:26-29). No more are non-believers able to bring reproach on God's people on this account.

The redeemed will never forget the ugliness of the sinful life from which God has saved them. Having experienced the cleansing of God, the empowerment of his Spirit, and fellowship with Yahweh, redeemed Israel will *loathe*, i.e., abhor their former life of sin (cf. 6:9). They make a complete break with their past life of rebellion.

The redeemed realize that they do not deserve the blessing that they receive from the hand of God. Their salvation is a pure act of divine grace. It is, therefore, appropriate that they be ashamed of their past conduct which, if dealt with by God in absolute justice, would have demanded complete and final rejection.

Desolated Places Populated 36:33-36

Thus says Lord Yahweh: In the day that I cleanse you from all your iniquities, I will cause cities to be inhabited, and the waste places to be built up. 34 And the desolate land will be tilled instead of remaining a desolation in the sight of all who pass by. 35 And they will say: This land that was desolate has become like the Garden of Eden; and the waste and desolate and ruined cities are fortified and inhabited. 36 The nations that remain round about you will know that I Yahweh have built the ruined places, and planted the places that were desolate; I Yahweh have spoken it, and I will do it.

The day of cleansing is marked by the repopulation of the desolate land of Canaan. Even those areas thought by passers-by to be beyond reclamation will be productive again.

The transformation in the land causes amazement on the part of those outside the nation. The once ugly and barren land suddenly becomes as beautiful as the Garden of Eden. The ruined and defenseless cities are filled and fortified. Some think that 38:11 (no walls, bars or gates) contradicts this description of the fortification of the land. Zimmerli suggests that *fortified* here refers figuratively to the protection that, according to Zech 2:9, Yahweh offers to Jerusalem like a wall of fire.[637]

Certain *nations* remain round about restored Israel. Obviously Israel's neighbors were not totally destroyed in the judgments previ-

---

[637]Zimmerli, *Ezekiel*, 2:250.

ously announced by the prophet. They remain to be witnesses of Yahweh's faithfulness to his people. These nations recognize the hand of God in Israel's restoration. Through his prophets God had announced beforehand what he planned to do. He who cannot lie always performs his word. Thus it is that through the fulfillment of prophecy non-believers come to see the works of God in history.

Petitions Answered 36:37-38

Thus says Lord Yahweh: I will yet for this be petitioned by the house of Israel to do it for them. I will increase them with men like a flock. 38 As a holy flock, as the flock of Jerusalem in her appointed times, so will the waste cities be filled with flocks of men; and they will know that I am Yahweh.

Earlier Ezekiel had insisted that God would not allow himself to be petitioned by the hypocritical leaders of the exilic community.[638] Here Yahweh allows himself to be petitioned to act on behalf of the redeemed house of Israel. They are a small band at first; but they pray for an increase in numbers (cf. 36:11). One of the principal concerns of those who know Yahweh as Savior is that others might share in the blessings of salvation. God here promises to hear that prayer and answer it.

The city of Jerusalem swarmed with sacrificial animals before one of the appointed national festivals. So the waste areas reclaimed by God's people will swarm with men (cf. Zech 2:8). Ezekiel describes this flock as *holy*, i.e., a population that is a living sacrifice to God. The fulfillment of this promise strengthens the faith of God's people. They join the nations (cf. v 36) in acknowledging the supremacy of Yahweh.

The promises of the repopulation of Canaan began to be fulfilled in the return of the Jews to Canaan in 538 BC. Earthly Canaan, however, was but a type of that better country promised to the people of God from the time of Abraham (Heb 11:9-10, 16). The return to Canaan after Babylonian exile was at the same time a fulfillment of a promise and the down payment of a promise. True Israelites, through faith in Christ, have left the bondage of the world. They have come

[638]See 14:3, 7, 10; 20:3, 31.

into spiritual Canaan (Heb 12:22). Ezek 36:22-38, properly understood, points to the spiritual realities of the present gospel age.

EZEKIEL 37
REBIRTH OF THE NATION

Ezekiel had been promising God's people a bright future with new leadership in a new Canaan. These promises, however, were met with as much skepticism as his earlier message announcing the 586 BC overthrow of Jerusalem. The destruction of the temple led to the shattering of faith. The Judeans were absolutely convinced that their dead and disjointed nation could never live again.

By means of a vision (vv 1-14) and a symbolic action and an oracle (vv 15-28) Ezekiel responded to their despondency.[639]

VALLEY OF DRY BONES[640]
37:1-14

Observation of the Bones
37:1-3

The hand of Yahweh was upon me, and Yahweh brought me out in the Spirit, and set me down in the midst of the valley. It was full of bones. 2 He caused me to pass by them round about. Behold there were very many upon the surface of the valley; and, behold, they were very dry. 3 He said unto me, Son of man, can these bones live again? I said, O Lord Yahweh, You know.

---

[639]Joseph Grassi, "Ezekiel XXXVII.1-14 and the New Testament," *NTS* 11 (1965): 162-64.

[640]Cf. Michael Fox, "The Rhetoric of Ezekiel's Vision of the Valley of the Bones," *HUCA* 51 (1980): 1-15; M. Dijkstra, "The Valley of Dry Bones: Coping with the Reality of the Exile in the Book of Ezekiel" in Bob Becking and Marjo Korpel eds. *The Crisis of Israelite Religion* (Leiden: Brill, 1999), 114-33; Leslie Allen, "Structure, Tradition and Redaction in Ezekiel's Death Valley Vision" in Philip Davies and David Clines, eds. *Among the Prophets* (Sheffeld, JSOT, 1993), 127-42.

Thanks to the Negro spiritual Ezekiel's vision of the dry bones is perhaps the best known passage in the book. The prophet felt *the hand of Yahweh*, i.e., God's power overwhelmed him.[641] He was carried *in the Spirit*,[642] i.e., mentally, to the middle of *the valley*, perhaps the same valley where Ezekiel earlier had seen a vision (cf. 3:22). The floor of that valley was littered with the bones of dead men.

Yahweh directed his prophet to move about in that valley. As he did so Ezekiel was impressed with two facts: the bones were numerous; and they were very dry, having lain exposed to the elements for many long years.

In order to heighten the prophet's interest and give him a fore gleam of what was about to transpire, God asked Ezekiel a question: *Can these bones live?* From the human standpoint nothing seemed more improbable. Ezekiel, however, did not underestimate the power of God. If Yahweh so willed those moldering bones could live.

Prophecy to the Bones
37:4-6

He said unto me, Prophesy over these bones. Say unto them, O dry bones, hear the word of Yahweh. 5 Thus says Lord Yahweh to these bones, Behold I am about to cause spirit to enter into you, and you will live. 6 I will put sinews upon you, and bring upon you flesh. I will cover you with flesh, and put spirit in you. You will live; and you will know that I am Yahweh.

Ezekiel was told to prophesy to the bones—to bid them to hear God's word. What discouraged people most need to hear is his word. God will resurrect those skeletons by means of a process that he describes in reverse order. Life-giving spirit will be imparted to those corpses. Perhaps this is mentioned first so as to underscore the point that God is the source of life for his people. Of course *sinew, flesh* and *skin* must first cover those skeletons. This miraculous and mass resurrection once again underscores the deity of the only God who can dare to make such a prediction.

---

[641]On the expression *hand of Yahweh*, see on 1:3.

[642]The key word in this vision is *rüach, wind, spirit, breath.* It occurs 10x in vv 1-10 in all its shades of meaning. The first and last usage, however, point to God's Spirit.

Resurrection of the Bones
37:7-10

So I prophesied as I was commanded. As I prophesied there was a sound. Behold a shaking! Bones came together bone to its bone. 8 I saw, and, behold, sinews and flesh came upon them. Flesh covered them above; but no spirit was in them 9 He said unto me, Prophesy unto the spirit, prophesy, son of man, and say to the spirit, Thus says Lord Yahweh: Come from the four winds, O spirit, and breathe on these slain ones that they may live. 10 So I prophesied as he commanded me. The spirit, came on them. They lived! They stood on their feet an exceeding great host.

Ezekiel did as he was told. As he prophesied he heard a *sound*. Suddenly a commotion—a *shaking*—erupted all over the valley as the bones began to unite. Then over those naked skeletons flesh began to appear. Still there was no life in the corpses.

Again Ezekiel was told to *prophesy*, this time to the *spirit* or breath of life. Ezekiel was to command the spirit to *come* and *breathe* upon the *slain*. The term *slain* is used because the bones have become bodies again. They are now lying there like corpses. The breath of life that once had animated those corpses is thought of as having been scattered to *the four winds*, i.e., in all directions.[643] Through this mighty prophetic prayer Ezekiel summoned the life-giving spirit to return from wherever it may be.[644]

The prophet again did as he was told. The breath of life returned to the corpses, and they lived. A great host all over that valley stood up.

Explanation of the Bones
37:11-14

He said unto me, Son of man, these bones are the whole house of Israel. Behold they are saying, Our bones are dry; our hope has perished; we are cut off. 12 Therefore prophesy and say unto them,

---

[643]On the *four winds* as a description of the four points of the compass, see also 42:20; Zech 2:10; 6:5; 1 Chr 9:24; Dan 8:8; 11:4.

[644]Another possible interpretation: the wind from the four corners of the earth is but a symbol of the universal life-giving Spirit of God.

Thus says Lord Yahweh: Behold I am about to open your graves, and bring you up from your graves, O my people. I will bring you unto the land of Israel. 13 You will know that I am Yahweh when I open your graves, and bring you up from your graves, O my people. 14 I will put my Spirit in you, and you will live. I will place you in your own land; and you will know that I Yahweh have spoken and done it (oracle of Yahweh).

The dry and disjointed bones are a sad symbol of the entire people of Israel. The northern kingdom of Israel, and now the southern kingdom of Judah as well, had been destroyed and left desolate. The scattered survivors of the two kingdoms could in no sense be considered a nation any longer.

Using the language of Psalms and Proverbs the people lament their sad condition in Babylon. *Bones* are representative of the whole person (e.g., Ps 31:10). *Our bones are dried up*, they cried. A downcast spirit dries up the bones (Prov 17:32). The *hope* of ever again existing as a nation had *perished* (cf. 19:5). They compare themselves to limbs severed from the body—*cut off* never again to be united in a living organism. Nationally they were dead and disjointed with no prospect of anything better.

Ezekiel begins, not by belittling the exiles' assessment of their situation, but by confirming it. He speaks of their *graves*. Politically they are dead!

God had a positive word for those discouraged exiles. The *graves* (i.e., the foreign lands) where God's people were languishing in captivity will be opened. Israel will be resurrected from those metaphorical graves and restored to Canaan. This stupendous miracle of national resurrection will cause the people's faith in Yahweh to be firmly established.

Only the impartation of God's life-giving Spirit can effect such a revival. Only the action of God can bring them back to their own land. The God of Israel not only has the prescience to predict the future, he has the power to perform his word.

ORACLE OF THE TWO STICKS 37:15-28

The preceding vision portrayed Israel's restoration from exile as a miracle equivalent to a mass resurrection of corpses. Now Ezekiel goes a step further. He describes this resurrection as a reunion into one kingdom of the two kingdoms (Israel and Judah) that had been hostile neighbors for over two hundred years.

Instructions to the Prophet 37:15-17

The word of Yahweh came unto me, saying, 16 Now as for you, son of man, take for yourself a stick. Write upon it: For Judah and for the children of Israel his companions. Then take another stick. Write upon it, For Joseph, the stick of Ephraim and all the house of Israel his companions. 17 Bring them near one to the other into one stick that they may become one in your hand.

Revived Israel will be a unified nation. The schism that occurred in 931 BC between the northern tribes and Judah will be a thing of the past. To symbolically portray this reunion of the tribes, Ezekiel was told to take two sticks—emblems of the royal scepters[645]—and to label each.

The first stick represented *Judah* and those of the children of Israel who had allied themselves with Judah. The tribe of Benjamin, though related to the northern tribes, chose to remain loyal to the Davidic dynasty in 931 BC. The second stick represented *Joseph*, the northern kingdom. Here, as frequently in the Old Testament that kingdom is called *Ephraim* after the largest and most influential tribe of the north.[646] *All the house of Israel* refers to the other nine tribes that joined Ephraim in constituting the northern kingdom.

---

[645]Others understand *stick* (*'ēts*) to be two property title deeds placed together to form one title deed (Zimmerli). The ancient Aramaic paraphrase renders *stick* as tablet, i.e., two leaves of one tablet joined together to form a folding tablet (cf. NEB).

[646]Ezekiel does not use the name *Israel* for the northern kingdom because he uses that name for the covenant nation as a whole.

The prophet was to take the newly inscribed sticks and *bring them near one to the other*. This is the same verb (r. *qrb*) that describes the joining together of the bones in v 7. Ezekiel was to hold the sticks end-to-end to make it appear that they were one stick.

Declaration to the People 37:18-20

When the children of your people say to you: Will you not declare to us what you mean by these things? 19 Say unto them: Thus says Lord Yahweh: Behold I am about to take the stick of Joseph that is in the hand of Ephraim and the tribes of Israel his companions, and I will put them upon the stick of Judah. I will make them to be one stick. They will be one in my hand. 20 The sticks upon which you have written will be in your hand before their eyes.

Ezekiel's actions were designed to provoke interrogation and provide a preaching point. When asked about the sticks Ezekiel was to explain the parable thusly: All the tribes that had joined Ephraim in the secession of 931 BC will be joined with Judah to form a single kingdom. This reunification will be a divine act brought about by the *hand* (power) of God. Holding the sticks together in his hand Ezekiel was to amplify this reunification theme.

Unified Nation 37:21-23

Say unto them: Thus says Lord Yahweh: Behold I am about to take the children of Israel from among the nations where they went. I will gather them from round about, and bring them into their land. 22 I will make them one nation in the land upon the mountains of Israel. One king will be king to all of them. They will no longer be two nations, nor will they be divided anymore into two kingdoms. 23 They will not defile themselves anymore with their idols, their abominations and all their transgressions. I will save them out of all their dwelling places where they have sinned. I will cleanse them. They will be my people, and I will be their God.

Israelites as well as Judeans will be gathered up from exile and brought to Canaan. There they will form one nation with the tribe of Judah. All citizens of that kingdom will pay homage to one *king*. Here (and in v 24) Ezekiel uses the term *king* (*melek*)[647] to refer to the ruler of restored Israel. The term he previously used for this person is *prince* (cf. 34:24).

Passages similar to this are interpreted in the New Testament to refer to the gathering together of Jews and Gentiles into the one body of Christ. See Rom 9:25-26; 1 Pet 2:10.

The citizens of the new Israel are dedicated to Yahweh. Heathen practices absorbed from the pagan environment of captivity are purged from their midst. God rescues them out of those pagan lands where they are currently dwelling. The cleansed and redeemed people enter into a new relationship with Yahweh. He will be their God—the object of their devotion and worship—and they will be his people—the object of his concern and blessing. In Old Testament language, this v anticipates the cleansing power of the gospel in the lives of those God brings out of the kingdom of darkness.

Enduring Nation
37:24-27

Beginning in v 24 there is a subtle but clear shift from the theme of unity to that of *permanence.* The key word in the closing vv of ch 37 is *forever* (*lᵉ ʻōlām*).

A. Davidic Nation (37:24-25)

My servant David will be king over them. There will be one shepherd to all of them. They will walk in my ordinances, keep my statutes, and do them. 25 They will dwell upon the land that I gave to Jacob my servant, where your fathers dwelled. They will dwell therein, they, their sons and their grandsons forever. David my servant will be prince forever.

The king who rules the united kingdom is now identified. He is *my servant David.* This is not David in the flesh of course, but a scion of David's house (cf. 34:23). This king is their spiritual as well as their political ruler for he will be their *shepherd.* Under the tender leadership of this shepherd-king God's people faithfully carry out the commandments and ordinances of Yahweh.

[647]See Paul M. Joyce, "King and Messiah in Ezekiel" in John Day, ed. *King and Messiah* (JSOTSup 270; Sheffield: Sheffield Academic Press, 1998), 323-37.

To Jacob, the ancestor of Israel, God had promised a land. The physical terrain of Canaan was but a preview of that land. The patriarchs knew this. Abraham looked for a city whose maker and builder was God (Heb 11:10). The redeemed children of Israel and Judah (converted Jews and Gentiles) dwell in that land forever. What land is that? Ezekiel refers to the territory (kingdom, nation) over which the glorious Prince of the house of David rules. The *David* of this prophecy is Christ. The *land* over which he rules is his kingdom.

B. Covenantal Nation (37:26-28)

I will make a covenant of peace with them—it will be an everlasting covenant with them. I will establish [them] and multiply them. I will set my sanctuary in their midst forever. 27 My dwelling place will be over them. I will be their God, and they will be my people. 28 The nations will know that I Yahweh sanctified Israel when my sanctuary will be in their midst forever.

Other blessings of the coming age are spelled out in the closing vv of ch 37. First, the citizens of Messiah's kingdom are under a new covenant—*a covenant of peace* that is *everlasting* (cf. 16:60). No covenant, other than that one inaugurated by the death, and ratified by the resurrection, of Jesus Christ, could possibly be intended. Through Christ peace with God becomes a reality and peace with man a possibility.

Second, Messiah's subjects enjoy security under the new covenant for God *establish*es (lit., "gives") them. Third, the numbers of those who recognize the authority of David's greater Son will be ever increasing (cf. 36:10f, 37). This echoes the old promise to the patriarchs (e.g., Gn 12:2). God multiplies them in that Holy Land. The Book of Acts records the thrilling fulfillment of this blessed promise.

Fourth, the *dwelling place*[648] of God will be in the midst of his people (Messiah's subjects) *forever*. The physical temple erected by Zerubbabel after the return from exile was but a preview of the true sanctuary where Jesus ministers (Heb 8:2). This promise receives its highest realization first in the incarnation (Jn 1:14), next in God's inhabitation of the church through the Spirit (2 Cor 6:16), and finally in his tabernacling with redeemed men in the heavenly Jerusalem (Rev 21:3, 22). The old temple towered over the inhabitants of Jerusalem.

[648]Ezekiel uses the term *miškān* that originally described the tent of meeting in the days of Moses. This term may have been used because it stresses the *dwelling* of Yahweh among his people.

So in the messianic age God's dwelling place is over his people. This figure sets forth the idea of God's protective grace.

Fifth, the people of God will enjoy intimate communion with their Maker in the messianic day. Once again the promise only attains complete realization in the relationship of Christian believers to the Father of Yahweh Jesus Christ (2 Cor 6:16).

Finally, the establishment of the new Israel has a profound effect upon the heathen world round about. They see the sanctuary of God (see fourth promise above) in the midst of "Israel." They will recognize in the lives of the redeemed the power of God to sanctify people. Having recognized this they seek admittance to the fellowship of God's spiritual Israel, the church of Christ.

EZEKIEL 38
FINAL DELIVERANCE

Apparently the messages delivered on the night prior to the arrival of the fugitive from Jerusalem continue in chs 38-39 (cf. 33:21-22). These chs[649] deal with the efforts of some archenemy of God's people to invade and devastate the land of Israel. The tranquil scene with which the previous ch closed does not go unchallenged. The new Israel of God undergoes testing, as did national Israel of Old Testament times. These chs are apocalyptic in nature. The language is highly symbolical and at times deliberately shadowy and even cryptic.[650] These two chs are one of the most difficult parts of this book.[651]

The theme of these oracles reappears in Zech 15:1-5 and Dan 11:40-45. Outside the Old Testament the picture of a final eschatological battle in which God's enemies are utterly destroyed is found in 1 Enoch 90:20ff, 2 Esdras 13:5, 8ff, and the Assumption of Moses 10:1ff. In the New Testament Gog and Magog are named as hosts led by Satan in the final battle following the thousand years (Rev 20:7-10). From the earliest periods of Israel's history God revealed himself

---

[649]Recent study of Ezek 38-39: Reuben Ahroni, "The Gog Prophecy and the Book of Ezekiel," *HAR* 1 (1977): 1-27; Ralph Alexander, "A Fresh Look at Ezekiel 38 and 39," *JETS* 17 (1974): 157-169; Michael Astour, "Ezekiel's Prophecy of Gog and the Cuthean Legend of Naram-sin," *JBL* 95 (1976): 567-579; J. Hugh Michael, "Gog and Magog in the 20th Century," *ET* 61 (1949): 71-73; J. Paul Tanner, "Rethinking Ezekiel's Invasion by Gog," *JETS* 39 (1996): 29-46.

[650]Taylor, *Ezekiel*, 243.

[651]Eichrodt, *Ezekiel*, 519.

in word and deed as the God who triumphs over all enemies. The Exodus and subsequent conquest of Canaan are both described in military terms. Yahweh achieved his intermediate goals for his people through battle. Through Ezekiel God reveals that without a final battle in which all of Yahweh's enemies are decisively defeated there can be no consummation of Yahweh's purposes.[652]

In these chs Ezekiel develops two great themes from his prophetic predecessors. First, he makes use of the concept of a foe from the north, one of the prominent themes of Jeremiah.[653] Second, he works with Isaiah's theme of Yahweh destroying a great enemy on the mountains of Israel and thus delivering his people.[654]

Chs 38-39 consist of seven oracles, each introduced with the formula, *Thus says Lord Yahweh.*[655] For the purpose of this discussion, the material can be divided into four major units: 1) the invasion by Gog (38:1-13); 2) the overthrow of Gog (38:14-23); 3) the destruction of Gog (39:1-16); and 4) the results of Gog's destruction (39:17-24). To this is appended a note of consolation for the exiles in Babylon (39:25-29).

INVASION BY GOG 38:1-9

Introduction 38:1-2

The word of Yahweh came unto me, saying, 2 Son of man, set your face toward Gog from the land of Magog, prince of Rosh, Meshech and Tubal. Prophesy against him…

Ezekiel is to address an oracle to Gog.[656] Scholars have wrestled with the etymology of the name *Gog*. Among the more interesting suggestions are the following: 1) Gog is derived from the Sumerian *gug*, i.e., *darkness*. Gog would then be a "personification of all that is

---

[652]B. Erling, "Ezekiel 38-39 and the Origins of Jewish Apocalyptic," *Ex Orbe Religionum; Studia Geo Widengren* (Leiden: Brill, 1972), 109.

[653]Jer 1:14; 4:6; 6:1, 22; 10:22; 13:20. See also Zeph 2:13; Joel 2:20.

[654]Isa 14:24-25; 17:12-14; 31:8-9.

[655]38:3-9, 10-13. 14-16. 17-23; 39:1-16, 17-24. 25-29.

[656]The name appears elsewhere in the Old Testament only in 1 Chr 5:4 where it refers to a Reubenite prince.

dark and evil."[657] 2) Gog is the exact equivalent of the Assyrian name *Gugu,* king of Lydia in Asia Minor from 685-652 BC.[658] 3) Gog is a name artificially constructed from Magog, the land over which this anonymous ruler is said to have ruled.[659]

In truth there probably never will be general acceptance of any etymology for the name *Gog.* More important, however, is the question: who is *Gog*? Almost every character of note in the Hellenistic period has been nominated. Probably Gog should not be identified with any figure of history. Gog is an apocalyptic figure of the end-time.

Concerning the identification of Gog only two clues are given. First, he is from a distant land. *Magog, Meshech* and *Tubal* are mentioned in the Table of Nations in Gn 10 as being among the sons of Japheth (cf. 1 Chr 1:5). Many scholars follow Josephus (*Ant.*1.6.1) in identifying the Magogites as the ruthless Scythians. These warriors were infamous in the ancient world for their practice of pausing to drink the blood of the first enemy soldier killed in battle.

Gog is introduced, not as the ruler of some vast empire, but as the leader of a number of confederated national groups. This shadowy figure was not a contemporary of Ezekiel. Gog will irrupt into history *after many days, at the end of years* (cf. v 8). Probably the original readers of Ezekiel's book had no more idea who Gog is than does a modern reader.

Gog is prince of Rosh,[660] Meshech and Tubal. The identification of *Rosh* (*chief, head*) is problematic. A country called *Rashu* is mentioned in one Assyrian text that also mentions *Mushki* and *Tubal.*[661] This identification is likely. On the other hand, some scholars believe that *Rosh* is a general designation for all northern territories.[662]

A more positive identification can be made for *Meshech* and *Tubal*, two other lands ruled by Gog. In Assyrian literature these peo-

---

[657]H.H. Rowley, *The Relevance of Apocalyptic* (London: Lutterworth, 1944), 32.
[658]Pfeiffer. *Introduction,* 562.
[659]Keil, *Biblical Commentary*, 2:159.
[660]KJV; ASV; NASB. Another rendering is "chief prince" of Meshech and Tubal, taking *rō'š* as an adjective meaning *chief* or *first.* Cf. NRSV; BV; NJPS; NIV.
[661]David Luckenbill, *Ancient Records of Assyria and Babylonia* (Chicago: University Press, 1927), 2:48.
[662]Alexander (*Expositor's Bible Commentary*, 930) holds that the accentual system and syntactical constructions of the Hebrew language strongly indicate an appositional relationship between the words *prince* and *chief*: He renders the phrase as "the prince, the chief [`head' or `ruler'] of Meshech and Tubal."

ples were known as *Mushki* and *Tubal*.[663] They inhabited the region of central and eastern Anatolia near the headwaters of the Tigris. The *Mushki* entered the Near East in the twelfth century BC. During the time of Sargon II the *Mushki* were ruled by the famous King Mita—Midas of classical and mythical fame.[664]

Announcement of Hostility 38:3-5

And say: Thus says Lord Yahweh: Behold I am against you, O Gog, prince of Rosh, Meshech and Tubal. 4 I will turn you about, put hooks in your jaws and bring you and your army out—horses and horsemen, all of them clothed gorgeously, a great company with buckler and shield, all of them handling the sword: 5 Persia, Cush and Put with them, all of them with shield and helmet; Gomer, and all her bands; the house of Togarmah in the uttermost parts of the north, all his bands; even many people with you.

Ezekiel is to address Gog with the challenge or encounter formula *I am against you*. These ominous words indicate that Gog is antithetical to Yahweh, his people, and all for which he stands. Unlike the Assyrians in Isaiah, or Nebuchadnezzar in Jeremiah, there is no hint here that Gog in any way serves as God's instrument of chastisement against Israel.

Ezekiel is using the thought-forms of his day as vehicles for this eschatological prophecy. Throughout Old Testament history prophets warned of an attack upon God's people from the north (cf. Jer 4:5-6:26). Ezekiel anticipates that God's people will face one last dreadful onslaught by the forces of evil out of the north, the traditional region of national Israel's enemies.

The evil designs of Gog against God's people cannot succeed. Like a wild beast captured and led about by *hooks* in the jaws,[665] Gog is forcefully turned back. His force is well-equipped, vast in number and gloriously arrayed. Nevertheless, Gog cannot defeat the people of God.

---

[663]Texts mentioning one or both of these people are found in Luckenbill, *Ancient Records*, 1:74, 138-44; 2:4, 12, 21-23, 46-48, 61.

[664]Herodotus (1:14) has Midas as king of the Phrygians. Mita (Midas) must have been a dynastic title preserved by the Phrygians from the *Mushki* who apparently earlier had occupied parts of Asia Minor.

[665]The image of hooks to control a beastly nation comes from 19:4; and 29:4.

Five allies of Gog are named. The Persians were an Indo-European people who entered the Iranian plateau late in the second millennium BC. They were located east of the Persian Gulf. The Cushites were a Hamitic nation (Gn 10:6-8; 1 Chr 1:8-10) residing south of Egypt. *Cush* is roughly equivalent to Ethiopia. The war-like inhabitants of *Put* were a Hamitic people (Gn 10:6; 1 Chr 1:8). They are mentioned elsewhere as allies of Egypt (Nah 3:9; Jer 46:9; Ezek 30:5) and Tyre (Ezek 27:10). Put was certainly an African nation, but its location is disputed. Probably Put is Libya in North Africa.[666]

Gomer was a Japhethic people (Gn 10:2-3). They probably are to be identified with the ancient Gimirrai (Cimmerians).[667] These people invaded the Fertile Crescent from their Ukrainian homeland sometime before the eighth century BC. *Togarmah* were a Japhethic people (Gn 10:3; 1 Chr 1:6) mentioned earlier by Ezekiel as trading partners with Tyre (Ezek 27:14). In the fourteenth century Tegarama is described as lying between Carchemish and Haran on a main trade route through southwest Armenia. Some refer to the house of Togarmah as the Armenians.

Announcement of Future Invasion 38:7-9

Be prepared, and prepare yourself, you and all your congregation who have congregated about you, and for whom you are a guard 8 After many days you will be mustered for service, at the end of the years you will come against the land that is brought back from the sword, that is gathered out of many peoples, against the mountains of Israel, that have been a continual waste; but they have been brought forth from peoples, and they dwell safely all of them. 9 You will go up, you will come like a storm, you will be like a cloud to cover the land, you and all of your bands, and many people with you.

God exhorts Gog to prepare for the invasion of Israel and to assume the guardianship or command of the various people who had assembled about him. Verse 8 serves to underscore the timeframe of

[666]Kitchen, *NBD*, 1066.

[667]This identification is based on statements made by Herodotus (1:6, 15, 103; 4:1, 11, 12).

the entire prophecy. The attack will take place *after many days*. This phrase suggests that, for a long period of time, Gog and his confederates will be dormant. At the appropriate time, however, they will be mustered for service, i.e., they will reappear on the stage of history. The attack will transpire *at the end the years*, i.e., the conclusion of the period consisting of years (Zimmerli). This points to the final end-time period.

Gog's attack is treacherous for three reasons. First, it will occur after the restoration of the people of God. Gog will attack a people that had been rescued from the sword of national death by being gathered out of all peoples where they had been held captive. Second, Gog's attack is against a land that already had suffered immeasurably, having been uninhabited a long time. Finally, the attack is against a land that enjoyed security and peace.

Restored Israel is a type of the kingdom of Christ. Here is another clue regarding the timeframe of Gog's invasion. The phrase *dwell safely* (*yāšebhū lābhetach*; cf. vv 11, 14; 39:26) is used in Ezekiel as a description of messianic security of the new Israel of God. The author of the Book of Revelation seems to allude to this same event, viz. the last battle between the powers of evil and the church of God. He placed this battle immediately before the final judgment and the emergence of the new heavens and the new earth (Rev 20:8).

At the conclusion of the future golden age the awesome armies of Gog come up against the land of Canaan (kingdom of God) like a terrible storm cloud.[668]

Intentions of Gog
38:10-13

Thus says Lord Yahweh: It will come to pass in that day, that things will come up upon your heart. You will devise an evil plot. 11 You will say, I will go up against the land of unwalled villages. I will come upon those who are quiet, who dwell safely, all of them dwelling without walls, having neither bars nor gates; 12 to take spoil and seize prey; to turn your hand against the waste places that are now inhabited, and against the people that are gathered from the nations, that have acquired cattle and goods, that dwell in the

---

[668]Jeremiah described the foe coming down from the north with the same imagery (Jer 4:13). Cf. also Isa 10:3.

middle of the earth. 13 Sheba and Dedan, and the merchants of Tarshish, with all its powerful ones, will say to you: Have you come to take spoil? Have you assembled a congregation to seize prey? to carry away silver and gold, to take cattle and goods, to take great spoil?

Ezekiel shifts back in time to the point where Gog first hatched the plot to attack Israel. In that day when Israel was dwelling safely in Canaan Gog devised an evil plan against the people of God.

The security of God's people is such that they had not made any preparation to meet such an onslaught. The defenseless, unwalled villages are an open invitation to tyrants like Gog to invade the land. Even before the attack Gog counted the spoil and captives he would take. He would *turn* his *hand*, i.e., take strong measures, in this campaign. Yet those who are the objects of his wrath—God's people—certainly had done nothing to raise the ire of Gog. He came from the distant north; Israel lived in the center (lit., "navel") of the earth.[669] Certainly a people so far removed from Magog could pose no threat. The attack of Gog is an act of naked aggression.

In his evil scheme Gog is encouraged by neighboring merchant nations—Sheba, Dedan, Tarshish (cf. 27:12, 15, 22). They hoped to enrich themselves by purchasing and reselling the plunder of Israel.

OVERTHROW OF GOG 38:14-23

God's Purpose for Gog 38:14-16

Therefore, son of man, prophesy, and say to Gog: Thus says Lord Yahweh: In that day, when my people Israel dwell safely, will you not know it? 15 You will come from your place, from the uttermost parts of the north, you and many people with you, all of them riding on horses, a great congregation and a mighty army. 16 You will go up against my people Israel like a cloud to cover the land; it will be at the end of days that I will bring you against my land in

[669]All the international highways converged in Canaan. The phrase is also used in Judg 9:37.

order that the nations might know me when I am sanctified through you before their eyes, O Gog.

Gog takes note of the unpretentious and peaceful people. He anticipates no difficulty in overwhelming them. With his vast armies coming from the north he arises suddenly and ominously against Israel, like a storm cloud.

The more common *at the end of days*[670] replaces the unique formula *at the end of the years* of v 8. Apparently the two formulas mean the same thing. Little do the heathen realize that they are unwittingly carrying out the plans of God. He had brought them in the sense that he had permitted them to make this attack.[671] Through the destruction of this vast throng God will prove conclusively to all that he is king of the universe. He will be *sanctified* i.e., honored as holy, through the destruction of Gog's forces.

God's Wrath against Gog
38:17-19a

Thus says Lord Yahweh: Are you he of whom I spoke in former days by the hand of my servants the prophets of Israel who prophesied in those days for (many) years that I would bring you against them? 18 It will come to pass in that day when Gog comes against the land of Israel (oracle of Lord Yahweh) that my wrath will rise up in my nostrils. 19 For in my jealousy, in the fire of my wrath, I have spoken.

The invasion by Gog was part of God's foreordained plan for self-vindication. Long before the invasion occurred, the servants of Yahweh predicted such an invasion. The prophecy here in Ezekiel is certainly in view, and possibly passages in Zephaniah (ch 1) and Jeremiah (4:5ff) as well.[672] In a variation of the final assault theme Joel

---

[670]The formula *the end of days* appears 12x in the Old Testament.

[671]Here, as throughout the Old Testament, the active or causative will of God must be distinguished from the permissive will. All things that happen do so because God either causes them to happen, or allows them to happen. Thus is removed the moral difficulty of having God lead these heathen into a crime for which he must punish them.

[672]There is no record that earlier prophets prophesied specifically that Gog will invade Israel, unless Gog is a metaphor for a greedy, militaristic power. If Gog is such a metaphor then all the great prophets so prophesied. Cf. D.I. Block, "Gog in Prophetic Tradition: a New Look at Ezekiel xxxviii 17," *VT* 42 (1992): 154-72.

Joel (ch 3) and Zechariah (ch 14) depict final attempts of hostile armies to crush Jerusalem.

The fate of Gog, as well as the fact of the invasion, is announced by Ezekiel. The furious wrath of God will be manifested against Gog. *In that day* is used 5x in chs 38-39.[673] It refers to the day of Yahweh, the day of judgment or salvation (cf. 7:7-19; 30:2-18). Divine *jealousy* or *zeal* was aroused whenever man outraged his immutable law. The linkage between anger and jealousy/zeal was previously used in describing Edom's wrath against Israel (cf. 35:11). The *fire of my wrath* is used of Yahweh's anger (21:36; 22:21, 31).

God's Weapons
38:19b-23

Surely in that day there will be a great shaking upon the land of Israel. 20 Fish of the sea, birds of the heavens, beasts of the field, and every creeping thing that creeps upon the ground, and every man who is upon the face of the earth will shake at my presence. The mountains will be ripped open. The steep places will fall. Every wall will fall to the ground. 21 I will call against him a sword throughout all my mountains (oracle of Lord Yahweh); every man's sword will be against his brother. 22 And I will enter into judgment with him with pestilence, and with blood. An overflowing shower, great hailstones, fire and brimstone I will rain upon him and upon his bands, and upon the many peoples who are with him. 23 Thus I will magnify myself, and sanctify myself and make myself known before the eyes of many nations; and they will know that I am Yahweh.

Yahweh brings a *great shaking*, i.e., an earthquake, in the land. The shaking causes consternation and confusion in man and beast alike. Mountains and massive walls crumble. In the panic caused by this awesome display of divine power the enemy soldiers engage in suicidal strife with one another.[674] In this judgment against Gog God employs pestilence and bloodshed. A violent, overflowing storm of hailstones, fire and brimstone (cf. 13:11, 13) finally brings about the demise of Gog.

---

[673]38:10, 14, 18, 19; 39:11.
[674]Cf. Judg 7:22; 1 Sam 14:20.

The stroke against Gog, and consequent rescue of Israel, causes citizens of many nations to recognize the majesty and power of Yahweh.

EZEKIEL 39
FINAL DELIVERANCE

Ch 39 contains three more messages pertaining to the Gog invasion—that final showdown between the forces of darkness and the people of God.

DESTRUCTION OF GOG
39:1-20

Certainty of Destruction
39:1-8

A. First Oracle (39:1-5)

As for you, son of man, prophesy against Gog, and say. Thus says Lord Yahweh: Behold I am against you, O Gog, prince of Rosh, Meshech and Tubal. 2 I will turn you about, lead you on, and bring you up from the uttermost parts of the north. I will bring you against the mountains of Israel. 3 I will smite your bow from your left hand. I will cause your arrows to fall from your right hand. 4 Upon the mountains of Israel, you will fall, you and all your bands and peoples that are with you. I will give you to birds of prey of every sort and to beasts of the field to be devoured. 5 Upon the face of the ground you will fall; for I have spoken (oracle of Lord Yahweh).

Ch 39 begins with a declaration of divine hostility directed toward Gog (cf. 38:3). God will *turn* Gog *about*, i.e., frustrate his purpose. God will lead him to his destruction upon the *mountains of Israel*. Earlier God threatened those mountains with judgment because of their idols (cf. 6:4-5). After those mountains were made desolate, however, God promised their redemption (36:1-15).

Gog's skillful archers are of no value in the battle. Gog and all his confederates will fall on the redeemed *mountains of Israel*. Once and for all time the violent, imperialist powers of this world are crushed by God. The corpses of Gog are left unburied, a prey to beast and bird alike. By no means will Gog be able to avert this calamity, for this destruction had been decreed by Yahweh.

B. Second Oracle (39:6-8)

And I will send fire against Magog and against the inhabitants of the isles who dwell safely; and they will know that I am Yahweh. 7 My holy name I will make known in the midst of my people Israel. I will not defile my holy name again; and the nations will know that I am Yahweh, the Holy One in Israel. 8 Behold it comes, and it will come to pass (oracle of Lord Yahweh); that is the day of which I have spoken.

Even the lands from which the invaders came experience divine judgment. God sends *a fire* against those lands. The fire here, as frequently in the Old Testament, symbolizes warfare. No more will the heathen profanely mock the impotence of Israel's God. The divine presence in the midst of Israel will be obvious to all when Yahweh makes known his name, i.e., his character, person, presence, in this mighty judgment upon Gog.

The destruction of Gog was a foregone conclusion; it was as good as accomplished. The Lord cannot lie, and he had announced it.

Completeness of Destruction 39:9-16

In stressing the completeness of the destruction of Gog, Ezekiel flashes two gruesome pictures before his readers.

A. Immense Quantity of Spoils (39:9-10)

The inhabitants of the cities of Israel will go out. They will burn the weapons and make fuel of them, even the shields, bucklers, bows, arrows, hand staves, and spears. They will make fires of them seven years. 10 They will not take wood from the field, nor will they cut down any out of the woods; for they will make fires of the weapons. They will take spoil of those who spoiled them. They will plunder those who plundered them (oracle of Lord Yahweh).

Ezekiel points out the immense quantity of spoil that God's people obtain from the fallen foe. So vast is the multitude of the enemies slain that the wood of their weapons serves God's people as fuel for *seven years*. During the seven years it is not necessary for men to re-sort to their usual sources of firewood.

God's people take spoil from those powerful enemies who previously had plundered Israel. Usually weapons left by a defeated enemy were added to the victor's cache of arms. God's people, however, have no need for weapons of war. There will be no further battles to fight. Ezekiel is building on the old motif of the destruction of weapons of war (Isa 9:5; Ps 46:10). Ezekiel, however, goes a step further. The weapons of Gog are converted to domestic use by God's people.

B. Problem of Burial (39:11-16)

It will come to pass in that day that I will give to Gog a place
there for burial in Israel, the valley of those who pass through east
of the sea. It will stop those who pass through. They will bury there
Gog and all his multitude. They will call it the valley of Hamon-gog.
12 In order to cleanse the land, the house of Israel will bury there
seven months. 13 Yea, all the people of the land will bury there. It
will acquire for them a reputation, in the day when I am glorified
(oracle of Lord Yahweh). 14 And they will set apart men of contin-
ual employment who will pass through the land burying those who
remain upon the face of the ground to cleanse it. At the end of the
seven months they will search. 15 When they that pass through have
passed through the land and see the human bones, then a sign will
be erected beside it until the buriers have buried it in the valley of
Hamon-gog. 16 Hamonah will be the name of a city. Thus they will
cleanse the land.

In order to cleanse the land, the corpses of Gog's soldiers needed to be buried. God provides a burial place for them. That spot is identified as *the valley of those who pass through*, i.e., it was a major thoroughfare. The valley is said to be *east of the sea*. If Ezekiel means the Dead Sea then the burial took place outside the normal borders Israel. NIV renders *east toward the sea*, i.e., a valley through which one would travel east in the direction of the Dead Sea. In this case, the Esdraelon Valley in lower Galilee might be nominated as a likely candidate. On the other hand, if the sea is understood as the Mediterranean then the specific valley could be any valley in the land of Israel east of that sea. Perhaps the geography is deliberately vague because it contributes nothing to the main point. The multitude of bodies blocks that thoroughfare. The valley receives the name *Hamon-gog*, i.e., the multitude of Gog.

For *seven months* the house of Israel transports dead bodies to this remote burial spot. An unburied corpse was a defilement of the land (Dt 21:23) that had to be removed. The whole population takes part in this mass burial. They will be famous for this noble and horrendous effort. They share the glory of their God in that day of victory.

After the seven-month period a permanent burial committee is appointed. They scour the land looking for unburied bones. Travelers aid the committee by marking any spot where they noticed bones. Near that valley of Hamon-gog, a city is built to commemorate the victory over Gog.[675] That city is called *Hamonah*, i.e., multitude.[676]

RESULTS OF GOG'S DESTRUCTION 39:17-24

Sacrificial Feast 39:17-20

As for you, son of man, thus says Lord Yahweh: Say to the birds of every sort, and to every beast of the field: Assemble yourselves! Come! Gather yourselves on every side to my feast that I am preparing for you, even a great feast upon the mountains of Israel, that you may eat meat and drink blood. 18 The flesh of the mighty you will eat. The blood of the princes of the earth you will drink. Rams, lambs, goats, bullocks, fatlings of Bashan are all of them. 19 You will eat fat until you are full. You will drink blood until you are intoxicated because of my feast that I have prepared for you. 20 You will be filled at my table with horses and horsemen, with mighty men, and with all men of war (oracle of Lord Yahweh).

Ezekiel depicts the horrible carnage that results from the overthrow of Gog. The slaughter of the multitude is regarded as a sacrificial feast to which the birds and beasts are the invited guests. The flesh and blood of the fallen men of Gog serve as the sacramental

---

[675]Alexander (*Expositor's Bible Commentary*, 936) suggests that the city might be viewed as a city of the dead.

[676]Cf. Margaret Odell, "The City of Hamonah in Ezekiel 39:11-16: the Tumultuous City of Jerusalem," *CBQ* 56 (1994): 479-89.

elements. The victims of this sacrificial *feast* are described as *rams, lambs, goats* and the like. These are figures for the mighty warriors of Gog. The birds and beasts of prey will eat of God's sacrificial feast, God's *table*.

Future Revelation
39: 21-24

I will set my glory among the nations. All the nations will see my judgment that I have executed, and my hand that I have set against them. 22 So the house of Israel will know that I am Yahweh their God from that day and forward. 23 The nations will know that the house of Israel went into captivity because of their iniquity, because they acted treacherously against me. I hid my face from them, and gave them into the hand of their adversaries. All of them fell by the sword. 24 According to their uncleanness and their transgressions I dealt with them. I hid my face from them.

The overthrow of Gog is regarded as a divine act revealing God's *glory, judgment*, and *hand*. Israel's faith will thereby be confirmed. The nations at last are convinced that Israel's captivity experience was not due to any lack of power on God's part. Rather Yahweh had allowed Israel to suffer because *they acted treacherously against me*. God hid his face[677] from them, refusing to aid them against their enemies. The idea is that Israel will prosper only when God's face is toward them. As a result *all of them,*[678] i.e., a great number of them, fell by the sword.

Perversity on the part of the people, not powerlessness on the part of God, was responsible for their abandonment by Yahweh.

---

[677]Ezekiel borrows this imagery from the blessing of Aaron in Nm 6:25-26. It is common in the Psalms (e.g., Ps 13:1).

[678]An example of biblical hyperbole. Ezekiel already has made clear that the house of Israel went into captivity. He was himself one who had survived the slaughter of the sword.

PRESENT CONSOLATION
39:25-29

***Therefore thus says Lord Yahweh: Now I will reverse the cap-
tivity of Jacob. I will have compassion on all the house of Israel. I
will be zealous for my holy name. 26 They will bear all of their
shame, and all their treachery that they have committed against me
when they dwell upon their land safely. None will terrify them 27
when I have brought them back from the peoples, and gathered
them out of the lands of their enemies. I have been sanctified in
them in the eyes of many nations. 28 They will know that I am
Yahweh their God when I have caused them to go captive unto the
nations, and then have gathered them unto their own land. I will
not leave any of them anymore there. 29 I will not hide anymore my
face from them; for I have poured out my spirit upon the house of
Israel (oracle of Lord Yahweh).***

The captivity was a time when God was hiding his face from his people. Using vv 23-24 as a transition, Ezekiel brings the focus back to his own time for the final movement of thought in this section. It was needful that the exiles in their distress see at the close of this far-reaching prophecy the first step in the long course of events leading to its fulfillment. That step was one of special interest and comfort to them; but even this promise is mingled with predictions that still look beyond to the distant future.

Ezekiel has spoken previously of the promised restoration. He alluded to the glory of Yahweh abiding with his people in their own land. In chs 38-39 he has indicated that these promises do not go unnoticed nor unchallenged by other nations. Yahweh's presence does not preclude aggression against the Canaan of God. The difference is this: Yahweh will not withdraw from his people as he had done in 586 BC.

God's new positive relationship to his people is about to begin. He will *reverse the captivity of Jacob*, i.e., reverse the fortunes of his people. *All the house of Israel*, i.e., all the tribes, will experience the compassion of Yahweh. God will be jealous or zealous for his name or reputation. His reputation is most enhanced by the prosperity of his worshipers.

In their homeland, God's people enjoy peace and security. Their sense of gratitude toward Yahweh makes them keenly ashamed of their own former waywardness. God was about to bring his people back from the lands of their enemies.

The restoration of Israel will cause God's name to be reverenced by many peoples. Gentiles will come to see that Yahweh God reveals himself in history. Yahweh brought about the captivity of his people. He also engineered their restoration to their homeland. Not one of his true people was left in foreign lands.

No more does God hide his face from his people, i.e., they will enjoy fellowship with Yahweh. This glorious state of affairs exists in the age of the Holy Spirit when God pours out his Spirit upon the house of Israel. Ezekiel repeats the promise made earlier in 36:27 and 37:14. Joel was the first prophet to make such a prediction (Joel 2:28). After the time of Ezekiel that same promise was taken up by Zechariah (Zech 12:10).

The Gog prophecy speaks in concrete terms about the salvation that Ezekiel proclaimed after the destruction of Jerusalem in 586 BC. It therefore forms a fitting conclusion to the oracles of salvation that began in ch 33.

SPECIAL NOTE INTERPRETATION OF EZEKIEL 38-39

In chs 38-39 Ezekiel predicts an unparalleled invasion by a dreadful foe. Commentators generally concede that these chs contain an apocalyptic element. In apocalyptic literature the setting is usually the end of the age. This kind of literature is full of symbols, especially numerical symbols. Great catastrophes befalling God's people and dramatic rescues by divine agencies characterize this type of writing. Most of the characters are painted much larger-than-life in these word pictures. Deliberate vagueness and purposeful incongruities are further identifying marks of apocalyptic.

One can note at least three incongruities in the Gog-Magog chs. First, in 38:4 Yahweh brings Gog forth, but in 38:10 Gog himself devises the plan of attack. Second, in 38:18-22 Gog is overthrown by earthquake and storm, but in 39:1-2 Gog is still very much active. Third, in 39:4 Gog and company are devoured by birds and animals, while in 39:11-16 the bodies of the fallen host are buried; but again in

39:17-20 the carcasses of the fallen enemy are picked clean by birds and beasts.

As in apocalyptic literature in general, "the final catastrophe is looked at from various angles, without any attempt to trace a logical order in the sequence of events."[679] The purpose of apocalyptic writing such as this is the "unveiling" of the future, not in the sense of chronicling every event prior to its occurrence, but in the sense of showing God's lordship over the future. It serves the function of letting the faithful know that God knows where history is heading, and that he is ultimately in control of the situation. Thus apocalyptic literature guides and strengthens God's people in dark days of uncertainty.

Having recognized the apocalyptic elements within these two chs, commentators are still divided as to the fulfillment of the prediction here made. Four major categories of conclusions have been formulated.

Historical Views

Some commentators hold that the invasion of Gog was an actual event, future from the standpoint of Ezekiel, but ancient history from the present-day vantage point. Gog has been identified with every outstanding general from the time of Ezekiel to the time of Christ and even beyond. Among those suggested are Cambyses king of Persia, Alexander the Great, Antiochus the Great, Antiochus Epiphanes, Antiochus Eupator, and Mithridates king of Pontus. Within this general category of approach perhaps the strongest case can be made for equating Gog with Antiochus Epiphanes.

Antiochus Epiphanes was a bitter opponent of the Jews in the second century before Christ. The center of his kingdom was in Antioch on the Orontes River. To the east his territory extended beyond the Tigris. To the north his reign extended over Meshech and Tubal, districts of Anatolia.

In his excellent commentary on the Book of Revelation William Hendriksen argues that Ezekiel's Magog represents Syria, and Gog, Antiochus. He comments as follows on the relationship between the Gog invasion of Ezekiel and that recorded in the Book of Revelation: "...The Book of Revelation uses this period of affliction and woe as a

[679]Cooke as cited by Blackwood, *Ezekiel*, 228.

symbol of the final attack of Satan and his hordes upon the church."[680] That Ezekiel's description of the defeat of Gog (Antiochus) is an appropriate type of the final overthrow of the enemies of God can be seen in the following parallels pointed out by Hendriksen:

1. The last great oppression of the people of God under the Old Testament era was sufficiently severe to typify the *final* attack of anti-Christian forces upon the church in the New Testament age.

2. The armies of Gog and Magog were very numerous and came from wide-ranging territories. This is appropriate to symbolize the world-wide opposition to the church in the days just preceding the second coming.

3. The persecution under Antiochus was very brief, but very severe. The tribulation through which God's people will pass toward the end of the present dispensation will apparently also be of short duration, but extremely severe (cf. Rev 11:11).

4. Defeat of Gog and Magog was unexpected and complete. It was clearly the work of God. So also will be the sudden overthrow of the eschatological Gog and Magog of the Book of Revelation.

Linking the invasion forces of Ezek 38-39 with the hosts of Antiochus Epiphanes is an interpretation not as easily overturned as some commentators seem to think. It will not do, for example, to argue that the timeframe for the Ezekiel passage is the *latter years* or *latter days* (38:8, 16). These expressions are clearly used in the Book of Daniel to include events that transpired after the Babylonian captivity.[681] Especially weak is the argument that the apocalyptic character of these chs necessitates a prophecy dealing with the end-time. Clearly Daniel uses highly symbolic (apocalyptic?) language to describe certain events in the intertestamental period (Dan 8), as does Zechariah as well (Zech 9:11-17). Furthermore, the ruthless assault of Antiochus against Israel and the divine protection of God's people in the midst of that assault are major themes in the prophecies of Ezekiel's contemporary Daniel (Dan 8:9-27; 11:21-35). Why should it then be thought strange that Ezekiel would devote two chs to describing, in highly idealized language, this same invasion?

---

[680]W. Hendriksen, *More than Conquerors* (Grand Rapids: Baker, 1967), 233.

[681]See Dan 2:28 and 10:4. Similar expressions clearly referring to the closing days of the Old Testament era: "time of the end" (Dan 8:17; 11:35, 40; 12:4, 9); "end of years" (Dan. 11:6).

Literal Futuristic View

Some believe that the invasion of Gog and Magog has not yet occurred. Ezekiel is describing the final invasion of the land of Israel by a ruthless coalition following the Millennium. C.I. Scofield popularized this view. He writes:

> That the primary reference is to the northern, (European) powers, headed up by Russia, all agree 'Gog' is the prince, 'Magog,' his land. The reference to Meshech and Tubal (Moscow and Tobolsk) is a clear mark of identification. Russia and the northern powers have been the latest persecutors of dispersed Israel, and it is congruous both with divine justice and with the covenants that destruction should fall at the climax of the last mad attempt to exterminate the remnant of Israel in Jerusalem. The whole prophecy belongs to the yet future 'day of Jehovah' and to the battle of Armageddon ..., but includes also the final revolt of the nations at the close of the kingdom-age . . . .[682]

A disciple of Scofield, John F. Walvoord, cites two reasons for believing that a Russian invasion of Israel is being prophesied. First, he points out that 3x in chs 38-39 the invading armies are said to come from the extreme north (38:6, 15; 39:2). Second, he points to the fact that Gog is said to be "the prince of Rosh." The nineteenth century lexicographer Wilhelm Gesenius is cited as the authority for equating Russia with Rosh.[683]

The geographical argument offered by Walvoord is weak. Jeremiah frequently speaks of armies coming from *the uttermost parts of the earth* by which he means no more than Babylonia.[684] In some sense Mount Zion itself is said to be situated in the uttermost part of the north (Ps 48:2).

The etymological argument offered by Walvoord linking Russia with Rosh is also weak. For one thing, the precise translation of the Hebrew term *rosh* is uncertain. Several modern versions render the word as an adjective modifying the word *prince*.[685] Even conceding that Rosh is a proper name[686] here (as in ASV and NASB), that by no

---

[682]*Scofield Reference Bible,* comments on Ezek 38.

[683]John Walvoord, *The Nations in Prophecy* (Grand Rapids: Zondervan, 1977), 106-108.

[684]See Jer 6:22; 25:32; 31:8; 50:41.

[685]KJV, RSV, and NASB margin have "chief prince of Meshech."

[686]The Greek Old Testament supports *Rosh* as a proper name.

means proves that Rosh is to be identified with Russia. For one thing hard etymological evidence for this identification is lacking. Rosh is here connected with Meshech and Tubal, now generally accepted as being regions in eastern Anatolia.

Gesenius was making an intelligent guess at the identification of Rosh, but he was writing at a time when Assyrian texts mentioning these places were not available. His etymologies are now generally disregarded. Even the dispensational writer Feinberg rejects the Rosh = Russia identification.[687] A cylinder text of the Assyrian king Sargon mentions a land of Râshi on the Elamite border. The same text speaks of Tabalum (Ezekiel's Tubal) and the land of Mushki (Ezekiel's Meshech).[688] Could this Râshi be Ezekiel's Rosh? In any case, the evidence seems to point to Rosh as a region of Anatolia far north of Israel, but far south of Russia.

Patrick Fairbairn does perhaps the best work in setting forth the arguments against any literal interpretation of Ezek 38-39. He enumerates six arguments that are here summarized:

1. It is impossible to identify Gog and Magog with any historical person or place.

2. It is improbable that such a conglomerate army as is here described would ever form a military coalition.

3. The size of the invading force is disproportionate to that of Israel or any spoil that they might have derived from Israel.

4. The mind cannot imagine a situation in which it would take seven months to bury slain soldiers, much less the utilization of discarded weapons for seven years as fuel. Fairbairn conservatively estimates that the corpses would have to number over three hundred million. How would any living thing survive the pestilential vapors arising from such a mass of corpses?

5. The gross carnality of the scene is inconsistent with messianic times.

6. This prophecy was the same that had been spoken in old times by the prophets (38:17). While no prophecies concerning Gog and Magog are recorded elsewhere, prophecies of a final assault against God's people and the miraculous overthrow of the invaders is a constant burden of prophecy.[689]

---

[687]Feinberg, *Ezekiel*, 220.

[688]Luckenbill, *Ancient Records*, 2:48.

[689]Patrick Fairbairn, *Exposition of Ezekiel* (Grand Rapids: Sovereign Grace, 1971 reprint), 204-205.

Future Idealistic View

Since there are no clearly identifiable historical events to which the prophecy can be attached, it is possible that this invasion is yet future. The commentators holding to the future idealistic view distinguish between what is of primary and what is of secondary significance in the two chs. The primary significance is that the ruthless enemies of God's people will attack with the avowed intention of utterly destroying them. God will rescue his people by divine agencies. The secondary or "representative" elements in the two chs are the place names, the weapons used, the chronological statements and the like.

The future idealistic school interprets Ezek 38-39 this way: God's people will face implacable enemies; the leader of the enemy will not necessarily have the name Gog, nor will he fight with bows and arrows.[690] By his use of the same names, and a short summary of the same description, the Apostle John has shown that he regarded Ezekiel's vision as typical, and its fulfillment still future.

Thus the commentators holding the future idealistic view see in Ezek 38-39 the final climatic struggle between the forces of good and evil. With the help of their God, Israel (God's people) will ultimately be victorious in this struggle.

Prophetic Parable View

The parabolic view of Ezek 38-39 is very popular among conservatives as well as liberals. These chs illustrate a great truth but refer to no specific event in time and space. Israel can have assurance from these chs that once restored the power of God will protect her from the worst foe. At the same time the church can gain strength from this passage in that here is a promise of God's deliverance from the most severe attacks. Gardiner sets forth this view when he states that

> There are several clear indications that he did not confine his view in this prophecy to any literal event, but intended to set forth under the figure of Gog and his armies all the opposition of the world to the king-

---

[690]Hall, *Wesleyan Bible Commentary*, 470.

> dom of God, and to foretell, like his contemporary Daniel, the final and complete triumph of the latter in the distant future.[691]

Blackwood adds these words:

> If the passage is apocalyptic, the identity of Gog becomes meaningless. He represents every force of evil that is marshaled against God. It is immaterial whether or not Ezekiel had in mind a historical prototype.[692]

From the more liberal camp Allen writes:

> The chs should be treated as an elaborate piece of symbolism, an attempt to portray some of the ultimate problems of human life with the help of figures and incidents borrowed from the repertoire of mythology.[693]

Thus according to this view Ezek 38-39 speaks of concepts, not events, the clash of ideologies rather than armies. Those who seek to identify Gog with some ancient tyrant, and those who seek here specific predictions of some imminent attack upon the Zionist state of Israel are equally wide of the mark. This apocalypse "deals with every threat to faith in every time and every nation."[694]

In criticism of the parabolic view three points can be made.

1. Many of those holding this view fail to take the oracle as a serious teaching of the word of God. Within these two chs, however, there are seven distinct claims to inspiration. This is a divine revelation and not Ezekiel's speculations.

2. The parabolic view does not unite the interpretation of these chs with a real return of God's people to their land. Yet history records the fulfillment of many items in the background and setting of this prophecy.

3. Those holding this view do a rather poor job of correlating the predictions of Ezekiel with the Gog-Magog prophecy of Rev 20:9.

---

[691]F. Gardiner, "Ezekiel," in vol. V of *An Old Testament Commentary for English Readers* (ed. Charles John Ellicott; New York: Cassell, 1901), 352.

[692]Blackwood, *Ezekiel*, 227.

[693]H.G. May and E. L. Allen, "The Book of Ezekiel," *The Interpreter's Bible* (Nashville: Abingdon, 1956), 272-274.

[694]Blackwood, *Ezekiel*, 228.

Conclusion

Ezekiel's prophecies regarding the invasion of Gog are enigmatic and difficult. Honest and capable expositors will continue to have differences of opinion regarding the specific fulfillment of the prediction. Probably Ezekiel is speaking about a specific event that has not yet transpired. That he employs hyperbole, symbolism and apocalyptic imagery is readily admitted. That the passage has an application to any situation in which God's people are under trial may also be readily admitted. What Ezekiel had in mind, however, was an eschatological event—the final showdown between God's people and their enemies.

EZEKIEL 40
GOD'S FUTURE TEMPLE[695]

The Book of Ezekiel ends as it began with a vision. In chs 1-3 Ezekiel saw a vision illustrating how God had visited his people in exile; these last chs depict God dwelling in the midst of his people who have been re-established in their own land. Earlier in vision Ezekiel had seen the departure of the divine glory from the profaned temple (8:1-11:25). In these final chs God again dwells in the midst of his temple (43:5). Thus chs 40-48 are not a superfluous appendix to the book but rather the climax of Ezekiel's prophetic thought.[696]

In the angelic guided tour of the Zion-to-be the tedious details are not especially significant. The subject of the closing chs of Ezekiel is the restitution of the kingdom of God. This theme unfolds in a vision in which are displayed in concrete detail a rebuilt temple, reformed priesthood, reorganized services, restored monarchy, reapportioned territory, and a renewed people.

Because chs 40-48 form a veritable continental divide in biblical interpretation it is necessary first to survey the various approaches that have been taken in interpreting these chs. This introductory section is followed by a description of the new temple envisioned by Ezekiel.

---

[695]See R.J. McKelvey, *The New Temple* (London: Oxford, 1981).
[696]Cf. Rimmon Kasher, "Anthropomorphism, Holiness and Cult: A New Look at Ezekiel 40-48," *ZAW* 110 (1998): 192-208.

INTERPRETATION OF EZEKIEL'S TEMPLE

The problem of the interpretation of Ezek 40-48 is one of the most difficult in biblical hermeneutics. Three main approaches to these chs have been taken by scholars: the literal prophetic, the literal futuristic, and the symbolic Christian.

Literal Prophetic View

The literal prophetic view argues that Ezekiel is here given the blueprints for the temple that God intended for his people to build upon their return to the Holy Land. Philip Mauro is perhaps the most forceful proponent of this view. He argues:

> God's plan had always been to give his people the exact pattern of the sanctuary they were to build for his name .... And now again a house was about to be built for the Name of Yahweh in Jerusalem. Therefore ... we should expect to find at this period a revelation from heaven of the pattern to be followed in the building of that house. And just here we *do* find the revelation from God of the complete pattern and appointments of a temple, with directions to the prophet to show the same to the house of Israel.[697]

It is sometimes argued against this view that too many details are omitted if Ezekiel intended these chs to be a set of blueprints. This is certainly true; but it is no less true of the tabernacle specifications given to Moses at Sinai. Plumptre, however, points to a more telling indictment of the literal prophetic view of the temple vision. He points out that

> there is no trace in the after history of Israel of any attempt to carry Ezekiel's ideal into execution. No reference is made to it by the prophets Haggai and Zechariah, who were the chief teachers of the people at the time of the rebuilding of the temple. There is no record of its having been in the thoughts of Zerubbabel, the Prince of Judah, and Joshua the high priest, as they set about that work. No description of the second

[697]Philip Mauro, *The Hope of Israel* (Reprinted by Pastors Library Foundation, n.d.), 119.

temple or its ritual in Josephus or the rabbinical writings at all tallies with what we find in these chs.[698]

In rebuttal to this line of argument Mauro points out that

> there is no evidence now available as to the plan of the temple built in the days of Ezra. Herod the Great had so transformed it in the days of Christ ... as to destroy all trace of the original design. That question, however, which we cannot now answer, does not affect the question of the purpose for which the pattern was revealed to Ezekiel.[699]

Literal Futuristic View

Much support in recent years has been given to the Dispensational view, or what might be dubbed the literal futuristic view of Ezekiel's temple. According to this view God still has physical Israel very much in his plans. All prophecies pertaining to a glorious future for Israel are to be literally fulfilled in a millennial dispensation that is to follow this present age.

Dispensationalists believe that Messiah or the Jews will one day rebuild the temple in Jerusalem following the specifications given by Ezekiel. The Old Covenant blood sacrifices, festivals and rituals will be restored. Among those holding this position regarding Ezekiel's temple, the statement of G.L. Archer is typical:

> Much caution should be exercised in pressing details, but in the broad outline it may be reasonably deduced that in a coming age all the promises conveyed by the angel to Ezekiel will be fulfilled in the glorious earthly kingdom with which the drama of redemption is destined to close.[700]

Erich Sauer adds this thought:

> We stand here really before an inescapable alternative: Either the prophet himself was mistaken in his expectation of a coming temple service, and his prophecy in the sense in which he meant it will never be fulfilled; or God, in the time of the Messiah, will fulfill literally these

---

[698]Cited by Whitelaw, *Pulpit Commentary*, xi.
[699]Mauro, *Hope*, 121.
[700]Gleason Archer, *A Survey of Old Testament Introduction* (Chicago: Moody, 1964), 363.

prophecies of the temple according to their intended literal meaning. There is no other choice possible.[701]

According to Dispensational principles of interpretations all prophecies pertaining to physical Israel that have not been carnally or materially fulfilled are to be assigned to the millennial age. The Millennium becomes a convenient dumping ground for every prophecy that offers any difficulty. The unhappy result of this procedure is that many prophecies that were fulfilled at the first coming of Christ, or are being fulfilled even now, are relegated to some distant future. This postponement system is popular because it is safe and easy. It is safe because no one can conclusively refute it until the Millennium arrives. It is easy because it requires little spiritual discernment.

The Dispensational view fails to come to grips in any meaningful way with certain basic New Testament principles. The first principle is that the once-for-allness of the sacrifice of Christ nullified all animal sacrifices forever (Heb 10:18).[702] Hebrews (7:18-19; 9:6-10; 10:1-9) argues that the Old Testament sacrificial system was abolished by Christ's death. If the sacrifices of Ezekiel 40-48 are interpreted literally it would be impossible to place Ezekiel's temple in any dispensation subsequent to Calvary The Dispensational retort that the animal sacrifices of the millennial temple will be sacramental—a memorial to the sacrifice of Christ—is weak. All five offerings of the Levitical system are mentioned. It is a gratuitous assumption that these sacrifices serve some different function in Ezekiel's temple than in the Old Testament Levitical system.

Another New Testament principle to which the Dispensationalists fail to do justice is that the heirs of the kingdom are not national Jews (Mt 21:43). True Jews (Rom 2:28-29) are those who confess Jesus as Messiah. These, along with converted Gentiles, constitute the new Israel of God (Gal 6:16; 1 Pet 2:9-10). Ezekiel's temple visions present difficulties of interpretation as is generally recognized; but whatever they may or may not mean, they certainly afford no support for the doctrine of a political future for the earthly Israel in the period just before and just after "the rapture."

---

[701]Erich Sauer, *From Eternity to Eternity* (Grand Rapids: Eerdmans, 1954), 181.

[702]For a more recent Dispensational attempt to harmonize animal sacrifices with the sacrifice of Christ, see Jerry Hullinger, "The Problem of Animal Sacrifices in Ezekiel 40-48," *BS* 152 (1995): 279-89.

The Dispensational view also fails to come to grips with the reality of God's present-age temple, the church of Jesus Christ. That temple is real, it is literal; but it is not physical (1 Pet. 2:5; 2 Cor 6:16; Eph 2:13-22).

Symbolic Christian View

Many of the older commentators held that the entire vision of these final chs was fulfilled symbolically in the gospel age and the Christian church. Much of the symbolism of these chs has been borrowed by the apostle John in Revelation as he pictures the new Jerusalem, the kingdom of God (Rev 21:9-22:5). As John repaints the picture he removes all traces of Judaism. Beasley-Murray sets forth this view as follows:

> The conclusion of Ezekiel's prophecy, therefore, is to be regarded as a true prediction of the kingdom of God given under the forms with which the prophet was familiar, viz. those of his own (Jewish) dispensation. Their essential truth will be embodied in the new age under forms suitable to the new (Christian) dispensation. How this is to be done is outlined for us in the book of Revelation 21:1-22:5-6.[703]

To this may be added the appropriate comments of Young:

> It is obvious that the prophet never intended these descriptions to be taken literally. It is clear that he is using figurative or symbolic language. Every attempt to follow out his directions literally leads to difficulty.[704]

Ezekiel himself may have anticipated that his plans would be carried out to the letter. The real question, however, is not what Ezekiel may have had in his mind, but what the Holy Spirit, who is the ultimate author of this temple vision, intended to convey through these chs. A literal interpretation of the New Testament teaching regarding Christ's present-day temple (the church) surely suggests, if not demands, that one view these chs as preparatory for the establishment of this spiritual, but nonetheless real, worship edifice.

---

[703]Beasley-Murray, *New Bible Commentary*, 664.
[704]Edward J. Young, *An Introduction to the Old Testament* (Grand Rapids: Eerdmans, 1960), 264-65.

The hermeneutical principle involved is this: fullness of promised blessing is here expressed in terms of restorative completeness. The vision, then, must be viewed as strictly *symbolical*, the symbols employed being the Mosaic ordinances. This is not spiritualization but realization. In 2 Cor 6:16 Paul is not merely borrowing Old Testament language (Lv 26:12; Ex 29:45; Ezek 37:27); he is proclaiming fulfillment. The material and physical fulfillment of some prophecies does not demand the material and physical fulfillment of all prophecy.

Conclusion

All things considered the symbolic Christian view of chs 40-48 seems the best alternative. The vision then pertains to the church of Christ upon earth, and perhaps in heaven as well. The prophets of the Old Testament often employed dark speeches and figurative language. They spoke in shadowy forms of the Old Covenant; but they spoke of Christ. Here Ezekiel in his own unique way is preaching Christ. The temple vision is an elaborate representation of the messianic age.

Regardless of the interpretation to which one is inclined certain great truths are expressed in these chs. First, worship is central in the new age. Second, God dwells in the midst of his people. Third, blessings flow forth from the presence of God to bring life to the most barren regions of the earth. Fourth, responsibilities as well as privileges belong to God's people in the messianic age.

Why does Ezekiel give such exact details of the plan of the city and the temple? There is no evidence that the measurements of the exalted city contain any spiritual symbolism. Nonetheless, Ezekiel was a preacher, not an architect. In these tedious details these truths are underscored:

1. The details underscore the reality of the future city and temple. Much religious teaching is unimpressive because it is too general and abstract.

2. The details emphasize the definiteness of the future city and temple. The new Jerusalem does not exist in the ephemeral land of clouds. The man with the measuring line underscores the truth that the Israel of the future will have a definite shape and a divine design. Man's ideas are generally hazy; but God's are definite.

3. The details depict the order that prevails in God's kingdom. There is a place for everything, and everything is in its place. These chs stress the principle of 1 Cor 14:40.

4. The details force the conclusion that in God's kingdom all things are arranged by divine directive. Moses was to make the tabernacle after the pattern shown to him in the mount (Ex 25:40). Ezekiel wants us to know that God cares for the smallest details of his people's life and work. We should seek his guidance in these matters.[705]

5. The details signal the inauguration of a new covenant. At Mount Sinai God gave Moses similar details for constructing the tabernacle. The old covenant commenced with tedious details of worship and structure. A similar section here, in the midst of discussion of the last days, suggests that God will enter into a new covenant with his people.

Ezekiel 40-43 contains the second of three great architectural visions in the Bible.[706] For the exiles, this temple vision fueled hope. It was a celebration of faith. Ezekiel provided the exiles with the raw material that permitted them mentally to visualize the temple.

INTRODUCTION
40:1-4

In the twenty-fifth year of our captivity, in the beginning of the year, in the tenth day of the month, in the fourteenth year after the city was smitten, on that very day the hand of Yahweh came upon me, and he brought me there. 2 In the visions of God he brought me unto the land of Israel. He set me down on a very high mountain, upon which was something like the frame of a city on the south. 3 He brought me there, and behold, a man. His appearance was as the appearance of bronze, with a line of flax and a measuring reed in his hand. He was standing in the gate. 4 The man said unto me, Son of man, look with your eyes, and hear with your ears, and consider all that I am about to show you, for you have been brought

---

[705]These thoughts have been adapted from W.F. Adeney in *Pulpit Commentary*, 2:329.

[706]The other two architectural visions are 1) Moses' vision of the tabernacle pattern (Ex 25-30); and 2) John's vision of the New Jerusalem (Rev 21:9-27). Cf. Susan Niditch, "Ezekiel 40-48 in a Visionary Context," *CBQ* 48 (1986): 208-224; Bruce Vawter, "Ezekiel and John," *CBQ* 26 (1964): 450-58; Steven Tuell, "Ezekiel 40-42 as Verbal Icon," *CBQ* 58 (1996): 649-64.

here in order that I might show them to you. Declare all that you see to the house of Israel.

The temple vision is dated to April 29, 573 BC, fourteen years after the destruction of Jerusalem. *Beginning of the year* probably means the first month of the year. Ezekiel again experienced the overwhelming power (*hand*) of Yahweh.

The prophet was transported in the visionary experience to the land of Palestine. He found himself on the top of a *very high mountain.* This is "theological geography." It points to Yahweh's supremacy.[707] Mount Zion is in view. There Ezekiel could see what appeared to be the outline of a city on the southern end[708] of the mountain.

On Mount Zion Ezekiel met *a man.* The description of this man makes it clear that he is a supernatural being. His appearance was *like bronze* (cf. 1:4; Dan 10:6). He carried *a line of flax* for measuring long distances, and a *measuring reed* as well (cf. Rev 21:10-15). This angelic agent acts as both guide and interpreter for the prophet in these chs. The man was standing *in the gate*—the eastern gate of the temple's outer court. This is the spot from which Ezekiel's visionary tour commences.

Four imperatives are given to the prophet in this vision. He is to *look*, *hear*, *consider*, and *declare*. Since the most used verb in the entire account is *measured* (29x) the first imperative is preeminent.

The temple tour proceeded in silence except for five occasions when the tour guide (the angel) broke the silence and addressed Ezekiel.[709] All that Ezekiel saw and heard he was to *consider* (lit., "set your heart") so that he might fulfill the fourth imperative, to *declare,* "not Yahweh's word as was usual, but Yahweh's architecture."[710] These visionary "blueprints" were designed to help the exiles face the discouragement engendered by the destruction of their beloved temple.

---

[707]Leslie C. Allen, "Ezekiel 20-48" in vol. 29 *Word Biblical Commentary* (Dallas: Word, 1990), 229.

[708]The LXX reads "opposite" me instead of *on the south.* For this reason some scholars prefer to identify the mountain as the Mount of Olives rather than Mount Zion. Alexander (*Expositor's Bible Commentary*, 953) prefers to leave the city and the mountain unidentified.

[709]40:45; 41:4, 22; 42:13; 43:7.

[710]Lind, *Ezekiel*, 327.

OUTER COURT AND ITS GATEWAYS 40:5-27

Outer Wall 40:5[711]

Behold a wall on the outside of the house round about, and in the man's hand a measuring reed six cubits long, of a cubit and a handbreadth each: so he measured the thickness of the building, one reed; and the height, one reed.

The measurements of the temple area are given in *cubits*. The cubit varied in length from time to time. A *handbreadth* is the width of four fingers. The standard cubit was six handbreadths (tip of finger to elbow), about eighteen inches. Apparently here the long cubit, equal to about 20.5 inches, is being used. The *measuring reed* carried by the angelic agent was ten feet and three inches long.

A wall surrounded the courtyard. This wall was one reed thick and one reed high. The height of the wall reflects its external measurement. The higher level of the ground in the outer court (vv 6, 22) meant that from the inside the wall was only about two cubits high.[712]

The court could be entered by three identical gateways in the north, east and south sides of the wall. No description of the gates of Solomon's temple has survived. The gates that Ezekiel sees resemble those that have been discovered in Solomon's fortress cities (e.g., Hazor) rather than any known temple gates of biblical times. Ezekiel transforms those immense gates from a military to a religious setting. These gates symbolically guard the temple. They proclaim that no profane person will be admitted into the presence of the holy God.[713]

---

[711]At this point the American Standard Version of 1901 has been followed with only slight modification.
[712]Allen, *Word Biblical Commentary*, 229.
[713]Lind (*Ezekiel*, 238) quoting Klein.

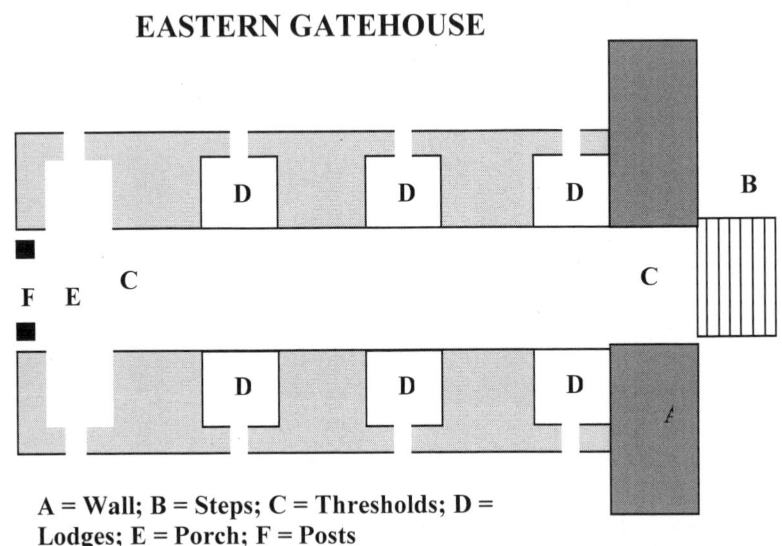

Eastern Gatehouse
40:6-16

*Then he came unto the gate that looks toward the east, and went
up the steps thereof: and he measured the threshold of the gate, one
reed broad; and the other threshold, one reed broad. 7 Every lodge
was one reed long, and one reed broad; and the space between the
lodges was five cubits; and the threshold of the gate by the porch of
the gate toward the house was one reed. 8 He measured also the
porch of the gate toward the house, one reed. 9 Then measured he
the porch of the gate, eight cubits; and the posts thereof, two cubits;
and the porch of the gate was toward the house. 10 The lodges of
the gate eastward were three on this side, and three on that side; the
three were of one measure: and the posts had one measure on this
side and on that side. 11 He measured the breadth of the opening of
the gate, ten cubits; and the length of the gate, thirteen cubits; 12
and a border before the lodges, one cubit on this side, and a border,
one cubit on that side; and the lodges, six cubits on this side, and six
cubits on that side. 13 He measured the gate from the roof of the
one lodge to the roof of the other, a breadth of twenty-five cubits;
door against door. 14 He made also posts, sixty cubits; and the court
reached unto the posts, round about the gate. 15 From the forefront*

of the gate at the entrance unto the forefront of the inner porch of the gate were fifty cubits. 16 There were closed windows to the lodges, and to their posts within the gate round about, and likewise to the arches; and windows were round about inward; and upon each post were palm-trees.

The description began from the outside of the eastern gate and worked inward. The technical Hebrew terms used in this account are not decipherable. Some uncertainty exists, therefore, about the exact meaning of each item and the corresponding relationship of each dimension.

The gateways were approached by seven steps (vv 22, 26). Seven is the number of perfection in biblical symbolism. The gateway itself consisted of a corridor with three square recessed *lodges* or guardrooms on either side.

A barrier of some kind—probably a low wall—separated the guardrooms from the corridor.

The corridor opened into a large porch (eight by twenty cubits) that in turn opened into the outer court of the temple.

The verb *made* in v 14 has been given two interpretations. Some think it points to the fact that the one who is explaining this building had fashioned it previously. Another view is that the verb *made* is equivalent to *estimate*. It was not possible to measure the posts from bottom to top so the angel *made* an estimate.

The posts within the gate were decorated with palm trees (cf. 1 Kgs 6:29-35).

Lower Pavement
40:17-19

Then he brought me into the outer court; and, behold, there were chambers and a pavement, made for the court round about: thirty chambers were upon the pavement. 18 The pavement was by the side of the gates, answerable unto the length of the gates, even the lower pavement. 19 Then he measured the breadth from the forefront of the lower gate unto the forefront of the inner court without, a hundred cubits, both on the east and on the north.

Immediately inside the wall of the outer court was a paved area called the *lower pavement*. Thirty chambers were built on this pavement around the perimeter of the wall on the north, south and east.

Probably these rooms were intended for the use of Levites who served in the temple.

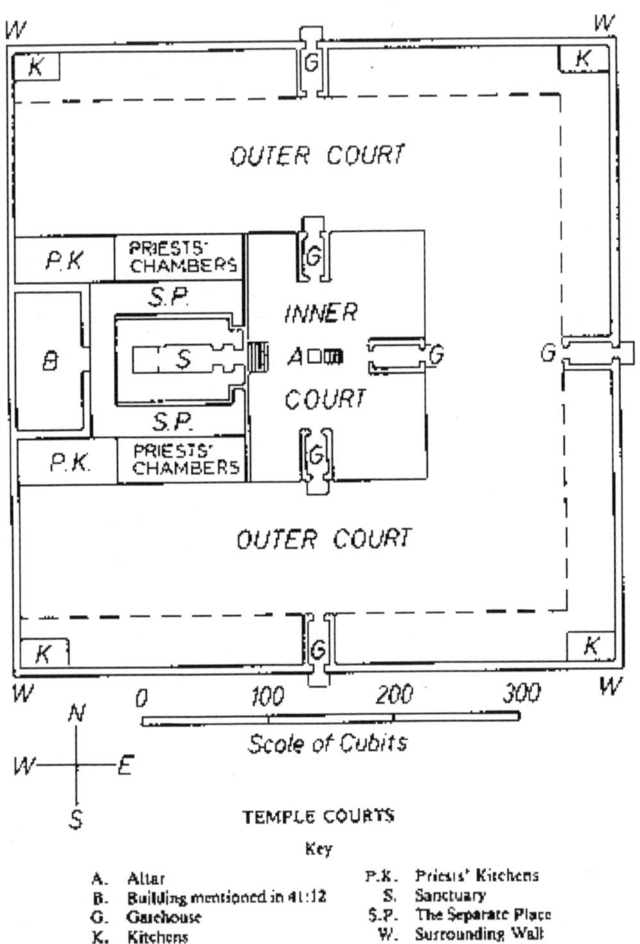

TEMPLE COURTS

Key

A. Altar
B. Building mentioned in 41:12
G. Gatehouse
K. Kitchens
P.K. Priests' Kitchens
S. Sanctuary
S.P. The Separate Place
W. Surrounding Wall

Northern Gatehouse
40:20-23

As for the gate of the outer court facing north, he measured the length thereof and the breadth thereof. 21 The lodges thereof were three on this side, and three on that side: and the posts thereof and the arches thereof were after the measure of the first gate: the

length thereof was fifty cubits, and the breadth twenty-five cubits. 22 The windows thereof, and the arches thereof, and the palm-trees thereof, were after the measure of the gate facing east; and they went up unto it by seven steps; and the arches thereof were before them. 23 There was a gate to the inner court over against the other gate, both on the north and on the east; and he measured from gate to gate a hundred cubits.

The northern gatehouse was identical to the eastern gatehouse.

Southern Gatehouse 40:24-27

Then he led me toward the south; and, behold, a gate toward the south: and he measured the posts thereof and the arches thereof according to these measures. 25 And there were windows in it and in the arches thereof round about, like those windows: the length was fifty cubits, and the breadth twenty-five cubits. 26 There were seven steps to go up to it, and the arches thereof were before them; and it had palm-trees, one on this side, and another on that side, upon the posts thereof. 27 There was a gate to the inner court toward the south: and he measured from gate to gate toward the south a hundred cubits.

The southern gatehouse was identical to the eastern and northern gatehouses.

INNER COURT AND ITS GATEWAYS 40:28-47

The temple tour now examines the gates of the inner court on the south (40:28-31), east (40:32-34), and north (40:35-46). The descriptions are similar to those of the outer gates.

Southern Gate 40:28-31

Then he brought me to the inner court by the south gate: and he measured the south gate according to these measures; 29 and the

lodges thereof, and the arches thereof, according to these measures: and there were windows in it and the arches thereof round about; it was fifty cubits long, and twenty-five cubits broad. 30 There were arches round about, twenty-five cubits long and five cubits broad. 31 The arches thereof were toward the outer court; and palm trees were upon the posts thereof: and the ascent to it had eight steps.

Although no mention is made of it one must assume that a wall surrounded the inner court. One entered the inner court through three gateways that were of similar construction to the gates that led to the outer courtyard except in two respects. First, the vestibule of these interior gateways was on the front rather than the back side as one approached from without. Second, *eight* steps led up to the inner court (vv 31, 34, 37).

Eastern Gate
40:32-34

Then he brought me into the inner court toward the east: and he measured the gate according to these measures; 33 and the lodges thereof and the posts thereof, and the arches thereof, according to these measures: and there were windows therein and in the arches thereof round about; it was fifty cubits long, and twenty-five cubits broad. 34 The arches thereof were toward the outer court; and palm-trees were upon the posts thereof, on this side, and on that side: and the ascent to it had eight steps.

The eastern gate that led to the inner court was identical to the southern gate.

Northern Gate
40:35-37

Then he brought me to the north gate: and he measured it according to these measures; 36 the lodges thereof, the posts thereof, and the arches thereof: and there were windows therein round about; the length was fifty cubits, and the breadth twenty-five cubits. 37 The posts thereof were toward the outer court; and palm-trees were upon the posts thereof, on this side, and on that side: and the ascent to it had eight steps.

The northern gate that led to the inner court was similar to the southern and eastern gates.

Sacrificial Work Area
40:38-43

A chamber with the door thereof was by the posts at the gates; there they washed the burnt offering. 39 In the porch of the gate were two tables on this side, and two tables on that side, to slay thereon the burnt-offering, the sin-offering, and the trespass-offering. 40 On the one side without, as one goes up to the entry of the gate toward the north, were two tables; and on the other side, which belonged to the porch of the gate, were two tables. 41 Four tables were on this side, and four tables on that side, by the side of the gate: eight tables where upon they slew the sacrifices. 42 There were four tables for the burnt-offering, of hewn stone, a cubit and a half long, and a cubit and a half broad, and one cubit high; whereupon they laid the instruments wherewith they slew the burnt-offering and the sacrifice. 43 The hooks, a handbreadth long, were fastened within round about; and upon the tables was the flesh of the oblation.

Two factors indicate that the temple tour now reaches a climax: the amount of space devoted to the description of the sacrificial work area; and the first break in the silence of the tour guide.

Inside the northern gateway that led to the inner court was a special chamber where the burnt offerings were to be washed. The intestines and legs of the burnt offering had to be washed before being brought to the altar (Lv 1:9).

Eight tables on which sacrifices were slaughtered were situated in the northern gateway.[714] Four were within the porch or vestibule, and four beyond the porch and within the gateway. Four smaller tables of hewn stone were also found in the northern gateway. These tables held the sacrificial instruments, i.e., knives and receptacles for collecting the blood. Within the northern gateway, slabs or hooks were fixed to pillars to allow the animal carcasses to be suspended while being flayed. The sacrificial meat, once cut from the carcass, was placed on tables previously mentioned.

---

[714]Fisch (*Ezekiel*, 275-76) thinks v 41 refers to eight additional tables. This means there was a total of sixteen sacrificial tables.

Three types of offerings were prepared in the work areas. In the *burnt offering* (*'ōlāh*), the entire animal (minus the hide) was consumed on the altar. This offering symbolized the consecration of the worshiper. The *sin offering* (*chattā't*) made atonement for unintentional sin (Lv 1:3-4). The *trespass offering* (*'āšām*) was a restitution offering (Lv 5:14-6:7).

Explanations
40:44-46

Outside the inner gate were chambers for the singers in the inner court, which was at the side of the north gate; and they faced north. 45 He said unto me, This chamber, facing south, is for the priests, the keepers of the charge of the house; 46 and the chamber facing north is for the priests, the keepers of the charge of the altar: these are the sons of Zadok, who from among the sons of Levi come near to Yahweh to minister unto him.

On the northern and southern sides of the inner court were the chambers of the *singers*. Choirs of Levites provided musical accompaniment during sacrificial ceremonies.

The interpreting angel explains that in this future temple these chambers will be occupied by the descendants of *Zadok*.[715] Zadok was high priest in the days of Solomon. He was a descendant of Phinehas, the son of Aaron, to whom God had given the covenant of an everlasting priesthood (Nm 25:13). Ezekiel implies that there are two categories of priests. One group deals with the maintenance and security of the temple. The other manages the more important sacrificial worship. Those priests who ministered within the house (i.e., offering incense) occupied one of the priestly chambers; those who served at the altar of sacrifice in the courtyard, lived together in another chamber.

Measurements of Inner Court
40:47

Then he measured the court, a hundred cubits long, and a hundred cubits broad, foursquare; and the altar was before the house.

[715]Raymond Abba, "Priests and Levites in Ezekiel," *VT* 28 (1978): 1-9.

The inner courtyard was a square of one hundred cubits. This court had the *altar* as its center,[716] and the front of the temple as its western edge.

PORCH OF THE SACRED HOUSE 40:48-49

Then he brought me to the porch of the house, and measured each post of the porch, five cubits on this side, and five cubits on that side, and the breadth of the gate was three cubits on this side, and three cubits on that side. 49 The length of the porch was twenty cubits, and the breadth eleven cubits; even by the steps whereby they went up to it: and there were pillars by the posts, one on this side, and another on that side.

The description of the *porch* (*'ulām*) or vestibule is ambiguous, and various configurations are possible. The front wall, on which the gates were hung, was five cubits on each side, and each leaf of the gate was three cubits, giving sixteen cubits (5 x 2 + 3 x 2) for the whole exterior breadth of the porch.

The interior breadth of the porch was eleven cubits. To harmonize this figure with the previous v one must conclude that the walls of the porch were 2.5 cubits thick. *Steps*[717] led up to the porch, but the exact number is not given. *Pillars* are mentioned in connection with the porch. They correspond to the famous pillars (Jachin and Boaz) that decorated the porch of Solomon's temple (cf. 1 Kgs 7:21).

---

[716]A more complete description of the altar is found in 43:13-27.

[717]Following the LXX, the number of steps is assumed to have been ten. The temple tour ascends ever higher to this focal point: from the outside to the outer court (seven steps; 40:22), to the inner court (eight steps; 40:31), to the temple proper (ten steps; 40:49) for a total of twenty-five steps.

EZEKIEL 41
SACRED HOUSE

GENERAL STRUCTURE
41:1-15a

Holy Place
41:1-2

And he brought me to the temple, and measured the posts, six cubits broad on the one side, and six cubits broad on the other side, which was the breadth of the tabernacle. 2 And the breadth of the entrance was ten cubits; and the sides of the entrance were five cubits on the one side, and five cubits on the other side: and he measured the length thereof, forty cubits, and the breadth, twenty cubits.

Walking westward through the porch Ezekiel entered the *temple* proper (*hēkhāl*). This area he calls the *tabernacle* or tent "because the posts were shaped like an arch at the top like a tent."[718] The prophet does not mention the contents of this area, only its dimensions. The holy place—the area between the porch and the holy of holies—was forty cubits long and twenty cubits wide corresponding to the same room in Solomon's temple (1 Kgs 6:2-3).

Most Holy Place
41:3-4

Then went he inward, and measured each post of the entrance, two cubits; and the entrance, six cubits; and the breadth of the entrance, seven cubits. 4 He measured the length thereof, twenty cubits, and the breadth, twenty cubits, before the temple: and he said unto me, This is the most holy place.

Only the angel entered *the most holy place*, i.e., the holy of holies. The entrance to the holy of holies was but seven cubits wide. The holy of holies was twenty cubits square corresponding to the dimensions of the same room in Solomon's temple (cf. 1 Kgs 6:16-17).

---

[718]Fisch, *Ezekiel*, 279.

The guide breaks the silence for the second time on this temple tour to identify the area he has just measured. There is no mention of the ark of the covenant that was housed in this area in Solomon's temple. This harmonizes with Jeremiah's prophecy that the ark will be missing in the messianic age (Jer 3:16).

THE SACRED HOUSE

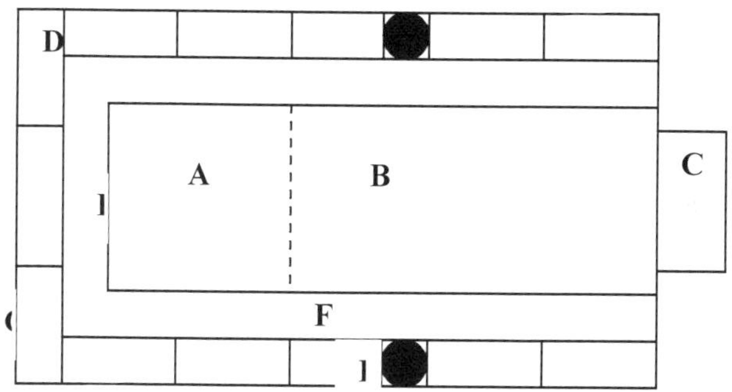

A = Holy of Holies; B = Holy Place; C = Porch; D = Side Chambers; E = Spiral Staircase; F = Corridor; G = Wall of Side Chambers; H = Wall of House

Side Chambers
41:5-12

A. Side Chambers Proper (41:5-7)

Then he measured the wall of the house, six cubits; and the
breadth of every side-chamber, four cubits, round about the house
on every side. 6 The side-chambers were in three stories, one over
another, and thirty in order; and they entered into the wall which
belonged to the house for the side-chambers round about, that they
might have hold therein, and not have hold in the wall of the house.
7 And the side-chambers were broader as they encompassed the
house higher and higher; for the encompassing of the house went
higher and higher round about the house: therefore the breadth of
the house continued upward; and so one went up from the lowest
chamber to the highest by the middle chamber. 8 I saw also that the
house had a raised basement round about: the foundations of the
side-chambers were a full reed of six great cubits.

As in Solomon's temple, attached to the wall of Ezekiel's visionary temple on three sides were side-chambers (cf. 1 Kgs 6:5-6). They were in three stories. The chambers of the second story were slightly larger than those on the ground floor, while those of the third story were still larger. This was possible because of abatements in the wall.

Along the back or western wall there were three large chambers, one on each of the three levels. There were fifteen along the south wall, and fifteen along the north wall, five chambers on each tier.[719] The wall of the temple was six cubits thick at the base; but at two points it diminished as it ascended. These abatements served as supports for the beams of the second and third stories.

The upper-most story was reached by a spiral staircase. It passed from the ground floor through the middle tier.

B. Other Details (41:9-11)

The thickness of the wall, which was for the side-chambers on the outside, was five cubits: and that which was left was the place of the side-chambers, that belonged to the house. 10 Between the chambers was a breadth of twenty cubits round about the house on every side. 11 The doors of the side-chambers were toward the place that was left, one door toward the north, and another door toward the south: and the breadth of the place that was left was five cubits round about.

A thick wall surrounded the chambers on the outside. Thus, the chambers were constructed between two massive walls.

Between these side-chambers and the chambers of the priests mentioned in 40:44-46 was a space of twenty cubits called in KJV "the separate place" and in the RSV the "temple yard."

The side-chambers were entered from without through two doors, one in the north wall, and one in the south wall. These probably were located at the mid-point of the wall. Connecting doors made passage from one chamber to another possible.

[719]Others understand the text to say there were thirty chambers per story.

Hinder Building
41:12

The building that was before the separate place at the side toward the west was seventy cubits broad; and the wall of the building was five cubits thick round about, and the length thereof ninety cubits.

At the rear of the temple was a large separate building (seventy by ninety cubits) that probably served as a storage area.

External Dimensions
41:13-15a

So he measured the house, a hundred cubits long; and the separate place, and the building, with the walls thereof, a hundred cubits long; 14 also the breadth of the face of the house, and of the separate place toward the east, a hundred cubits. 15 He measured the length of the building before the separate place which was at the back thereof, and the galleries thereof on the one side and on the other side, a hundred cubits.

The total length of the temple from east to west, from the wall of the porch to the back western wall, was one hundred cubits.[720] The pavement and building at the rear of the temple extended westward another one hundred cubits.[721] The front of the temple, along with its yard, was one hundred cubits.[722] The overall breadth of the building at the rear of the temple was also one hundred cubits.[723] Galleries or balconies were built along the outside of the wall.

---

[720]Post 5 (40:48) + vestibule 12 (40:49) + post 6 (41:1) + holy place 40 (41:2) + post 2 (41:3) + holy of holies 20 (41:4) + wall 6 (41:5) + side-chambers 4 (41:5) + outer wall 5 (41:9) = 100 cubits.

[721]Yard 20 (41:10) + building 70 (41:12) + two walls of building 10 (41:12) = 100 cubits.

[722]The temple yard to the north and south 40 + the paved areas to north and south 10 + the two outer walls of side-chambers 10 + the two side-chambers 8 + the north and south walls of the house 12 + the interior of the house 20 = 100.

[723]Interior breadth of the room 90 + two side walls 10 = 100 cubits.

TEMPLE INTERIOR
41:15b-26

Measuring
41:15b-17

[He measured] the inner temple, and the porches of the court; 16 the thresholds, and the closed windows, and the galleries round about on their three stories, over against the threshold, ceiled with wood round about, and from the ground up to the windows, (now the windows were covered) 17 to the space above the door, even unto the inner house, and without, and by all the wall round about within and without, by measure.

The holy place, holy of holies and the porches of the court all had jambs, narrow windows and balconies. The stone walls were covered with paneling from floor to ceiling.

Decorations
41:18-21

It was made with cherubim and palm-trees; and a palm-tree was between cherub and cherub, and every cherub had two faces; 19 so that there was the face of a man toward the palm-tree on the one side, and the face of a young lion toward the palm-tree on the other side: thus was it made through all the house round about. 20 From the ground unto above the door were cherubim and palm-trees made: thus was the wall of the temple. 21 As for the temple, the floor posts were squared; and as for the face of the sanctuary, the appearance thereof was as the appearance of the temple.

As in Solomon's temple (1 Kgs 6:29), the wooden panels were decorated with carved figures of cherubim and palm-trees from floor to ceiling. These cherubim had two faces—that of a man and that of a lion—that were turned in opposite directions. Each palm-tree was between the human face of one cherub and the lion's face of another cherub.

The jambs or doorposts of the temple were square rather than round.

Altar
41:22

The altar was of wood, three cubits high, and the length thereof two cubits; and the corners thereof, and the walls thereof, were of wood: and he said unto me, This is the table that is before Yahweh.

For the third time the guide breaks silence to designate the altar as *the table that is before Yahweh*. Opinions differ as to whether the altar of incense is being described metaphorically as a *table*,[724] or the table of showbread is being described metaphorically as an altar.[725]

Doors
41:23-26

The temple and the sanctuary had two doors. 24 And the doors had two leaves apiece, two turning leaves; two leaves for the one door, and two leaves for the other. 25 There were made on them, on the doors of the temple, cherubim and palm-trees, like as were made upon the walls; and there was a threshold of wood upon the face of the porch without. 26 There were closed windows and palm-trees on the one side and on the other side, on the sides of the porch: thus were the side-chambers of the house, and the thresholds.

The holy place and the holy of holies each had a double door. Each door had *two leaves* that could be folded back independently. It would be possible for a door to be opened only a quarter of the full width of the entrance. The doors, like the walls, were decorated with cherubim and palm-trees.

Beams[726] extended before the porch making a kind of overhang.

---

[724]Fisch, *Ezekiel*, 285.
[725]Taylor, *Ezekiel*, 263.
[726]Meaning of the Hebrew word is uncertain. RSV renders it "canopy;" KJV "planks."

EZEKIEL 42
PRIESTS' CHAMBERS

DESCRIPTION
42:1-14

Northern Chambers
42:1-9

***Then be brought me forth into the outer court, the way toward
the north: and he brought me into the chamber that was over
against the separate place, and which was over against the building
toward the north. 2 Along the length, which was a hundred cubits,
was the north door; the width was fifty cubits. 3 Over against the
twenty cubits which belonged to the inner court, and over against
the pavement which belonged to the outer court, was gallery against
gallery in the third story. 4 Before the chambers was a walk of ten
cubits' breadth inward, a way of one cubit; and their doors were
toward the north. 5 Now the upper chambers were shorter; for the
galleries took away from these, more than from the lower and the
middlemost, in the building. 6 For they were in three stories, and
they had not pillars as the pillars of the courts: therefore the uppermost was straitened more than the lowest and the middle-most
from the ground. 7 The wall that was without by the side of the
chambers, toward the outer court before the chambers, the length
thereof was fifty cubits. 8 For the length of the chambers that were
in the outer court was fifty cubits: and, behold, before the temple
were a hundred cubits. 9 And from under these chambers was the
entry on the east side, as one goes into them from the outer court.***

Across the temple yard directly opposite the side-chambers were the priests' chambers. These chambers were briefly mentioned in 41:10. The priests' chambers consisted of two blocks or complexes of chambers separated from one another by a passageway ten cubits wide. Closest to the temple was a rather large one-story building (a hundred by fifty cubits) that was divided into smaller chambers.

Across the passageway was a three-storied complex of chambers fifty cubits long. For aesthetic reasons a dividing wall extended another fifty cubits so that this second complex of chambers would balance in appearance the first block of priestly chambers. Apparently these priestly chambers could be entered from the outer court and from the passage between the two complexes of chambers.

Southern Chambers
42:10-14

In the thickness of the wall of the court toward the east, before
the separate place, and before the building, there were chambers. 11
The way before them was like the appearance of the way of the
chambers which were toward the north; according to their length so
was their breadth: and all their egresses were both according to
their fashions, and according to their doors. 12 According to the
doors of the chambers that were toward the south was a door at the
head of the way, even the way directly before the wall toward the
east, as one enters into them.

The chambers on the south side of the temple are the exact replica of those on the north.

Purpose of the Chambers
42:13-14

Then said he unto me, The north chambers and the south
chambers, which are before the separate place, they are the holy
chambers, where the priests that are near unto Yahweh shall eat the
most holy things, and the meal-offering, and the sin-offering, and
the trespass-offering; for the place is holy. 14 When the priests en-
ter in, then shall they not go out of the holy place into the outer
court, but there they shall lay their garments wherein they minister;
for they are holy: and they shall put on other garments, and shall
approach to that which pertains to the people.

The tour guide breaks the silence for the fourth time to describe the function of the buildings he has just measured. First, they were used for dining rooms. Here the priests partook of their portion of the sin-offering, the trespass-offering (cf. 40:39) and *meal offering* (*minchāh*), an offering of grain prepared in various ways that accompanied one of the blood offerings (cf. Lv 2:1-3). Twice the text emphasizes that these chambers are *holy*.

Second, the chambers served as a kind of transit zone between the inner and outer courts. The priests paused there to change from their holy garments worn in ministry to ordinary clothing.

Total Dimensions of the Temple Area 42:15-20

Now when he had made an end of measuring the inner house, he brought me forth by the way of the gate that faced east, and measured it round about. 16 He measured on the east side with the measuring reed five hundred reeds, with the measuring reed round about. 17 He measured on the north side five hundred reeds with the measuring reed round about. 18 He measured on the south side five hundred reeds with the measuring reed. 19 He turned about to the west side, and measured five hundred reeds with the measuring reed. 20 He measured it on the four sides: it had a wall round about, the length five hundred, and the breadth five hundred, to make a separation between what was holy and what was common.

The measurements of the inner house, including its courts and associated buildings, are now complete. The angel returned to the eastern gate, the point at which the measuring had begun. He now measures the entire area surrounding the wall.

Apparently another wall surrounded the entire temple complex as it previously has been described. This third wall formed a square of *five hundred reeds*. A reed is thought to have been about six cu-bits. So this outer area measured three thousand square cubits.[727] The symmetry is perfect.

The temple tour ends as it began with the measurement of a wall. The purpose of the wall is the purpose of this unit, viz. *to make a separation between what was holy and what was common.*[728] Ezekiel's vision reinforces the teaching that there are degrees of holiness. The entire land is holy, the temple precincts yet more holy. The inner chamber of the temple depicts the unapproachable holiness of God himself.

[727]By comparison, the size of Solomon's temple was only five hundred cubits square.
[728]Lind, *Ezekiel*, 331f.

The painfully detailed description of the ideal temple underscores the importance of this sacred structure to the exiles. By means of the temple God's presence in the world became tangible. Everything about that temple—its symmetry, decorations, elaborate architecture—inspired awe. Yet these buildings, like the bones in the valley, have no life in them without the presence of God. The palace awaits its King.

EZEKIEL 43
TEMPLE GLORY RESTORED

RETURN OF THE DIVINE GLORY 43:1-12

Ezekiel at the Eastern Gate 43:1-4

Afterward he brought me to the gate, even the gate that looks toward the east: 2 and behold, the glory of the God of Israel came from the way of the east: and his voice was like the sound of many waters; and the earth shined with his glory. 3 It was according to the appearance of the vision that I saw, even according to the vision that I saw when I came to destroy the city; and the visions were like the vision that I saw by the river Kebar; and I fell upon my face. 4 The glory of Yahweh came into the house by the way of the gate that faced east.

After he had witnessed the measuring of the outer wall the interpreting angel brought Ezekiel back to the eastern gate of the temple where the tour had begun (cf. 40:6). There he witnessed an awe-inspiring scene. Nineteen years earlier Ezekiel had seen the glory of God leaving the temple by that eastern gate (10:18-22; 11:22-24). The return of God's glory is the ultimate sign of a new chapter in the relationship with his people.

The prophet sees *the glory* of God returning to sanctify the new structure as his holy dwelling. The roar of the cherubim in their flight sounded like the roar of many waters. The splendor of the divine presence illuminated the earth. On two previous occasions Ezekiel had seen this vision of the throne-chariot—once at his call by the River Kebar (ch 1), and again when he saw in vision the destruction of Jerusalem (chs 8-11).

The prophet attributes the destruction of Jerusalem to himself in v 3 because he had prophesied it.

Ezekiel was awe-stricken at the sight of the divine glory entering that eastern gate. The words *the glory of Yahweh came into the house* "are the most significant that the prophet has uttered, for they give ultimate meaning to his entire life and ministry."[729]

Ezekiel in the Inner Court 43:5-9

The Spirit took me up, and brought me into the inner court; and, behold, the glory of Yahweh filled the house. 6 I heard one speaking unto me out of the house; and a man stood by me. 7 He said unto me, Son of man, this is the place of my throne, and the place of the soles of my feet, where I shall dwell in the midst of the children of Israel forever; and the house of Israel shall no more defile my holy name, neither they, nor their kings, by their whoredom, and by the dead bodies of their kings in their high places; 8 in their setting of their threshold by my threshold, and their door-post beside my door-post, and there was but the wall between me and them; and they have defiled my holy name by their abominations which they have committed: wherefore I have consumed them in my anger. 9 Now let them put away their whoredom, and the dead bodies of their kings, far from me; and I shall dwell in the midst of them forever.

After viewing the divine throne-chariot Ezekiel was whisked away into the inner court by *the Spirit* (cf. 2:2; 8:3). From that vantage point Ezekiel could see that the glory of God completely filled the temple.

A man—probably the interpreting angel of the previous chs—stood beside Ezekiel there. Here the silence of the tour was broken for the fifth and last time. The voice of God could be heard from within the sanctuary. The word from God is the climax of the temple tour.

---

[729]Vawter and Hoppe, *Ezekiel*, 194.

The voice spoke of the significance of the new temple. The former temple had served as God's footstool; his throne was in heaven (Isa 60:13; Ps 132:7; Lam 2:1; 1 Chr 28:2). The new temple will serve as God's *throne* as well as his footstool.[730] There he will dwell with his people forever.

In the new temple age the Israel of God will no longer defile God's holy name by their disgusting *whoredom*, i.e., idolatry. In days gone by kings were buried in close proximity to the temple. Contact with the dead produced ritual impurity (Nm 5:2-4; 19:11-13). The new temple will be insulated from such defilement.[731]

In the pre-exilic Jerusalem the royal palace abutted the temple. Only a wall separated the holy sanctuary from the royal palace. This was an intolerable infringement on Yahweh's space. The *abominations* (idolatrous practices) of the palace defiled the temple. This was the reason God had consumed these kings.

The sanctity of the new temple is safeguarded by a large area of outer and inner courts. In these areas the priests and other sacred personnel dwell. When his people put away their whoredom (idolatry), God can dwell forever in their midst.

Instructions for Ezekiel 43:10-12

As for you, son of man, show the house to the house of Israel, that they may be ashamed of their iniquities; and let them measure the pattern. 11 If they be ashamed of all that they have done, make known unto them the form of the house, and the fashion thereof; the egresses and entrances, and all the forms thereof; all the ordinances, and all the forms thereof; and all the laws thereof. Write it in their sight; that they may keep the whole form thereof, and all the ordinances thereof, and do them. 12 This is the law of the house: upon the top of the mountain the whole limit thereof round about shall be most holy. Behold this is the law of the house.

A new commission is given to Ezekiel. He is commanded to describe the temple of his vision to his fellow exiles in all its particulars. His purpose in doing so was to cause them to *be ashamed of their in-*

---

[730]Elsewhere the footstool of God is the ark (1 Chr 28:2); Zion (Lam 2:1); the sanctuary (Isa 60:13); and the earth (Isa 66:1).

[731]Another interpretation is that the graves of the kings became pagan high places where idolatrous rites were performed

iquities.[732] This vision serves to remind the exiles of the loss of their former sanctuary. Their hearts will be filled with contrition as they contemplate the reasons why God allowed their former temple to be destroyed.

The vision of God's glory returning to the temple is a summons to commitment and loyalty.[733] The exiles are *to measure the pattern* (ASV). The Hebrew term (*tokhnît*) is better translated "proportion." The exiles are to measure the temple's relationships and degrees of access.[734] Thus they will learn the standard of God's holiness that is clearly set forth in the structure and design of the temple.

If the people appeared to be moved to repentance by Ezekiel's temple preaching he was to give them all the details concerning the new structure: *the form of the house*, i.e., the general appearance of the new temple; *the fashion thereof*, i.e., the various sections, chambers and cells; the egresses (gates) and entrances; *the ordinances thereof*, i.e., the function and use of the various parts of the temple complex; *the forms thereof*, i.e., the cherubim and palms that decorate it; and *all the laws* that regulated the use of that facility.

Write it in their sight suggests that Ezekiel may have sketched out the temple plan (on the ground?) even as he described the details of it to the exiles. The Jews were expected *to keep the whole form* of that temple, i.e., remember the shape and design of the structure; and to implement, when it became possible, the ordinances pertaining to those sacred precincts.

Verses 10-12 are a bridge from the vision of the new temple and the cultic legislation to follow. The higher standards of these laws reflect the greater sanctity of the new temple. Ezekiel anticipates that the cultic ordinances shall be followed. This prevents any future departures of God's glory from his temple. God permanently resides in his temple.

---

[732]The four references to *shame* in Ezekiel are all in the context of Israel's salvation. Cf. 16:54, 61; 36:32; 43:10. *Shame* is intended to lead to repentance.
[733]Vawter and Hoppe, *Ezekiel*, 194.
[734]Donna Stevenson as cited by Lind, *Ezekiel*, 333.

CENTER OF WORSHIP: ALTAR 43:13-27

Ezekiel first describes the altar (43:13-17), and then speaks at length about the dedication of that sacred spot (43:18-27).

Altar Measurements 43:13-17

These are the measures of the altar by cubits: (the cubit is a cubit and a handbreadth:) the bottom shall be a cubit, and the breadth a cubit, and the border thereof by the edge thereof round about a span; and this shall be the base of the altar. 14 From the bottom upon the ground to the lower ledge shall be two cubits, and the breadth one cubit; and from the lesser ledge to the greater ledge shall be four cubits, and the breadth a cubit. 15 The upper altar shall be four cubits; and from the altar hearth and upward there shall be four horns. 16 The altar hearth shall be twelve cubits long by twelve broad, square in the four sides thereof. 17 The ledge shall be fourteen cubits long by fourteen broad in the four sides thereof; and the border about it shall be half a cubit round about; and the steps thereof shall look toward the east.

The altar was mentioned previously in 40:47. It was located in the center of the inner court directly in front of the temple entrance. The arrangement of the Ezekiel's altar is different from that of the Mosaic altar (Ex 20:25-26). The messianic temple has an altar of a new design (cf. Heb 13:10).

The Hebrew terms used in vv 13-17 are obscure. There is no unanimity among scholars about the dimensions and design of this structure. The following points are more or less clear:

1. The measurements of the altar are specified as being by the longer cubit. A *handbreadth* or span was half a cubit. The previously given temple measurements include only the ground plan. The altar measurements include height as well.

2. The altar was built on a *base*. This foundation platform was set in the pavement of the court, its upper surface being apparently level with the surrounding pavement. A rim or border distinguished this foundation platform from the surrounding pavement.

SACRIFICIAL ALTAR

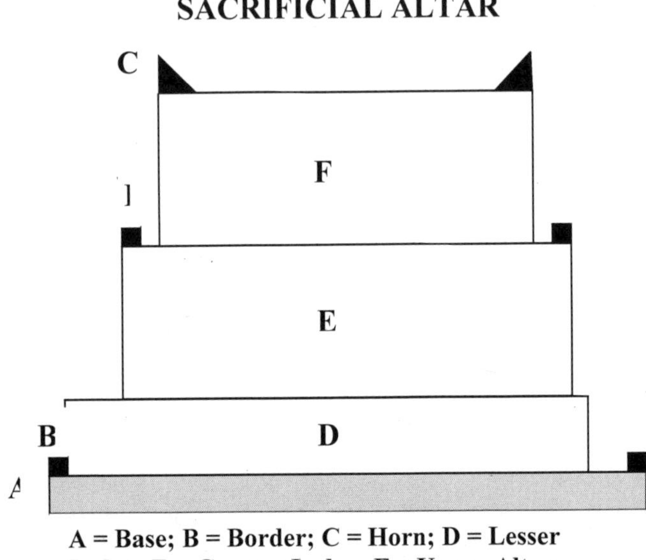

A = Base; B = Border; C = Horn; D = Lesser Ledge; E = Greater Ledge; F = Upper Altar

3. The altar was built in three square stages, each with a side two cubits shorter than the stage below it. The sides of the three stages were twelve, fourteen and sixteen cubits long respectively. The altar had a step-like appearance.

4. The total height of the altar proper was thirteen cubits.[735] The *horns* that projected upward another cubit were regarded as the most sacred part of the altar. Here the blood was smeared in the various sacrifices.

5. The hearth area, where the sacrifices were placed, measured twelve by twelve cubits or 144 square cubits.

6. The approach to the altar was on the east side. *Steps* were forbidden in early altars (Ex 20:24-26). The increased size of later altars made them a necessity. Since the steps faced east a priest on the steps faced west toward God's throne. That is opposite the direction pagan priests faced while ministering.

---

[735]Base 1 (v 13) + elevation 2 (v 14) + lesser ledge 1 (v 14) + elevation 4 (v 15) + greater ledge 1 (v 14) + upper altar 4 = 13 cubits. If the base was in a depression of one cubit, than the height of the altar was twelve cubits.

Altar Dedication
43:18-27

A. Cleansing (43:18-22)

He said unto me, Son of man, thus says Lord Yahweh: These are the ordinances of the altar in the day when they shall make it, to offer burnt offerings thereon, and to sprinkle blood thereon. 19 You shall give to the priests the Levites that are of the seed of Zadok who are near unto me, to minister unto me (oracle of Lord Yahweh), a young bullock for a sin-offering. 20 You shall take of the blood thereof, and put it on the four horns of it, and on the four corners of the ledge, and upon the border round about: and thus shall you cleanse it and make atonement for it. 21 You shall also take the bullock of the sin-offering, and it shall be burnt in the appointed place of the house, without the sanctuary. 22 On the second day you shall offer a he-goat without blemish for a sin-offering; and they shall cleanse the altar, as they did cleanse it with the bullock.

In the Old Testament worship system the altar was used two ways: burnt offerings were offered on it; and blood was smeared on it. The altar needed to be consecrated in order to make it suitable for these two important functions. Moses[736] carried out the consecration of the Israel's first altar (Ex 29:36-37; 40:9-11; Lv 16:18-19). So Ezekiel was to organize the consecration of the new altar. He was to assign the various consecration functions to the Levitical priests[737] who were descendants of Zadok.[738] Non-Zadokites were debarred from priestly ministry for reasons that are stated in the following ch (44:10).

On the first day of the dedicatory rites a bullock was to be used as a sin-offering. The blood of that sacrificial beast was to be smeared on the four horns, on the four corners of the (greater) ledge and on the rim or border that surrounded the greater ledge. This shed blood cleansed the altar and made atonement for it. The remainder of the sacrificial bullock was to be burned in another, unspecified spot within the walls of the temple mount.

A he-goat was to be sacrificed on the second day of the dedicatory rites. The blood of the he-goat was to be sprinkled on the altar in

[736]Other similarities to Moses: Ezekiel speaks of a new exodus, a new covenant, a new allocation of land. Like Moses Ezekiel sees the Promised Land from a distance.
[737]All priests were Levites, but not all Levites were priests.
[738]Zadok was the first high priest in Solomon's temple.

the same manner as was done with the blood of the bullock. Thus the altar was purified a second time.

B. Consecration (43:23-27)

When you have made an end of cleansing it, you shall offer a young bullock without blemish, and a ram out of the flock without blemish. 24 You shall bring them near before Yahweh. The priests shall cast salt upon them, and they shall offer them up for a burnt-offering unto Yahweh. 25 Seven days you shall prepare every day a goat for a sin-offering: they shall also prepare a young bullock and a ram out of the flock, without blemish. 26 Seven days shall they make atonement for the altar and purify it; so shall they consecrate it. 27 When they have accomplished the days it shall be that upon the eighth day, and forward, the priests shall make your burnt-offerings upon the altar, and your peace-offerings; and I shall accept you (oracle of Lord Yahweh).

Whole burnt offerings of a bullock and a ram were to be offered on the purified altar. The whole burnt offering symbolized complete consecration. Salt was to be sprinkled upon these burned offerings[739] by the priests. This preservative may symbolize the everlasting covenant between God and his people.[740]

These three sacrifices—the goat, bullock and ram—were to be repeated six more times during the dedicatory week. By this means the new altar was to be set apart for its sacred functions.[741]

After these rites had been performed then the regular sacrificial service could begin. Burnt-offerings and peace-offerings[742] had as their primary aim acceptance by God. The devout and obedient worshipers of the new temple era find that acceptance with God.

[739]Cf. Lv 2:13; Mk 9:49.

[740]Fisch, *Ezekiel*, 300.

[741]The altar of the tabernacle was consecrated by anointing (Ex 30:28; 40:10) as well as with sacrificial blood (Lv 8:14ff). The altar in Solomon's temple was consecrated by a seven-day feast of burnt-offerings and peace-offerings (2 Chr 7:1-9).

[742]The peace-offering symbolized fellowship with God.

EZEKIEL 44
MINISTERS OF WORSHIP

The empty temple complex of chs 40-42 comes alive. Now that God has returned to the temple (43:1-12) his people can meet with him there. The laws set forth in the present unit underscore that the temple of the preceding chs is not a lifeless monument. It is the hub of worship and service. Having already focused his attention on the center of worship (43:13-27) Ezekiel now speaks of the ministers of worship (44:1-45:8).

After briefly discussing the relationship of the prince to the sanctuary (44:1-3), Ezekiel speaks of the qualifications of the temple ministers (44:4-14), the regulations for the Zadokite priests (44:15-27); the provision for the Zadokite priests (44:28-31), and the allocation of land that was theirs (45:1-8).

PRINCE AND SANCTUARY
44:1-3

Then he brought me back by the way of the outer gate of the sanctuary that faces east; and it was shut. 2 Yahweh said unto me, This gate shall be shut; it shall not be opened, neither shall any man enter in by it; for Yahweh, the God of Israel, has entered in by it; therefore it shall be shut. 3 As for the prince, he shall sit therein as prince to eat bread before Yahweh; he shall enter by the way of the porch of the gate, and shall go out by the way of the same.

The angel now brought Ezekiel back from the inner court to the outer eastern gate that only shortly before he had entered (43:1). He found that gate shut now that the glory of God had reentered the temple. Never again will that gate be open. God's glory will never again depart from his temple. No man will be permitted to enter the gate through which the divine presence had come.

The future leader of God's people—*the prince*[743]—will be permitted to *eat bread before Yahweh* within the eastern gate complex. The phrase hints of the priestly prerogatives of the future prince.[744] Not even the prince, however, will be allowed to enter by the sealed gate. He will enter the gate complex from the rear or west by the way of the porch of the gate.

PRIESTLY QUALIFICATIONS 44:4-14

Word of Admonition 44:4-5

Then he brought me by the way of the north gate before the house; and I looked, and, behold, the glory of Yahweh filled the house of Yahweh: and I fell upon my face. 5 Yahweh said unto me, Son of man, mark well, and look with your eyes, and listen with your ears all that I say unto you concerning all the ordinances of the house of Yahweh, and all the laws thereof; and mark well the entrance of the house, with every egress of the sanctuary.

The architectural tour of the temple is over; but the heavenly guide continues to lead Ezekiel. From the outer court the prophet was led by his angelic guide around through the northern gate (the eastern gate was to be kept perpetually closed) to the inner court. For the last time in the book Ezekiel observed the glory of God filling the house. The prophet falls on his face in reverence.

At this juncture God spoke to Ezekiel again, this time concerning the qualifications of those who approach him in his holy temple. Previously the emphasis was on what the guide showed Ezekiel; here it is upon what Yahweh tells him. Ezekiel was bidden to make careful note ("mark, look, listen") of these *ordinances*, particularly those *laws* governing the approaches to the house.

---

[743]The *prince* (*nāśî'*) is mentioned 17x in chs 44-48. Jewish commentators regarded this prince as Messiah. Most Christian commentators have rejected this view because the prince 1) offers a sin offering for himself (45:22), 2) has sons (46:15), and 3) is distinct from the priests. For a defense of the messianic interpretation of the prince, see Smith, *Promised Messiah*, 372-377.

[744]Certain bread could not be eaten by non-priests (e.g., Lv 2:3; 24:9). Cf. Ex 29:32 where the Aaronic priests were to eat a religious meal by the door of the tabernacle.

Word of Condemnation 44:6-8

You shall say to the rebellious, even to the house of Israel, Thus says Lord Yahweh: O house of Israel, let it suffice you of all your abominations, 7 in that you have brought in foreigners uncircumcised in heart and uncircumcised in flesh, to be in my sanctuary, to profane it, even my house, when you offer my bread, the fat and the blood. They have broken my covenant, to add unto all your abominations. 8 You have not kept the charge of my holy things; but you have set keepers of my charge in my sanctuary for yourselves.

In the former temple aliens[745] had been permitted to discharge priestly functions. This abomination must not persist in the age of the new temple. Those *uncircumcised in heart and...flesh* profaned the holiness of that sacred shrine. Circumcision of the flesh was the sign of the Abrahamic covenant. Moses, however, called for Israelites to be circumcised in their hearts as well as in the flesh (Lv 26:41; Dt 10:16; 30:6; cf. Jer 4:4; 9:25). Such a change of heart was necessary for the Israelite and the foreigner if they were to enter into a proper relationship with Yahweh.

God's *bread*, i.e., sacrifices of *fat* and *blood*, was not to be offered by the uncircumcised, i.e., the unfaithful and unconverted. To allow them to do so was to violate the covenant and commit abomination.

Apparently the use of foreign temple servants such as the Carites (2 Kgs 11:4) is here being proscribed. It may have been that in times when the priesthood was at low ebb some priestly duties actually had been assigned to these foreigners. In so doing God's people had been more concerned about what was convenient to them rather than what conformed to the instructions of God.

---

[745]The use of aliens for menial temple service can be traced back to Joshua. He made the Gibeonites temple servants (Josh 9:23, 27). Israel seems to have continued this practice through the time of Ezra (Ezra 8:20).

Word of Judgment
44:9-15

Thus says Lord Yahweh, No foreigner, uncircumcised in heart, and uncircumcised in flesh, shall enter into my sanctuary, of any foreigners that are among the children of Israel. 10 But the Levites that went far from me, when Israel went astray, that went astray from me after their idols, they shall bear their iniquity. 11 Yet they shall be ministers in my sanctuary, having oversight at the gates of the house, and ministering in the house: they shall slay the burnt-offering and the sacrifice for the people, and they shall stand before them to minister unto them. 12 Because they ministered unto them before their idols, and became a stumbling block of iniquity unto the house of Israel; therefore have I lifted up my hand against them, says Lord Yahweh, and they shall bear their iniquity. 13 They shall not come near unto me, to execute the office of priest unto me, nor to come near to any of my holy things, unto the things that are most holy; but they shall bear their shame, and their abominations which they have committed. 14 Yet shall I make them keepers of the charge of the house, for all the service thereof, and for all that shall be done therein.

The menial temple work, formerly done by aliens, must in the future be performed by the Levites.[746]

The duties of the Levites in Ezekiel's temple were threefold. First, they were to have charge of the temple gates, i.e., they were to police the crowds who entered for worship. Second, they were to minister *in the house*, i.e., courtyard, by slaying the sacrificial animals.[747] Third, they were to stand before the worshipers to minister to them by helping them in their ritual responsibilities.

The demotion of the Levites in the new temple was a punishment for previous transgression on their part. They had gone far away from God. They had ministered at idolatrous shrines. They had been stumbling blocks to the people of God. God had taken an oath (*lifted up my hand*) against the Levites that they must bear the consequences of their iniquity in the new temple age.

---

[746]Cf. J. Gordon McConville, "Priests and Levites in Ezekiel: A Crux in the Interpretation of Israel's History," *TB* 34 (1983): 3-31.

[747]The slaughtering of the animal for sacrifice was not a priestly function. It could be performed by a layman.

In effect the penalty against the once wayward Levites was reduction in status to that of lay servants in the temple. They will not be allowed to come near Yahweh, i.e., enter the inner courtyard, or minister at the sacrificial service, or come near any holy thing in the temple.

The Levites are *keepers of the charge of the house,* i.e., they are restricted to functions in the outer court.

PRIESTLY REGULATIONS 44:15-27

Ministerial Privileges 44:15-16

But the priests the Levites, the sons of Zadok, that kept the charge of my sanctuary when the children of Israel went astray from me, they shall come near to me to minister unto me; and they shall stand before me to offer unto me the fat and the blood (oracle of Lord Yahweh): 16 they shall enter into my sanctuary, and they shall come near to my table, to minister unto me, and they shall keep my charge.

Only the sons of Zadok[748] will be allowed to minister before and within the sanctuary proper. They alone had remained faithful when the rest of the nation had gone into idolatry. The Zadokites are permitted to 1) *come near* to God to minister unto him; 2) *stand before* God to offer the sacrificial portions of animals and the blood; 3) enter into the sanctuary itself and minister there; and 4) approach the *table* of showbread (cf. 41:22). Whereas the Levites were to keep the *charge of the house* the Zadokites were to *keep my charge.*

Older critics saw in these vv evidences of a political conflict between priests and Levites. Supposedly Ezekiel took the side of the priests. The main concern here, however, is the holiness of a temple liturgy that far surpasses in holiness anything known during the days of the previous temple.[749]

---

[748]The genealogy of Zadok is found in 1 Chr 6:50-53. Zadok was a priest in David's day, alongside Abiathar (2 Sam 8:17; 15:24ff). He became the high priest under Solomon.

[749]Vawter and Hoppe, *Ezekiel*, 200.

Ministerial Dress
44:17-20

It shall be that, when they enter in at the gates of the inner court they shall be clothed with linen garments. No wool shall come upon them, while they minister in the gates of the inner court, and within. 18 They shall have linen turbans upon their heads, and shall have linen undergarments upon their loins; they shall not gird themselves with anything that causes sweat. 19 When they go forth into the outer court, even into the outer court to the people, they shall put off their garments wherein they minister, and lay them in the holy chambers; and they shall put on other garments, that they sanctify not the people with their garments. 20 Neither shall they shave their heads, nor suffer their locks to grow long; they shall only cut off the hair of their heads.

In the new temple, the Zadokite priests were to serve clothed only in *linen*. They will not be permitted to wear the partly woolen garments worn by priests in the former temple. Linen is light and clean in appearance. The heavier wool caused perspiration that in turn resulted in ritual defilement.

The holy linen garments were to be removed and stored in the holy chambers before the priests joined the lay people in the outer court. Holiness was communicated by direct contact (cf. Ex 29:37; Lv 6:20). If the priests mingled with the lay people in those holy garments the people would be sanctified. Holy and profane were never to meet in the new age.

The priests were to be examples of holiness to the people of God. They were not permitted to shave their heads, or let their hair grow long. Those customs were associated with heathen practice (cf. Lv 21:5, 10).

Ministerial Restrictions
44:21-22

Neither shall any of the priests drink wine, when they enter into the inner court. 22 They shall not take for their wives a widow, nor her that is put away; but they shall take virgins of the seed of the house of Israel, or a widow that is the widow of a priest.

As in the Law of Moses priests were not allowed to drink wine before performing their sacrificial ministry in the inner court.

Rigid marriage restrictions prohibited a priest from marrying anyone but an Israelite virgin[750] or the widow of a fellow priest. These strict marriage regulations were perhaps designed to preserve the purity of the priestly families.

Ministerial Responsibility 44:23-24

They shall teach my people the difference between the holy and the common, and cause them to discern between the unclean and the clean. 24 In a controversy they shall stand to judge; according to my ordinances shall they judge it: and they shall keep my laws and my statutes in all my appointed feasts; and they shall hallow my sabbaths.

The priests were teachers.[751] They were responsible, by word and example, for constantly reminding the people of the difference between the holy and the common, the clean and the unclean. In civil cases the priests acted as judges.[752] In this capacity they were to render each verdict in accordance with the law of God.

The primary function of the priests was strictly to observe the regulations concerning the sacrifices that were to be offered on special festivals and sabbaths.

Ministerial Defilement 44:25-27

They shall go in to no dead person to defile themselves; but for father, or for mother, or for son, or for daughter, for brother, or for sister that has had no husband, they may defile themselves. 26 After he is cleansed, they shall reckon unto him seven days. 27 In the day that he goes into the sanctuary, into the inner court, to minister in the sanctuary, he shall offer his sin-offering (oracle of Lord Yahweh).

---

[750]In the Law of Moses this regulation applied only to the high priest (Lv 21:13f).
[751]Cf. Dt 33:10; Mal 2:7.
[752]Cf. Dt 17:8ff; 19:17; 21:5.

As in the Law of Moses the priests of the new temple age must avoid contact with dead bodies. Exceptions were made in the case of close relatives. Contact with a corpse defiled priests and rendered them temporarily unfit to perform their priestly function. A seven-day separation and ritual washing was necessary to cleanse a priest defiled by death in the Law of Moses. Ezekiel's regulations call for an additional seven-day period after the cleansing. Upon resuming his ministry in the inner court the priest was to offer a sin-offering for his defilement. These additional regulations are intended to portray the greater sanctity of the future temple.

PRIESTLY PROVISIONS 44:28-31

They shall have an inheritance: I am their inheritance; and you shall give them no possession in Israel; I am their possession. 29 They shall eat the meal-offering, the sin-offering, and the trespass-offering; and every devoted thing in Israel shall be theirs. 30 The first of all the first-fruits of everything, and every oblation of everything, of all your oblations, shall be for the priest: you shall also give unto the priests the first of your dough, to cause a blessing to rest on your house. 31 The priests shall not eat of anything that dies of itself, or is torn, whether it be bird or beast.

Other tribes received their inheritance in land tracts; but the priesthood itself was the inheritance of the Zadokites.[753] Spiritual privilege is greater blessing than material possession.

The priests received a portion of the various offerings for their daily maintenance. Every *devoted thing* (*cherem*)—any property consecrated to God—belonged to the priests.

The *first-fruits* of the land—a token portion of the crop—belonged to the priests.[754] The *oblation* or "heave-offering" was the priest's portion of first-born clean animals that were killed and sacrificed to God. The first cakes baked with the grain from the threshing floor were also to be given to the priests (cf. Nm 15:20). Those who

---

[753]The Pentateuch gives this spiritual inheritance to the Levites in general (Dt 10:9; 18:2). Pointing to the greater sanctity of the future age Ezekiel limits this inheritance to the priests.

[754]Cf. Dt 8:8 and Nm 18:13.

were faithful in presenting these offerings to the priests received a special blessing (cf. Mal 3:10).

Appended to the list of what priests could eat is a prohibition. No Israelite could eat any animal that died a natural death or that had been killed by wild beasts (cf. Ex 22:30; Lv 7:24; Dt 14:21). It is not clear why the regulation is repeated here in connection with the priests.

EZEKIEL 45
SPECIAL OFFERINGS

LAND OFFERING
45:1-8

Holy Portion
45:1-4

Moreover, when you shall divide by lot the land for inheritance, you shall offer an oblation unto Yahweh, a holy portion of the land; the length shall be the length of twenty-five thousand reeds, and the breadth shall be ten thousand: it shall be holy in all the border thereof round about. 2 Of this there shall be for the holy place five hundred in length, square round about; and fifty cubits for the suburbs thereof round about. 3 Of this measure you shall measure a length of twenty-five thousand, and a breadth of ten thousand; and in it shall be the sanctuary, which is most holy. 4 It is a holy portion of the land; it shall be for the priests, the ministers of the sanctuary, that come near to minister unto Yahweh; and it shall be a place for their houses, and a holy place for the sanctuary.

Ezekiel anticipates an apportionment of the holy land among the tribes of Israel. The central portion of that land was to belong to Yahweh. This rectangular area, twenty-five thousand by ten thousand reeds,[755] was to be reserved for the priests and the new temple. This portion of the land is viewed as more holy than the rest of the land.

---

[755]Actually the unit of measurement is missing in the Hebrew text. Some scholars think the unit is the cubit.

In the center of this priestly portion of ground was a square (500 x 500 reeds) where the temple was to be located. It was separated from the area where the priests dwelled by fifty cubits of open space.[756]

Ezekiel's vision of the Promised Land shows more concern for symmetry than for the realities of geography. His idealism has a pedagogical function. Pre-exilic Israel got into trouble for ignoring God. Ezekiel paints the picture of God in the center of things in the new era.[757]

Levitical Portion
45:5

And twenty-five thousand in length, and ten thousand in breadth, shall be unto the Levites, the ministers of the house, for a possession unto themselves, for twenty chambers.

The Levites will occupy a portion of land equal in extent to and adjoining that of the priests. Scholars differ as to whether this area was north or south of the priests' portion. At the extreme end of the Levites' portion, twenty chambers[758] were to be built. These chambers were to house the gate-keepers so that they were near the temple.[759]

City Portion
45:6

You shall appoint the possession of the city five thousand broad, and twenty-five thousand long, side by side with the oblation of the holy portion: it shall be for the whole house of Israel.

The city of Jerusalem was allocated a rectangular portion of land (25,000 x 5,000 reeds) adjacent to the portion of the priests on the south. This section of the land could be inhabited by any Israelite without regard to tribe. The total territory of the holy portion—the

---

[756]It is not clear whether v 3 refers to an additional portion of 25,000 x 10,000 reeds, or whether this is the same portion mentioned in v 1.

[757]Vawter and Hoppe, *Ezekiel*, 202.

[758]The RSV, following the Greek Old Testament, reads "for cities to live in."

[759]In v 5 the Levites are again called *ministers of the house* in contrast to the priests who were *ministers of the sanctuary that come near to minister unto Yahweh* (v 4).

territory allocated to the holy city, to the priests, Levites and temple—comprised an area 25,000 reeds square.

Prince's Portion
45:7-8

Whatsoever is for the prince shall be on the one side and on the other side of the holy oblation and of the possession of the city, in front of the holy oblation and in front of the possession of the city, on the west side westward, and on the east side eastward; and in length answerable unto one of the portions, from the west border unto the east border. 8 In the land it shall be to him for a possession in Israel: and my princes shall no more oppress my people; but they shall give the land to the house of Israel according to their tribes.

In Ezekiel's symbolic scheme of things the center of the land was a rectangle called the *holy oblation* (i.e., "offering"[760]) that has been described in the previous vv. The ideal city and temple occupy this oblation. As if guarding the approaches to both the prince's inheritance was on either side of the oblation in the very center of the land.

The Law of Moses made no special inheritance provision for kings. Old Testament kings were constantly attempting to expand their personal holdings at the expense of the citizens. This will not be the case in the future envisioned by Ezekiel. The portion of the prince was equal in size to that assigned to entire tribes, except that the holy portion was carved out of his territory (cf. 48:21).

Taking their cue from the prince, other leaders in the future Israel (*my princes*) are God-fearing men. They do not *oppress* God's people by trying to appropriate their inheritances. On the other hand, they see to it that all of God's people occupied their God-given share in the holy land, i.e., the kingdom.

PRINCELY OFFERINGS
45:9-25

At this point in his vision of the new temple Ezekiel sets forth the regulations pertaining to the rights and duties of the prince (vv 9-17);

---

[760]The Hebrew *t*ᵉ*rūmāh* is frequently translated "heave-offering." A more accurate translation is "levy" or compulsory contribution. See Taylor, *Ezekiel*, 273.

the festival offerings (45:18-25); and the offerings on the Sabbath and new moon (46:1-7).

Integrity in Office
45:9-12

Thus says Lord Yahweh: Let it suffice you, O prince of Israel: remove violence and spoil, and execute justice and righteousness; take away your exactions from my people (oracle of Lord Yahweh). 10 You shall have just balances, and a just ephah, and a just bath. 11 The ephah and the bath shall be of one measure. That the bath may contain the tenth part of a homer, and the ephah the tenth part of a homer: the measure thereof shall be after the homer. 12 The shekel shall be twenty gerahs; twenty shekels, twenty-five shekels, fifteen shekels, shall be your maneh.

The future leader of God's people will abandon the greed and corruption of his predecessors who did violence to the helpless. There will be no more *exactions*—unjust seizure of property. He will rule in *justice and righteousness*.

The most common means of defrauding people was by means of unjust measures. The prince will eliminate this evil. He will demand that just weights and measures be used throughout the land.

The *ephah* was a dry measure, the *bath*[761] a liquid measure. Both were equal to a tenth of a *homer*,[762] which was the standard unit of measure.

A *shekel* (about 0.4 ounces) was equal to twenty *gerahs*. Sixty *shekels* made up a *mina*.[763] The *shekels* were in use in denominations of twenty, twenty-five and fifteen in the days of Ezekiel.

Faithful in Temple Provisions
45:13-17

This is the oblation that you shall offer: the sixth part of an ephah from a homer of wheat; and you shall give the sixth part of an ephah from a homer of barley; 14 and the set portion of oil, of

[761]An *ephah* and *bath* were equal to about five gallons.

[762]*Homer*, literally "donkey-load," was equal to about six bushels.

[763]Elsewhere it is "fifty shekels" that equals a *mina*. Perhaps the Jewish shekel had been devalued during the exile to bring it into harmony with the Babylonian *shekel*.

the bath of oil, the tenth part of a bath out of the cor, which is ten baths, even a homer; (for ten baths are a homer); 15 and one lamb of the flock, out of two hundred, from the well-watered pastures of Israel—for a meal-offering, and for a burnt-offering, and for peace-offerings, to make atonement for them, (oracle of Lord Yahweh). 16 All the people of the land shall give unto this oblation for the prince in Israel. 17 It shall be the prince's part to give the burnt-offerings, and the meal-offerings, and the drink-offerings, in the feasts, and on the new moons, and on the sabbaths, in all the appointed feasts of the house of Israel: he shall prepare the sin-offering, and the meal-offering, and the burnt-offering, and the peace-offerings, to make atonement for the house of Israel.

The reasons for concern about weights and measures are set forth. The people are to present offerings to their prince. He in turn had the responsibility of supplying the needs of the temple service. A sixth of an *ephah* of wheat and barley was required, a tenth of each *bath* of oil out of the *cor,*[764] and one lamb out of a flock of two hundred. These required dues were to be used in temple offerings to make atonement for the people. When these vv are compared to the stipulations of the Mosaic Law it becomes clear that "the demands of Ezekiel's torah surpass those of the earlier or Mosaic torah in quantity as well as quality."[765]

The people render special tribute to the prince. He in turn provided the communal sacrifices offered throughout the year, as well as those special sacrifices offered on festival days. He will *prepare*[766] the various sacrifices that result in atonement. No mention is made in these chs of the people bringing sacrifices to the temple. Apparently all offerings are given to God through the prince.

---

[764]The *cor* was identical to the *homer*. Cf. v 11.

[765]Plumptre, *Pulpit Commentary*, 2:414.

[766]The verb r. *'sh* is frequently used in the technical sense of preparation of sacrifice (e.g., Lv 5:10; 9:7). It is also used in a more general sense of providing the material for sacrifice (e.g., Lv 14:30).

Festival Offerings
45:18-25

The regulations regarding festival offerings sketched out here presuppose the more detailed instructions found in the Pentateuch.[767] Some of the sacrifices spoken of here and in the next chs were unknown in Solomon's temple. The considerable differences between Ezekiel's ordinances and the Mosaic laws again signal that the worship system of the messianic era is substantially different from that of the mosaic era.

Some scholars hold that the sacrifices outlined here were intended to be replacement for the Mosaic regulations regarding these holy days. Others see these sacrifices as being in addition to those stipulated in the Mosaic Law. Still others see these sacrifices as authorized only for the period of the dedication of the new temple.

A. New Year (45:18-20)

Thus says Lord Yahweh: In the first month, in the first day of the month, you shall take a young bullock without blemish; and you shall cleanse the sanctuary. 19 The priest shall take of the blood of the sin-offering, and put it upon the door-posts of the house, upon the four corners of the ledge of the altar, and upon the posts of the gate of the inner court. 20 So you shall do on the seventh day of the month for every one that errs, and for him that is simple: so shall you make atonement for the house.

The blood of a bullock is used to purify the sanctuary on New Year's Day. The blood of that sin offering is smeared on the door-posts of the temple, on the four corners of the greater ledge of the altar (cf. 43:20), and on the post of the gate[768] of the inner court. These actions were to be repeated on the seventh day of the month. This ritual served to cleanse the holy area from those who through ignorance had wandered into a restricted area of the temple courtyard.

B. Passover (45:21-24)

In the first month, in the fourteenth day of the month, you shall have the Passover, a feast of seven days; unleavened bread shall be

---

[767]Ezekiel does not mention Pentecost, one of the three annual pilgrimage feasts of pre-exilic days.

[768]The word *gate* may be used here in a collective sense of all three gates of the inner court.

eaten. 22 Upon that day shall the prince prepare for himself and for all the people of the land a bullock for a sin-offering. 23 The seven days of the feast he shall prepare a burnt-offering to Yahweh, seven bullocks and seven rams without blemish daily the seven days; and a he-goat daily for a sin-offering. 24 He shall prepare a meal-offering, and ephah for a bullock, and an ephah for a ram, and a hin of oil to an ephah.

Passover commemorated the deliverance of the Israelites from Egypt. It was celebrated on the fourteenth day of *Nisan*, the first month. This spring festival lasted seven days during which only unleavened bread was eaten. The prince was *to prepare*, i.e., provide, a bullock as a sin-offering *for himself and for the people*. If the prince is a messianic figure this can only mean that the prince provided the sin offering for the people. The provision of that offering was in some sense necessary for the fulfillment of his mission. That the prince himself was a sinner is not a necessary conclusion drawn from the text. No such sacrifice was connected with Passover in the Mosaic Dispensation.

In the future worship Ezekiel has the sin offering coming before, and presumably taking precedence over, the Paschal feast proper. Clearly the sin offering is more prominent in the new age. Messiah was made to be a sin offering for guilty men (2 Cor 5:21). He accomplished all that the animal sin offerings of the old covenant could not accomplish.

In addition to the sin-offering bullock the prince was to provide seven bullocks and seven rams for burnt-offerings on each of the seven days of the festival. He was also to provide a he-goat each day for a sin-offering. Along with each bullock and ram the prince was to provide an *ephah* of grain and a *hin* of oil.

C. **Tabernacles** (45:25)

In the seventh month, in the fifteenth day of the month, in the feast, shall he do the like seven days; according to the sin-offering, according to the burnt-offering, according to the meal-offering, and according to the oil.

The Feast of Tabernacles was observed during *Tishri*, the seventh month. During this joyous seven-day festival the prince was to duplicate the offerings required during Passover.

EZEKIEL 46
WORSHIP REGULATIONS

MORE OFFERINGS
46:1-7

Sabbath Offerings
46:1-5

Thus says Lord Yahweh: The gate of the inner court that looks toward the east shall be shut the six working days; but on the Sabbath day it shall be opened, and on the day of the new moon it shall be opened. 2 The prince shall enter by the way of the porch of the gate without and shall stand by the post of the gate; and the priests shall prepare his burnt-offering and his peace-offerings, and he shall worship at the threshold of the gate: then he shall go forth; but the gate shall not be shut until the evening. 3 The people of the land shall worship at the door of that gate before Yahweh on the sabbaths and on the new moons. 4 The burnt-offering that the prince shall offer unto Yahweh shall be on the Sabbath day six lambs without blemish and a ram without blemish. 5 The meal-offering shall be an ephah for the ram, and the meal-offering for the lambs as he is able to give, and a hin of oil to an ephah.

On Sabbath and new moon (first day of the month) the eastern gate of the inner court was to be opened.[769] On these occasions *the prince* was allowed to enter the eastern gate. He was the official representative of the people who presented to the priests the sacrifices that were to be offered on behalf of the nation. From his vantage point at the *post of the gate* (i.e., the western end of the gateway) he worshiped as the priests offered his sacrifices within his view upon the altar. Even after he departed from the temple the inner gate was to be left open until evening.

---

[769]This gate is not to be confused with the eastern gate of the outer court that was never to be opened (44:2).

Clearly Ezekiel envisioned a ruler in his Zion-to-be. He prefers to call him a *prince* (*nāsî'*), rather than a *king* (*melek*),[770] probably to hint that he is a ruler of a different kind. His leadership is ratified by the people he rules (cf. 1 Sam 10). The prince has no palace. The only building associated with him in these chs is the temple. He devotes himself entirely to the worship of his people.[771] In fact, he joins his people in their worship. "In effect, the prince acts as a high priest, an official that does not appear elsewhere in Ezekiel's portrayal of messianic worship."[772] The coming of the prince causes the gate to be opened for his subjects to worship from without. The people are allowed to come to the door of that inner gate. They worshiped behind the prince. Through the open gate they could observe the priests preparing the sacrifices provided by the prince. Here again the prince appears as the leader in worship.

The offerings prescribed for Sabbath and new moon of the new temple age do not correspond with those prescribed in the Law of Moses (cf. Nm 28:9, 11-15).[773] The prince is to offer each Sabbath six lambs and a ram, an *ephah* of meal with the ram, an unspecified amount of meal for each lamb, and at least a *hin* of oil.

New Moon Offerings
46:6-7

On the day of the new moon it shall be a young bullock without blemish, and six lambs and a ram; they shall be without blemish: 7 and he shall prepare a meal-offering, an ephah for the bullock, and an ephah for the ram, and for the lambs according as he is able, and a hin of oil to an ephah.

On the new moon, the prince is to offer the regular Sabbath offerings, but add to them an unblemished bullock and another *ephah* of meal.

---

[770]Ezekiel uses the word *nāsî'* several times when speaking of the Davidic head of state (12:10, 12; 19:1; 21:25). It is Ezekiel's favorite designation for the ruler of the Zion-to-be (34:24; 37:25 + 14x in chs 40-48). In 7:27 he uses it in parallel with *melek*.

[771]Cf. Dt 17:18-20 where the ideal king devotes himself entirely to the study of the Mosaic Law.

[772]Vawter and Hoppe, *Ezekiel*, 204.

[773]To reconcile this account with the Pentateuch some Jewish scholars have proposed that these sacrifices are special, additional sacrifices required during the sabbaths of the dedication period for the new temple.

WORSHIP REGULATIONS
46:8-24

In this unit Ezekiel learns the regulations that govern the more sanctified worship of the messianic era. He is instructed regarding the entrance and exit of the worshipers (46:8-10); the offerings of the prince on behalf of the people (46:11-15); the inheritance of the prince (46:16-18); and the preparation of the sacrificial meals (46:19-24).

Movement of Worshipers
46:8-10

When the prince shall enter, he shall go in by the way of the porch of the gate, and he shall go forth by the way thereof. 9 But when the people of the land shall come before Yahweh in the appointed feasts, he that enters by the way of the north gate to worship shall go forth by the way of the south gate; and he that enters by the way of the south gate shall go forth by the way of the north gate: he shall not return by the way of the gate whereby he came in, but shall go forth straight before him. 10 The prince, when they go in, shall go in the midst of them; and when they go forth, they shall go forth together.

The prince is accorded honor in that he alone is permitted to enter and leave by the same route on weekly and monthly worship occasions. On the Sabbath and new moon the prince enters by the porch of the (inner) eastern gateway and leaves by the same way.

The outer eastern gate is not open. There is no western gate. In the *appointed seasons* (Passover, Pentecost, and Tabernacles),[774] the worshipers are required to enter the outer court by one of the side gates and leave by the gate on the opposite side. This made for orderly flow of traffic across the inner court. It also symbolized that those who truly worship God should leave the experience a new person.

During the great annual feasts the prince was to enter the temple when the people did. The prince joins with his people in their wor-

[774]On these festivals every male Israelite was required to appear at the temple.

ship. The law of attendance of the prince suggests that worshipers should approach God in worship only *with* and *in* and *through* their great mediator, Christ Jesus. *When they go forth, they shall go forth together.* Whether at worship, work or recreation, the prince is in the midst of his people.

Prince's Offering
46:11-15

In the feasts and in the solemnities the meal-offering shall be an ephah for a bullock, and an ephah for a ram, and for the lambs as he is able to give and a hin of oil to an ephah. 12 When the prince shall prepare a freewill-offering, a burnt-offering or peace-offerings as a freewill-offering unto Yahweh, one shall open for him the gate that looks toward the east; and he shall prepare his burnt-offering and his peace-offerings, as he does on the Sabbath: then he shall go forth; and after his going forth the gate shall be shut. 13 You shall prepare a lamb a year old without blemish for a burnt-offering unto Yahweh daily: morning by morning you shall prepare it. 14 You shall prepare a meal-offering with it morning by morning, the sixth part of an ephah, and the third part of a hin of oil, to moisten the fine flour; a meal-offering unto Yahweh continually by a perpetual ordinance. 15 Thus shall they prepare the lamb, and the meal-offering, and the oil, morning by morning, for a continual burnt-offering.

On all *feasts* (e.g., Pentecost) and *solemnities*, i.e., appointed seasons (e.g., New Years, Day of Atonement) the prince had the obligation to provide meal offerings as well as animals for sacrifice. He was required to offer an *ephah* of meal for each bullock or ram. For each lamb he would make a voluntary contribution of meal. Each *ephah* of meal was to be accompanied by a *hin* of oil.

If the prince should desire to offer a free-will offering on a weekday the eastern gate of the inner court was opened for him. Apparently that too was a special privilege that was his alone. Upon his departure the gate was to be closed again. Only on Sabbath days was the eastern gate left open all day so that worshipers might view the sacrificial ritual. Clearly the prince surpasses all his people in liberality. He sets for them a princely example. His position as prince affords him special access to God. He practices personal worship seasons above and beyond the stated times of public worship.

Everyday sacrifices were to be offered by the priests upon the great temple altar. A lamb was to be offered and a meal-offering as well. No mention is made here of an evening offering (cf. Nm 28:4 f).[775]

Prince's Inheritance 46:16-18

Thus says Lord Yahweh: If the prince gives a gift unto any of his sons; it is his inheritance. It shall belong to his sons. It is their possession by inheritance. 17 But if he gives of his inheritance a gift to one of his servants, it shall be his to the year of liberty; then it shall return to the prince; but as for his inheritance, it shall be for his sons. 18 Moreover, the prince shall not take of the people's inheritance, to thrust them out of their possession; he shall give inheritance to his sons out of his own possession, that my people be not scattered every man from his possession.

Ezekiel has enumerated the offerings that the prince might give to God. Now he speaks about gifts that the prince might make to others. There are three regulations. They are introduced by *Thus says Yahweh.*

A gift of property given by the prince to his sons was to be regarded as a possession by inheritance in perpetuity. The property did not revert to the prince under any circumstances.

Royal property given to a servant was to be regarded as a temporary loan. It reverted back to the prince in *the year of liberty* (Jubilee year) that occurred every fiftieth year.

The prince in all cases must make his land grants out of his own, not out of his subjects' possessions. He was to respect the property rights of his subjects. Confiscations of property by the crown, as in the case of Naboth's vineyard (1 Kgs 21), will be a thing of the past. Ezekiel did not want a repeat of pre-exilic seizure of property by the crown.

[775]The amount of the meal offering also differs from that prescribed in Numbers.

Sacrificial Meals
46:19-24

A. Inner Kitchen (46:19-20)

Then he brought me through the entry, which was at the side of the gate, into the holy chambers for the priests, which looked toward the north: and, behold, there was a place on the hinder part westward. 20 He said unto me, This is the place where the priests shall boil the trespass-offering and the sin-offering, and where they shall bake the meal-offering; that they bring them not forth into the outer court, to sanctify the people.

Ezekiel's conducted tour of the temple resumes in these vv. He was taken by his angelic guide into the priests' chambers that ran parallel to the temple on the north and south. This block of chambers faced north. He was led to the extreme western end of this structure. There Ezekiel was shown a special chamber. In this chamber the priests were to boil the meat of the guilt-offering and sin-offering, and bake the meal of the meal-offering. These meats and cakes were only be eaten by the priests. They were to exercise care not accidentally to carry these sanctified foods into the outer court where they might communicate holiness to the people (44:19).

B. Outer Kitchens (46:21-24)

Then he brought me forth into the outer court, and caused me to pass by the four corners of the court; and, behold, in every corner of the court there was a court. 22 In the four corners of the court there were courts enclosed, forty cubits long and thirty broad; these four in the corners were of one measure. 23 And there was a wall round about in them, round about the four, and boiling-places were made under the walls round about. 24 Then said he unto me, These are the boiling-houses, where the ministers of the house shall boil the sacrifice of the people.

The angel next brought Ezekiel to the outer court. He observed in each of the four corners of this court enclosures or small courts. Each of these courts was forty by thirty cubits. The courts are said to be *qᵉturōt*, which the KJV renders "enclosed." Some rabbis thought the word meant "uncovered," i.e., the corner structures were roofless to allow the smoke to freely ascend. These small courts are called *boiling places*, i.e., fire places where large boiling pots could be placed.

The ministers of the house—the Levites boiled the people's sacrifices for them. This part of the sacrificial animal was eaten by the worshipers in a communal meal in the temple courtyards.

EZEKIEL 47
FUTURE LAND

In his last vision Ezekiel observes the blessing that the people of God will enjoy in the new temple age. In that blessed land the tribes of Israel have eternal possession. Here Ezekiel discusses the transformation of the Promised Land (47:1-12); the boundaries of the Promised Land (47: 13-21); and the place of aliens in the land (47:22-23).

LAND TRANSFORMATION
47:1-12

Since 44:4 Ezekiel has been setting forth the legislation that will govern the future temple. The entire purpose of that legislation is to underscore the superior holiness of the temple and priesthood of the messianic age. Now Ezekiel resumes recounting the vision that he had of the temple and its environs. The theological architecture of the previous chs gives way to theological geography.[776]

Water of Life
47:1-7

Ezekiel picks up a theme first introduced by Isaiah—that of a fabulous stream that gushes forth from Zion (Isa 8:6-7; 33:20-24). What Isaiah mentioned without much comment Ezekiel develops at length. The point is that the return of God to the temple brings healing and bountiful blessing to the land.

A. Source of the Water (47:1-2)

He brought me back unto the door of the house; and, behold, waters issued out from under the threshold of the house eastward;

[776]Allen, *Word Biblical Commentary*, 285.

(for the forefront of the house was toward the east); and the waters came down from under, from the right side of the house, on the south of the altar. 2 Then he brought me out by the way of the gate northward, and led me round by the way without unto the outer gate, by the way of the gate that looks toward the east; and, behold, there ran out waters on the right side.

The angelic guide brought Ezekiel back to the inner court and the door of the house. There he saw a stream issuing forth from under the threshold of the house. The waters were flowing in a southeasterly direction past the altar and out into the outer court.

Ezekiel was led out the northern gate of the inner court (the nearer eastern gate was closed; cf. 44:2; 46:1). He was taken around the outside wall of the temple complex to the east gate of the outer court. There he saw the waters trickling[777] forth.

B. Increasing Depth (47:3-5)

When the man went forth eastward with the line in his hand, he measured a thousand cubits, and he caused me to pass through the waters, waters that were to the ankles. 4 Again he measured a thousand, and caused me to pass through the waters, waters that were to the knees. Again he measured a thousand, and caused me to pass through the waters, waters that were to the loins. 5 Afterward he measured a thousand; and it was a river that I could not pass through; for the waters were risen, waters to swim in, a river that could not be passed through.

At a thousand cubits east of the eastern gate Ezekiel was directed to wade into the waters. They were ankle deep. At two thousand cubits the waters were knee deep; at three thousand cubits, waist deep; at four thousand cubits (about a mile and a third) the waters were so deep that the prophet could not get across them without swimming.

C. Lush Vegetation (47:6-7)

He said unto me, Son of man, have you seen this? Then he brought me, and caused me to return to the bank of the river. 7 Now when I had returned, behold, upon the bank of the river were very many trees on the one side and on the other.

By means of a rhetorical question the angelic guide underscored the amazing increase in the depth of the water. No mention is made of

---

[777]The Hebrew word is found only here. Its exact meaning is doubtful.

any tributaries, yet the river increased in volume as it descended eastward through the mountains toward the Dead Sea.

Apparently the banks of the river were bare when Ezekiel tested the depth of the water. Now he observed a thick growth of trees shooting up on both banks of the river. These were no ordinary trees. They produced a new crop every month. Furthermore, the leaves of these trees had curative powers (cf. v 12).

Dead Sea Cleansed
47:8-11

Then he said unto me, These waters issue forth toward the eastern region, and shall go down into the Arabah; and they shall go toward the sea; into the sea shall the waters go which were made to issue forth; and the waters shall be healed. 9 It shall come to pass, that every living creature which swarms in every place where the rivers come, shall live; and there shall be a very great multitude of fish; for these waters are come thither, and the waters of the sea shall be healed, and everything shall live wherever the river comes. 10 It shall come to pass, that fishers shall stand by it: from En-gedi even unto Eneglaim shall be a place for the spreading of nets; their fish shall be after their kinds, as the fish of the great sea, exceeding many. 11 But the miry places thereof, and the marshes thereof, shall not be healed; they shall be given up to salt.

The prophet is informed that the river of life flowed far beyond his range of vision to the Arabah[778] and the Dead Sea. The lifeless waters of that body of water were healed, i.e., purified, by the fresh flowing water of life. The point that Ezekiel is making is this: the transformation produced by the new covenant gospel will be as dramatic as the transformation of the briny waters of the Dead Sea into sweet water that supports life.

Where previously no aquatic creatures could exist swarms of fish will be found. Commercial fishermen flock to the shore of the once dead sea. They find the catch as abundant as that to which they were accustomed on the Great (Mediterranean) Sea. Along the shoreline of the Dead Sea they spread their nets from En-gedi (mid-point on the

---

[778]*Arabah* is the technical name for the deep depression through which the Jordan River flows and in which the Dead Sea is located.

western shore of the Dead Sea) to En-eglaim (exact location unknown).

Even though the waters of the sea are healed the marshy areas about the sea remain in their former state so as to provide the people with salt.

Abundant Fruitfulness 47:12

By the river upon the bank thereof, on this side and on that side, shall grow every tree for food, whose leaf shall not wither, neither shall the fruit thereof fail: it shall bring forth new fruit every month, because the waters thereof issue out of the sanctuary; and the fruit thereof shall be for food, and the leaf thereof for healing.

Those who try to interpret the vision of the life-giving stream physically have missed completely the point of the passage. This is a clear instance of symbolism. Fertility and water are virtually interchangeable (Ps 46:4; 65:9; Isa 33:20f). The sheer physical impossibility of a stream increasing in volume without aid of tributaries is a clue to the symbolic import of the text. Furthermore, fruit trees that bear a new crop every month are hard to interpret physically. The main point is that in the new age the temple of God is the source of life, healing and fruitfulness.

LAND DELINEATION 47:13-21

Very little of the legislation in Ezekiel 40-48 influenced the decisions of the community of Jews that returned from exile in Babylon. This is not a body of functional legislation; it is an eschatological vision. Ezekiel saw Israel, not restored to former glory, but to a permanent relationship with Yahweh.[779]

---

[779]Vawter and Hoppe, *Ezekiel*, 208.

General Principles
47:13-14

Thus says Lord Yahweh: This shall be the border whereby you shall divide the land for inheritance according to the twelve tribes of Israel: Joseph shall have two portions. 14 You shall inherit it, one as well as another; for I swore to give it unto your fathers: and this land shall fall unto you for inheritance.

In the new age the land of promise is to be divided fairly between the twelve tribes.[780] It was noted in 44:28 that the Levites were to receive no land inheritance. God had provided for their needs in the temple offering system.

Joseph was given two portions because his sons Ephraim and Manasseh were reckoned as separate tribes. Thus was retained the number *twelve* for the tribes of Israel. In this new allocation each tribe was to receive an equal portion of land.[781] God had made a promise to the Patriarchs—had *lifted up* his *hand* in the gesture of an oath—that the land was to belong to their descendants. God keeps that promise. The land of promise finally and forever belongs to his people.

That each tribe has an equal portion within the holy land is further evidence that this is a symbolic vision. It was never intended to be literally implemented. The topography of the land, so carefully followed in the land allocation to the tribes under Joshua, is here completely ignored. Ezekiel is making the point that all of God's people share equally in the kingdom of God.

Northern Border
47:15-17

This shall be the border of the land: On the north side, from the great sea, by the way of Hethlon, unto the entrance of Zedad; 16 Hamath, Berothah, Sibraim, which is between the border of Damascus and tbe border of Hamath; Hazer-hatticon, which is by the border of Hauran. 17 The border from the sea, shall be Hazarenon

---

[780]David Engelhard, "Ezekiel 47:13-48:29 as Royal Grant" in Joseph Coleson and Victor Matthews, eds. *Go to the Land I will Show You; Studies in Honor of Dwight S. Young* (Winona Lake, IN: Eisenbrauns, 1996), 45-56.

[781]In the first apportionment of the Promised Land numerical strength of the tribes was taken into account (cf. Nm 26:54).

at the border of Damascus; and on the north northward is the border of Hamath. This is the north side.

Not all the towns mentioned in this verbal sketch of the northern border can be located with certainty. The northern boundary stretched roughly from *Tyre* on the west to the headwaters of the Jordan. *Hamath* (i.e., the entrance of Hamath, v 20)[782] marks the northern-most point.

Other Borders 47:18-21

The east side, between Hauran and Damascus and Gilead, and the land of Israel, shall be the Jordan; from the north border unto the east sea shall you measure. This is the east side. 19 The south side southward shall be from Tamar as far as the waters of Meribath-kadesh, to the brook of Egypt, unto the great sea. This is the south side southward. 20 The west side shall be the great sea, from the south border as far as over against the entrance of Hamath. This is the west side. 21 So shall you divide this land unto you according to the tribes of Israel.

Below the Sea of Galilee the eastern boundary of the ideal land was formed by the Jordan River. The southern boundary extended from *Tamar* near the southern end of the Dead Sea to Meribath-kadesh (lit., "the waters of strife," i.e., Kadesh-barnea), to the Brook (i.e., the Brook of Egypt) that ran into the Mediterranean Sea. The great sea (Mediterranean) formed the western boundary of the ideal land.

INCLUSION OF ALIENS 47:22-23

It shall come to pass, that you shall divide it by lot for an inheritance unto you and to the strangers that sojourn among you, who shall beget children among you; and they shall be unto you as the

[782]Cf. Nm 34:8. The entrance of Hamath is generally thought to refer to the one-hundred-mile long valley leading up to Hamath. In Solomon's day, the entrance of Hamath actually served as the northern border of Israel (1 Kgs 8:65).

home-born among the children of Israel; they shall have inheritance with you among the tribes of Israel. 23 And it shall come to pass, that in what tribe the stranger sojourns, there shall you give him his inheritance, (oracle of Lord Yahweh).

The Pentateuch prescribes humane treatment for aliens living in Israel. Such treatment is mandated because of Israel's experience as aliens in Egypt.[783] Ezekiel, however, goes beyond benevolent toleration. He foresaw a fully integrated society. Aliens who live among the Israelites will receive an inheritance within the Promised Land. Proselytes who embraced the worship of the true God have the same privileges as native-born Israelites. Similar broadminded statements are found in 14:7 and 22:7. The unification of Jew and Gentile in the kingdom of Jesus Christ is thus foreshadowed.

EZEKIEL 48 HOLY LAND AND HOLY CITY

LAND APPORTIONMENT 48:1-29

Now that the boundaries of the Promised Land have been spelled out, the prophet deals with the division of that land among the tribes. There was to be a new exodus (20:32-38) and a new covenant (34:23-30; 37:21-28); so also there will be a new allotment of land to the various tribes. The whole territory west of Jordan is to be divided into twelve parallel portions running from east to west. No mention is made of the width of these tribal areas.[784]

Seven Northern Tribes 48:1-7

Now these are the names of the tribes: From the north end, beside the way of Hethion to the entrance of Hamath, Hazarenan at

---

[783]Cf. Ex 22:21; 23:9; Lv 19:10, 33-34; 23:22; Dt 14:29; 24:14-15, 17-22.

[784]The rabbis gave the width of these portions as 25,000 reeds. They equated the dimensions of the *holy portion* (48:8) with those of a tribal tract.

the border of Damascus, northward beside Hamath, (and they shall have their sides east and west,) Dan, one portion. 2 By the border of Dan, from the east side unto the west side, Asher, one portion. 3 By the border of Asher, from the east side even unto the west side, Naphtali, one portion. 4 By the border of Naphtali, from the east side unto the west side, Manasseh, one portion. 5 By the border of Manasseh, from the east side unto the west side, Ephraim, one portion. 6 By the border of Ephraim, from the east side even unto the west side, Reuben, one portion. 7 By the border of Reuben, from the east side unto the west side, Judah, one portion.

Ezekiel's ideal allotment differs from that implemented by Moses and Joshua. First, the three Transjordanian tribes (Reuben, Gad and half of Manasseh) are now to be located west of the Jordan.[785] Second, the order of the allotments does not follow any historical precedent.

Seven tribes are assigned territories north of the holy portion of the land, i.e., the temple area and domains of the priests, Levites and prince. From north to south, these seven tribes are 1) Dan, 2) Asher, 3) Naphtali, 4) Manasseh, 5) Ephraim, 6) Reuben, and 7) Judah. The three tribes farthest away from the sanctuary are those descended from Jacob's concubines.[786]

Because of the messianic blessing of Gn 49:8-12 Judah was given the honor of inheritance nearer to the sanctuary. Judah has been transposed north of Benjamin. This signals that the age-old conflict between the tribes in the north and those in the south is over. These tribal relocations again suggest that Ezekiel's intent is symbolic and not programmatic.

Oblation: Priests' Portion 48:8-12

By the border of Judah, from the east side unto the west side, shall be the oblation which you shall offer, twenty-five thousand reeds in breadth, and in length as one of the portions, from the east side unto the west side: and the sanctuary shall be in the midst of it. 9 The oblation that you shall offer unto Yahweh shall be twenty-five

[785]The occupation east of the Jordan is represented in the earlier books as an anomaly. See Nm 32; Josh 22).

[786]Dan and Naphtali were born to Rachel's maid Bilhah and Asher to Leah's maid Zilpah (Gn 30:5-13).

thousand reeds in length, and ten thousand in breadth. 10 For these, even for the priests, shall be the holy oblation; toward the north twenty-five thousand in length, and toward the west ten thousand in breadth, and toward the east ten thousand in breadth, and toward the south twenty-five thousand in length: and the sanctuary of Yahweh shall be in the midst thereof. 11 It shall be for the priests that are sanctified of the sons of Zadok, that have kept my charge, that went not astray when the children of Israel went astray. 12 It shall be unto them an oblation from the oblation of the land, a thing most holy, by the border of the Levites.

The Oblation

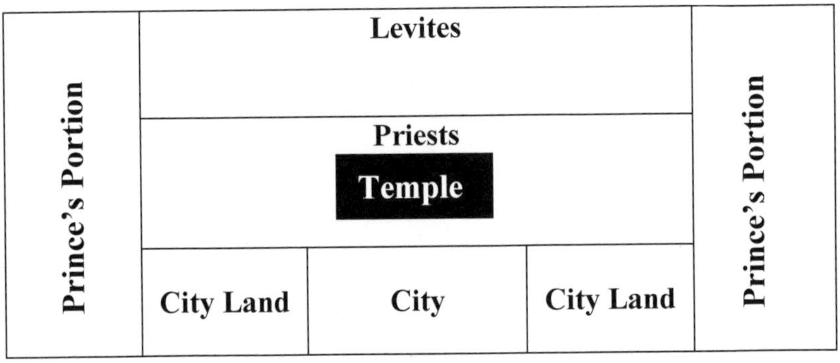

<table>
<tr><td rowspan="3">Prince's Portion</td><td colspan="3">Levites</td><td rowspan="3">Prince's Portion</td></tr>
<tr><td colspan="3">Priests
Temple</td></tr>
<tr><td>City Land</td><td>City</td><td>City Land</td></tr>
</table>

Just south of the tribal area of Judah was a tract 25,000 cubits square. Like the tribal areas this tract occupied the entire length of the land from east to west. This area was known as the "offering" or *oblation.*

Within the oblation was a smaller oblation or offering. This area measured 25,000 cubits east and west and 10,000 cubits from north to south. The sanctuary was situated in the midst of this inner oblation. The smaller oblation was to be the possession of the faithful priests of the line of Zadok. The larger oblation area was holy; but the smaller oblation within it was *most holy*.

Oblation: Levites' Portion 48:13-14

Answerable unto the border of the priests, the Levites shall have twenty-five thousand in length, and ten thousand in breadth: all the

length shall be twenty-five thousand, and the breadth ten thousand. 14 They shall sell none of it, nor exchange it, nor shall the first-fruits of the land be alienated; for it is holy unto Yahweh.

The Levites will no longer be scattered throughout the land in forty-eight cities (Josh 21). They live in the region immediately surrounding the temple. A section of the larger oblation was set aside for the Levites. It was comparable in size to the area set aside for the priests, 25,000 by 10,000 cubits. It is not clear whether this Levite area was north or south of the priestly area.

The areas inhabited by the priests and Levites were holy. For this reason they could not be sold or exchanged by them. This area was called the *first-fruits* (lit., "first;" *rē'šîth*)[787] as well as the *oblation*.

Oblation: Jerusalem's Portion 48:15-20

The five thousand that are left in the breadth, in front of the twenty-five thousand, shall be for common use, for the city, for dwelling and for suburbs; and the city shall be in the midst thereof. 16 These shall be the measures thereof: the north side four thousand and five hundred, and the south side four thousand and five hundred, and on the east side four thousand and five hundred, and the west side four thousand and five hundred. 17 The city shall have suburbs: toward the north two hundred and fifty, and toward the south two hundred and fifty, and toward the east two hundred and fifty, and toward the west two hundred and fifty. 18 The residue in the length, answerable unto the holy oblation, shall be ten thousand east-ward, and ten thousand westward; and it shall be answerable unto the holy oblation; and the increase thereof shall be for food unto them that labor in the city. 19 They that labor in the city, out of all the tribes of Israel, shall till it. 20 All the oblation shall be twenty-five thousand: you shall offer the holy oblation four-square, with the possession of the city.

The city of Jerusalem was assigned the territory south of the priestly area within the oblation. This area measured 5,000 cubits north to south and, like the other sections of the oblation, 25,000 cubits east to west. This area contained the city proper, (a square of

[787]The priestly dues from the crops are called *first-fruits (rē'šîth)* in Dt 18:4.

4,500 cubits), *for common use*[788] about the city (250 cubits on all sides), and two tracts of arable land on either side of the city (10,000 by 5,000 cubits each). These latter areas were to be cultivated by the inhabitants of the city. Regardless of tribal affiliation every citizen of the city was expected to work that ground for the good of all.

The entire oblation area with all of its subdivisions formed a square of 25,000 cubits. This is equivalent to about fifty square miles if the conventional cubit is intended, sixty-nine square miles if the longer cubit is intended.

Oblation: Prince's Portion 48:21-22

The residue shall be for the prince, on the one side and on the other of the holy oblation and of the possession of the city; in front of the twenty-five thousand of the oblation toward the east border, and westward in front of the twenty-five thousand toward the west border, answerable unto the portions, it shall be for the prince: and the holy oblation and the sanctuary of the house shall be in the midst thereof. 22 Moreover from the possession of the Levites, and from the possession of the city, being in the midst of that which is the prince's, between the border of Judah and the border of Benjamin, it shall be for the prince.

On the east and west sides of the oblation was a large territory belonging to the prince. To state the matter differently, the territories of the priests, the Levites, the sanctuary and the city were situated between the two halves of the domain of the prince.

Five Southern Tribes 48:23-29

As for the rest of the tribes: from the east side unto the west side, Benjamin, one portion. 24 By the border of Benjamin, from the east side unto the west side, Simeon, one portion. 25 By the border of Simeon, from the east side unto the west side, Issachar, one portion. 26 By the border of Issachar, from the east side to the west side, Zebulun, one portion. 27 By the border of Zebulun, from the

788 Hebrew *chōl* refers to *common-land*, perhaps for grazing cattle.

east side unto the west side, Gad, one portion. 28 By the border of Gad, at the south side southward, the border shall be even from Tamar unto the waters of Meribath-kadesh, to the brook of Egypt, unto the great sea. 29 This is the land that you shall divide by lot unto the tribes of Israel for inheritance, and these are their several portions (oracle of Lord Yahweh).

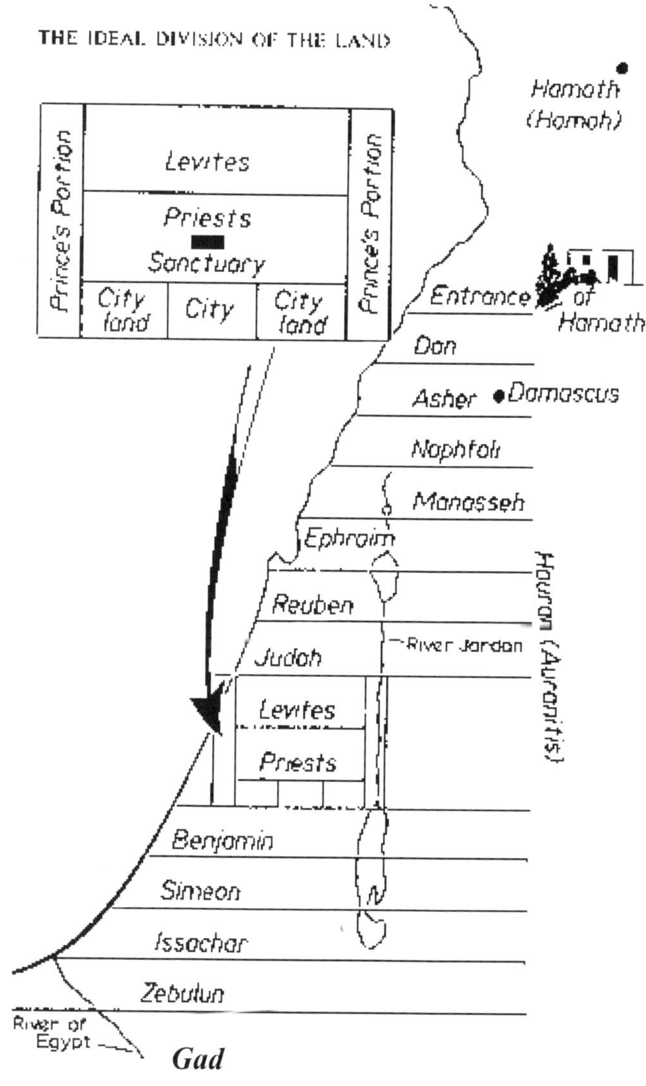

To the south of the oblation were the territories of 1) Benjamin, 2) Simeon, 3) Issachar, 4) Zebulun, and 5) Gad. Benjamin received the favored position near the oblation because that tribe had descended from Jacob's youngest son by Rachel, the beloved wife. Two of the tribes that formerly had been in the north (Zebulun and Issachar) have come south to join Benjamin and Simeon. This is another hint that the new Israel will be a united people. Gad, formerly a Transjordanian tribe, is now occupying the territory to the extreme south. The Gadites were descendants of the son of the concubine Zilpah. Perhaps that is why this tribe's territory is farthest away from the holy portion.

NEW JERUSALEM
48:30-35

These are the egresses of the city: On the north side four thousand and five hundred reeds by measure; 31 and the gates of the city shall be after the names of the tribes of Israel, three gates northward: the gate of Reuben, one; the gate of Judah, one; the gate of Levi, one. 32 At the east side four thousand and five hundred reeds, and three gates: even the gate of Joseph, one; the gate of Benjamin, one; the gate of Dan, one. 33 At the south side four thousand and five hundred reeds by measure, and three gates: the gate of Simeon, one; the gate of Issachar, one; the gate of Zebulun, one. 34 At the west side four thousand and five hundred reeds, with their three gates: the gate of Gad, one; the gate of Asher, one; the gate of Naphtali, one. 35 It shall be eighteen thousand reeds round about: and the name of the city from that day shall be, Yahweh-shammah.

The new Jerusalem as envisioned by Ezekiel had twelve gates, three on each side. These gates were named after the twelve tribes. The gates on the north and south are named after the sons of Leah:

Northern Gates	Southern Gates
Reuben Gate	Simeon Gate
Judah Gate	Issachar Gate
Levi Gate	Zebulun Gate

The two sons of Rachel are honored by having the eastern gates of the city named after them.[789] The third gate was named for the son of Rachel's handmaid Bilhah. The gates on the west were named for the sons of handmaids, Zilpah and Bilhah, viz. Gad, Asher and Naphtali.

Eastern Gates	Western Gates
Joseph Gate Benjamin Gate Dan Gate	Gad Gate Asher Gate Naphtali Gate

It should be noted in the enumeration of gates that Ephraim and Manasseh have been united under the designation *Joseph*.

The Jerusalem of' the future receives a new name. She is called *Yahweh-shammah*, i.e., *Yahweh is there*. God will never again depart from that holy city.

The description of Ezekiel's new Jerusalem, points forward to that new Jerusalem described by John in Rev 21. John's city had twelve gates named after the twelve tribes of Israel. It also had twelve foundations that bore the names of the twelve apostles (Rev 21:12-14). Like his prophetic predecessor, John foresaw the day when God will dwell with his people finally and forever (Rev 21:3).

[789]The temple was to face the east (43:1-5; 44:1-3; 46:1-3) and the "glory" of God entered the temple by the eastern gate (43:2).

BIBLIOGRAPHY

Albright, W.F. *From the Stone Age to Christianity*. Second edition. Garden City, New York: Doubleday, 1957.

Alexander, Ralph. "Ezekiel" in vol. 6 *The Expositor's Bible Commentary*. Ed. Frank E. Gaebelein. Grand Rapids: Zondervan, 1986.

Allen, Leslie C. "Ezekiel 20-48" in vol. 29 *Word Biblical Commentary*. Dallas: Word, 1990.

Archer, Gleason. *A Survey of Old Testament Introduction*. Chicago: Moody, 1964.

Beasley-Murray, G.R. "Ezekiel" in *The New Bible Commentary*. Ed. F. Davidson. Grand Rapids: 1954.

Beck, A.B. et al. eds. *Fortunate the Eyes that See; Essays in Honor of David Noel Freedman*. Grand Rapids: Eerdmans, 1995.

Becking, Bob and Marjo Korpel eds. *The Crisis of Israelite Religion*, Leiden: Brill, 1999.

Becking, Bob and M. Dijkstra eds. *On Reading Prophetic Texts*. Leiden: Brill, 1996.

Bentzen, Aage. *Introduction to the Old Testament*. Fifth ed.; Copenhagen: Gad, 1959.

Blackwood, Jr., Andrew W. *Ezekiel, Prophecy of Hope*. Grand Rapids: Baker, 1965.

Brownlee, W.H. "Ezekiel 1-19" in vol. 28 *Word Biblical Commentary*. Waco, Tx: Word, 1986.

Carley, Keith. *The Book of the Prophet Ezekiel*. Cambridge: University Press, 1974.

Coleson, Joseph and Victor Matthews. *Go to the Land I will Show You; Studies in Honor of Dwight S. Young*. Winona Lake, IN: Eisenbrauns, 1996.

Coogan, M.D. et al. eds. *Scripture and Other Artifacts: Essays in Honor of Philip J. King*. Ed. Louisville: Westminster, 1994.

Cooke, George A. *A Critical and Exegetical Commentary on the Book of Ezekiel*, "International Critical Commentary." Edinburgh: T. and T. Clark, 1936.

Currey, G. ‘‘Ezekiel,” in vol. VI of *The Holy Bible with Explanatory and Critical Commentary*, ed. F.C. Cook. New York: Scribner, 1892.

Davidson, A.B. *The Book of Ezekiel*. “The Cambridge Bible for Schools and Colleges.” Cambridge: University Press, 1896.

Davies, Philip and David Clines, eds. *Among the Prophets*. Sheffeld, JSOT, 1993.

Day, John ed. *King and Messiah*, JSOTSup 270, Sheffield: Sheffield Academic Press, 1998.

Eichrodt, Walther. *Ezekiel, a Commentary* in "The Old Testament Library." Philadelphia: Westminster, 1970.

Ellison, H.L. *Ezekiel: The Man and His Message*. Grand Rapids: Eerdmans, 1956.

_______. "Ezekiel, Book of," *The New Bible Dictionary,* Ed. J.D. Douglas. Grand Rapids: Eerdmans, 1962.

Fairbairn, Patrick. *Exposition of Ezekiel*. Grand Rapids: Sovereign Grace, 1971 reprint.

Fausset, A.R. "Ezekiel" in *A Commentary: Critical, Experimental, and Practical* by Robert Jamieson, A.R. Fausset, and David Brown. Hartford, Conn.: S. S. Scranton, 1877.

Feinberg, Charles Lee. *The Prophecy of Ezekiel*. Chicago: Moody, 1969.

Fohrer, George. *Introduction to the Old Testament*. Trans. David Green. Nashville: Abingdon, 1968.

Fisch, S. *Ezekiel*, "Soncino Books of the Bible." London: Soncino, 1950.

Fuller, J.F.C. "Tyre," *Encyclopedia Britannica*, 14th ed., 22:652-53.

Gardiner, F. "Ezekiel," in vol. V of *An Old Testament Commentary for English Readers*. Ed. Charles John Ellicott. New York: Cassell, 1901.

Greenberg, Moshe *Ezekiel 1-20* in Anchor Bible. Garden City: Doubleday, 1983.

Grider, J. Kenneth. "The Book of the Prophet Ezekiel," in vol. 4 of *Beacon Bible Commentary*, ed. A.F. Harper, *et al.* Kansas City: Beacon Hill Press, 1966.

Hall, Bert. "The Book of Ezekiel," in vol. III of *The Wesleyan Bible Commentary*. Ed. Charles W. Carter. Grand Rapids: Eerdmans, 1967.

Harrison, R.K. *Introduction to the Old Testament*. Grand Rapids: Eerdmans, 1969.

Hendriksen, W. *More than Conquerors*. Grand Rapids: Baker, 1967.

Kaufman, Yehezkel. *The Religion of Israel*. Chicago: University Press, 1960.

Keil, C.F. *The Prophecies of Ezekiel*. "Biblical Commentary on the Old Testament." Grand Rapids: Eerdmans, 1950 reprint.

Lind, Millard. *Ezekiel,* "Believers Church Bible Commentary." Scottdale, Pa: Herald, 1996.

Luckenbill, David. *Ancient Records of Assyria and Babylonia.* Chicago: University Press, 1927.

Matthews, I.G. *Ezekiel* in "An American Commentary on the Old Testament." Chicago: American Baptist Publishing, 1939.

Mauro, Philip *The Hope of Israel.* Reprinted by Pastors Library Foundation, n.d.

May, H.G. and E.L. Allen, "The Book of Ezekiel," *The Interpreter's Bible.* Nashville: Abingdon, 1956.

Payne, Barton. *Encyclopedia of Biblical Prophecy.* New York: Harper and Row, 1973.

Pfeiffer, Robert. *Introduction to the Old Testament.* New York: Harper, 1948.

Plumptre E.H. and Thomas Whitelaw, *Ezekiel*, 2 vols. "Pulpit Commentary." New York: Funk and Wagnals, 1909.

Rowley, H.H. *The Relevance of Apocalyptic.* London: Lutterworth, 1944.

Sauer, Erich. *From Eternity to Eternity.* Grand Rapids: Eerdmans, 1954.

Seitz, Christopher and K. Green-McCreight eds. *Theological Exegesis: Essays in Honor of Brevard S. Childs.* Grand Rapids: Eerdmans, 1999.

Smith, James E. *The Promised Messiah.* Nashville: Nelson, 1993.

Smith, Wilbur. *Egypt in Biblical Prophecy.* Grand Rapids: Baker, 1957.

Taylor, John B. *Ezekiel*, "Tyndale Old Testament Commentaries." London: Tyndale, 1969.

van Ruiten, J. and M. Vervenne eds. *Studies in the Book of Isaiah: Festscrift Willem A.M. Beuken.* Leuven: Leuven University Press, 1997.

Vawter, Bruce and Leslie Hoppe, *Ezekiel: A New Heart.* "International Theological Commentary." Grand Rapids: Eerdmans, 1991.

Walvoord, John. *The Nations in Prophecy.* Grand Rapids: Zondervan, 1977.

Weis, Richard and David Carr eds. *A Gift of God in Due Season: Essays on Scripture and Community in Honor of James A. Sanders.* Sheffeld: Sheffeld Academic Press, 1996.

Wevers, John W. *Ezekiel, The Century Bible, New Series*. Camden, New Jersey: Nelson, 1969.

Young, Edward J. *An Introduction to the Old Testament*. Grand Rapids: Eerdmans, 1960.

Zimmerli, Walther. *A Commentary on the Book of the Prophet Ezekiel*, "Hermeneia"; 2 vols. Philadelphia: Fortress, 1979, 1983.

OTHER BOOKS BY THE AUTHOR

Available from College Press, Joplin, Mo.

The Pentateuch, 1993, 534 pp.
The Books of History, 1995, 747 pp.
The Wisdom Literature and Psalms, 1996, 873 pp.
The Major Prophets, 1992, 637 pp.
The Minor Prophets, 1994, 653 pp.
1 & 2 Samuel in "The College Press NIV Commentary," 2000. 541 pp.

Available from Restoration Press, Florida Christian College 1011 Bill Beck Blvd. Kissimmee, Fl 34744. 407-847-8966

What the Bible Says about the Promised Messiah 1991, 522 pp.

Available from Amazon.com

Bible History Made Simple, 2007, 180 pp.
Old Testament Books Made Simple, 2007, 272 pp.
New Testament Books Made Simple, 2008, 196 pp.
Biblical Protology, 2007, 530 pp.
Postexilic Prophets, 2007, 268 pp.
Daniel; a Christian Interpretation, 2008, 418 pp.